BUDDHISMS AND DECONSTRUCTIONS

BUDDHISMS AND DECONSTRUCTIONS

Edited by
JIN Y. PARK

Afterword by
ROBERT MAGLIOLA

MOTILAL BANARSIDASS PUBLISHERS
PRIVATE LIMITED • DELHI

*First Indian Edition: Delhi, **2011***
Published by arrangement with Scarecrow Press

ISBN: 978-81-208-3386-9

MOTILAL BANARSIDASS
41 U.A. Bungalow Road, Jawahar Nagar, Delhi 110 007
8 Mahalaxmi Chamber, 22 Bhulabhai Desai Road, Mumbai 400 026
203 Royapettah High Road, Mylapore, Chennai 600 004
236, 9th Main III Block, Jayanagar, Bangalore 560 011
Sanas Plaza, 1302 Baji Rao Road, Pune 411 002
8 Camac Street, Kolkata 700 017
Ashok Rajpath, Patna 800 004
Chowk, Varanasi 221 001

Printed in India

By Jainendra Prakash Jain at Shri Jainendra Press,
A-45 Naraina, Phase-I, New Delhi 110 028
and Published by Narendra Prakash Jain for
Motilal Banarsidass Publishers Private Limited,
Bungalow Road, Delhi 110 007

CONTENTS

Abbreviations

"AT" Jacques Derrida, "Of an Apocalyptic Tone Recently Adopted in Philosophy"
B&N Jean-Paul Sartre, *Being and Nothingness*, trans. Hazel Barnes, 1956
"CHW" Geshe Rabten, "The Commentary to the Heart of Wisdom"
CJ *Chanzong jicheng*
"Comment" Jacques Derrida, "Comment ne pas parler"
CZT Lu K'uan Yu, *Chan and Zen Teaching: First Series*
D Jacques Derrida, *Dissemination*
DC Harold Bloom et al., *Deconstruction and Criticism*
DH Denshin hōyō, *Ui Hakujū yakuchū zenseki shūsei maki*
"Differance" Jacques Derrida, "Différance" in *Speech and Phenomena and Other Essays on Husserl's Theory of Signs*
"Differentialism" Robert Magliola, "Differentialism in Chinese Ch'an and French Deconstruction: Some Test-Cases from the Wu-men-kuan"
DLW Robert Magliola, *On Deconstructing Life-Worlds*
DOM Robert Magliola, *Derrida on the Mend*
EDY *Erdi yi.*
"EW" Cadava, Connor, Nancy, eds. "'Eating Well', or the Calculation of the Subject"
"FDD" Robert Magliola, "French Deconstruction with a (Buddhist) Difference"
GCM Emmanuel Levinas, *Of God Who Comes to Mind*
HCP Yu-Lan Fung, *A History of Chinese Philosophy*
HTC *Hsu Tsang Ching*
I Edmund Husserl, *Ideas*
IB The Interpreter's Bible
JBC Jerome Biblical Commentary
JD Bennington and Derrida, *Jacques Derrida*
JYP Jin Y. Park
KJV King James Version of the Bible
"Letter" Jacques Derrida, "Letter to a Japanese Friend"
LH G.W.F. Hegel, *The Logic of Hegel*
ME Jeffrey Hopkins, *Meditation on Emptiness*
MMK Nāgārjuna, *Mūlamadhyamakakārikā*
MP Jacques Derrida, *Margins of Philosophy*

NIB The New Interpreter's Bible
NIDNTT The New International Dictionary of New Testament Theology
NRSV The New Revised Standard Version
NS John R. McRae, *The Northern School and the Formation of Early Ch'an Buddhism*
OD Jonathan Culler, *On Deconstruction*
ODE Ven. Khyabje Thrangu Rinpoche, *The Open Door to Emptiness*
OG Jacques Derrida, *Of Grammatology*
P Jacques Derrida, *Positions*
PEW *Philosophy East & West*
POM G.W.F. Hegel, *Phenomenology of Mind*
PS Wing-tsit Chan, trans. *The Platform Scripture*
PSSP Philip B. Yampolski, trans. *The Platform Sutra of the Sixth Patriarch*
RSML Ruth Fuller Sasaki, trans. *The Recorded Sayings of Ch'an Master Lin-chi Ḥui-chao of Chen Prefecture*
RSV Revised Standard Version of the Bible
SB Wing-tsit Chan, ed. *A Source Book in Chinese Philosophy*
SHCL Yang Zengwen, ed. *Shenhui Heshang Chanhua lu*
Shoki Yanagida Seizan, *Shoki no zen shi 2: Rekidai hōbōki*
Signs D. Lehman, *Signs of the Time*
SLXY *Sanlun xuanyi*
SLXYJS *Sanlun xuanyi jiaoshi*
SP Jacques Derrida, *Speech and Phenomena*
"Statements" Jacques Derrida, "Some Statements and Truisms about Neologisms, Newisms, Postisms, Parasitisms, and other small Seismisms,"
T *Taishō shinshū daizōkyō*
TE Jean-Paul Sartre, *The Transcendence of the Ego*
Tojo Kamata Shigeo, ed. *Zengen shosenshū tojo*
"Tsung-mi" Jan Yun-hua, "Tsung-mi: His Analysis of Ch'an Buddhism"
"TT" Jacques Derrida, "The Time of a Thesis"
UBD Unger's Bible Dictionary
"Ulysses" "Ulysses Gramophone"
"Vacuité," J. May, "La philosophie bouddhique de la vacuité"
VV Nāgārjuna, *Vighrahavyāvartanī*
W *Windbell*
WD Jacques Derrida, *Writing and Difference*
WNO Trinh Thi Minh-ha, *Women, Native, Other*
WO Bernard Faure, *The Will to Orthodoxy*
ZTML Burton Watson, trans. *The Zen Teachings of Master Lin-chi*

ACKNOWLEDGMENTS

This volume grew out of a close encounter panel on "Buddhism, Deconstruction and the Works of Robert Magliola" held at the twenty-second annual conference of the International Association for Philosophy and Literature. Half of the essays in the volume are revised versions of the papers presented at the panel and the rest are contributions solicited for this volume. I am grateful to Hugh J. Silverman, who originally proposed the idea of the panel to me and who has been strongly supportive throughout the process of transforming the panel into the current volume. I thank Robert Magliola, who accepted my proposal for the panel without hesitation and helped me in various ways with the creation of this volume. I am greatly indebted to Hwa Yol Jung whose advice has been essential for this volume to take the present form. Many thanks are due to the contributors to the volume for their patience and support. Most of the editorial work for this volume was done during my tenure as Mellon Fellow at Vassar College. I would like to thank the Mellon Fellowship for the opportunity and Vassar College for hosting me as a fellow. I also thank American University, College of Arts and Sciences, which provided me with the computer equipment necessary for the preparation of this manuscript on such short notice. I thank Eve DeVaro in Roman & Littlefield who has helped me in various ways in the preparation of this manuscript. Last, but not least, I thank Emily A. Vezina and David Howe who read the entire manuscript and provided me with much editorial help.

General Introduction

Jin Y. Park

A comparative study of Eastern and Western thought is not a phenomenon that belongs exclusively to our era. However, the nature of current philosophical discourse has inspired some scholars with the idea that the project can be better executed and the results more meaningful in today's environment, and they are not wrong.

Limiting the scope to the comparative study between Buddhism and deconstruction, we notice that the publications in this field during the past two decades far exceed those in any other period both in terms of the number of publications and the diversity of topics discussed. Until recently, East-West comparative philosophy has been at best sporadic gestures marked by an imbalance in the way the Eastern and Western ideas were presented. A rather unsuccessful pattern in comparison was partly due to the socio-political and historical relationship between the East and the West. The philosophical orientation of the West's Continental metaphysical thinking and the nature of the project of modernity and enlightenment have also played a significant role in creating this pattern. It would be premature to say that such a practice has completely disappeared. However, along with the emergence of nonsubstantialist philosophy in the West, a new direction in comparative philosophy is definitely on the horizon. *Buddhisms and Deconstructions*, with its acknowledgment of the plurality of both Buddhist traditions and deconstructive philosophy, is an attempt to mark such a change. The thirteen essays in this volume attest to a new relationship between Eastern and Western thought, expand the scope of our understanding of each philosophical tradition, and thus offer a new framework for both.

Buddhist studies in the West have a relatively short history.[1] The motivation that initiated this scholarship was complicated as well. Socio-political issues aside, the first generation European Buddhist scholars encountered difficulty in understanding Buddhist doctrines because of the different frames of thought between Buddhism and Judeo-Christian/Greek-metaphysical thinking. Attempts to interpret Buddhist doctrines from a European perspective without considering the gap existing between the different modes of thinking in the East and the West resulted in a negative evaluation of Buddhism as reflected in the first generation European Buddhist scholars' understanding of Buddhism. European scholars of Buddhism in the nineteenth century described Buddhism as being full of negative and even horrible tenets characterized by the disappearance of the individual. The negation of self reaches its culmination, they speculated, in Buddhist *nirvāṇa* which Europeans understood as a desire for "the absolute nothing."[2]

The negative portrayal of Buddhism is also found in the Continental philosophers' interpretation of the tradition. In his lectures on the philosophy of religion, G. W. F. Hegel (1770-1831) placed Buddhism in the primitive stage in the evolution of world religions, defining it as a religion of "annihilation."[3] This tendency was carried over to the twentieth century, as we witness, for example, in Karl Jaspers (1883-1969), who declared the impossibility of being a Western Buddhist: "To participate in the essence of Buddha's truth, we should have to cease to be what we are. The difference lies not in rational position but in the whole view of life and manner of thinking."[4] Reading Jaspers' portrayal of Buddhism, we wonder what made him feel such a distance from Buddhism that he thought it stands in direct opposition to the identity of Westerners. A brief review of basic Buddhist doctrines will help us shed some light on this question.

One most comprehensive theoretical basis of Buddhist philosophy can be found in the Buddhist doctrine of "dependent co-arising" (Sanskrit: *pratītya-samutpāda*, literally "in dependence, things rise up"). Dependent co-arising resembles the concept of causation except that in dependent co-arising, the causation takes place in multi-dimensional levels. A being in Buddhism is always already a result of co-arising (simultaneous happening) of different elements that together construct what we call a "self." In various works of Buddhist literature, the Buddha emphasizes that one's understanding of being and the world is seriously impaired by one's "determination" and "desire" to grasp something permanent. In an attempt to demonstrate the impossibility of affirming any enduring entity in one's being, the Buddha analyzes a human being in terms of five categories known as the Five Aggregates: matter, feeling, perception, mental formations, and consciousness.

The fact that none of these five elements can independently represent an entity but that an individual is constructed through the inter-dependent functioning of these five aggregates leads us to the Buddhist doctrine of no-self. As a major Buddhist belief, the theory of no-self in Buddhism requires a careful understanding for us to fully grasp its meaning. Unlike the common misunderstanding that the idea of no-self locates itself at the opposite of the theory of self, Buddhist tradition is keenly aware of the problem entailed in this dualism. If we understand the theory of no-self as a "lack" of self, we are already presupposing the existence of self. The difference in this case is that the theory of enduring self affirms, whereas the no-self theory—if it is understood as a lack of self—negates the existence of self. In both cases, self should exist. The Buddha presents the reality of no-self, not as a lack of self but as the "middle path" between affirmation and negation of self.

In the *Sūtra of Kindred Sayings*, the Buddha is asked whether there is a self. He does not respond. His student asks the same question three times, to which the Buddha remains silent. At this point, Kāśyapa, one of the Buddha's disciples, tells the Buddha that his silence might be interpreted as an evidence of his inability to deal with the issue. The Buddha replies: "If I say the self exists from the beginning, I make [the mistake of affirming] the view of permanent self; if I say that now the self does not exist, I make [the mistake of proposing] the view of annihilation. The Tathāgata teaches the middle path which cuts off both poles. In other words, I say, because of this, that happens; because this arises, that arises."[5]

There being no possibility of the existence of an enduring entity in a being, Buddhism proposes non-self. In this sense, Buddhism does not deny the existence of an individual being in the empirical world. The phenomenology of being in Buddhism, however, does not extend itself into a transcendental ontology that affirms the existence of permanent substance behind and/or beyond the empirical being, be it Being, Idea, or Existence per se.

One reason for the frequent misunderstanding of the Buddhist theory of no-self as the lack of self lies in our dualistic concept which maintains that "~A" is the opposite of "A." However, "A" and "~A" are not actually binary opposites as dualist thinking has assumed, but they fall into the same category in the sense that both presuppose the existence of "A." That language is the main culprit for such a tendency has also been noticed by Buddhist traditions, which, accordingly, have developed philosophies of language addressing the issue.

The fact that language is capable of leading one to the mistaken concept of opposites does not suggest that one should not use language or should totally mistrust the linguistic system. The second century Buddhist thinker Nāgārjuna thus makes a distinction between "declaration" and "expression" in our use of language. According to Nāgārjuna, both being and non-being, or self and non-self, can be understood as "*prajñapti*" (provisional explanation or linguistic communication or expression). The use of such expressions, however, does not presuppose that they exist as independent entities.

In order to emphasize the fact that a being is always already in the web of movement without a moment's possibility of creating a "presence" of "entity," Nāgārjuna introduces and foregrounds the concept of "emptiness" (*śūnyatā*). Emptiness is another name for dependent co-arising and the middle path that emphasizes the impossibility of exhausting the multilevel causations which we call existence.

As a philosophical doctrine, Buddhism provides a vision of interconnectedness of all beings with an emphasis on differential notion and temporality as the groundless-grounding of the world and being. As a religion, Buddhism awakens one to the reality of this differential and temporal ground of existence and teaches two opposite consequences that come about as a result of one's understanding (or misunderstanding) of this reality: either one is bound in the confusion of reality and phenomenon, or one is emancipated from the traditional concept of self.

If we place side by side the basic concepts of Buddhism and Continental metaphysical thinking, it is not too difficult to imagine the possible conflict between the two philosophies. For example, from the perspective of Continental metaphysics, the concept of Buddhist non-self is "horrible" because it demands the "annihilation" of the self, the Ego-Cogito, which is the very ground of one's existence in the tradition. From the Buddhist perspective however, there is nothing to annihilate since the self was not there in the first place. The Buddhist denial of the existence of any enduring entity beyond the phenomenal world will be problematic to transcendental ontology and metaphysics. Further the Buddhist identity of non-identity will be understood as a violation of the Aristotelian logic, the ground of philosophical reasoning. In order for these different perspectives and philosophies from the East and the West to be properly evaluated by the other side, we needed to wait for changes in the direction of our philosophical discourse. One such change was facilitated by an emergence of new philosophical thinking in Western philosophy which we identify here as deconstruction.

Derridean deconstruction created a rupture in the Continental philosophy. However, it was also a result of the developments that had been evolving in Europe for more than half a century before the first trilogy of Jacques Derrida's works was published in the late nineteen sixties. Before deconstruction appeared on the scene of Continental philosophy, Freudian psychoanalysis had discovered the unconscious, the unknown realm within an individual, threatening the concept of Cartesian modern man who has anchored the certainty of his existence on reason. Later, Jacques Lacan's theory of the split subject declared the impossibility of carrying on with the Ego-Cogito as a ground for the certainty of one's existence. Further, the post-structuralism of Michel Foucault prophesied the disappearance of the human episteme, the main player in Continental modernist philosophy, from the shore of human science.[6] What is more, the postmodern philosophy of Jean-François Lyotard has symbolically defined the nature and the result of modernist philosophy when he declares that Auschwitz is a "paradigmatic name for the tragic 'incompletion' of modernity."[7] Auschwitz cannot be explained with reason; it scorns Cartesian belief in human subject as a rational being.

According to Jacques Derrida, the turning point in Continental philosophy accommodated by the thinkers in the twentieth century is marked by the notion of "difference" with which Derrida characterizes our epoch. Whereas the European modernist thinkers grounded their philosophical investigation on the principle of identity, post-modern philosophers have turned the direction of their investigation to the relationship between identity and non-identity, inside and outside, and self and its other. Philosophers of "difference" view a being as a differential notion in which identity is constructed by its relation to non-identity, and, thus announces the dethronement of the metaphysical concept of the subject.

The idea of "difference" is well articulated in de Saussure's semiological difference and Heidegger's ontico-ontological difference. In the field of linguistics, de Saussure's semiology challenges the metaphysical understanding of the sign. By setting forth the arbitrariness of signs and their differential character as principles of general semiology, de Saussure subverts the traditional concept that a sign is identical with a word. In the semiological difference, each sign obtains its identity by its difference from the other signs in a linguistic system. Signification arises not by an act of consciousness or an act of the subject, but by signs participating in a signifying chain. Thus, "in language there are only differences ... without positive terms."[8] By denying the possibility of any positive values which are not produced from the system of the difference, the semiological difference undermines the function of the signifying subject in traditional linguistics.

Heideggerian ontico-ontological difference plays a similar role in the history of metaphysics. To Heidegger, the history of metaphysics is the history of the oblivion of the relation of Being to beings. Heidegger contends that to reinstate the question of Being from its oblivion and thus from the reduction of being into an essentialized transcendental entity is to think about the relationship between Being and beings. In Heidegger's ontology, one's existence is this relationship, the difference between being and Being, the nature of which Heidegger identifies not with the relationship of ownership but of "the event of appropriation."[9] Existence, thus, is not identity but difference, or the happening of ontico-ontological difference.

To Derrida, however, de Saussure's semiological difference and the Heideggerian ontico-ontological difference present their own limit. They still remain in the realm of the metaphysics of identity and presence in the form of structure (in the case of de Saussure) and onto-theology (in the case of Heidegger). Marking the limits of his predecessors in the philosophy of "difference," Derrida presents his own version of "difference," which he names *différance*. *Différance* differs/defers. In this neologism, Derrida combines the difference in kind ("to differ") and that in temporality ("to defer")–which are two meanings of the French verb, *différer*–symbolically re-presenting the inexhaustible "movements" of "difference" which are constantly and always already charged with traces. "*Différance* is the systematic play of differences, of the traces of differences, of the *spacing* by means of which elements are related to each other," Derrida observes in his interview with Julia Kristeva.[10]

Derridean deconstruction takes place by marking a gap in a discourse which becomes possible with the consideration of function of *différance* and trace in a discourse and signifying process. Derrida points out that once language, the medium of philosophy, is accepted as functioning on a differential base, no discourse can enjoy the privilege of coherence or the purity of unity. By marking the gap and fissure in a discourse through a close examination of how signification takes place, a deconstructive reading dismantles, destabilizes, and delimits the scope of a text and further inscribes the limits of metaphysical thinking.

Metaphysical thinking in particular and western philosophy in general has maintained itself as discourse on Truth, the presence of which is located in the presence of the enduring entity. Derrida thus identifies the history of western philosophy as the history of the metaphysics of presence. Philosophy is a guarantor of the existence and presence of Truth in the enduring being which protects the subject from the contingency of existence. Philosophy, in this context, has contributed to appropriate the mutability of being, and that was made possible through a positing of the atemporal *Being* as presence of *Truth*. Derrida announces this transcendental metaphysics as the result of our "determination." *Différance* and trace constantly remind us of the contextuality in which existence takes place and in which the presencing of Truth cannot survive. Here we already notice the similarities the Derridean project shares with the Buddhist.

Marking a gap in the discourse in a deconstructive reading is the procedure of marking the limits and nature of *prājñapti*. In both Buddhist and Derridean deconstruction, there is awareness that the field of existence as well as existence itself cannot be exhausted. Huayan Buddhism calls this field *dharmadhātu* (the realm of reality) and Derrida calls it context: "there is a context, but one cannot analyze it exhaustively; the context is open because 'it comes' [*ça vient*], because there is something to come [*il y a de l'avenir*]."[11] Like dependent co-arising in Buddhism, Derridean *différance* is the name which attests to the impossibility of drawing a line between things, between events and beings, because there is always something to come. That is the very inexhaustibility of contexts of one's existence.

The current volume begins by outlining the ground of the comparison between Buddhism and deconstruction. Part One provides a general outline of the comparative study between Buddhisms and deconstructions and prepares the reader for other chapters in the volume. Jin Y. Park's essay sets the tone of this comparative philosophy by investigating the "spirit" shared by these two philosophical endeavors. Park illuminates the nature of deconstructive philosophy as she discusses the Buddhist "middle path" and "dependent co-arising" in comparison with the Derridean "middle voice" and "*différance*." Ian Mabbett's essay further delineates the basic similarities or resemblances of these two philosophies. By juxtaposing the Indian Buddhist thinker Nāgārjuna's philosophy with deconstructive operation (which he does not limit to Derridean), Mabbett summarizes their similarities on eight points.

Some Buddhist scholars claim that Derridean deconstruction has not been deconstructive enough because of the over-consciousness of its relationship with the metaphysical tradition. Two essays in Part Two, one by Zong-qi Cai and the other by David R. Loy, take such a position. Both Cai and Loy provide in-depth discussions on the similarities between Buddhism (Mādhyamika Buddhism in

Cai and Huayan Buddhism in Loy) and deconstruction. In conclusion they contend that textual deconstruction exercised by Derrida should be compensated for by "religious discipline," especially by the Buddhist practice of meditation and "religious enlightenment beyond language and conceptuality." Elsewhere, Loy also claimed that Derridean deconstruction has "open[ed] up paths that he [Derrida] himself has been unwilling or unable to explore." Loy suggested that these tasks Derridean deconstruction has been incapable of carrying out can be performed especially by *praxis* in Buddhist tradition, which balances and complements the *theory* of deconstruction.[12]

Regarding the relationship between praxis and theory, Derrida will argue against the idea of any kind of "leap"—whether it is a leap from metaphysics to deconstruction, from theory to practice, or from *saṃsāra* to *nirvāṇa.* This brings up the issue of genre in the comparative project of Buddhism and deconstruction. Some might argue that the project was off-balance from the beginning. By juxtaposing the religio-philosophical tradition of Buddhism with the philosophy of deconstruction, the project might have attempted to cross the border of genre as much as that of geographic specifics, which could damage the value of this project. However, we should keep in mind that the demarcation between religion and philosophy has not been clear in Asian tradition, unlike in the West. Further, Derridean deconstruction has been a philosophy that defies the very definition of philosophy, which I would contend as one of the most important contributions of Derrida's work to Western "philosophy."[13] Further, more and more scholars are beginning to address the religious dimension in Derrida's writing.[14] Considering these factors, the differences between Buddhism and deconstruction which Cai and Loy address in their essays offer us an occasion to reconsider not only the relationship between philosophy and religion, but also the problem involved with the reification of the "institutionalized categorization" in academia (such as philosophy and religion) and in our society (e.g., gender, ethnicity, or social class).[15]

From the perspective of Derridean deconstruction, however, Buddhism is not deconstructive enough. One problem of Buddhism as a deconstructive operation arises with the fact that within Buddhist doctrines are encompassed both deconstructive and onto-theological aspects. This dual tendency in Buddhism is clearly reflected in the orientation of the comparative study of Buddhism and deconstruction. The majority of publications and research in this field have been done on the Mādhyamika school of Buddhism. The fact that Buddhist deconstruction is mostly identified with Mādhyamika Buddhism is in turn suggestive of the essentialist nature of other Buddhist schools. For example, the Tathāgatagarbha theory in the Yogācāra School or the theory of the Buddha-nature in Chan Buddhism entails an element that can be interpreted as endorsing an enduring entity in a being. An attempt to sort out different characteristics of different Buddhist schools in this context is helpful to understand the status of Buddhism in this comparative study. Roger R. Jackson in Part Three of this volume investigates the issue. Through an examination of Indian and Tibetan Buddhism, Jackson demonstrates that most deconstructive discourse also contains a foundationalist element in that it remains as a discourse (philosophical system or religious tradition) which exists in this world. In this sense, Jackson's idea goes together with what Ian Mabbett takes as the two levels of truth of deconstruction: deconstruction as a deconstructive operation on the one hand and deconstruction, on the other, as a written text, being discussed in lectures, and taught in academic institutions. Ellen Zhang also notices that in the *śūnyatā* speech of Chinese Sanlun Buddhism, the discourse on emptiness is "deconstructive in its methodological negation yet un-Derridean in that *śūnyatā* 'points to' an experiential dimension that is not confined to language, or even thought." The question then remaining is how we deal with this "experiential dimension" in Buddhism in the context of a deconstructive operation.

From the Derridean deconstructive perspective, an onto-theological tendency in a thought system cannot be dismissed merely because the deconstructive operation is part of the system. Derrida has clearly demonstrated this issue in his discussion of Heidegger's texts, among others. The issue of the deconstructive nature of Buddhism is still open to debate, especially because if it is true that an onto-theological tendency exists in certain forms of Buddhism, it is also true that the history of Buddhism itself has been a series of deconstructive movements against the human being's tendency towards reification. Two essays in Part Four demonstrate the deconstructive endeavor in Buddhist tradition as a self-deconstruction of Buddhism. Youru Wang asserts a deconstructive operation as an essential motive in the development of early Chan Buddhism, and Frank W. Stevenson explores the Chan technique of questions and answers, known as *gong'an,* as another of such instances in Buddhism.

Whether the Derridean project has strictly remained within a textual analysis, shutting itself off from the deconstruction of the problems of the "life-worlds," is a debatable issue. It is true that Derridean deconstruction is heavily involved with textual analysis. It is also true that from the very beginning of his career, Derrida's works have been strongly charged with issues of the life-worlds such as gender, race, hierarchy, power, and so on. At the very beginning of *Of Grammatology* (1967), Derrida mentions "ethnocentrism" as an immediate corollary of the "logocentrism" of the metaphysics of presence. If one thinks that Derrida was not clear enough in articulating his concern for the life-world in his early works, one can turn to his later publications for more explicit discussions of the issues of justice and ethics.[16]

As a different approach to the issue, a relationship between deconstruction and the life-world is well articulated in Robert Magliola's book, *Deconstructing Life-Worlds*, in which Magliola deconstructs the double-binding of his own life which he sees as a life caught in the double-cross, the chiasm between philosophy and experience, the conventional truth (Sk. *saṃvṛti-satya*) and the ultimate truth (Sk. *paramārtha-satya*), *saṃsāra* and *nirvāṇa*. Two essays in Part Five discuss the relationship between deconstruction and the life-worlds at the juncture of Buddhism, Christianity, Judaism, deconstruction, commitment, and ethics. Jane Augustine discusses the deconstructive operation in the life-world, taking Robert Magliola's work/life as an example, and Gad Horowitz explores the possibility of ethics in Buddhism and deconstruction. Both Buddhism and deconstruction (and postmodern thought) have faced a challenge from the traditional ethics, which claims that the non-existence of the independent entity in non-substantialist philosophy implies the absence of ethical agency and thus the lack of ethics itself. The criticism as to the ethical position of non-substantialist philosophy has been especially noticeable in the process of Buddhism's acculturation in the West. During the early stage of Buddhism's introduction to the West, questions were raised as to whether Buddhist philosophy can accommodate ethics.[17] However, no religio-philosophical system can survive long without having some kind of ethical mode within its system. What should be asked, then, is not whether or not a thought system has ethics, but what kind of ethics it provides for.[18]

After all these endeavors to read deconstruction in line with Buddhism and *vice versa*, we still need to ask whether this comparative study is justifiable at all. In order to consider this issue, essays in Part Six launch a self-critical approach to the comparative study of Buddhism and deconstruction by discussing Buddhism in connection with Continental thinkers other than Derrida. Simon Glynn discusses the Buddhist theory of no-self in comparison with Sartre's existential phenomenology; Steven Laycock explores the relationship between the Buddhist concept of self and the idea of consciousness and reflexivity in modern subjectivity drawn from diverse Continental thinkers; and E. H Jarow meditates on the act of inter-religious dialogue itself.

As Jarow tells us, in order for a comparative study between the two philosophies to take place, a "totalizing process" of each tradition is inevitable. Both Buddhism and deconstruction, however, refute any generalization, because generalization inevitably involves appropriation and reification. In the process of generalization we walk on a thin line of essentialization that defies the functioning of dependent co-arising or *différance*. Jarow tries to resolve the problem by turning to the issue of the life-worlds and asks how to hold the encounter dialogue "in the flesh as well as in the word" so that one can see through a "culture of awakening" which is "willing to abandon the separate certainty of its own position," "willing to listen without the customary forms of protections," and "willing to relate… to enter the stream."

Comparative philosophy in the format of the East-West dialogue is in the end an endeavor to open ourselves up to the possibilities we fail to explore because of the self-closure involved in any kind of discourse. Maurice Merleau-Ponty once wrote: "Western philosophy can learn from [India and China] to rediscover the relationship to being and the initial option which gave it birth, and to estimate the possibilities we have shut ourselves off from in becoming 'Westerners', and perhaps reopen them."[19] The same can be said of Buddhism. The cultural-philosophical orientation in our time seems to provide us a better condition in which we can carry out such a self-critical project of comparative philosophy. *Buddhisms and Deconstructions* witnesses our endeavor to make it happen.

Notes

1. Although a fragment of Buddhism was known to Europeans before Buddhism became a field in academic research, it was not until the nineteenth century that Buddhism in Pāli and Sanskrit was studied in any serious manner. For a history of the study of Buddhism in Europe, see J. W. de Jong, *A Brief History of Buddhist Studies in Europe and America* (Tokyo, Japan: Kensei Publishing Co., 1997). Roger-Pol Droit divides the nineteenth century European understanding of Buddhism into three periods—the birth (1784-1831), the threat (1832-1863), and the decline (1864-1893)—in his *Le culte du néant: Les philosophes et le Bouddha* (Paris: Éditions du Seuil, 1997); English translation, *The Cult of Nothingness: The Philosophers and the Buddha,* trans. David Streights and Pamela Vohnson (Chapel Hill: University of North Carolina Press, 2003). Also see Henri dc Lubak, *La rencontre du bouddhisme et de l'Occident* (Paris: Éditions Montaigne, 1952; Les Éditions du Cerf, 2000). For the history of Buddhism in America, see Rick Fields, *How the Swans Came to the Lake: A Narrative History of Buddhism in America* (Boston: Shambhala Publications, Inc, 1981) and Charles S. Prebish, *Luminous Passage: The Practice and Study of Buddhism in America* (Berkeley & Los Angeles, CA: California University Press, 1999).

2. See for example Guy Richard Welbon, *The Buddhist Nirvana and Its Western Interpreters* (Chicago: University of Chicago Press, 1968) for the evaluation of Buddhism by the first generation European Buddhist scholars, such as Saint Hillaire, Eugène Burnouf (1801-1852) or his student Marx Müller (1823-1900).

3. Hegel gave four lectures on the philosophy of religion in 1821, 1824, 1827, and 1831. In the lectures of 1821, he did not include any Asian religions. In the lectures of 1824 and 1827, Buddhism is categorized as the religion of "The Being-within-Self" and in the 1831 lectures, Hegel identifies it as the religion of "annihilation." See G. W. F. Hegel, *Lectures on the Philosophy of Religion*, 3 vols. Ed. Peter C. Hodgson, trans. R. F. Brown, P. C. Hodgson, & J. M. Stewart with the assistance of H. S. Harris (Berkeley, CA: University of California Press, 1995), 303-316, 562-579, 735-736. Also see G.W. F. Hegel, *Philosophy of History*, trans. J. Sibree (Buffalo, NY: Prometheus Books, 1991), 103-172.

4. Karl Jaspers, *Socrates, Buddha, Confucius, Jesus: The Paradigmatic Individuals* (1957/1962), trans. Ralph Manheim (San Diego: A Harvest Book, 1990), 40.

5. *Za ahan jing* (*Sūtra of the kindred sayings*), Taishō shinshū daizōkyō 2.99.245b.

6. Michel Foucault, *The Order of Things: An Archaeology of the Human Sciences* (1966) (New York: Vintage Books, 1973), 387. Foucault writes: "man would be erased, like a face drawn in sand at the edge of the sea."

7. Jean-François Lyotard, *The Postmodern Explained* (1988) (Minneapolis, MN: University of Minnesota Press, 1992/1993), 18.

8. Ferdinand de Saussure, *Course in General Linguistics* (1916), trans. Wade Baskin (New York: MacGraw-Hill, 1959), 120.

9. Martin Heidegger, *Identity and Difference*, translated by Joan Stambaugh (New York: Harper & Row, 1969), 36.

10. Jacques Derrida, *Positions* (1972), trans. Alan Bass (Chicago: University of Chicago Press, 1981/1982), 27.

11. Jacques Derrida & Maurizio Ferraris, *A Taste for the Secret* (1997), trans. Giacomo Donis (Polity, 2001), 13.

12. David Loy, ed. Healing Deconstruction: Postmodern Thought in Buddhism and Christianity (Atlanta: Scholars Press, 1996), 2.

13. See for example, "Tympan," an introduction to his book *Margins of Philosophy* (1972) in which Derrida asks whether philosophy can have margins, or whether that which has margins can be philosophy. (Trans. Alan Bass, Chicago, IL: University of Chicago Press, 1982, ix-xxix). Also see Jacques Derrida, *Who's Afraid of Philosophy?: Right to Philosophy 1* (1990), translated by Jan Plug (Stanford, CA: Stanford University Press, 2002).

14. For example, see John D. Caputo, *The Prayers and Tears of Jacques Derrida: Religion without Religion* (Bloomington & Indianapolis: Indiana University Press, 1997). Also see Jacques Derrida and Gianni Vattimo, eds. *Religion* (1996) (Stanford, CA: Stanford University Press, 1998), and Jacques Derrida, *Acts of Religion*, edited by Gil Anidjar (New York: Routledge, 2002).

15. In terms of the crossing of borders and conventional categorization, it is not only the boundary between philosophy and religion that Derridean deconstruction has been crossing. The traditional boundary between logos and mythos represented in the West by philosophy and literature has also been problematized by Derrida. (See for example, Jacques Derrida, "I have a Taste for the Secret" in *A Taste for the Secret*, Jacques Derrida & Maurizio Ferraris, translated by Giacomo Donis [Polity, 2001], 7-12.).

16. See for example Derrida's criticism of Eurocentrism and phallocentrism in "Faith and Knowledge: The Two Sources of 'Religion' at the Limits of Reason Alone" in *Acts of Religion,* 42-103; Derrida's response to the general criticism of deconstruction for its lack of political/ethical agenda: "Force of Law: The 'Mystical Foundation of Authority'" in *Acts of Religion,* 228-298; Jacques Derrida, *On Cosmopolitanism and Forgiveness* (London and New York: Routledge, 2002); Also see Geoffrey Bennington, *Interrupting Derrida* (New York: Routledge, 2000), and Richard Beardsworth, *Derrida & the Political* (London, New York: Routledge, 1996).

17. For example see James Whitehill, "Is there a Zen Ethics?" *The Eastern Buddhist* 20 (1987): 9-33; Lee Stauffer, "Is an ethical theory possible within Zen Buddhism?," *Southwest Philosophical Studies* (1977): 80-84; Christopher Ives, *Zen Awakening and Society* (Honolulu: University of Hawaii Press, 1992). For a positive answer to these questions, see Daniel Palmer, "Masao Abe, Zen Buddhism, and Social Ethics," *Journal of Buddhist Ethics* 4 (1997): 112-137; Charles Prebish, "Ethics and Integration in American Buddhism," *Journal of Buddhist Ethics* 2 (1995): 125-139.

18. Discourse on Buddhist ethics and Buddhism's social commitment is one of the distinctive features of American Buddhism and Western Buddhist scholarship. See for example, Damien Keown, ed., *Contemporary Buddhist Ethics* (Richmond, Surrey: Curzon, 2000); Charles Prebish, Damien Keown, Wayne R. Husted, eds., *Buddhism and Human Rights* (Taylor & Francis, Inc, 1997); Christopher S. Queen, ed., *Engaged Buddhism in the West* (Boston: Wisdom Publications, 2000); Christopher S. Queen & Sallie B. King, eds., *Engaged Buddhism: Buddhist Liberation Movements in Asia* (Albany: State University of New York Press, 1996).

19. Maurice Merleau-Ponty, "Everywhere and Nowhere." In *Signs,* trans. Richard C. McCleary (Evanston: Northwestern University Press, 1964), 139.

Part One

Buddhism and Deconstruction

Introduction

The essays in Part One provide a general outline of the comparative study of Buddhism and deconstruction by exploring major issues involved in this discourse. Jin Y. Park's essay elaborates the mode of thinking that Buddhism and deconstruction share. Park identifies this as "the unnamable." Note that "the unnameable" in both Buddhism and deconstruction has less to do with the negation of language than the reality of our existence. Hence, both name the unnameable. The paradox involved in the naming of the unnamable captures the spirit of Buddhism and deconstruction.

One example of this can be found in the Buddhist doctrine of "dependent co-arising." Buddhism sees that existence is contingent upon and conditioned by the innumerable different factors that constitute a being. There are multiple causes and effects, each of which carries with it its own temporal dimension. A being is a result of multi-level causation on the horizontal level together with temporal dimensions on the vertical level. At the crossroads of these multi-dimensional functions lies one's existence.

What this suggests is that a being has never been a self-sufficient entity. Buddhism explains the situation through the doctrine of non-self. A being in Buddhism is always already a result of co-arising (simultaneous happening) of different elements that together construct what we call for the sake of convenience a "self." In a being, there is no one specific essence, be it Ego or reason, with which a self can be identified. A being is always already an "inter-being," to borrow Thich Nhat Hanh's term. Beings inter-are, and interactions among the members of the cosmos function at a level that cannot decisively distinguish the identity of the one from that of another: The identity of a being is always "between identity" and hence identity is non-identity. The Buddhist concept of non-identity is also articulated as "the middle path" in the sense that this non-identity is neither affirmation nor negation of identity. While dualism may be a convenient mode of thinking, it is to be negated in the "middle path" because the middle path is not the same as a meridian point between the two poles. Dualism has to be negated because if a being is not an "independent entity," dualism loses its ground to support the system of binary opposites. (The negation of dualism will again be negated in order to prevent its self-reification, which we will see in the chapters later in this volume on Madhyamaka and Chan Buddhism.) Park identifies the Buddhist notion of interdependency as "the unnameable," for it violates the basic rules of language. However, "the unnameable" has such names as "dependent co-arising" and "the middle path" because they are part of both our empirical world and language game as well.

Derridean deconstruction shares the spirit of "the middle path," which Derrida calls *différance* or the "middle voice." Strategically speaking, Derridean deconstruction begins by marking a gap in a discourse. When the principle of identity is sustained as a ground for the thinking process, philosophical speculation, and linguistic theory, then a discourse can be presented as a coherent entity that carried with it a fixed meaning. However, once a possibility of contingency in any one element within a discourse is recognized and accepted, a possible gap and contradiction will emerge on the horizon and remain there. This is the point of departure in Derridean deconstruction, which was originally named grammatology, the science of writing (and reading). Derridean deconstruction articulates the non-identity of being by introducing the concept of "*différance*," a neologism, that demonstrates a differential notion ("to differ") combined with temporal difference ("to defer") caused by "trace." Like the Buddhist dependent co-arising, Derridean *différance* defies any attempt to see a being as an independent entity. This becomes a most noticeable feature of Derridean deconstruction inasmuch as Derrida executes the deconstructive operation in the context of the Continental metaphysical tradition in which a being has been understood as the presence of essence.

Ian Mabbett explores the "spirit" shared by Buddhism and deconstruction on eight counts by discussing the similarities between the Mādhyamika Buddhism of Nāgārjuna and deconstructive operations of Jacques Derrida, Paul de Man, Jonathan Culler, et al. In Mabbett's essay the "middle" in "middle voice" and "middle path" addressed by Park is interpreted with the concept of "voidness" (or "emptiness"). Voidness does not suggest either existence or nonexistence of a being. Voidness is the name for the "lack" of substantiality of a being. "Lack" is used with precautionary quotation marks because no sense of a being—either deprived, or, of a deficiency, of a being that is generally, normatively, and ideally there—should be connoted by the word. No sense of a negation from or privation of an already-existing plenum should be understood. In this sense, Derrida's idea of "context" as an environment and reality of being better explains the situation. Mabbett discusses this with the example of the reader-text relationship. The traditional attitude toward text gives privileges to text as an inviolable entity that contains a determinate message. The idea of the "Great Books" confirms this attitude. The Reader Response Theory on the other hand locates this privilege of meaning production within the reader. Unlike these two claims, in deconstruction and in Buddhism as well, text is always context; text in this case is not limited to written/printed material but includes existence and being in general. What this suggests is that not only can a text not be a closed system or pre-determined, but it is, in fact, inexhaustible. Hence, the Derridean dictum: "*Il n'y a pas de hors texte*" ("There is nothing outside of the text"; "There is no outside-text."). This insaturability of the context of being and the world is explained by Buddhists as "dependent co-arising," as "voidness," by Nāgārjuna, and *différance* by Derrida. Because the context of being does not have a fixed boundary but is expandable and inter-woven both temporally and spatially, the identity principle, the logic of binary opposites, and the self as essence and entity—which constitute continental metaphysics—become problematic in Derridean deconstruction. The binary opposites and the dualistic mode of thinking, together with essence-entity oriented metaphysics, become the target of deconstruction to the degree that the essentialist view has been deconstructed by Buddhism.

Park and Mabbett focus their discussions on the similarities between Buddhism and deconstruction, thus preparing us to think about the possibilities for comparative studies. These similarities will be further explored in Part Two, where the authors also bring our attention to the major differences between Buddhism and deconstruction. (JYP)

One

Naming the Unnameable: Dependent Co-arising and Différance

Jin Y. Park

In the *Diamond Sūtra*, one of major texts of Zen Buddhism, the Buddha teaches his disciple, Subhūti, the reality of Buddhist teachings with the following words: "Subhūti, do not say that the Tathāgata has this idea, 'I must set forth a teaching'. Do not think like that. Why is it so? Because if anyone says that the Tathāgata sets forth a teaching, he really slanders the Buddha and is unable to explain *what I teach*. Subhūti, as with any truth-statement, truth is undeclarable; so it is called a truth-statement" (emphasis mine).[1]

In this passage, the Buddha makes two seemingly contradictory claims: First, he denies the fact that he has set forth any teaching; and second, he accepts the fact of his having set forth teachings by expressing his worries that someone could misrepresent his teaching. If he has not set forth any teaching, why should he worry about a possible misinterpretation of his teaching? The Buddha seems to attribute the cause of this paradox to the role of language. He thus declares that "truth-statement" is just a name. Does this mean that he has a teaching with which he wants to enlighten people but which cannot be expressed in language? If truth is undeclarable in a truth-statement, how can we call it a truth-statement? That is only its name, the Buddha says. What is then the relationship between the name, truth, and reality? How does one get to "what I [the Buddha] teach" without being trapped by the undeclarability of truth and the naming of that truth? Since the Buddha denies that he set forth any teaching, the tradition maintains that during his forty-five years of teaching, the Buddha did not say a word. And yet Buddhist teaching continues to spread around the world twenty-five hundred years after his death.

***

"This, perhaps, is what I would have liked to say of a certain Mount Moriah—while going to Capri, last year, close by the Vesuvius of Gradiva,"[2] writes Jacques Derrida in parentheses attached to the end of his essay entitled "Faith and Knowledge: the Two Sources of 'Religion' at the Limits of Reason Alone," read at a conference on religion held in Capri. According to this note added by Derrida one year after the essay was presented,[3] what he had said in the essay might have been what he meant to say or might not have. As the editor of the volume, *Acts of Religion*, Gil Anidjar states, "Along with the 'perhaps,' 'what I would have wanted to say' not only suspends the ever having been present of the paragraph and of Derrida's words on religion."[4]

In the passage, Derrida shares with the Buddha his negation, or rather his "half-negation," of the possibility of articulation. In the *Diamond Sūtra*, the Buddha both affirms and negates the Buddhist teaching; so does Derrida in his talk on religion when he says that he un/said that which he "would have wanted to say."

Hesitation, avoidance, and evasion seem inevitable in Derrida and his voluminous writings as much as in the Buddha's discourse. The difficulty both Derrida and the Buddha are experiencing and try to convey through their un/said statements is not exclusively the issue of language as some might want to think it is. Nor can it be treated as a simple negation.

The confusion of Derridean discourse (especially *différance*, to which I will turn later in this essay) with negative theology,[5] and the Western characterization of Buddhism as annihilating theory,[6] size up the difficulty involved in the kind of discourses I have just presented: those of the Buddha and Derrida.

This essay sheds light on this unnameable area in the discourses of Buddhism and deconstruction. The unnameable has names, though, as will become clear as we move on, such as the "middle path," the "middle voice," "dependent co-arising," or "*différance*." They are names, however, of the unnameable. These concepts are unnameable because they violate the basic rules of language; but they have names because we need to discuss them. To illuminate the gap existing between the unnameable-ness of these names and the names themselves on the one hand, and the differences between the unnameability of those names/named and negative theology on the other, will be one topic of this essay, in which I will present the kinds of discourse that remind us of how to tell the unnameable without resorting to hyper-essentiality. This will be a test of and a challenge to our capacity to imagine movements without a subject, which we will call the play of *différance* and of dependent co-arising.

The Middle Path or the Middle Voice

Let me begin by discussing the seeming paradox in the previously quoted passage from the *Diamond Sūtra.* One clue for interpreting the Buddha's worries in that passage can be found in his conversation with Kaccāyana as recorded in one of the early Buddhist texts. In this text, Kaccāyana comes to ask the Buddha about the meaning of the "Right View," one of the eight steps in the Eightfold Path. In replying, the Buddha points out that the basic structure of people's construction of meaning is based on dualism: "This world, Kaccāyana, usually based [its view] on two things: on existence and on non-existence."[7] Such a dualism, the Buddha contends, arises with one's desire to grasp things as permanent entities. The Buddha points out that this is demonstrated in our "dogmatic bias" which causes a "mental standpoint." The Buddha tells Kaccāyana that when our thought stands still, it inevitably distorts reality, because the reality exists in the flux of constant changes. On the other hand, when one sees the inner changes of things that constitute being beyond the optical illusion of the seeming constancy of being, one has much chance to see through the reality. The Buddha thus states: "He, who with right insight sees the uprising of the world as it really is, does not hold with the non-existence of the world. But he, who with the right insight sees the passing away of the world as it really is, does not hold with the existence of the world."[8] The Buddha here again affirms both arising and ceasing, being and non-being. His affirmation, however, is characterized with a double affirmation: The Buddha is not affirming exclusively arising or exclusively ceasing. Arising is accepted together with cessation; by the same token, being is affirmed alongside non-being. The Buddha sums up: "Everything exists:—this is one extreme. Nothing exists:—this is the other extreme. Not approaching either extreme the Tathāgata teaches you a doctrine by *the middle* [way]"(emphasis mine).[9]

The Buddha here introduces Kaccāyana to the core of Buddhist teaching: the middle path. The "middle" here does not point to the meridian center of two ends. The traditional version of understanding the "middle path" as an endorsement of a moderate life that denies two extremes of the luxury of sensual pleasures (as young Gautama Siddhārtha experienced in his palace as a prince) and the asceticism of physical mortification (which he practiced during his post-palace, pre-enlightenment period) explains the middle path in only a limited way. The difficulty of identifying the "middle" the Buddha refers to in his conversation with Kaccāyana arises among other reasons from the fact that the Buddha applied the idea to the concept of "existence." To the Buddha, the position of viewing things from the perspective of "being" ("everything exists") and that of "non-being" ("everything does not exist") are both extremes. Unlike the moderate lifestyle that can be conceived of as a middle point between hedonism and asceticism, a medium between existence and nonexistence is not easy to grasp. What does exist between existence and non-existence? How do we find a middle path between being and non-being?

"The Buddha-nature neither exists nor non-exists/both exists and non-exists/ . . . being and non-being combined/This is what is called the middle path."[10] Thus is the middle path defined in the *Nirvāṇa Sūtra.* The passage unequivocally violates the Aristotelian logic of Identity, Contradiction, and the Excluded Middle. Not only does the passage violate the rule of logic by identifying "A" with "~A," it doubles the violation by articulating that (A · ~A) and ~(A · ~A) are non-conflicting. One thing we can glean from this passage is that, in the middle path, the identity of being and non-being needs to be understood in a manner that is different from their conventional senses.

In the *Miscellaneous Discourse of the Buddha,* the Buddha addresses the middle path in several different ways; On one occasion, he explains it as a middle path between the idea of permanence (which accepts the idea of the permanent self) and that of annihilation (which denies the existence of the permanent self). In another instance, he places the middle path as the path between the claims that suffering is caused by self and that it is caused by others. From the Buddha's perspective, these seemingly opposite positions of either accepting or denying permanent entity as a ground of one's being and actions are two sides of one coin. As the Buddha tries to explain to Kaccāyana, to say that there is no self is only another way of saying that there is self. Statements of "is" and "is not" confirm the existence of a being in the form of either affirmation or negation. By putting the affirmation and negation in the same category, Buddhist thought deviates from the dualistic discourse in which being and non-being, presence and absence, active and passive, form binary opposites.

Understood from this perspective, the focal point of the well-known Buddhist concept of no-self is not the issue of either accepting or denying the existence of self so much as it is how to change one's mode of thinking from a substantialist to a non-substantialist way. Along with Derrida, we can state that the major issue in the Buddhist concept of no-self is the matter of how to escape the "instituting question of philosophy" which is "what is. . . ."[11] Through the theory of no-self, Buddhism introduces a new mode of thinking that neither affirms nor negates the existence of being. Without accepting or denying the existence of self, Buddhist thought illuminates the impossibility of pinning down the moment when a self exists as a "substantial and self-sufficient entity." Through the idea of "the middle path" the Buddha expresses the impossibility of substantializing our being, and hence the impossibility of articulating that being through a linguistic system when the system functions by making distinctions and temporarily reifying things.

The Buddha thus explains the middle path in terms of mutual dependency of the constituents of a being. Existence is conditional and dependent upon various conditions at each and every moment, which makes existence possible. Existence is a result of a combination of various conditions; these conditions, or constituents, of a being exist dependent upon other constituents. This interdependency of things—interdependency of being and non-being—is what the Buddha calls "the middle path."

Derridean deconstruction joins Buddhism in its efforts to explain the state of being through its interdependency. According to Derrida, the history of Western philosophy has been the metaphysics of presence, whereby philosophy maintains itself by giving being an onto-theological essence. The onto-theological metaphysics of essence outlives the mutability of beings in the phenomenal world. This longevity—or rather, this immortality of essence—has been explained as grounded in the nature of essence. Be it as Plato's Idea, Descartes' ego-cogito, the Kantian *a priori*, or even Heidegger's crossed-out Being, philosophy has survived by identifying the unoriginated origin as the ground of our being and the world. The immortality of essence negates, denies, and even scorns any possibility of absence. Immortality of essence guarantees its never-dying presence. Superiority of essence is its capacity to overcome absence, because absence is death. Western metaphysics, Derrida argues, has survived throughout history by subscribing to this negation of death, negation of absence. Derridean deconstruction questions the priority of presence, and the immortality of essence, and thus demonstrates that the self-sufficient, self-identifying, and enduring entity that is ever present in the philosophy of essence is nothing other than the determination of philosophy, philosophy's appropriation of its own boundary.

In his disclosure of the nature of essence, Derrida frequently employs the system of binary opposites to reveal that the two poles of binary opposites sustain their positions through mutual *inclusion* and dependency instead of mutual *exclusion*. The binary opposite system is important to Derrida's investigation and deconstruction of the underlying mentality of Western philosophy, especially because of the imbalance of power assigned to each pole. Not only are binary opposites based on the idea of exclusion and self-sufficiency of being, they also function by establishing a hierarchy between the system's two poles. Derrida argues that philosophy has survived and maintained its assumed role as a seeker of Truth by creating binary poles in our mind and by suppressing the less-favored party in this system.

In *Of Grammatology*, Derrida illuminates this issue using an example of two modes of language: written and spoken. Speech, in its phenomenal manifestation, is characterized by the presence of the speaker. The history of philosophy expands this presence of the speaker into the realm of value and thus identifies it with the presence of Truth. The unmediated presence of Truth in speech establishes its superiority over writing, in which truth is mediated and then reproduced in spite of the absence of the speaker. Here, Derrida claims, speech-immediacy-presence and writing-mediation-absence create binary opposites, through which the philosophy of Truth maintains itself by suppressing writing, the secondary language. Derrida interprets the hierarchy between speech and writing—their further presence and absence, and their unmediated Truth and meditated truths— as a result of our determination. His argument is based on the following: Be it speech or writing, language functions through its iterability by nature; that is, the capacity to be repeated. To function as a language, any linguistic system should be able to generate meaning in the absence of the original speaker. When one says "I exist," the meaning of the expression "I exist" will survive its author. Even after the death of the author, the sentence "I exist" will have meaning all the same. What this suggests is that regardless of the format of language—whether speech or writing—language is and has always been repetition, which Derrida calls "arche-writing." In speech, then, writing is already inscribed. Speech cannot be thought of without writing, whether it is the writing in our mind, in the trace of our memory, or in the very neurons that enable us to repeat a linguistic system in our speech and, thus, send our message.

The relationship between speech and writing is only one of the many examples that Derrida cites in his writings to evidence how the traditional binary opposites are always working together and interdependent rather than functioning independently. The concept of presence cannot exist without knowing the concept of absence. Light cannot be light without darkness and thus within the light darkness is always already there.

In illuminating the mutual inclusion and dependency of the binary opposites two poles, Derrida introduces "the strategic note or connection," which he names "*différance*." Derrida created this coinage by combining the two meanings of the same French verb *différer*—namely, "to differ" and also "to defer." *Différance*—in which the middle "e" of "*différence*" (the noun form of the meaning "to differ" of the verb "*différer*") is replaced by an "a"—demonstrates a simultaneous operation of the meaning of distinction (or differences of "to differ") and the delay of the same of "to defer" ("Differance," 136-137). In explaining the construction of *différance*, Derrida writes:

> Here in the usage of our language we must consider that the ending *–ance* is undecided between active and passive. And we shall see why what is designated by "*différance*" is neither simply active nor simply passive, that it announces or rather recalls something like the *middle voice*, that it speaks of an operation which is not an operation, which cannot be thought of either as a passion or as an action of a subject upon an object, as starting from an agent or from a patient, or on the basis of, or in view of, any of these terms. ("Differance," 137, emphasis mine)

The "middle" in Derrida's "middle voice," like the "middle" in the Buddhist "middle path," cannot be the median of two end points. The Derridean "middle" also designates the impossibility of drawing a clear-cut demarcation between conditions that the history of philosophy has defined as binary opposites and that our linguistic convention has separated into two opposite realms. In the above passage, Derrida brings up a centuries-old issue of philosophy—namely, the relationship between subject and object.

Modern Continental philosophy has been constructed by inflating the subject in the form of ego-cogito. In the logic of Cartesian philosophy, the thinking subject constructs the objective world through its rational capacity to think about the world. As Derrida demonstrates, each different story of philosophy has been the philosophy that essentializes, inflates, and privileges one side of binary opposites, which suppresses not only the unfavored side in a pair but also the middle voice (*la voix moyenne*) which is neither present nor absent. Derrida states: "Philosophy has perhaps commenced by distributing the middle voice, expressing a certain intransitiveness, into the active and the passive voice, and has itself been constituted in this repression" ("Differance," 137).

Here we can remind ourselves of the way the Buddha articulated the middle path. The philosophy of presence, and thus of being, is one extreme—just as absence and non-being is another. While problematizing Western philosophy for its privileging presence, Derrida is cautious so as not to place deconstruction at the opposite end of onto-theological metaphysics. A philosophy created to locate itself at the other end of the metaphysics of presence will be yet another metaphysics. As the Buddha expounds in his explanation of the middle path, the articulation of absence, as much as that of presence, anchors itself in substantialized being. The role of Derridean deconstruction, then, is to mark the indecidability between presence and absence and thus to demonstrate the impossibility of drawing a clear and permanent line between the two. The "middle" in the middle voice, thus, witnesses the dissolution of the subject and object, and further announces their interdependence.

Différance and Dependent Co-arising

The "middle"—both in the "middle path" and the "middle voice"—attests to the limits of pursuing our thinking in a dualistic manner. While the middle path and the middle voice both announce interdependence as a condition of being, the nature of this dependency is further clarified through the media of "dependent co-arising" in Buddhism and "*différance*" in Derridean deconstruction.

We can distinguish Buddhist "dependent co-arising" and Derridean "*différance*" by characterizing the former as empirical realism and the latter as semiotic realism. In proposing this distinction, I have no intention of employing it as a value judgment on these two philosophical endeavors. While others have attempted to interpret the linguistic nature of *différance* as a limitation of Derridean deconstruction, I have reservations about such an interpretation, which create a competition between deconstruction and Buddhism. That approach plays the latter over against the former by crediting Buddhism's function as a religious discourse and further positing religious practice as the final goal to be achieved in deconstruction. While we will not go into detail on this issue here, we can say that the differences between "dependent co-arising" and "*différance*" are rather a positive indication that deconstruction does not belong to one school of thought but is a mode of thinking that can be found in various philosophical traditions.

That said, what is the relationship between the middle voice/*différance* in Derridean deconstruction and the middle path/dependent co-arising in Buddhism? In the "Kaccāyana" section quoted earlier, the Buddha explicates the meaning of the middle path by virtue of the dependency of phenomena/dharma in the world:

> Kaccāyana, without approaching either extreme, the Tathāgata teaches you a doctrine by the middle. Dependent upon ignorance arise dispositions; dependent upon dispositions arises consciousness; dependent upon consciousness arises the psychophysical personality; dependent upon the psychophysical personality arise the six senses; dependent upon the six senses arises contact; dependent upon contact arises feeling; dependent upon feeling arises craving; de-

> pendent upon craving arises grasping; dependent upon grasping arises becoming; dependent upon becoming arises birth; dependent upon birth arise old age and death, grief, lamentation, suffering, dejection and despair. Thus arises this entire mass of suffering.[12]

The passage illuminates what are now known as the twelve-links of dependent co-arising. Rather than pause to elaborate on the meaning of each stage of the twelve-links, we direct our attention to the expression "dependent upon," which links the twelve chains in the above passage. What does it mean to say that "A" is "dependent upon" "B"?

Dependent co-arising in terms of temporality indicates the causation of things happening. In this case, the temporality is not a linear movement subscribing to the idea that cause "A" produces cause "A-1" as its effect. Dependent co-arising proffers the multilevel causation for each and every moment to each and every existence. A being exists at the crossroads of a complicated web of causes that are both causes for future happenings as much as they are effects of previous happenings. The "next-previous" connection exists only in the linguistic convention, since no moment—however brief it may be—can stand still to be identified as past, present, or future. In this sense, the past has never existed; the present and future will not ever exist; but all the same the past, present, and future influence and are influenced by others. The "dependent co-arising" then demands a maximum level of awareness of the mutability of a being.

The causality in this case needs careful understanding, as David J. Kalupahana describes:

> The description of phenomena as "dependently arisen" constitutes a middle way in that it steers clear of two extremes. First, it avoids the assumption of a mysterious underlying substance relating the cause and the effect, an assumption involved in most theories that uphold absolute identity or identities. The Buddha rejected such a conception of identity (*ekatta*) as metaphysical. Second, it eschews the equally metaphysical absolute distinction (*puthutta*), thereby ruling out atomistic theories of existence, which are normally based on rationalistic rather than empiricist analysis of time into past, present, and future. Therefore the terms expressive of the concepts of atoms (*paramānu*) or moments (*khana*) are conspicuously absent in the early discourses.[13]

In Buddhism one's inability and failure to realize the dependent nature of existence is identified as "suffering." One generally attributes this "feeling" of suffering to the physical and mental pain experienced in daily life. By elaborating on this pain, Buddhism expands the notion of suffering to comprehend the endemic symptom of a human being's tendency to reify dependently arisen phenomena and, accordingly, attribute a substantial nature to them. Explained through dependent co-arising, the conditionality of a being denies any such possibility of a being as a substantive entity—metaphysical or theological—and further places a being in a web of a multilevel causation.

The concept of dependent co-arising has been frequently confused with an atomistic dependency of entities as Kalupahana explained in the passage above. Consider the model of beings—A, B, C, D, *ad infinitum* —that exist in dependence upon others. A's existence is dependent upon B, B's upon C, C's upon D, *ad infinitum*. Though supporting the idea of a being's dependency on others, this falls short of truly explaining Buddhism's dependent co-arising because, according to this model, we are constantly hypostatizing A then B then C, and so on, as independent entities while we simultaneously state that they are not. In order to understand the meaning of dependent co-arising in Buddhism, at least two points need to be emphasized: activity and non-substantiality.

Things exist in connection with others. It is important in this context to imagine this connection *without* constructing a substantial entity—either as a subject or an object—that acts as an agent of this connection. Mutual-connections and inter-dependency in the web of dependent co-arising are movements without agent. To understand dependent co-arising as an activity means to recognize that dependent co-arising cannot have a name and thus is unnameable and, at the same time, self-deconstructing. In Derridean deconstruction, these self-deconstructing activities are indicated through the function of *différance*. *Différance*, writes Derrida, "has neither existence nor essence. It belongs to no category of being, present or absent" ("Differance," 134), because *différance* refutes any attempt to reify it. It refuses without refuting, for refuting itself presupposes an agent that does the act of refuting. *Différance*, then, is an indication, a movement in itself. From its birth, *différance* violates linguistic convention and, perhaps, the very rule of language, as Derrida replaces the normal "e" with an "a" in order to incorporate a "temporal" dimension. This "a" in *différance* is a reminder of the temporality that functions in each and every word in our language and thus in our thought process itself—the end result of which is the loss of innocence. The innocence of the human mind and of philosophy, which constantly appropriates its own limits within itself so that it can "receive name[s] only from within itself,"[14] witnesses through the functioning of *différance* that the identity has always already been a non-identity. As dependent co-arising reminds us of heterogeneity of being, *différance* attests to the non-innocence of language and naming.

The issue, then, is how to illustrate the heterogeneity that exists within, instead of outside of, identity. Heterogeneity existing inside of identity is the power that is immanent, at all times ready for rupture. Each and every moment, like the shade of darkness in the light or the glow of light in the darkness, heterogeneity peeps out of each and every name given—sometimes hidden, sometimes exposed and thus is suppressed and forgotten. Intentional forgetting of the heterogeneity of one's identity has been a precondition of the determination that metaphysical thinking has inscribed in philosophy through its foregrounding of the presence and purity of unity and, thus, of essence. Identity itself has already been invaded and even constructed by heterogeneity within the identity. Derrida gives name *différance* to the activities of this heterogeneity.

At the very beginning of "Differance" Derrida has identified five precursors of *différance*:

> Différance is neither a word nor a concept. In it, however, we shall see the juncture—rather than the summation—of what has been most decisively inscribed in the thought of what is conveniently called our "epoch": the difference of forces in Nietzsche, Saussure's principle of semiological difference, differing as the possibility of [neuron] facilitation, impression and delayed effect in Freud, difference as the irreducibility of the trace of the other in Levinas, and the ontic-ontological difference in Heidegger. ("Difference," 130)[15]

In several places in this essay, Derrida brings our attention to the nature of our "epoch," which he defines as that of "difference." According to Derrida, the concept of difference plays a major role in all five thinkers he named as precursors of *différance*. These endeavors mark the turning away from the metaphysics of essence, of presence, and of the presence-absence dualism. In the history of modern Continental philosophy, the Cartesian ego-cogito searches its way out of the confinements of subjectivity through Hegelian dialectics as the subject and object inter-act in dialectical movements. Hegelian revolution, however, remains in the domain of subjectivist philosophy because the project of dialectics always returns to the identity of the subject as an agent of dialectics and to the expectation that the subject will eventually incorporate the object. Efforts to overcome subject-object dualism continue from the philosophy of Nietzsche to Heidegger, *via* Freud, de Saussure and Levinas. By proposing *différance* as yet another stage of our epoch, Derridean deconstruction begins by marking the meaning of these differences as well as the difference between them and *différance*.

Derridean *différance*—yet another version of the philosophy of difference in the epoch of difference—functions as a reminder of the degree of our enslavement to metaphysical thinking. To think about *différance* in our discourse is to imagine the invisible and inaudible sounds of the "functioning" of difference that is the play of "trace" and of *différance*:

> Differance is what makes the movement of signification possible only if each element that is said to be "present" appearing on the stage of presence, is related to something other than itself but retains the mark of a past element and already lets itself be hollowed out by the mark of its retaliation to a future element. This trace relates no less to what is called the future than to what is called the past, and it constitutes what is called the present by this very relation to what it is not, to what it absolutely is not. ("Differance," 142-143)

Through *différance*, Derrida facilitates the interruption of metaphysical thinking, announcing its closure, but which is not an end.

The Unnameable and Negative Theology

"[D]ifférance remains a metaphysical name," writes Derrida. Even *différance*, so far as it is a name that we use to communicate and talk about beings, is metaphysical, because "all the names that it receives from our language are still, so far as they are names, metaphysical" ("Differance," 158). However, *différance* "is not a name, . . . is not a pure nominal unity, and continually breaks up in a chain of different substitutions" ("Differance," 158). Here we can remind ourselves of the Buddha's words, quoted at the beginning of this essay: "Subhūti, with any truth-statement, truth is undeclarable; so it is called truth-statement." In this passage (and in many others in Buddhist literature), the issue is not so much "the truth" as the *nature* of the truth. The nature of truth has little to do with the authority and power that have always been connected with the name "truth." When the unnameability of names, hence, the non-name-ness of such names as "dependent co-arising" or "*difference*," is understood in the style of transcendental onto-theological metaphysics, the unnameability obtains the power all the more because of its evasiveness and its beyond-name-ness. When Buddhism was/still is misunderstood as a tradition of nihilism, and when "*différance*" is assessed as a kind of negative theology, we once again remember how strong our tie is with history.

The difference between *différance* and negative theology could be "infinitesimal" as much as "infinite," as Derrida notes.[16] All the same, the unnameability of dependent co-arising and *différance* is to be distinguished from negative theology, because negative theology is a movement toward hyper-essentiality. Negative theology is another reflection of our determination to identify Being and essence as existing beyond the confinement of our language, whereas dependent co-arising and *différance* obviate such a possibility. Like "dependent co-arising," *différance* is not a "thing" nor a "concept" or an "idea." Thus again we are reminded of the passage quoted earlier concerning the "middle path" and the "middle voice," which are neither passive nor active, neither exist nor do not exist, and which are neither present nor absent.

Why is presence and the philosophical assumption of the existence of nonchanging entity so problematic for Derrida? There are at least two ways to explain this. First, in our thinking process, philosophy is done through language and language itself functions through differences and trace. Once the differential notion of language is accepted, the idea of presence in onto-theological discourse is possible only when we seize the movements of *différance* and trace that have been always already at work.

Secondly, to Derrida, the problem of presence (and the present) is the problem of the future as well. If presence exists in the present, then presence should provide a predictable future. Presence is not merely a predictability of future, but the future itself, because presence is timeless. However, the future is a "monster" as Derrida attests at the end of his "exergue" in *Of Grammatology*. The future is utter unpredictability, clear evidence of which appears in one's death. In *Of Grammatology*, the "monstrosity" of death is articulated through the movement of *différance*.[17] In "Signature Event Context," death reveals itself through the "iterability" of writing. The text outlives its author, and the capacity of the text to survive its author's absence and the death of the author in language is a "pyramid."[18] To remember the face of death—its presence and absence in our being—is to refresh the existential condition of the human being all over again. Here we realize a theme that runs through both Buddhism and deconstruction in a manner that is not too obvious but still visible: the mortality of our existence.

Though implicit and sometimes even disguised, Derridean deconstruction has waged a war against the philosopher's futile dream to reify our existence and thus create immortality out of one's finite and mortal life. The names Derrida has assigned to the tradition of Western metaphysics—such as ethnocentrism, logocentrism, metaphysics of presence, phallocentrism and so on—are all marked by the extension of the power of the dominant party in the field into eternity and thus into *the* Truth. That the immortality of their power is inevitably based on the identity principle, which is constructed through the suppression of their respective Others, make both Buddhism and Derridean deconstruction emphasize the middle path/middle voice, in which identity cannot be understood except as non-identity. Identity is constantly in the process of being created without giving us a chance to name it *as* "identity," for dependent co-arising or *différance* is always already at work, before we name it.

Marking the juncture between Buddhist and Derridean deconstruction of the essentialist view of life and the world, we are asked to remember once again the reality of our existence. The immeasurability of life remains with us, sometimes silent, sometimes palpable, but all the time defying human beings' desire to create a pyramid and domesticate others. Our existence is marked by an open ending. Without openness toward the inconceivability of the world, we are trapped. As Derrida tells us, this is a dangerous play. Buddhists know that it is not easy for us to give up the illusory "self" we have created since the beginningless beginning of the phylogeny of the human mind. Danger and difficulty, however, do not change the reality. It might be only through a constant engagement with them that we may be able to peep into a fragment of the groundless ground which we call "our existence."

Notes

1. *The Diamond Sūtra, Taishō shinshū daizōkyō.* [Hereafter *T*] 8.235.751 c.

2. Jacques Derrida, *Acts of Religion*, ed. Gil Anidjar (New York: Routledge, 2002).

3. The essay was presented at a conference on religion held in Capri on February 28 and March 1, 1994, and the note was added on April 26, 1995. The note in its entirety says: "This, perhaps, is what I would have liked to say of a certain Mount Moriah—while going to Capri, last year, close by the Vesuvius of Gradiva. Today I remember what I had just finished reading in Genet at Chatila, of which so many of the premises deserve to be remembered here, in so many languages, the actors and the victims, and the eves and the consequence, all the landscapes and all the specters: 'One of the questions I will not avoid is that of religion'" (*Acts of Religion,* 101).

4. Derrida, *Acts of Religion*, 23.

5. When Derrida first introduced "*différance*" before the French Society of Philosophy he was fully aware that *différance* could be confused with negative theology. He was also well aware of the importance of distinguishing between the two, as he states: ". . . the detours, phrases, and syntax that I shall often have to resort to will resemble,—will sometimes be practically indiscernible from those of negative theology. Already we had to note that differance is not, does not exist, and is not any sort of being-present (on). And

we will have to point out everything that it is not, and consequently, that it has neither existence nor essence. It belongs to no category of being, present or absent. And yet what is thus denoted as differance is not theological, not even in the most negative order of negative theology. The latter, as we know, is always occupied with letting a supraessential reality go beyond the finite categories of essence and existence, that is, of presence, and always hastens to remind us that, if we deny the predicate of existence of God, it is in order to recognize him as a superior, inconceivable, and ineffable mode of being." (Jacques Derrida, "Differance" [Hereafter "Differance"] in *Speech and Phenomena and Other Essays on Husserl's Theory of Signs,* trans. David B. Allison [Evanston, Ill: Northwestern University Press, 1973], 134).

Also see "The Original Discussion of 'Différance' (1968)," trans. David Wood, Sarah Richmond, and Malcom Bernard, in *Derrida and Différance*, eds. David Wood and Robert Bernasconi (Evanston, Ill: Northwestern University Press, 1988), 83-95; and *Derrida and Negative Theology*, eds. Harold Coward and Toby Foshay (Albany: State University of New York Press, 1992).

6. See my "General Introduction" to this volume for a discussion on this issue.

7. "The Kaccāyana" in *Samyutta-nikāya* vol. 2, 12, §15. English translation, *The Book of the Kindred Sayings*, trans. Rhys Davids (Oxford: Pali Text Society, 2000), vol. 2, 12.

8. *Samyutta-nikāya,* vol. 2, 12-13

9. *Samyutta-nikāya*, vol. 2, 12-13. This passage is repeated several times in the text with several variations. For example, the chapter on "Jānussoni" (*Samyutta-nikāya*, XII, §47 (7)) has almost the same expression as in "The Kaccāyana." The section 48 (8) "The Brahmin wise in world-lore" shows a variation on the theme:

'What [say you] here, Master Gotama: — everything is?'

'"Everything is"— that, brahmin, is the chief world-wisdom.'

'Well then, Master Gotama:—nothing is?'

'"Nothing is":— that, brahmin, is the second world-wisdom.'

'"Everything is a unity":— that, brahmin, is the third world-wisdom.'

'Well then, Master Gotama: — everything is a plurality?'

'"Everything is a plurality": — that, brahmin, is the fourth world-wisdom.

The Tathāgata, not approaching any of these extremes, teaches you a Doctrine by a middle [way].'

10. *Daban niepan jing* (*The Nirvana Sūtra*), *T* 12.375.819b. Earlier in the same text, it was also stated: "The Buddha nature is neither inside, nor outside, both inside and outside, therefore it is called the middle path"(*T* 12.375.819b).

11. Jacques Derrida, *Of Grammatology*, trans. Gayatri Chakravorty Spivak (Baltimore: The Johns Hopkins University Press, 1974), 19; *De la grammatologie* (Paris: Les Éditionsde Minuit, 1967), 31

12. "The Kaccāyana" in *Samyutta-nikāya* vol. 2, XII, §15. English translation by David J. Kalupahana, *A History of Buddhist Philosophy: Continuities and Discontinuities* (Honolulu: University of Hawaii Press, 1992,), 58-59.

13. Kalupahana, *A History of Buddhist Philosophy*, 54.

14. Jacques Derrida, *Margins of Philosophy* (1972), trans. Alan Bass (Chicago: University of Chicago Press, 1982), x.

15. This passage was omitted when "Differance" was reprinted to be included in the *Marges de la philosophie* (1972). The version in *Théorie d'ensemble* (1968) and the English translation in *Speech and Phenomena* contain the passage.

16 David Wood and Robert Bernasconi, eds. *Derrida and Différance* (Evanston, Ill: Northwestern University Press, 1988), 85.

17. Derrida thus writes: "Differance does not *resist* appropriation, it does not impose exterior limit upon it. Differance began by broaching alienation and it ends by leaving reappropriation *breached.* Until death. Death is the movement of differance to the extent that that movement is necessarily finite" (*Of Grammatology*, 143, emphasis original; *De la Grammatologie*, 206).

18. See Jacques Derrida, "Signature Event Context" and "The Pit and the Pyramid: Introduction to Hegel's Semiology" in *Margins of Philosophy.*

Two

Nāgārjuna and Deconstruction[1]

Ian Mabbett

In July 1992, the Mongolian People's Revolutionary Party discarded its former icons Marx and Lenin and installed Nāgārjuna in their place. This all goes to show that the great sage and *siddha* revered in the lamaist tradition has something to say to an age when the old certainties, east and west, are being busily deconstructed.

No doubt the former Communist party was anxious to improve its image with the Mongolian Buddhist faithful, but it remains to be seen how successfully the doctrine of the void can be applied to the problems of falling production and soaring prices. Critics of Nāgārjuna might complain that a currency made of voidness must make little impression in the market-place of economic reality. It is not hard to find a western parallel: hostile critics of deconstruction like to ask, similarly, what this teaching has to do with the problems of the real world. Rather like Samuel Johnson kicking a large stone to demonstrate the alleged fatuity of Berkeley's subjective idealism,[2] they appeal to all-too-solid things like buses and large stones to emphasize the contrast between the real world and the flossy Gallic tissue of verbiage which they take deconstruction to be.[3]

Nāgārjuna followed Marx eastwards to Mongolia; deconstruction followed Berkeley westwards to America. Indeed, as Jacques Derrida (who is certainly honored in America, if not in his own country) said, America *is* deconstruction. "L'Amérique, mais *c'est* la déconstruction."[4] As Berkeley said, "Westward the course of empire takes its way."

Eastward and westward: opposites meet. Perhaps the apostle of the Middle Way and the prophet of infinite deferral have something in common.

Nāgarjuna, the possibly second-century Mahāyāna Buddhist teacher who provided a foundation for the doctrine of the void, has been compared to most western thinkers from Zeno to Wittgenstein. In principle, there is no reason why such comparisons should not often enough be illuminating. At all events, it is surely timely, since almost all other possible terms of comparison have been ransacked, that the magic void-making spells of the Mādhyamikas and the deconstructionists should be tested together. Of course, the tests must be conducted with extreme caution, for the spells are dangerous to their users. Nāgārjuna himself warned us: "Like a snake when it is not properly grasped, or a magical spell when it is not properly executed, voidness when it is not properly apprehended can be the ruin of a person of weak intelligence."[5]

There have already been a few essays in the comparison.[6] In setting out to add to their number, I began with the belief that the comparison between two systems of thought from such different cultural environments must be radically incommensurable, and that the plotting of similarities could only be a *jeu d'esprit*. The further I advanced, however, the more genuinely significant the similarities seemed to be. In some important sense, it seemed that people like Jacques Derrida and people like Nāgārjuna are seeking to give form—a self-referring and self-canceling form—to the same vision. In a sense, no doubt, the fundamental differences of world view and intellectual purpose set them in different universes; yet the tracing of similarities is not just a game. In what follows, I seek to identify a number of areas of similarity, and to argue that in these areas the juxtaposition of deconstruction and Mādhyamika allows us to recognize a type of vision which can be shared by widely different cultures.

For the purposes of the comparison, some assumptions must be made. So far as deconstruction is concerned, the authority claimed for the characterizations to be offered lies in some of the writings of Jacques Derrida, Paul de Man, Jonathan Culler, Barbara Johnson and a few other scholars generally considered to be of the same persuasion.

So far as the Madhyamaka philosophy of Nāgārjuna is concerned, the authority claimed for what follows lies primarily in my study of the *Mūlamadhyamakakārikās* (with some account of other texts credibly attributed to the same author, principally the *Vigrahavyāvartanī*). Detailed justification of the interpretation of this philosophy must wait on separate publication of the results of this study.[7] There has recently been much discussion of Nāgārjuna's philosophy, often showing a tendency to assimilate it to modern empirical ideas. David Kalupahana considers that the *Kārikās* offer essentially pragmatic arguments about the meaning of experience and deny the value of metaphysical inquiry into supposed realities or non-realities that cannot be demonstrated.[8] Quite a few other scholars have taken the chief concern of Madhyamaka philosophy to be with validating the language of ordinary experience in one way or another, particularly in a Wittgensteinian way; but it is not clear that Wittgenstein would have accepted the views here attributed to him.[9]

Clearly there is no room here, in comparing a particular view of deconstruction with a particular view of Madhyamaka, to justify and document properly the interpretation of Madhyamaka adopted. I shall have to give short shrift to some of the authorities often cited in philosophical discussion. The interpretation of Nāgārjuna's thought which I adopt is not influenced by those who interpret it as pragmatic or empirical, but draws support at various points from some other scholars who have made close textual studies—for example, J. W. de Jong,[10] D. Ruegg[11] and Jacques May[12]—although no identity is claimed for my interpretation with all of theirs.

The assumption I make here is that Nāgārjuna's teaching was anti-metaphysical in one sense but not in another. He did consider it possible to say important things about metaphysics, and he engaged in metaphysical discussion; he believed, not that metaphysical *arguments* are without practical value, but that they can be used to dismantle any metaphysical *claim* about the existence or non-existence of any particular thing alleged to be real; such claims conceal contradictions (specifically, in Husserl's sense, *Widersinnigkeit*; "The supplement" 91f.). This demolition of categories was carried out in the name of rational analysis, not intuition or practical utility. Nāgārjuna certainly believed in the over-riding importance of Buddhist cultivation, *bhāvanā*, to which ultimately rational analysis was only an accessory. However, this should not blind us to the rational character of his philosophical writing, which must be judged by the standards appropriate to its purposes.

Here, then, is a characterization of the various ways in which Nāgārjuna's dismantling of concept-reifying views can be compared to that of the deconstructionists.

Questioning Determinate Reality

Both Nāgārjuna and deconstruction avoid any claim about a determinate reality. Nāgārjuna insists that, in arguing that all alleged real things are void, he is nevertheless advancing no dogma of his own. He is committed to no doctrine or systematic belief about reality (*dṛṣṭi*). The method that he follows in criticizing any *dṛṣṭi* is not to advance some argument of his own against it; instead, he proceeds by putting himself into his opponent's sandals and setting them going in order to show how the opponent's argument works. The sandals march straight over the edge of a cliff. Essentially, his method is the *reductio ad absurdum*, which in Madhyamaka is regarded, not as an argument different from the one which it exposes, but as the same, recast in a form that allows us to see its absurdity.

In the *Vigrahavyāvartanī*, he confronts squarely the objection that he is contradicting himself when he proclaims the voidness of all things, including his own claim that all is void. This is not a contradiction, he maintains. Something unreal or false may have its unreality or falseness exposed by something which is itself unreal or false. We may imagine a puppet show in which one puppet tears apart another, revealing it to be just a puppet, not a sentient being.

> Suppose that a person, artificially created, should do away with another artificial person; or that a magic man should do away with another man created by his own magic (*svamayayā*). Of the same nature would be this negation.[13]

Though it is a commonly held view, the notion that Nāgārjuna's "voidness" means either "non-existence" or "falsity" must be rejected; it is easy to show, from the *Vigrahavyāvartanī*, that by "void" Nāgārjuna did not mean "non-existent." What is void is unreal, lacking substance; it is not exactly existent (being unreal) and not exactly non-existent (being manifest, however delusively). An unreal figure (a robot, or a phantom, or a figure seen in a dream) may utter a true statement; similarly, though all things are void including the utterance of the teaching of voidness, this utterance can serve as the vehicle for truth. This is made quite clear in *VV* XXII (autocommentary).

It has often been debated whether Nāgārjuna means to offer any views of his own at all. The view that he somehow manages to teach the doctrine of voidness without saying anything seems to rest upon a misunderstanding of some passages in the *Kārikās* and, especially, the *Vigrahavyāvartanī*.[14] What Madhyamaka teaches is that concepts, dogmas, rational constructions of all sorts that presuppose the existence of things fail to capture the ultimate truth. The truth must always defeat any attempt to shut a door upon it, to give it a fixed and final shape. Those who make a dogma of voidness itself are making a grave mistake: "The vanquishers [the Buddhas of the past] have proclaimed that vacuity is the purgative of all views. But they declared those who hold vacuity as (itself) a view to be incurable" (*MMK* 13.8).

Like Nāgārjuna stepping into his opponent's sandals, the deconstructionists seek to take an object of thought and show it for what it is, allowing its inconsistencies to discredit it. They, like Nāgārjuna, expressly dissociate themselves from theories about things; or rather, in examining "theory" in inverted commas, they seek to transcend theories without offering rival theories.[15]

What ultimately legitimizes a proposition about a thing is the meaning it derives from its context. The context is constituted by an infinite play of differences which cannot be fixed and determined. Therefore, as soon as we seek to describe something, what happens is not exactly the utterance of a truth or an untruth; it is rather an arbitrary construction that cannot be attached to any absolute framework of objective fact.[16]

Derrida is therefore seeking to elicit a sense of a reality which always steps aside from itself. One cannot speak of it, but one can point to the conceptual space it occupies which constitutes the condition of speaking about it, the possibility of a quest.[17]

Discourse and Reality

Both Nāgārjuna and deconstruction identify their teaching with what is really the case. All this looks uncommonly like the enlightenment, *bodhi*, which (perhaps rather than the too-much-discussed *nirvāṇa*) is at the heart of the Buddhist message. After the Buddha had transcended the realms of being and non-being, of consciousness and non-consciousness, he entered the realm that is pure enlightenment, which is not a knowing of facts but a disappearance of ignorance, leaving only what *is* (in a special sense distinct from existence and non-existence). What, then, is it that *is*? The early schools which Nāgārjuna criticized taught that from the standpoint of enlightenment the phenomenal world of change and appearances (*saṃsāra*) is unreal; what is real is the transcendent state of *nirvāṇa*. Mahāyāna thought, which Nāgārjuna as much as anybody mapped out,[18] declares on the other hand that *saṃsāra* and *nirvāṇa* are coterminous.[19] There is no place or state separate from the world we know, with its chaos, its inconsistencies, its texts waiting to be deconstructed. *Nirvāṇa* does not introduce us to some new state; the difference is simply that enlightenment shows us all the old states (including the states of our "selves") as they really are.

The only word recognized in Buddhism as meaning anything like "Buddhism" is *dharma*, which originally meant what holds things up. It is the substratum, the foundation, the bedrock of reality. In Buddhism, *dharma* became the teaching, the doctrine, the bedrock of knowledge, the way taught by the Buddhas. In some of the early schools, the term came to signify the bedrock of apprehended reality—*dharmas* were real things, which could be counted. In Mahāyāna Buddhism, the *dharmakāya* was the body of the Buddha which is one with the ultimate truth, the ultimate reality. Hence we see ontological and epistemological categories doubling one another: the teaching or way taught by the Buddhas is also what is the case; it is the universe.

In the case of the deconstructionists, likewise, what they do is often described as a way of recognizing what is, rather than a theory or view about it. Deconstruction, it has been said, is simply what is the case. If this is true, we must remember that (according to the deconstructionist approach) "what is the case" is not a given reality, eternally different from specific alternatives that are not the case: "Deconstruction is neither theory nor philosophy. It is neither a school nor a method. It is not even a discourse, nor an act, nor a practice. It is what happens, what is happening today" ("Some statements," 20).

Elsewhere, Derrida suggests that he might ("with a smile") say that deconstruction is America. It follows then that America is what happens, what is happening today. It is *saṃsāra*, a monster text ripe for deconstruction.

But what sort of thing can deconstruction really be? It is not even a *method*, because after all methods use tools, which are real, solid entities, on the same plane of reality as the things upon which they are used, and different from them. Deconstruction, however, has no existence as an activity separate from the phenomena whose nature it recognizes, which it deconstructs. It is a non-thing in itself. Derrida acknowledges the criticism of John Searle that for twenty years deconstruction had not been in existence, had been a "mist hiding everything." He cordially agreed. "Yes, it has neither consistency nor existence" ("Some Statements," 93f.). Elsewhere he affirmed: "All sentences of the type: 'Deconstruction is X' or 'Deconstruction is not X' *a priori* miss the point" ("Letter," 4). When we speak of deconstruction, then, there is no unique given reality with which we can identify it apart from the phenomenal world itself, which is a text, a structure or seeming structure whose real nature can be recognized to be incapable of consistent characterization once it is seen for what it is. "Reality," or all that can be recognized as such, is not something that *comes to be known*, having existed previously. It is a construction of knowing. The ghosts of Nietzsche and Heidegger breathe upon "what happens, what is happening today": knowledge,

Wissen, constructs realities as part of the will to control. Deconstruction, which employs a special type of contemplative thought, *Denken* we might call it, gives us the eye of insight to see that this is what is happening. It is really like the Buddha eye, which sees all things, and the enlightenment it promises is really like *bodhi.*

Inter-dependency of Beings

According to both Nāgārjuna and deconstruction, things are not intrinsically real but exist only in relation to other things. Everything is relative.[20] This is a fundamental doctrine of Buddhism, maintained as an axiom (with important variations of detail) throughout Buddhist history. The Buddha sought to formulate this notion with the doctrine of "dependent co-production," *pratītyasamutpāda*, according to which things must be understood as arising in dependence upon each other. They are not absolutes; they are conditioned by causes. Given that one thing is present, another thing arises. Phenomena are not solid and permanent things; they are transient, appearing and disappearing in mutual dependence.

Possibly, according to the realism of the *abhidharma* (philosophical dogma) schools whose influence Nāgārjuna was vigorously challenging, the interdependence of the phenomena of the world was seen as an interdependence of real, substantive entities, even if they were impermanent and subject to iron laws that ruled their brief life. Nāgārjuna, however, denied the intrinsic substantive reality of anything, however brief, and insisted that the very existence of any phenomenon is only relative. It is relative to other phenomena, which in turn exist only in relation to others.

Two images will help to capture something of this notion of radical relativity. One is the paradoxical interdependence of things in an Escher drawing. For example, there is his famous picture *Drawing Hands*, which depicts one hand holding a pen to draw a picture of a second hand, which is holding a pen and drawing the first. Or there is the battlement staircase, where, impossibly, every step is below every other step (or, equally, above every other step), so that the men trudging up the staircase are always ascending yet always going in circles. Perhaps the images are not radical enough; for Nāgārjuna, nothing is real and solid—not just its position but its very being belongs not to it but to something else.

Again, consider the cliché scene of innumerable cartoon films in which some fleeing victim, running blindly and furiously, continues successfully to run for several paces through empty air even after going over the edge of a precipice. After a few moments of this paradoxical locomotion, the victim looks down, registers comical dismay, and *only then* plummets through the void. The Buddhist message is clear. The phenomenal world continues to hold us up only so long as we are ignorant. When we gain knowledge, we see that it is not solid and capable of holding us up. The solidity of things is an illusion: each thing is held up by something else, but if we analyze the chain of holding-up completely we find that it is circular, and there is nothing holding up the whole world. When we see that, we understand the truth of the void. Things exist, but only relatively.

Deconstruction, of course, is playing a different game by different rules. It is not a system of methodical thought pursuing a logically constructed programme.[21] Nevertheless, it too ends up with radical relativity.

This can be seen, pre-eminently, in the area of textual criticism, which is deconstruction's home ground. Jonathan Culler, for example, insists upon the essential relativity of text and reader, neither of them absolutely real, each taking on essential reality and definition from the other. He warns us against the two sorts of monism which can tempt those who one-sidedly emphasize either of two complementary themes in deconstructive criticism.[22]

On the one hand, there is a temptation to treat the reader alone as real and the text essentially as an artifact of the reader's imagination—it is not something fixed and absolute, but something re-created by each reading. This version of deconstructive criticism is a fallacy.

On the other hand, there is a temptation to treat the text alone as real ("the author is dead"[23]); properly analyzed, it is seen not to conform to the facile expectations brought to it by the reader but to be inexorably alien. At every step it defeats the images of it produced by the reader's imagination, stepping back into absolute otherness. This version too, maintained exclusively, is also a heresy.

What is needed, says Jonathan Culler, is a sort of dualism of text and reader, a relativity: neither is absolutely real, yet both are necessary.[24] This relativity is implicit in the dualism of context and meaning that runs through Derrida's thought and has already been alluded to above. Meaning must be supplied by a reconstitution of the context, but there is an infinite play of possibly appropriate context. One must take into account all aspects of a statement which could affect its meaning: language, allusions, stress on words, the identity of the speaker and the reader, and so forth. Derrida wrote that a "text" is not really confined by any boundary, but is part of a total context. "This is my starting-point: no meaning can be determined out of context, but no context permits saturation."[25] There is no meaning without context and *vice versa*. Derrida's essay plays on the concept of the double bind.

This relativity is particularly apparent also in the fundamental deconstructionist routine that can be used to dismantle any given system of symbols ("marks," as Derrida prefers to call them, rather than the earlier "signs"), such as language itself. Within an integrated system of symbols, the essential reality of each element is actually constituted by its relation to the other elements, not by anything intrinsic to it, for in practice its structure can vary a great deal; only its relation to its context defines it. "No element," says Derrida, "can function as a sign without referring to another element which itself is not simply present. This interweaving results in each element... being constituted on the basis of the trace within it of the other elements of the chain or system."[26] Since the phenomenal world is created for us by our concepts, and our concepts by language, the world itself is composed of elements that exist only in relation to each other, like Escher's drawing hands or like the "Twelve Nidānas" of Buddhist doctrine.

Criticism of Binary Opposites

Both Nāgārjuna and deconstruction criticize the logic of binary oppositions. Nāgārjuna's *Mūlamadhyamakakārikās* are founded upon the analysis of a series of asymmetrical relationships between paired terms. Each chapter attacks one such pair, or a cluster of related pairs. Generally speaking, each exhibits the same logic: the relationship in question is examined and declared to entail a contradiction or a logical impossibility. In each case, one term (*x*) is primary; it is substantive, or prior, while the other (*y*) is modal, or dependent. Nāgārjuna explores the meaning of the claim that *x*R*y*, where R is the relationship that is conventionally held to obtain between the two terms, and seeks to demonstrate that the claim is essentially absurd. Ultimately, his method is one that could be used to discredit any existential proposition that attributes a particular predicate to a particular subject.

The topics of his chapters show the repetitive technique. Nāgārjuna's juggernaut mows down sacred cow after sacred cow, leaving a shambles where the palace of Hīnayāna abhidharma philosophy once stood. Cause and effect, subject and verb, sensation and object of sense, entity and property, agent and action, thing that changes and successive states of that thing, earlier time and later time, Buddha and constituents of the Buddha's person, even *nirvāṇa* and life or becoming are all declared to be void, meaningless, mere empty expressions.[27]

Where deconstruction is concerned, it is enough to recall that the dismantling of binary oppositions is a stock routine. Wherever a relationship is supposed to inhere between two terms, one of which is primary and the other dependent or secondary, this relationship is systematically dismantled; each term is examined and declared to be unintelligible except insofar as it turns into a form of the other term. If *x* and *y* show a tendency to turn into each other, more happens than that *x*R*y* is inverted; the whole system that underpins the relationship is shown to be unstable; there is no fixed structure of determinate categories to which we can appeal. In textual criticism, this logic is repeatedly applied to such pairs as reality and appearance, truth and fiction, signified and signifier, man and woman, speech and writing, cause and effect, system and event, metaphor and metonymy. An interesting example is the case of cause and effect; Nietzsche suggested that the chronological relationship between them is inverted from the point of view of phenomenology;[28] Paul de Man and Jonathan Culler pursued a deconstructionist analysis of the relationship;[29] Jonathan Searle criticized this analysis.[30]

Emptiness

Both Nāgārjuna and deconstruction celebrate emptiness. Voidness (*Śūnyatā*) is Nāgārjuna's hallmark; he rides upon its back, as on a tiger, and his fame as a *siddha*, a perfect being endowed with supernatural faculties, must owe a great deal to his fearlessness in seeking to plumb the ultimate emptiness of the universe. The void is the protagonist of the major works that are most reliably attributable to him, the *Mūlamadhyamakakārikās* and the *Vigrahavyāvartanī*.

There are naturally problems in understanding his version of voidness, which can scarcely be addressed satisfactorily without undertaking an extended textual study. One such problem, surprisingly little analyzed, is in understanding exactly *how* Nāgārjuna seeks to prove this voidness (or, as he would have it, allows anybody else's arguments to expose themselves as void).[31]

At any rate, Nāgārjuna is quite clear that, however hard we look, we cannot discover any real things: "In no case are any things ever observed, whether they be (considered as) coming into existence autonomously, or derivatively, or both, or without any cause" (*MMK* I.1).

Here, "things" translates *bhāva*,[32] which has the general sense of "what arises or comes into being," "phenomenon." Why can we not observe things? Is it because they do not exist to be observed, or because our words or concepts are unequal to the task of identifying them accurately? This is one of the more contentious problems in the interpretation of the *Kārikās*; here there is room only to sketch a particular understanding of Nāgārjuna's teaching without detailed discussion of the views of others.

Madhyamaka is not idealism, and it is not nihilism either.[33] The "four-cornered negation," to be described shortly, proves as much: it was as important to Nāgārjuna to deny that things are inexistent as it was to deny that they are existent. "Not existing" is not an adequate characterization of what is void. The Madhyamaka void is supposed to be different from both existing and not existing; it designates the ontological status of a network of interdependent phenomena, rigorously governed by the rules of production but without the supporting framework of any first cause, divine power or immanent absolute.

This much is metaphysics, but there was a soteriological dimension to Mahāyāna practice not emphasized in the *Kārikās*. The application of Madhyamaka's metaphysics to the quest for salvation is to be found in the cultivation of *prajñā*, a Buddhist conception of insight or wisdom which is not specifically a mystical faculty but rather an intellectual intuition which can break down the barriers between the practitioner's consciousness and the ultimate truth (*paramārtha*). This insight is promoted by the proper realization of voidness.[34] The result of the insight can perhaps be described as a stepping aside from existence and inexistence; it is the place or condition that is presupposed by the possibility of either existing or not existing.

This teaching is important to the comparison with deconstruction, whose conception of "absence" needs to be understood similarly: it is not a simple nihilism. Deconstructionists do not argue flatly that things do not exist. The deconstructionist move is, rather, to point to the impossibility of finding original and ultimate referents for our words; what words succeed in referring to consists of traces, and these traces are traces of traces.

For Derrida, truth is not grasped by a mere negation. On the contrary, the right move employs an affirmation, albeit a paradoxical double affirmation: "Yes, yes." A statement, if it asserts something, contains an affirmation of it; but this affirmation can take on meaning only from a context—that is, by being endorsed, validated, by something outside itself, and the endorsement or validation is a second affirmation, a mention which is not the same thing as a use. In principle, the series is endless: "Et le *oui* se relance à l'infini" ("Ulysse," 143).

Our traditional world-view is said to be "logocentric": words are used as if each one corresponded to some stable and accessible feature of the real universe. On the contrary, rigorous analysis of the structures and relationships contained in any representation shows that they are inherently unstable and contradictory. The "presence" of the things supposed to be designated by words or other signs always retreats. There is no presence or *svabhāva*; there is only absence, and the real nature of things we seek to define must remain forever indeterminate.

It is a typical deconstructionist move to invert (albeit only provisionally, on the way to deconstruction) the relationship between archetype and ectype, origin and derivation. Origins and archetypes are, in the "logocentric" tradition, supposed to be actually existent determinate things, but they turn out on analysis to be constructions after the event (*vijñaptimātra*, Nāgārjuna would call them—mere verbal constructs), accessible only indirectly, and at a remove, through the derivations and ectypes that come to supplement them or transmit their effects. Thus, things are known only through the verbal conceptions with which we seek to pin them down. These conceptions are supposed to be dependent upon the alleged realities which they represent, but in fact the conceptions are all we have; the realities are absent. Where are they? All we can say is that they can never be tied down to a place; they are known only by their effects. Hence the principle (though it is really only a provisional formulation) that there are only representations; the thing represented cannot be definitively identified. Often quoted is Jacques Derrida's saying: "Il n'y a pas de hors-texte" (*OG*, 158). A page later, he writes (in G. Spivak's translation): "There has never been anything but writing; there have never been anything but supplements, substitutive significations which could only come forth in a chain of differential references, the 'real' supervening, and being added only while taking on meaning from a trace and from an invocation of the supplement, etc." (*OG*, 159). A previous reader of the library copy in which I read this had added his own exasperated supplement in the margin: "We are all figments of J. D.'s imagination. Solipsist ad nauseam. Real author, real reader, not you, not me, just HIM." This is not fair to Derrida, for whom the concept of us or him is just as much an unwarranted logocentric hypostatization as anything else.

Four-cornered Logic of Indeterminacy

Both Nāgārjuna and deconstruction use the same four-cornered logic. This is an Indian term, designating the tetralemma (*catuṣkoṭi*) by which it is shown that a given concept can have no fixed or determinate referent in reality. It is an extension of the simple dilemma, which succeeds in showing that there can be no such thing as a subject S if it is known that S with predicate P is impossible and also that S *without* P is impossible. The Indian tetralemma, part of the armory of Buddhist scepticism, is more thorough. It negates four possibilities: that there can be S with P, that there can be S without P, that there can be S both with and without P, and that there can be S neither with nor without P.

There has been a great deal of discussion of Nāgārjuna's use of the *catuṣkoṭi* from the point of view of logic.[35] It is an important part of his stock demonstration of the voidness of things, which can figure as subjects in no sentences.

Without attempting to display the actual logic of his attempted demonstration of the voidness of all things, we can review the pattern in its typical form as Nāgārjuna deploys it time and time again in the *Kārikās* to demonstrate the inconsistency of logocentric conceptions.

The technique takes the conception which is to be rendered void and shows step by step that its subject is impossible. Let us call its subject S and its predicate P. This formula, it will be noticed, can be used to render unintelligible any statement whatsoever about any alleged real entity if it can be used to destroy anything at all. ("*Nirvāṇa* exists;" "Buddhas have taught;" all is grist to the mill.)

In the first place, Nāgārjuna demonstrates that S cannot be without P, because by definition S is with P. This was taken as the premise. To claim that S lacks P would be contradictory. It is worth the observation that Nāgārjuna is not here (or anywhere else, despite the claims sometimes made) introducing a new three-valued logic as a part of his method. His logic is here quite conventional.[36]

In the second place, Nāgārjuna argues that S cannot be *with* P, because this involves doubling S (a sort of *dédoublement*). In his paradigm chapter on movement, for example, he says that the locus of a movement cannot be characterized by moving because this would entail two movements, and therefore two movers (*gantārau*) (*MMK* II.5, 6), which is false by definition—the discussion started with the case of just one mover. The distinctive method by which he reaches this result can be passed over here, but it may be noticed again that, given the result, the treatment of it follows conventional logic: if there must be two movers, this contradicts the premise and is therefore false if the premise is true.

In the third place, if S cannot be without P and if S cannot be with P, it follows that S cannot be both with and without P.

In the fourth place, S cannot be neither with nor without P, as this is absurd. Throughout, Nāgārjuna is appealing to the normal rules of logic.

The avowed technique of Madhyamaka, then, is to show by the use of the "four-cornered" logic that there can be no statement about a determinate subject S made by applying the predicate P.

There is a real similarity in deconstruction, which likewise seeks to allow the internal inconsistency of any 'logocentric' statement to reveal itself. David Lehman points out that in seeking to demonstrate that a conception X is contradictory, deconstruction is neither affirming nor denying X—it is, rather, seeking to show that X escapes both affirmation and denial (*Signs*, 82). Barbara Johnson wrote: "Instead of a simple 'either/or' structure, deconstruction attempts to elaborate a discourse that says *neither* 'either/or' *nor* 'both/and' nor even 'neither/nor', while at the same time not abandoning these logics either."[37]

Is this to propose for deconstruction a new set of rules of logic, in which the middle between affirmation and denial is allowed? Probably not. As with Madhyamaka, the answer seems to be that, where contradictory statements appear, they do not reflect a new sort of logic that is adopted to analyze statements. Normal logic is used to analyze statements. The statements are allowed to discredit themselves by their own rules. However, when the discrediting is achieved, this analysis leads to the conclusion that the realities to which the statements ostensibly refer are indeterminate. At this point, a variety of statements, contradictory or otherwise, are seen to be as good or bad as each other.

A careful examination of Barbara Johnson's options will show that deconstruction is credited with, precisely, the technique of the *catuṣkoṭi*. The matter is clinched by the words of Derrida himself: "Every time I say: X is neither this nor that, neither the contrary of this nor that, neither the simple neutralization of this nor of that with which it has *nothing in common*, being absolutely heterogeneous to or incommensurable with them, I would start to speak of God" ("Comment," 6). On this point, no more need be said.

Dismantling Self

Both Nāgārjuna and deconstruction dismantle the concept of the self. "Non-self" (*anātman*) is a traditional and fundamental Buddhist doctrine. There has always been room for debate about the meaning of *anātman* as it is presented in the canonical texts; these deny the identification of the self with any of five supposed constituents of personality severally, but one can still speculate that it might be identical with something else. On the other hand, the question of the fate of the self is one of the questions claimed elsewhere in the scriptures to have been declared by the Buddha to be unprofitable and not to be explained.[38] To ask such questions is already to miss the point. The truth comes in the space before the possibility of asking arises.

There is no particular difficulty about "non-self" for Nāgārjuna (*MMK* XVIII, *Ātmaparīkṣā*). *Ātma*, self, is like any other concept that identifies and constructs seemingly solid realities in the world. It is void, indeterminate. The constituents of the self are merely *prapañca*, projections. *Nivṛttam abhidhātavyaṃ, nivṛttaś cittagocaraḥ* (*MMK* XVIII, 7)—what is to be asserted ceases, the mind-field ceases. What is this "ceasing?" Perhaps it is a sort of absence, but not a non-existence; both self and not-self are provisional teachings; actually there is not self or not-self; nor are there both together, or neither one.

This resembles deconstruction insofar as the latter denies the validity of the logocentric concept of "self" as the designation of a knowable identifiable entity. The concept of the self, author or reader, can be deconstructed like any other. We find the relationship between the writing or reading self and language falling prey to the same juggernaut as other binary oppositions. Ostensibly, the self is the given reality, the substance, and language is its mode; but, being analyzed, language turns out to be (provisionally) what is given, indeed to be all that is given, and the self is a mode of language. "Language . . . thinks man and his 'world', including poems, if he will allow it to do so."[39]

The activities of modern critical thought, especially those that have developed in the wake of semiotics, are considered to have dissolved the absoluteness of the self, which can now be seen to be an epiphenomenon, a construct, indeed a projection or *prapañca*; as Foucault wrote: "The researches of psychoanalysis, of linguistics, of anthropology, have 'decentred' the subject in relation to the laws of its desire, the forms of its language, the rules of its actions, or the play of its mythical and imaginative discourse."[40] The point of view has changed. There is no fixed point of all reference marked by a seat of consciousness, from which the rest of the world can be observed; its place has been taken by a point of convergence, but the lines which converge are always shifting, and the self which they define is always retreating.

Perhaps the clearest deconstructionist statement of something like the principle of *anātman* is Derrida's: "'I' always means, at heart, 'I am dead.'"[41]

Two Levels of Truth

Both Nāgārjuna and deconstruction recognize a conventional and a higher truth. Nāgārjuna makes much use of his doctrine of "two truths." This is characteristically Mahāyāna in its distinction between higher and lower claims or teachings, which are offered according to the capacity of the hearer to understand. Nāgārjuna distinguishes between those propositions which have the truth of ultimate meaning (*paramārthasatya*) and those which on the other hand are advanced for a practical purpose, such as assisting the hearer along the path; these latter are pragmatic, valid for social intercourse; they are conventional truth (*samvṛtisatya*).[42]

Paramārtha, supreme truth, is the truth of voidness, the truth that all statements about what *is* are inherently flawed, incapable of identifying any real thing about which anything can be said. When we understand this truth in our bones, we begin to qualify for enlightenment.

Samvṛtisatya, conventional truth, is truth for the traffic of social convention; it is truth embodied in the particular. One needs to accept the conventions of the logocentric world view in order to embark upon the process that leads to its destruction or ceasing (which is not really annihilation but something else which sidesteps being and non-being). One must live in the world in order to conquer the world. Thus, from Nāgārjuna's point of view, one should not step in front of a "bus" even if the "bus" is, considered from the standpoint of ultimate truth, no more solid than a bubble of foam, a flower growing in the sky, or the son of a barren woman.[43]

The Mādhyamika can argue that his doctrine of two truths is not contradictory. The relation between the two is not that of contradiction. Suppose that provisional truth declares that something exists (or, alternatively, that it does not exist). It is not in the nature of ultimate truth to deny this. It is not affirmed and it is not denied. It is not both affirmed and denied, nor is it neither affirmed nor denied.

When we turn to deconstruction, it would be unwise to attempt to insist that what we find is *just the same thing*. We are, we must never forget, dealing with different systems that belong to different cultural worlds and, ultimately, work in different ways. There is, however, a real kinship which deserves to be admitted.

Seen from outside, deconstruction has an awkward relationship with the real world of solid objects like buses, just as Madhyamaka does.

Paul de Man wrote that "Death is a displaced name for a linguistic predicament."[44] The realist, the man of common sense, thinks that there is something more to it than this. Until the very moment of death, the experience of being run over by a "bus," for example, demands the services of Aesculapius, not Derrida (or, in Indian terms, *Bhaiṣajyaguru*, not *Pāṇini*). If the collision of solid determinate bodies is the lower truth, and the resolution of a linguistic predicament the higher, then the lower seems so cogent as to rob the higher of any pretension to be actually "true."

Yet, if we are going to be rigorous about the matter, we must acknowledge that Johnson's common-sense answer to Berkeley's subjective idealism, however appealing to common sense, is not a disproof. We see a large stone; it is said to be in the mind. Very well; we kick it, and obtain a strong tactile sensation. How can this demonstration, of itself, tend in the slightest degree to prove that the stone is *not* in the mind? Vision and tactile sense are alike sensation; if, *ex hypothesi*, all sensations have no origin outside the mind, then the fact that two senses can produce the same illusion is not a difficulty. Similarly, if all statements of the form "Determinate subject S has determinate property P" are susceptible to deconstruction, then the possibility of making a statement of the type "X is run over by a bus" is simply an example, not a disproof.

There may indeed come a point when abstract speculation comes to seem altogether too airy-fairy, and we desire to place our feet upon the ground. David Hume often had this feeling. When it came upon him, he liked to play backgammon; but this does not prove that his speculations were pointless.

What, then, are deconstruction's two truths? The higher truth, which is not bound or restricted by determinate categories, is the truth of what *is*, properly understood; it is an absence of theory, method, doctrine; it is not an affirmation or dogma. It takes in all theories, but does not enter a determinate relationship with any one; it transcends them all, seeing through their indeterminacy.

The truth of deconstruction in the world, on the other hand, consists of the concrete facts that belong in a historical framework. From this point of view, deconstruction is institutionalized, has books, methods, styles of argument, disciples and enemies, teachers and pupils; yet all of this is ultimately only provisional; it is the springboard from which the seeker after knowledge can jump into the void of truth, not the void itself.

To anybody familiar with Mahāyāna thought, all this might seem to be an attempt to squeeze deconstruction into a Buddhist mould, yet in fact it is no more than a reasonably literal summary of what Jacques Derrida says in his article "Some statements." In this article, he plays with the word *jetée*, which can mean "jetty" or "breakwater," and distinguishes between two senses of deconstruction. The first is like a jetty or pier that "throws" (*jeter*) itself across the watery void. It is not determinate or stationary, has no stasis, is not a fixed state and does not commit itself to absolute statements; it pervades all intellectual positions, but tends to deva*state* them. (The puns are, naturally, in the original.) The second is solid, founded upon pillars or piers of concrete fact, institutionalized. It is a necessary condition for activity in the world, a framework for learning. In the same vein, J. Hillis Miller points to the ambivalence of deconstruction as a method that tends to turn into one more "quasi-scientific discipline," "another archeology" (like the conventional truth), yet at the same time must "constantly put its own grounds in question," stepping aside from any disciplinary framework as soon as it begins to appear (like the higher truth) (*DC*, 249).

This completes a review of some categories of similarity between the two schools of thought. Both of them are subject to debate, and have no doubt been often misunderstood. (Both, incidentally, are in obvious ways radical, but in less obvious ways conservative: Nāgārjuna sought to defend the original teachings of the Buddha; deconstruction, despite the transient allegiance to it of revolutionaries who may ultimately be more at home with Marxism and the other "isms," steps back to the renaissance and values the old disciplines of rhetoric and grammar, showing a remarkable taste for poesy, theological texts, and Greek philosophy.)

My concern here has been with the similarities, and my purpose has been to show that these are instructive, and in some cases go beyond what has so far been recognized; but this is not to insist that the two teachings or styles are really the same thing. That is another matter, which must be left aside. The two schools come from widely different cultural *milieux*, and it is not to be thought that there are no significant differences in outlook or method between them. I leave undiscussed a complex of debatable related issues in respect to which there may be important contrasts. These issues include the questions how far each school has the essential character of soteriology, negative theology, mysticism, or poetry; these are four distinct questions, not all to be answered in the same way. In an obvious if superficial sense, Madhyamaka belonged to a soteriological tradition while deconstruction does not. Madhyamaka employs negation, but does not seem to be theology; nor for that matter does deconstruction, though there has been some discussion whether Derrida is a sort of negative theologian (in despite of what he says).[45] The concept of mysticism is too problematic to be broached here, but there is a good case to be made for the claim that Nāgārjuna is rational, not mystical, while the status of deconstruction in this respect is not easily determined. Nāgārjuna writes verse, but it is the austere, pithy sort of verse that is designed to fix the message for transmission and teaching; Derrida writes prose, but it is the sort of prose that proceeds by allusion, circumbendibus and resonance, like poetry. There is no room here for exploration of these comparisons.

I therefore conclude with the observation that the similarities are strong enough at least to suggest the operation of common social or cultural forces in a way that transcends the differences between civilizations. One can speculate, for example, that deconstruction and Madhyamaka both found adherents in societies where the integrity of the political order was threatened by seething racial and cultural pluralism, and where there were many ready for an orthodoxy that seemed to validate the old intellectual standards of knowledge (Buddhist truth in the one case, academic rigor in the other) yet at the same time subverted the whole apparatus of education and received wisdom that advantaged the existing intellectual elite. Whatever the truth of this may be, the comparison between deconstruction and Madhyamaka identifies a field wide open for exploration.

Notes

1. Responsibility for everything written here is mine alone, but I would like to express gratitude to Dr Kevin Hart for many valuable comments on a draft of this article.

2. J. Boswell, *Life of Johnson*, vol. I (Oxford: Oxford University Press, 1934), 471: "I observed that, though we are satisfied his [Berkeley's] doctrine is not true, it is impossible to refute it. I never shall forget the alacrity with which Johnson answered, striking his foot with mighty force against a large stone, till he rebounded from it, 'I refute it *thus*.'"

3. This is one of the many themes of D. Lehman, *Signs of the Times: Deconstruction and the Fall of Paul de Man* (New York: Poseidon, 1991). Henceforth *Signs*.

4. Jacques Derrida, *Memoires for Paul de Man* (New York: Columbia University Press, 1986), 18. The following abbreviations will be used for the works by Jacques Derrida:

"Comment": "Comment ne pas parler," in *Psyché: Inventions de l'autre* (Paris: Galilée, 1987).

"Letter": "Letter to a Japanese Friend," in *Derrida and Différance*, eds. David Wood and Robert Bernasconi (Evanston, IL: Northwestern University Press, 1988).

OG: *Of Grammatology*, trans. Gayatri Spivak (Baltimore: Johns Hopkins University Press, 1998).

P: *Positions*, trans. Alan Bass (Chicago: University of Chicago Press, 1981/1982).

"The supplement": "The supplement of origin," in *Speech and Phenomena, and other essays*, trans. David B. Allison (Evanston, IL: Northwestern University Press, 1973), 88-104.

"Statements": "Some statements and truisms about neologisms, newisms, postisms, parasitisms, and other small seismisms," trans. Anne Tomiche, in D. Carroll, ed., *The States of "Theory." History, Art and Critical Discourse* (hereafter *ST*) (New York: Columbia University Press, 1990), 63-94.

"Ulysses": "Ulysses Gramophone," in *Ulysses Gramophone: Deux Mots pour Joyce* (Paris: Galilée, 1987).

5. *Mūlamadhyamakakārikās* of Nāgārjuna, ed. J. W. de Jong, *Mūlamadhyamakakārikās* (Madras: The Adyar Library and Research Centre, 1977), 24.11. Henceforth *MMK*.

6. See Harold Coward, *Derrida and Indian Philosophy* (Albany: State University of New York Press, 1990); David Loy, *Non-duality: a study in comparative philosophy* (New Haven: Yale University Press, 1988); Robert Magliola, *Derrida on the Mend* (West Lafayette, Indiana: Purdue University Press, 1984).

7. But see I. W. Mabbett, "Nāgārjuna and Zeno on Motion" *Philosophy East and West* 34, no. 4 (1984): 401-420; "An annotated translation of Chapter XVI of Candrakīrti's *Prasannapadā*," *Journal of Ancient Indian History* 15, nos.1-2 (1984-5): 47-84; "An annotated translation of Chapters XII and XIV of Candrakīrti's *Prasannapadā*," *Journal of the Department of Pāli, University of Calcutta* 4 (1987-88): 113-146. Candrakīrti's commentary cannot be used uncritically as a source for Nāgārjuna's thought, but it is certainly useful.

8. D. J. Kalupahana, *Nāgārjuna: the Philosophy of the Middle Way* (Albany: State University of New York Press, 1986). See also Kalupahana, *A History of Buddhist Philosophy. Continuities and Discontinuities* (Honolulu: University of Hawaii Press, 1992), 160-169.

9. On these comparisons see T. Anderson, "Wittgenstein and Nāgārjuna's paradox," *Philosophy East and West* (Henceforth *PEW*) 35, no. 2 (1985): 157-169; P. Della Santina, "The Madhyamaka and Modern Western Philosophy," *PEW* 36, no.1 (1986): 41-54.

10. J. W. de Jong, *Cinq Chapitres de la Prasannapadā* (Paris: Buddhica, Première Série, 1949); de Jong, "Le problème de l'absolu dans l'école Madhyamaka," *Revue Philosophique de la France et de l'Etranger,* 140 (1950): 322-327.

11. David Seyfort Ruegg, *The Literature of the Madhyamaka School of Philosophy in India* (Wiesbaden: Harrassowitz, 1981).

12. Jacques May, ed., *Candrakīrti Prasannapadā Madhyamaka vṛtti* (Paris: Adrien-Maisonneuve, 1959); J. May, "La philosophie bouddhique de la vacuité," *Studia Philosophia* 18 (1959):123-137. Hereafter "Vacuité."

13. *Vigrahavyāvartanī of Nāgārjuna,* text ed. E. H. Johnston and A. Kunst in K. Bhattacharya, *The Dialectical Method of Nāgārjuna* (Delhi: Motilal Banarsidass, 1978), XXIII. Hereafter *VV*; cf. *MMK*, 17.31f.

14. Some have thought that Nāgārjuna claims to offer no views about anything; see for example L. Stafford Betty, "Nāgārjuna's masterpiece—logical, mystical, both or neither?," *PEW* 33, no. 2 (1983): 123-138. On the other hand, David Ruegg argues that, when Nāgārjuna says that he advances no proposition (*pratijñā*), what he means by "proposition" is a claim about alleged real entities, not any claim at all. See D. Ruegg, "On the Thesis and Assertion in the Madhyamaka/dBu ma," in *Contributions on Tibetan and Buddhist Religion and Philosophy,* eds. E. Steinkellner and H. Tauscher (Wien: Arbeitskreis für Tibetische und Buddhistische Studien, Universität Wien, 1983), 205-241.

15. In one article, Jacques Derrida makes play with the word *jetée*, describing deconstructionism as a jetty, in the special sense that it is something thrown (the verb is *jeter*) across the watery void of theories, provisionally united with theories but also separated from theories and leaving theories behind (see Jacques Derrida, "Statements"). The implications of this article will be noticed further below.

16. On the concept of *la différance*, see particularly Jacques Derrida, "Ulysse."

17. The ineffability of what is real, on this view, does not arise from its being a transcendent super-reality, such as some mystics might be supposed to intuit. Derrida points to the conditions that must exist before anything is said: see Jacques Derrida, "Comment," an important essay rich in implications for the comparison with Nāgārjuna which there is no space to explore here.

18. On conventional scholarly views, anyway; but see A. K. Warder, "Is Nāgārjuna a Mahāyānist?," in *The Problem of Two Truths in Buddhism and Vedanta*, ed. M. Sprung (Dordrecht: Reidel, 1973), 78-88.

19. *MMK* XXV:19: *na saṃsārasya nirvāṇātkiṃ cidasti viśeṣaṇaṃ* | *na nirvāṇasya saṃsārātkim cidasti viśeṣaṇam.* This identification is not accepted by all scholars; some interpret Nāgārjuna's claim, not as an assertion of numerical identity, but as something else.

20. Theodore Stcherbatsky is often criticized for calling the Buddhist doctrine of *pratītyasamutpāda* "relativity." He was no doubt too much influenced by the (then novel) theories propounded by Einstein. Nevertheless, the notion that things arise in dependence upon each other can fairly be called relativity.

21. The ordinary rules of activity in the world are not, however, simply rejected. On the contrary, Derrida is seriously concerned with them. See Jacques Derrida, *Du Droit à la Philosophie* (Paris: Galilée, 1990).

22. Jonathan Culler, *On Deconstruction: Theory and Criticism after Structuralism* (London: Routledge and Kegan Paul, 1983), 74-76. Henceforth *OD*.

23. The notion of the "death of the author" is attributable pre-eminently to Roland Barthes, who may have misunderstood Derrida. Derrida argued that the intuition of the

meaning of "I" is not necessary to the making of a statement containing the word "I," which exists independently as a trace. The condition of the existence of the trace is in a sense the non-existence of the author: "My death is structurally necessary to the pronouncing 'I'" (Jacques Derrida, "The supplement," 96).

24. *Tasmin sati, idaṃ bhavati*, one might say. ("Given the existence of this, that can come into being.")

25. Jacques Derrida, "Living On," in H. Bloom *et al., Deconstruction and Criticism* (New York: Seabury, 1979), 75-176 at 81. Hereafter *DC*.

26. J. Derrida, *Positions*, cited by J. Searle, "Review of J. Culler, *On Deconstruction*," *New York Review of Books* 30, no. 16 (Oct. 27th, 1983), 75.

27. David Loy argues that Madhyamaka deconstructs pairs such as self and no-self, substance and mode, no causality and all-conditionality, permanence and impermanence, time and things in time, whereas brahmanism asserted the substantive reality of the first in each pair and made of the second an illusion or mere seeming, while Hīnayāna Buddhism made an absolute of the second and denied the first. Madhyamaka, he claims, recognizes that in every pair each term, rigorously analysed, turns out to contain the seed or essence of the other, and thus cannot be made an exclusive absolute. His discussion raises questions which cannot be discussed here, but at least, in relation to the point at issue, it captures a distinctive feature of the Madhyamaka approach, which is not half-hearted or formal in its espousal of the *catuṣkoṭi* but insists upon it as axiomatic. For a summary of Loy's argument, see his "The Mahayana Deconstruction of Time," *PEW* 36, no. 1 (1986): 13-23.

28. F. Nietzsche, *Werke*, ed. Karl Schlechta, vol. 3 (Munich: Hansen, 1966), 804f.

29. P. de Man, *Allegories of Reading: Figural Language in Rousseau, Nietzsche, Rilke and Proust* (New Haven: Yale University Press, 1979), 106-111; and *OD*, 86-88;

30. J. Searle, "Review of J. Culler, *On Deconstruction*."

31. Not many studies have cogently addressed the actual structure of argument or come close to identifying the real issues. The most important contributions are in the articles by C. Oetke (e.g., "Rationalismus und Mystik in der Philosophie Nāgārjunas," *Studien zur Indologie und Iranistik* 75 (1989): 1-39). See also R. Jones, "The Nature and Function of Nāgārjuna's Arguments," *PEW* 28, no.4 (1978): 485-502. The discussions by R. Robinson (e.g. "Did Nāgārjuna Really Refute All Philosophical Views?," *PEW* 22, no. 3 (1972): 325-331, and even his "Some Logical Aspects of Nāgārjuna's System," *PEW* 6, no. 4 (1957): 291-308) are brief and make debatable assumptions.

32. This term is defined by Jacques May, one of the leading authorities on Madhyamaka, as "les modes d'être ou les modifications de la réalité absolue qu'ils designent par leur annulation." This is a rather Kantian or Murtiesque way of looking at things. In the term's occurrences in Candrakīrti's commentary on the *MMK*, May commonly translates it as "essence." In the *MMK*, it is used quite freely with the straightforward sense of "thing."

33. It has recently been argued (see Oetke, in endnotes # 30) that Nāgārjuna's teaching was, ultimately, the non-existence of things. There is no space here to explore the senses in which this might legitimately be maintained.

34. See de Jong, "Emptiness," *Journal of Indian Philosophy* 2, no. 1 (1972): 1-17; May, "Vacuité."

35. See for example, R.D. Gunaratne, "Understanding Nāgārjuna's *catuṣkoṭi*," *PEW* 36, no. 3 (1988): 213-234, with references to earlier discussions.

36. I am aware that some philosophers consider the "four-cornered logic" of Buddhism in general, and of Nāgārjuna in particular, to introduce alternatives alien to conventional logic. K.N. Jayatilleke sees Buddhism as offering a "two-valued logic of four alternatives." *Early Buddhist Theory of Knowledge* (London: Allen and Unwin, 1963),

350. B.K. Matilal (like a number of philosophers) emphasizes the special character of negation in Madhyamaka. *Epistemology, Logic and Grammar*, 162-165 (and in other writings). My own study of the *Kārikās* leads to the conclusion that Nāgārjuna uses entirely conventional logical principles, albeit with odd results. The most useful account of the "four-cornered logic" is probably David Ruegg's "The Uses of the Four Positions of the *Catuṣkoṭi* and the Problem of the Description of Reality in Mahāyāna Buddhism," *Journal of Indian Philosophy* 5 (1977): 1-71.

37. B. Johnson, *A World of Difference* (Baltimore: Johns Hopkins University Press, 1989), 12.

38. See for example *Saṃyutta Nikāya* 4.400f; *Majjhima Nikāya* 1.483-488.

39. J. Hillis Miller, "The Critic as Host," in *DC*, 224. This article provides evidence of other aspects of deconstruction adduced here: the interlinking of phenomena in paradoxical relationships, each term doubling as foundation and superstructure, as in the Buddhist linking of the twelve *nidānas* (224); deconstruction is not nihilism but "interpretation as such" (228-232) revealing the relationships of alternation and reversal between nihilism and metaphysics.

40. Michel Foucault, *L'Archeologie du Savoir* (Paris: Gallimard, 1969), 22.

41. Jacques Derrida, *Cahiers Confrontation* XX (1989), 91-114.

42. There has been much discussion of the meaning of this doctrine of two truths. See particularly M. Sprung, ed., *The Problem of Two Truths in Buddhism and Vedānta* (Dordrecht: Reidel, 1973).

43. Such images as these are to be found principally in commentaries such as the *Prasannapadā* by Candrakīrti; but Nāgārjuna himself likens creation, continuity, and destruction (i.e., the phenomenal world) to "an illusion, a dream, a fairy castle in the sky [*gandharvanagara*]." *MMK* VII: 34.

44. Paul de Man, *The Rhetoric of Romanticism* (New York: Columbia University Press, 1984), 81.

45. David E. Klemm argues for a "family resemblance," if not more, between Derrida's deconstruction and negative theology in "Open Secrets: Derrida and Negative Theology," in *Negation and Theology*, ed. R. Scharlemann (Charlottesville/London: University Press of Virginia, 1992), 8-24. See also the other contributions in the same volume, especially R. Scharlemann, "Response and Queries," 100-119, and David E. Klemm et al., "Replies," 120-148; also *Derrida and Negative Theology*, eds. H. Coward and T. Foshay (Albany: State University of New York Press, 1992), esp. 129-226 (H. Coward) and 227-253 (David Loy).

Part Two

Buddhism Deconstructs

Introduction

The essays in Part Two provide in-depth investigations on the thematic similarities between Buddhism and deconstruction along with contemplations on their differences. Zong-qi Cai explicates deconstructive operations in Derrida and Mādhyamika (Middle School) Buddhism. Noticeable here is the logical proposition the Mādhymika Buddhist employs as a demonstration of Buddhist non-substantialism. David Loy develops his discussion in the context of Huayan (Flower Garland) Buddhism. In line with the Huayan Buddhist vision of cosmic expansion of the Buddhist idea of dependent co-arising (dependent origination), Loy addresses the social implications of the non-substantial mode of thinking.

Cai begins his essay by bringing our attention to the "relationship between linguistic deconstruction and onto-theological criticism" in Derrida and Mādhyamika Buddhism. This is important to Cai, because later in his essay, he will use this relationship as a lever to explore major differences between the two. In terms of similarities, Cai provides four parallels between Derridean and Mādhyamika deconstruction: (1) Both Derrida and the Mādhyamika Buddhists employ differentialism (as we see in Derridean *différance* and Mādhyamika *differentiam*) in their deconstruction of Essentialists and (2) of Materialists; also (3) both set forth the logic of neither/nor ("tetrapharmakon" in Derrida and "tetralemma" in Madhyamaka) as a deconstructive process and (4) they further launch a self-deconstruction of this logic in order to avoid self-reification by employing the "supernumerary" (Derrida) and "octolemma" (the Mādhyamika). Cai explores differentialism by comparing Dignāga's and Candrakīrti's philosophy with that of Derrida and moves from there to Chinese Mādhyamika scholars, Seng Zhao and Ji Zang, to illustrate their logical arguments.

The Mādhyamika School is well known for their logical proposition called "four-cornered logic" (tetralemma). Ian Mabbett also touched upon it in his chapter, and Ellen Zhang will further discuss the idea in her essay on the Chinese version of Mādhyamika. "Tetralemma" is a form of logical argumentation whose use is not limited to Mādhyamika in the Buddhist tradition. Put in a simple way, it has a structure that "S" is: P; ~P; both P and ~P; and neither P nor ~P.

It is not difficult to notice, even in this simple presentation, that the tetralemma violates the basic Aristotelian logic of identity, contradiction, and the excluded middle. The middle in the logical proposition of the tetralemma cannot be excluded because no borderline exists to identify the middle. The middle is indecidable. The middle is the space between affirmation and negation, and between identity and non-identity.

The strategy Derrida has used in executing the deconstruction of a text has shown a pattern that leads to a conclusion similar to the one we just arrived at with the tetralemma of the Mādhyamika. As Hugh J. Silverman identifies it, Derridean strategy can be explained in three steps: the first step is to identify the conceptual opposites that operate within a metaphysical discourse in the form of dualism and tactically overturn the traditional hierarchy of the binary opposites. The second is to mark the indecidability of the relation between the two factors involved in the binary structure. And thirdly, by revealing mutual dependency of opposites in dualism, and thus showing the fabricated nature of hierarchy among them, a deconstructive reading demonstrates the limits of a discourse and metaphysical thinking similar to the way in which the Mādhyamika shows the impossibility of maintaining an essentialist viewpoint.

Appraising the postmodern spirit in terms of the Huayan concept of Indra's Net, one of the best known images visualizing the Buddhist doctrine of relationality of beings, Loy examines the major concepts in deconstruction and Buddhism in six categories: 1. Causality, 2. Non-abiding, 3. Truth, 4. Play, 5. Ethics, and 6. Meditation. The first two are introduced as a ground for Buddhist truth, which Loy sees as "deconstruct[ing] the socially-conditioned metaphysical system." Similarly, the postmodern Truth also "subverts… [the] socially constructed myth of rationality."

The category of ethics in Loy's essay merits serious attention from both Buddhism and deconstruction, given the fact that both schools, fairly or unfairly, have been criticized for their seeming lack of a clear blueprint for social commitment. Criticizing the ethics that is based on a dualistic belief that "'I' have privileged access to the correct moral principle," Loy attempts to provide a new ethical vision based on the bodhisattva ideal. Loy envisions the new morality as a "non-moral morality of bodhisattva" which is "effortless, purposeless and playful." As Loy says, such a non-dualistic morality which calls for everyone's "response-ability" toward life, community, and the world is exactly what the current state of our society and environment demands of us. This issue of ethics will be further discussed by Gad Horowitz in Part Five of this volume.

Both Cai and Loy conclude their essays by considering the difference between Buddhism and deconstruction. In both cases, this involves distinguishing between philosophy and religion on the one hand and theory and practice on the other. According to Cai, both Derridean and Mādhyamika deconstruction declare the "end" of philosophy and the beginning of "non-philosophy." However, Cai contends that by jettisoning philosophy itself, Derrida "led himself into the prison house of language," whereas to the Mādhyamika Buddhists, the end of philosophy is "synonymous with religious enlightenment beyond language and conceptuality." This endgame of philosophy, Cai continues, is something to celebrate for the Mādhyamika thinkers, contrary to Derridean deconstruction, which Cai views as falling into the "abyss of nihilism." Loy takes a similar position. In the section on "Meditation," he distinguishes Buddhism from "postmodern" thought in that "Derrida's critique of 'transcendental signifieds' includes doubts about the possibility of such 'mystical' experiences'" involved in meditation. Even though Loy suggests that the differences between Buddhism and deconstruction can provide a "place where fruitful dialogue can occur," he maintains the position that "the textual dissemination liberated by Derrida's deconstruction will not be satisfactory unless the dualistic sense-of-self—not just its discourse—has been deconstructed." (JYP)

Three

Derridean and Mādhyamika Buddhist Theories of Deconstruction[1]

Zong-qi Cai

A comparative study of Jacques Derrida's deconstructive philosophy and the Mādhyamika Buddhism—which was founded by the Indian thinker Nāgārjuna (c. 100-200) and established in China by Seng Zhao (374-414) and Ji Zang (549-623), and flourished in Korea from the sixth to the fifteenth century and in Japan from the seventh to the twelfth century and in Tibet from the eighth century to the present—probably no longer needs to be preceded by an apology.[2] The remarkable parallel between the Derridean logic and the Mādhyamika *prasaṅga* (*reductio ad absurdum*) has already been carefully examined by a number of specialists in comparative philosophy.[3] In Derrida-Mādhyamika studies, there are still many other important parallels awaiting our discovery and exploration. Here, I propose to consider the relationship between linguistic deconstruction and onto-theological criticism in these two (anti)philosophical traditions. In the course of my inquiry, I will identify four important parallels in the Derridean and Mādhyamika theories. First, both Derrida and Mādhyamika thinkers develop deconstructive theories of meaning based on the similar ideas of *différance* and *differentiam*, and seek to nullify the logos and the Name of Non-Existence reified by Western idealists and Buddhist essentialists. Second, they both apply the same theories of meaning to deconstruct Matter and Existence reified by Western materialists and Buddhist realists, respectively. Third, they both conceive of their double negation as an exercise of *neither/nor* logic and set forth their deconstructive formulas in similar terms of "tetrapharmakon" and "tetralemma" (*catuṣkoṭi*). Fourth, they both abolish their own tetrapharmakon and tetralemma and embark on their self-deconstructive course along an aimless "supernumerary" and along a linear "octolemma." While I discuss these four parallels, I shall also pinpoint the fundamental differences between the Derridean and the Mādhyamika theories and consider how these two deconstructive traditions lead to the "end" of philosophy in their own fashions.

Deconstructing Western Idealists and Buddhist Essentialists: Derrida's and the Mādhyamika Differentiam

Both Derridean and Mādhyamika theories are cast in terms of disagreements over language with idealists and materialists. Derrida holds that Western idealists from Plato to Heidegger operate through a false conception of language. They all invoke the logos, a linguistic sign, as an intermediary between the transcendental and the sensible, the divine and the human. Socrates in the *Phaedo*, Derrida observes, "tells of his fear of being blinded by looking at things directly. And he tells how, instead of turning directly to things, he turned rather to logoi in order to examine there the truth of beings."[4] To vindicate the logos as an embodiment of "truth of beings," Plato and later idealists adopt a two-fold strategy—to banish its corporeal "gram" (*gramme*, in the French) and to reify its intangible "phonè." Although the term "logos" contains the meaning of language as a whole, they do not employ it pertaining to the graphic form of language. This banishment of the gram from the logos stems from the fear that the visibly corporeal gram will contaminate the phonè, the transcendental signified. Plato unequivocally expresses such a fear when he denounces the gram as "the intrusion of an artful technique, a forced entry of a totally original sort, an archetypal violence: eruption of the *outside* within the *inside*, breaching into the interiority of the soul, the living self-presence of the soul within the true logos, the help that speech lends to itself.[5] While Plato and later idealists banish the gram as "an orphan or a bastard," they reify the phonè as "the legitimate and highborn son of the 'father of logos'"[6]—on the ground of the "proximity of voice and being, of voice and the meaning of being, of voice and the ideality of meaning" (*OG*, 39). As a result of such a phonocentric reification, the logos has assumed the onto-theological significance of, as Gayatri Chakravorty Spivak notes, "the Word, the Divine Mind, the infinite understanding of God, and infinitely creative subjectivity, and closer to our time, the self-presence of full self-consciousness" (*OG*, lxviii).

In the opinion of Derrida, the phonocentric reification of the logos presents a paradox. While such reification is intended to forestall "the eruption of the *outside* within the inside," it actually exposes the *outside* within the inside of all Western idealist metaphysics. For Derrida, the reason cannot be simpler. The privileged phonè is as much a linguistic sign as the denigrated gram and is subject to the same rules of lingüistic signification governing the gram. So, the logos is by necessity a linguistic sign external to the purported transcendental absolute. As such, it inevitably inscribes all metaphysics within a space of externality and precludes the possibility of any intrinsic absolute presence.

To expose how Western metaphysics "finds inscribed, rather than inscribing itself, within a space [the externality of the logos] which it seeks but is unable to control,"[7] Derrida coins the word *différance.* This neologism constitutes on the one hand the nominal form for the French verb *différer*, which means both "to differ" and "to defer," and on the other a dissimulation of the French noun *dif-*

férence (difference). Simple and playful as it seems, this neologism spells out Derrida's deconstructive theory of linguistic signification. First, *différance* calls into question of the privileging of the phonè by idealists, because it is not the phonè but the gram of the word that makes its meaning understood. If heard but not read in French, *différance* is bound to be confused with the noun *difference*. Second, *différance* underscores the prerequisite for linguistic signification. A sign cannot exist unless it *differs* spatially and is *deferred* temporally from the signified. This ever receding gap between the signifier and the signified disproves the alleged fusion of the phonè and the onto-theological essence in the logos. Third, the Latin root of *différance* (*differre*, in the sense of "to scatter, disperse") denotes the necessary play of opposing referents (the spatial vs. the temporal in *différance*) in linguistic signification. A name must contain its disputant meaning(s) in order to exist as a name (i.e. A cannot be called A unless A also signifies the existence of non-A). So, a name signifies absence as well as presence. This being the case, what a name signifies cannot be the pure signified of presence, but another signifier which in turn signifies absence as well as presence.[8] This goes on and on to infinitude. It follows that the very possibility of the transcendental signified or the onto-theological presence is to be denied. Given this operation of *différance*, Derrida contends that logocentric concepts—"*eidos*, *arche*, *telos*, *energeia*, *ousia* [essence, existence, substance, subject], *aletheia*, *transcendentality*, *consciousness or conscience*, *God*, *man*, and so forth"[9]—are all caught in an infinite circularity of signifiers and will never be able to presence the transcendental absolute.

Like Derrida, Mādhyamika thinkers seek to demolish the onto-theological arguments by the Buddhist Essentialists by exposing their false conception of language. Whereas Derrida invalidates the intrinsic nature of the logos by demonstrating the phonè as a conventional sign in *différance*, the Mādhyamika philosophers nullify the "intrinsic identity" (*svalakṣana*) of the Name of Non-Existence by showing its conventionality.[10] Candrakīrti, a great Indian Mādhyamika thinker of the seventh century, repudiates the essentialist claim of the intrinsic nature of the Name of Non-Existence. In the opinion of a Buddhist Essentialist, that the phrases "body of a statute" and "head of Rāhu" exist—despite that neither an inanimate statue has a body nor does Rāhu (a demon) have a head—attests to the non-representational, intrinsic identity of language. In response to such an essentialist view, Candrakīrti writes:

> When the words "body" and "head" normally occur in grammatical connection with companion entities like "hand" or "mind," the thought produced on the basis of the words "body" and "head" alone carries an expectation of the companion entities in the form, "Whose body?" and "Whose head?" . . . Furthermore, the terms "statue" and "Rāhu," which are the qualifiers, actually exist as part of conventional usage, and are accepted without analysis, as in the conventional designation "person." Therefore your example is incorrect.[11]

Here, Candrakīrti considers the two phrases as no more than ordinary words that can convey a meaning only through conventional association established by grammatical connections. He believes that "whatever meaning they [words] had was acquired by a process of mutual dependence (*parasparāpekṣā siddhiḥ*), with one word depending for its meaning on the network of those that were used before it."[12] These remarks of Candrakīrti seem to anticipate Derrida's theory of *différance*. Like Derrida, he conceives of linguistic signification as an interplay of signifiers, and argues on that ground against the notion that a word has an intrinsic essence within itself.

It is important to note that Candrakīrti's analysis of linguistic signification is based on his common-sense observations while Derrida's is developed from modern theories of semiology. For a more systematically developed Buddhist theory of language, we must turn to the differentiation theory of meaning (*apoha*) developed by Dignāga (c. 480-540), a phenomenal Indian Buddhist logician, under the influence of the early Mādhyamika school.[13] Whereas Candrakīrti explores the mutual dependence of words within a grammatical construction, Dignāga looks into the mutual dependence of opposing elements within a single word and yields a fresh insight into the nature of linguistic signification: "Indeed the name can express its own meaning only by repudiating the opposite meaning, as for instance the words 'to have an origin' designate their own meaning only through a contrast with things having no origin or eternal."[14] This statement seems at first sight to be an affirmation of the self-present meaning of a name. A closer examination of it will reveal that Dignāga is actually arguing the opposite because he sees that the very condition for any name to establish a meaning is the existence of a disputant meaning. This necessary dependence of a meaning upon its contrary is sufficient disproof of the alleged intrinsic meaning of a name. The deconstructive significance of this statement becomes much clearer in the following commentary by Jinendrabuddhi: "Indeed the aim of the text of Dignāga is that the word 'expresses *per differentiam*' its own meaning . . . (The words express only negations, only differences!), because a pure affirmation without any (implied) negation is senseless."[15] This commentary assures us that Dignāga indeed conceives of linguistic signification as a process of negation and difference akin to that of *différance*.[16] Considering all this, it seems no accident that Jinendrabuddhi uses *differentiam* to characterize Dignāga's differentiation theory of meaning, just as Derrida uses *différance* to characterize his own. Moreover, like Derrida, Dignāga and other Buddhist logicians go from linguistic deconstruction to ontological negation (*arthātmaka-apoha*). While Derrida annuls "*eidos*, *arche*, *telos*, *energeia*, *ousia* . . ." through a demonstration of *différance* in those sacred names, they disprove the essence of language through a revelation of *differentiam* in onto-theological names.

Deconstructing Western Materialisms and Buddhist Realisms: Derrida's Double Séance and the Mādhyamika Double Negation

Both the Derridean *différance* and the Mādhyamika *differentiam* illuminate the mutual dependence of signified and signifier, referent and non-referent, presence and absence. On the ground of this mutual dependence, both Derrida and Mādhyamika thinkers believe that intrinsic identity cannot be claimed for either the signified-referent-presence side or the signifier-nonreferent-absence side. They hold that all onto-theologies are necessarily false insofar as they ascribe intrinsic identity to one or the other side of this paradigm. For Derrida and the Mādhyamika thinkers, this paradigm of mutual dependence not only exposes the erroneousness of all onto-theologies but also provides a very convenient way to deconstruct them. All one has to do is to overturn the "hierarchization" of these two sides by a philosophical system. We have already seen how Derrida and Mādhyamika thinkers launch such a deconstructive attack against Western idealisms and Buddhist Essentialisms. Now, let us see how they return to deconstruct Western materialisms and Buddhist Realisms.

While Derrida seeks to overturn the superiority of the phonè at the first phase of his deconstruction, he re-marks the gram at the second phase to prevent the re-institution of logocentrism in the form of materialism. He writes: "nothing would be more ridiculously mystifying than such an ethical or axiological reversal, returning a prerogative or some elder's right to writing" (*P*, 13). He perceives the "counter-privileging" of the gram, the ostensibly corporeal signifier as emblematic of a metaphysical reification in the form of materialism. Such a reification is not dissimilar to that of the phonè as the transcendental signified by the idealists:

> . . . the concept of matter has been defined as absolute exterior or radical heterogeneity. I am not even sure that there can be a "concept" of an absolute exterior. If I have not very often used the word "matter," it is not, as you know, because of some idealist or spiritualist kind of reservation. It is that in the logic of the phase of overturning this concept has been too often reinvested with "logocentric" values, values associated with those of thing, reality, presence in general, sensible presence, for example, substantial plenitude, content, referent, etc. Realism or sensualism—"empiricism,"—are modifications of logocentrism. (I have often insisted on the fact that "writing" or the "text" are not reducible *either* to the sensible or visible presence of the graphic or the "literal.") In short, the signifier "matter" appears to me problematical only at the moment when its reinscription cannot avoid making of it a new fundamental principle which by means of theoretical regression, would be reinstituted into a "transcendental signified." (*P*, 64-65)

In this passage, Derrida aims to show how easily the rehabilitation of a signifier—be it "thing, reality or presence in general"—may go overboard and result in the reinstitution of logocentrism. Derrida mentions that the materialist texts of Marx and Lenin represent a typical case (cf. *P*, 72, 74-76). There, the signifier of "matter" has become the absolute cosmological and socio-historical principle. In other words, the signifier is reified and turned into a transcendental signified no less fictitious than the logos subscribed to by most idealists from Plato to Heidegger. To prevent his own *gramm*atology from being "re-invested with 'logocentric' values," Derrida advocates a *simultaneous* deconstruction of the gram and the phonè and calls such a practice "biface or biphase," "*double séance*," or "*double register*" in "grammatological practice" (*P*, 42, 45 passim, 35).

The Mādhyamika double negation bears close resemblance to the Derridean "double séance." At one phase, they seek to reduce onto-theological Names "to mere conventional negative signs of differentiation" and thereby deconstruct all Essentialist schools "whose valuation of Speech and of Names [Non-Being] had all the character of religious veneration—for whom the Word was an eternal positive Ens existing in an eternal union with the things denoted by it."[17]

At the other phase, they seek to reduce the Physical Phenomenon to a mere language-thought construct and thereby destroy all Realist schools which valorize Existence as the eternal Ens—what Derrida calls "thing, reality or presence in general." Mādhyamika thinkers pursue double negation more even-handedly than Derrida does. Derrida concentrates his attacks on idealisms and seldom takes on idealisms and materialism *simultaneously*, as he claimed. By contrast, Mādhyamika thinkers almost always seek to negate Essentialisms and Realisms in the same breath. For instance, Seng Zhao, founder of Chinese Mādhyamika, exploits the mutual dependence of a "name" and a "thing" to expose the illusory nature of both. He writes: "A name does not correspond to an actuality. An actuality does not correspond to a name."[18] On that ground, he goes on to criticize the "name"-valorizing schools—the School of Original Non-being propagated by Dao An (312-385), its Variant School of Original Non-being headed by Fa Chen (286-374), and the School of Non-being of Mind led by Fa Wen (fl. 374).[19] He considers all their theories "nothing but a talk partial to non-being" (*SB*, 352). Then, he takes on the "thing"-valorizing schools like the School of Matter As It Is represented by Zhi Daolin (314-366). He contends that these schools do "not understand that matter [including its conditional existence] is really not matter at all" (*SB*, 352).

Such a relentless double negation abounds in all Mādhyamika schools. After all, it is in reaction against the Essentialisms and Realisms that the Mādhyamika rose and developed as a deconstructive philosophy. Its exercise of double negation is the very raison d'être of its existence.

Deconstructive Formulae: Derrida's Tetrapharmakon and the Mādhyamika Tetralemma

Both Derrida and Mādhyamika thinkers describe their double-register deconstruction in terms of "neither/nor." In *Positions*, Derrida double negates a host of conceptual opposites endowed with onto-theological significance, and then sums up the principle of his biphase deconstruction as a practice of *neither/nor*.

> ... the *pharmakon* is neither remedy nor poison, neither good nor evil, neither the inside nor the outside, neither speech nor writing; the supplement is neither a plus nor a minus, neither an outside nor the complement of an inside, neither accident nor essence, etc.; the hymen is neither confusion nor distinction, neither identity nor difference, neither consummation nor virginity, neither the veil nor unveiling, neither the inside nor the outside, etc.; the gram is neither a signifier nor a signified, neither a sign nor a thing, neither a presence nor an absence, neither a position nor a negation, etc.; spacing is neither space nor time; the incision is neither the incised integrity of a beginning, or of a simple cutting into, nor simple secondarity. Neither/nor, that is simultaneously either or; . . . (*P*, 43)

Likewise, Seng Zhao characterizes the Mādhyamika double negation of the "Name" and "Thing" as an exercise of "neither-this-nor-that" logic:

> The Zhong lun [Treatise on the Middle Doctrine, Mādhyamika śāstra by Nāgārjuna] says, 'Things are neither this or that.' . . . Thus 'this' and 'that' do not definitely refer to a particular name, but deluded people would believe that they necessarily do. This being the case, [the distinction] between 'this' and 'that' is from the beginning nonexistent, but to the deluded it is from the beginning not nonexistent. If we realize that 'this' and 'that' do not exist, is there anything that can be regarded as existent? Thus we know that things are not real; they are from the beginning only temporary names. (*SB*, 356)

Not only do Derrida and Mādhyamika thinkers theorize about their deconstructive logic in the same terms of *neither/nor*, they also seek to distinguish their deconstructive formulas from other modes of philosophical thinking by invoking the same symbolic number of Four. In *Dissemination*, Derrida self-consciously defines his deconstructionism against other philosophical schools "through its insistence upon squares, crossroads, and other four-sided figures . . . [and its] violent but imperceptible displacement of the 'triangular'—Dialectical, Trinitarian, Oedipal—foundations of Western thought."[20] First, Derrida restates the different symbolic numbers adopted in onto-theological discourses. Numbers One and Two represent the classical opposition of Being and beings and its attendant duplicities ("remedy/poison, good/evil, intelligible/sensible, high/low, mind/matter, life/death, inside/outside, speech/writing, etc" (*D*, 24-25). Number Three emerges as a resolution of the duplicities—in religion as the Trinity (Hegel's word), in Kant as a lifeless "triadic" form (*Triplicität*, Schelling's word), in Schelling as the quasi-dialectic triplicity, and in Hegel as the living triplicity.[21] Then, Derrida compares his deconstructive enterprise to "a pharmacy in which it is no longer possible to count by ones, by twos, or by threes" (*D*, 24). There, all the twos "can be neither reduced to unity, nor derived from a primary simplicity, nor dialectically sublated or internalized into a third term" (*D*, 25). Similarly, all the threes "no longer give us the ideality of the speculative opposition but rather the effect of a strategic re-mark" (*D*, 25). While destroying the dualistic and trinitarian horizons, Derrida envisions his operation of *différance* or textual dissemination as "a fourth term" and "the supplementary four (neither a cross nor a closed square)" (*D*, 25). Indeed, Derrida is so fascinated with the idea of a fourth term that he renames "pharmakon"—one of his arch-examples of *différance*—as "tetrapharmakon" (*D*, 350). To elaborate on the significance of this fourth term, he cites the following passage from Philippe Sollers' *Nombres*: "Even though it is only a triangle open on its fourth side, the splayed square loosens up the obsidionality of the triangle and the circle which in their ternary rhythm (Oedipus, Trinity, Dialectics) have always governed metaphysics. It loosens them up; that is, it de-limits them, reinscribes them, re-cites them."[22]

That a fourth term marks off the Mādhyamika Buddhism from other philosophical systems is self-evident in the very name for which the Mādhyamika deconstruction is best known—*catuṣkoṭi*, rendered as tetralemma or the four-cornered method of argument. Like Derrida, Mādhyamika thinkers believe the Number Four represents a negation of the preceding three numbers representative of all onto-theological positions. To nullify the three existing kinds of onto-theological claims, Nāgārjuna introduces the *neither/nor* as a fourth term:

The world is finite.
The world is infinite.
The world is both finite and infinite.
The world is neither finite nor infinite.[23]

Like Derrida, Nāgārjuna and other Mādhyamika thinkers aim to destroy not only the fundamental opposition of Being and Non-being but all its attendant duplicities and triplicities. Indeed, just as Derrida rules against counting "by ones, by twos or by threes" in his pursuit of tetrapharmakon, Nāgārjuna consistently disposes of the onto-theological ones, twos, and threes in his exercise of tetralemma. He casts out—among numerous other sets—the ones, twos, and threes regarding the extension of the world, the form of soul, and the finality of death, and other important philosophical issues.[24]

Self-deconstructive Course: Derrida's "Supernumerary" and the Mādhyamika Octolemma

When Derrida and Mādhyamika thinkers reach the fourth term in their deconstructive process, they still face the danger of getting trapped in a new dualism between the three preceding terms and their own fourth terms. Unless this new dualism is disposed of, their deconstructive terms themselves are bound to become a fixed onto-theological thesis. To overcome such an onto-theological re-inscription, both Derrida and Mādhyamika thinkers undertake self-deconstruction. Derrida sloughs conceptuality off his deconstructive terms and sees to it that they get "imprinted and fractured" by their own logic. He writes:

> The motif of *différance*, when marked by a silent *a*, in effect plays neither the role of a "concept," nor simply of a "word." This does not prevent it from producing conceptual effects and verbal or nominal concretions. Which, moreover—although this is not immediately noticeable—are simultaneously imprinted and fractured by the corner of this "letter," by the incessant work of its strange "logic." (*P*, 40)
>
> [*Différance*] cannot be elevated into a master-word or a master-concept ... it blocks every relationship to theology.... (*P*, 40)
>
> In the final analysis *dissemination* means nothing, and cannot be reassembled into a definition. ... If dissemination, seminal *différance* cannot be summarized into an exact conceptual tenor, it is because the force and form of its disruption *explode* the semantic horizon. (*P*, 44-45)

Like Derrida, Mādhyamika thinkers stress the importance of abolishing their arguments and positions. In grappling with the same problem of re-inscription, they, too, attempt to turn their deconstructive terms against themselves. For instance, they use the term *śūnyatā* to deconstruct itself and develop a self-deconstructive doctrine of *śūnyatā-śūnyatā* ("the emptiness of the emptiness"). From the writings of Nāgārjuna and Candrakīrti, we can find these comments on *śūnyatā-śūnyatā*:

> "Empty" [*śūnya*], "non-empty" [*aśūnya*], "both" [*śūnya* and *aśūnya*], "neither" [*śūnya* nor *aśūnya*]—these should not be declared. It is expressed only for the purpose of communication.[25]
>
> This statement (viz. that nothing has self-existence) is not self-existent. ... Just as a magically formed phantom could deny a phantom. ... Just so (is) this negation.[26]
>
> Emptiness is not a property, or universal mark, of entities, because then its substratum would be nonempty, and one would have a fixed conviction (*dṛṣṭi*) about it. In fact, it is a mere medicine, a means of escape from all fixed conviction. ... It is not a positive standpoint, but a mere turning away from all views and thought-constructions.[27]

Neither Derrida nor Mādhyamika thinkers believe that they can truly abolish their own arguments merely by disclaiming them. Therefore, they both launch into a sustained, rigorous process of self-deconstruction. For Derrida, a true abandonment of positions, whether his own or others', must be achieved through a *kinesis* of mutual negations. To distinguish this deconstructive *kinesis* from the teleological *kinesis*, particularly the Hegelian one, Derrida characterizes it as a process of infinite regress. He contends that "*difference* ... is not a pure nominal entity, and unceasingly dislocates itself in a chain of differing and deferring substitutions."[28] For Derrida, the term "trace" best captures the infinitude and the drifting nature of his deconstructive *kinesis*: "The trace is in fact the absolute origin of sense in general. Which amounts to saying once again that there is no absolute origin of sense in general. The trace is the *différance*" (*OG*, 65). Like the "trace" described here, the Derridean deconstructive *kinesis* reaches no destination—always drifting amidst the phantoms of "the absolute origin of sense." It does not at any stage bear fruits comparable to the syntheses born of the Hegelian *kinesis*. To emphasize the barren nature of his deconstructive *kinesis*, Derrida compares it to "a sowing that does not produce plants, but is simply infinitely repeated" and to "a semination that is not *in*semination but *dis*semination, seed spilled in vain, an emission that cannot return to its origin in the father."[29]

Mādhyamika thinkers, especially later Chinese masters, also seek to subject their own tetralemma to a deconstructive *kinesis*. They also believe that they must treat *catuṣkoṭi* as "mere medicine" and "magically formed phantom" rather than a positive entity. Although Seng Zhao does not explicitly mention the deconstruction of *catuṣkoṭi*, he nevertheless advances the idea of a deconstructive *kinesis* when he stresses that one "communes with the spirit in between existence and nonexistence" in such a way that "one never gets trapped by what is determinable."[30] By pursuing such a deconstructive *kinesis*, Mādhyamika thinkers seek to avoid any attachment to a fixed conviction while undoing all views and thought constructions.

In their pursuit of deconstructive *kinesis*, Mādhyamika thinkers follow a direction totally different from that of Derrida. Whereas Derrida views his as a random drift, they treat theirs as a decidedly directional operation leading to an ultimate *stasis*, if you will, beyond language and conceptuality. We can discern this distinguishing trait of Mādhyamika deconstructive *kinesis* in the doctrine of Three Levels of Two Truths (*sanchong erdi*), presumably developed by Fa Lang (fl. 610), the teacher of Ji Zang. This doctrine divides all philosophical positions, including Mādhyamika tetralemma, into the mundane truths and absolute truths on three levels of spiritual progress:

Three levels of Two Truths

Mundane	Absolute
1. Existence	2. Nonexistence
3. Both Existence and Nonexistence	4. Neither Existence nor Nonexistence
5. BOTH (Both Existence and Nonexistence) AND (Neither Existence nor Nonexistence)	6. NEITHER (Both Existence and Nonexistence) NOR (Neither Existence nor Nonexistence)[31]

The first lemma (existence) represents the mundane truth; and the second lemma (nonexistence), the absolute truth on the first and the lowest level. The third lemma (both existence and nonexistence) combines the first two lemmas and registers as the mundane truth on the second level. The fourth lemma (neither existence nor nonexistence) negates the third lemma and reaches the absolute truth on the second level. Then, just as the third lemma combines the first and second lemmas, the fifth lemma combines the third and fourth lemmas and becomes the mundane truth on the third level. Significantly, this fifth lemma represents the initial stage of Ji Zang's deconstruction of his own *catuṣkoṭi* (tetralemma). The sixth lemma completes this self-deconstruction through the negation of the fifth lemma and rises to the absolute truth on the third level.

For Ji Zang, this deconstructive kinesis is a means of mind-cleansing "not limited to three levels but to be employed progressively to infinite levels until one is free of conceptual attachment."[32] In his *Profound Treatise of Mahāyāna* (*Dacheng xuanlun*), he develops his teacher's scheme into an even grander scheme of Four Levels of Two Truths (*sichong erdi*). Expounding this new scheme, Ji Zang writes,

> They [other schools] regard "existence" as the mundane truth and "emptiness" as the absolute truth. Now it is clear to us that "either existence or emptiness" is the mundane truth and that "neither emptiness nor existence" is the absolute truth. On the third level, [let us call] "both nonexistence and existence" as the "Two" and "neither emptiness nor existence" as the "Negative Two." Then, the [combination] of the "Two" and the "Negative Two" is the mundane truth [the fifth lemma]. The negation of the "Two" and the "Negative Two" is the absolute truth [the sixth lemma]. On the fourth level, these Three Levels of the Two Truths are all the categories of teaching. In speaking of these "Three Categories," the purpose is to inspire an awakening to the "Negative Three." Only if the state of no attachment and no gain is reached can we call it the principle [i. e. the eighth lemma as the absolute truth].[33]

Here Ji Zang does not explicitly describe the seventh lemma (the "Three Categories") and the eighth lemma (the "Negative Three") as he does the previous six lemmas. However, if we can see the fourth level as analogous to the third and the second, we may then figure out what the seventh and the eighth lemmas are constituted of:

Seventh lemma:
BOTH [Both (both Existence and Emptiness) and (Neither Existence nor Emptiness)] AND [Neither (Both Existence and Emptiness) nor (Neither Existence nor nonexistence)]

Eighth lemma:
NEITHER [Both (both Existence and Emptiness) and (Neither Existence nor Emptiness)] NOR [Neither (both Existence and Emptiness) nor (Neither Existence nor Nonexistence)]

The seventh lemma represents a "both/and" affirmation of the fifth and sixth lemmas on the preceding level, while the eighth lemma constitutes a "neither/nor" negation of the fifth and the sixth lemmas.[34] The seventh and eighth lemmas, like their counterparts at earlier levels, are taken as mundane and absolute truths respectively. In order to explain the eighth lemma intelligibly, some scholars choose to describe it as a string of negations rather than to set forth all its constituents as given above. For instance, in the "Preface" to his annotations to *Profound Meaning of the Three Treatises* (*San lun xuanyi*) Han Tingjie gives this description of the eighth lemma: "Not existence, not emptiness [fourth lemma], neither the Two nor the Negative Two [sixth lemma], not "neither the Two nor the Negative Two."[35]

If not truncated, the eighth lemma, the "Negative Three," should be: "NEITHER 'both the Two and the Negative Two' NOR 'neither the Two nor the Negative Two.'" Thanks to the use of the symbols the "Two" and the "Negative Two," this name of the eighth lemma seems less convoluted than the one given earlier. While Ji Zang conveniently uses these numeric symbols in setting forth his deconstructive *kinesis*, he seldom employs them when deconstructing specific onto-theological concepts. For instance, when he deconstructs birth/extinction (*shengmei*), two of the eight primary binary onto-theological terms constantly negated by Mādhyamika thinkers, Ji Zang makes little use of the numeric symbol and consequently does not pursue his deconstructive *kinesis* any further than the fifth lemma. By the time he reaches the stage of *catuṣkoṭi* or tetralemma, his mind seems to have been rendered incapable of much further language-thought formulations. From that point, he normally just negates *catuṣkoṭi* and reaches the fifth and final lemma. His customary exercise of this five-fold negation is later known as the "Five Statements" (*wuju*).[36]

For Ji Zang, how far one should pursue the deconstructive *kinesis* depends on how effectively it renders one speechless and thoughtless. In his *Profound Meaning of Three Treatises*, he elucidates this view of a deconstructive *kinesis*: "*San Lun* [Three Treatises] doctrine teaches that each thesis that may be proposed concerning the nature of truth must be negated by its antithesis, the whole process advancing step by step until total negation has been achieved ... until everything that may be predicated about truth has been negated."[37] "This forgetting of words and this elimination of thought," Ji Zang believes, "is the [ultimate] absolute truth."[38] When the deconstructive kinesis reaches this final stage, one attains to the state of enlightenment.

Given this ultimate stereological goal, Mādhyamika thinkers would not set their deconstructive *kinesis* adrift among traces of traces, less would they delight in an infinite play of deconstructions, and still less would they compare their deconstructive enterprise to a fruitless dissemination. As Derrida and Ji Zang perceive their deconstructive *kinesis* in radically different lights, they naturally describe it with different numeric symbols. Derrida invokes Sollers' "supernumerary" in the last section of *Dissemination* and concludes the book with this mathematical formula: "$(1+2+3+4)^2$. . . ." Here, with a squaring formula, Derrida seems to indicate the non-linear drift of his deconstructive *kinesis*. With the supernumerary "..." after the squaring formula, he seems to symbolize the perpetual delays of an outcome and hence the fruitfulness of his deconstructive kinesis. In contrast to Derrida's aimless, fruitless "supernumerary," Ji Zang's "octolemma" can be conceived of as a linear progression: 1-2-3-4-5-6-7-8. This simple formula betokens the reverse of Derrida's formula. It stands for the directional character, the finite duration, the *fruitful* promise of the Mādhyamika deconstructive *kinesis*.

The "End" of Philosophy: the Outcome of the Derridean and the Mādhyamika Deconstructions

Having examined the four important parallels in the Derridean and Mādhyamika deconstructive theories, we can now reflect upon some fundamental differences between these two deconstructive enterprises. The two deconstructive *kinesis* reveal that the Derridean and Mādhyamika deconstructive programs differ from each other with respect to their directions and goals.

In their rigorous pursuits of deconstruction and self-deconstruction, the Derridean and Mādhyamika philosophies inevitably reach a point where philosophy ends and "non-philosophy" begins. In the case of Derrida, "non-philosophy" takes the form of infinite textual proliferation beyond comprehension. This is the consequence Derrida knows he has to bear. "To risk meaning nothing is to start to play, and first to enter into the play of difference. . . " (*P*, 14).

However, it would be wrong to think that Derrida delights in such a consequence of "non-sense," because he confesses that "'meaning-to-say-nothing' is not, you will agree, the most assured of exercises" (*P*, 14) and he regrets that his deconstructive discourse has provoked "resistance or out-of-hand rejection even on the part of the best informed readers" (*P*, 68). His is a dilemma between "true to his own word" and "meaning-to-say-nothing." If he practices what he preaches, he falls to "meaning-to-say-nothing"; but if he tries to avoid "meaning-to-say-nothing," he goes against his own word and becomes a half-hearted deconstructionist. While we can sense a frequent wavering between these two choices in Derrida's early writings, we feel that he seems more inclined to risk "meaning-to-say-nothing" in his later works.

For instance, his *Glas* seems to exemplify a work "entangled in hundreds of pages of a writing simultaneously insistent and elliptical ... carrying off each concept into an interminable chain of differences, surrounding or confusing itself with so many precautions, references, notes, citations, collages, supplements" (*P*, 14). However, the "non-sense" that results from such verbiage takes on a philosophical meaning of its kind, even though it is intended to negate philosophical meanings and positions.

As to how to interpret the meaning of the Derridean "non-sense," critics are quite divided. Many take the meaning to be that of anti-philosophy or even nihilism, and hold Derridean deconstructionism responsible for what they call the fads of denying humanistic values in present-day literary studies. Some are more sympathetic to Derrida's deconstructive enterprise and seek to ascribe a positive philosophical purpose to the Derridean "non-sense." For instance, Coward holds that the Derridean "non-sense" is not an aimless linguistic play, but is "itself an ontological process."[39] While Derrida deconstructs "illusions of permanence, stasis, or presence" superimposed on language, Coward argues, he pursues the dynamic process of becoming of language as "the means for the realization of the whole ("the sign")."[40] When Derrida's faithful execution of his deconstructive theory results in nearly pure verbiage, one cannot resist to doubt his claim that he does not "believe in what today is so easily called the death of philosophy" (*P*, 6). One may even assume that he has jettisoned, along with ontotheologies, philosophy itself, and led himself into the prison-house of language, or even the abyss of nihilism.

Whether or not we interpret the Derridean "non-sense" in a negative or positive light, we would agree that it is fundamentally different from the kind of "non-sense" arising from Seng Zhao's lexical-syntactical deconstructions. Mādhyamika deconstructions and self-deconstructions follow a clearly directional path, defined by step-by-step negations of lemmas.[41] In the case of the Mādhyamika Buddhism, "non-philosophy" is synonymous with religious enlightenment beyond language and conceptuality. For Mādhyamika thinkers, it is not a consequence to be dreaded, but to be celebrated. The Mādhyamika deconstruction is geared to none other than this dawning of *nirvāṇa* upon the death of language, concept, and philosophy. In the light of this, we can very well see the transformation of the Chinese Mādhyamika into the Chan (Zen) Buddhism—"a practical, anti-intellectual, irrational, unconventional and dramatic religious movement"[42]—as a doctrinal fulfillment of the stereological promise of the Mādhyamika Buddhism.[43]

Notes

1. This paper is a revised and expanded version of my article "Derrida and Mādhyamika Buddhism: From Linguistic Deconstruction to Criticism of Onto-theologies," which appeared in *International Philosophical Quarterly* 33, no. 2 (1993): 183-95. I wish to thank the editors of *International Philosophical Quarterly* for their permission to reprint the article.

2. For a succinct account of the origin, major figures and scriptures of the Mādhyamika Buddhism, see C. W. Huntington and Gesh N. Wangchen, *The Emptiness of Emptiness: An Introduction to Early Indian Mādhyamika* (Honolulu: University of Hawaii Press, 1989), 25-67; Hsueh-li Cheng, *Empty Logic: Mādhyamika Buddhism from Chinese Sources* (New York: Philosophical Library, 1984), 9-32.

3. See Robert Magliola, *Derrida on the Mend* (West Lafayette, Indiana: Purdue University Press, 1984), 3-129; Harold Coward, *Derrida and Indian Philosophy* (Albany: SUNY Press, 1990); David Loy, "The Clôsure of Deconstruction: A Mādhyamika Critique of Derrida," *International Philosophical Quarterly* 27 (1987): 59-80.

4. John Sallis, *Deconstruction and Philosophy* (Chicago: University of Chicago Press, 1987), xi.

5. Jacques Derrida, *Of Grammatology*, trans. Gayatri Chakravorty Spivak (Baltimore: Johns Hopkins University Press, 1974), 34; hereafter *OG*.

6. Jacques Derrida paraphrasing Plato in *Positions,* trans. Alan Bass (Chicago: University of Chicago Press, 1972), 12; hereafter *P*. See also Derrida's discussion of this issue in *OG* 39.

7. Jacques Derrida, "The Time of a Thesis: Punctuations," in *Philosophy in France Today*, ed. Alan Montefiore (Cambridge: Cambridge University Press, 1983), 45.

8. See Murray Krieger, "Poetics Reconstructed: the Presence and the Absence of the Word," *New Literary History* 7 (1976): 347-376.

9. Jacques Derrida, *Writing and Difference*, trans. Alan Bass (Chicago: University of Chicago Press, 1978), 279-280.

10. See G. C. Nayak, "The Mādhyamika Attack on Essentialism: A Critical Appraisal," *Philosophy East & West* (hereafter *PEW*) 29, no. 4 (Oct., 1979): 477-490; Peter G. Fenner, "Candrakirti's Refutation of Buddhist Idealism," *PEW* 33, no. 3 (Jul., 1983): 251-261.

11. *Prasannapada*, in *Bibliotheca Buddhica*, ed. Louis de la Vallée Pousin (St. Petersburg: Akad. Nauk-Izd. Vostochnoi Lit-ry, 1913), IV, 16.

12. Malcolm D. Eckel, "Bhāvaviveka and the Early Mādhyamika Theories of Language," *PEW* 28, no. 3 (Jul., 1978): 323-337, 325.

13. On the influence of the early Mādhyamika on Dignāga's theory of *apoha*, see F. Th. Stcherbatsky, *Buddhist Logic* (New York: Dover, 1962), vol. I, 27-31.

14. *Pramāṣa-samuccaya*, V. 1; Stcherbatsky, *Buddhist Logic* I, 459.

15. *Pramāṣa-samuccaya-vrtti* ad V. 11; Stcherbatsky, *Buddhist Logic* I, 463.

16. However, Dignāga does not pursue his *apoha* to the point of a total denial of all onto-theological positions. It is probably for this reason that Stcherbatsky puts Dignāga on the side of the idealists in his schema of the three phases of Indian Buddhism (Stcherbatsky, *Buddhist Logic* I, 14). Dhirendra Sharma discusses how Dignāga's followers pursue the *apoha* to different ontological conclusions in his *The Differentiation Theory of Meaning in Indian Logic* (The Hague: Mouton, 1969), 19-46. See also Bimal K. Matilal and Robert D. Evans, eds. *Buddhist Logic and Epistemology* (Dordrecht: D. Reidel, 1986), 77-87, 185-191, 229-237.

17. Stcherbatsky, *Buddhist Logic* I, 480.

18. "The Emptiness of the Unreal," collected in *A Source Book in Chinese Philosophy*, ed. W. T. Chan (Princeton: Princeton University Press, 1963), 356; hereafter *SB*. For comparison, see also *Zhao Lun: The Treatise of Seng Zhao*, trans. Walter Liebenthal, 2nd rev. ed. (Hong Kong: Hong Kong Univ. Press, 1968), 56.

19. For a brief introduction to these three Buddhist Essentialist schools before Seng Zhao, see *SB* chapter 20, 336-342; and appendix I of Liebenthal, trans., *Zhao Lun,* 133-150.

20. Jacques Derrida, *Dissemination*, trans. Barbara Johnson (Chicago: Chicago University Press, 1981), xxxii; hereafter *D*.

21. For Derrida's critiques of these trinitarian concepts, see *D*, 20-25.

22. Quoted without any documentation in *D*, 25. Derrida's italics.

23. Based on Nāgārjuna's *Mūlamadhyamakakārikā* (hereafter *MMK*), XXVII, 21, 25, 28, R. D. Gunaratne presents this form of *catuṣkoṭi* in "Understanding Nāgārjuna's catuṣkoṭi," *PEW*, vol. 36 (1986), 219. Cf. David J. Kalupahana, *Nāgārjuna: the Philosophy of the Middle Way* (Albany: State University of New York, 1986), 387-391.

24. See also the following important studies of *catuṣkoṭi*: R. D. Gunaratne: "The Logical Form of *catuṣkoṭi*," *PEW* 30, no. 2 (April 1980): 211-240; Ives Waldo, "Nāgārjuna and Analytical Philosophy," *PEW* 25, no. 3 (July 1975): 281-290; and "Nāgārjuna and Analytical Philosophy II," *PEW* 28, no. 3 (July 1978): 287-298; and Richard H. Jones, "The Nature and Function of Nāgārjuna's Arguments," *PEW* 28, no. 3 (July 1978): 485-502.

25. Nāgārjuna, *MMK* XXII, 11, trans. Kalupahana, in his *Nāgārjuna*, 307.

26. Nāgārjuna, *Vigrahavyāvartanī*, 23, 24, trans. by Frederick J. Streng, *Emptiness: A Study in Religious Meaning* (Nashville: Abingdon, 1967), 226.

27. Candrakīrti, *Prasannapadā*, 12, trans. by Edward Conze, *Large Sutra on Perfect Wisdom* (Berkeley: University of California Press, 1975), 144, n. 4.

28. Jacques Derrida, *Margins of Philosophy*, trans. Alan Bass (Chicago: University of Chicago Press, 1982), 25.

29. Spivak, "Translator's Preface," *OG*, lxv.

30. *Taishō shinshū daizōkyō* 1858, 45, 150. Hereafter *T*.

31. See a similar diagram drawn by Fung Yu-lan in his *A History of Chinese Philosophy*, trans. Derk Bodde, 2 vols. (Princeton, NJ: Princeton University Press, 1973), vol. 2, 295.

32. Cheng, *Empty Logic*, 51.

33. *T* 1853, 45, 15.

34. By adding these two lemmas to the diagram given above, we have a diagram of Ji Zang's "Four Levels of Two Truths." To be consistent with Ji Zang's wording, I have substituted "emptiness" for "nonexistence" in describing the seventh and eighth lemmas.

35. See Ji Zang, *Sanlun xuanyi jiaoshi* (Collation and Annotation to Profound Meaning of the Three Treatises), annot. Han Tingjie (Beijing: Zhonghua shuju, 1987), 25.

36. See Fang Litian, *Fojiao zhexue* (*Buddhist Philosophy*), Revised edition (Beijing: Zhongguo Remin Daxue chubanshe, 1991), 356-359.

37. *T* 1852, 46, 10; Cheng, *Empty Logic*, 51-52.

38. *T* 1853, 46, 15.

39. Coward, *Derrida and Indian Philosophy*, 140.

40. Coward, *Derrida and Indian Philosophy*, 139.

41. Taking note of this directional path, Robert Magliola writes, "I shall argue that Nagargjuna's *śūnyatā* ("devoidness") is Derrida's *différance*, and is the absolute negation which absolutely deconstitutes but which constitutes directional trace" (Magliola, *Derrida on the Mend*, 89).

42. Cheng, *Empty Logic*, 55.

43. See Hsüeh-li Cheng's observations on the historical and doctrinal relationship of the Mādhyamika and the Zen in his *Empty Logic*, chapter 3. For comparative studies of Derrida and Chinese Chan Buddhism, see Robert Magliolia, "Differentialism in Chinese Ch'an and French Deconstruction: Some Test-Cases from the Wu-men-kuan," *Journal of Chinese Philosophy* 17, no. 1 (1990): 87-97; and Steve Odin, "Derrida and the Decentered Universe of Chan/Zen Buddhism," *Journal of Chinese Philosophy* 17, no. 1 (1990): 61-86.

Four

Indra's Postmodern Net

David R. Loy

> What we mean by the sūtras is the entire universe itself, mountains and rivers and the great earth, plants and trees . . . (Dōgen)

Until recently, Western philosophy was largely a search for the one within the many, the Same that grounds Difference. Our century has seen the end of this project: not its realization but its abandonment. Perhaps the most dramatic refutation has come from psychology, in Freud's demonstration that our ego-consciousness is not Cartesian and autonomous but irretrievably split, buffeted by psychic forces it cannot control because it is a function of them. Others have questioned our supposedly self-sufficient self-consciousness by emphasizing the differences inherent within language. The Swiss linguist Saussure taught that meaning is a function not of any straightforward correspondence between signifier and signified, but of a complex set of phonetic and conceptual differences. Later the French critic Roland Barthes pointed out that each text is a tissue of quotations: not a line of words releasing the single "theological" meaning of an author-god but a multi-dimensional space where a variety of writings blend and/or clash. Jacques Derrida has argued that the meaning of such a multi-dimensional space can never be completely fulfilled, for the continual circulation of signifiers denies meaning any fixed foundation or conclusion. Hence texts never attain self-presence, and that includes the text that constitutes me.

What would happen if these claims about textuality were extrapolated into claims about the whole universe? A metaphor for such cosmic interpenetration and lack of self-presence is found in the *Avataṃsaka Sūtra* of Mahāyāna Buddhism: Indra's Net.

> Far away in the heavenly abode of the great god Indra, there is a wonderful net that has been hung by some cunning artificer in such a manner that it stretches out infinitely in all directions. In accordance with the extravagant tastes of deities, the artificer has hung a single glittering jewel in each "eye" of the net, and since the net itself is infinite in all dimensions, the jewels are infinite in number. There hang the jewels, glittering like stars of the first magnitude, a wonderful

> sight to behold. If we now arbitrarily select one of these jewels for inspection and look closely at it, we will discover that in its polished surface there are reflected all the other jewels in the net, infinite in number. Not only that, but each of the jewels reflected in this one jewel is also reflecting all the other jewels, so that there is an infinite reflecting process occurring.[1]

Indra's Net "symbolizes a cosmos in which there is an infinitely repeated interrelationship among all the members of the cosmos," according to Cook. Because the totality is a vast body of members each sustaining and defining all the others, "the cosmos is, in short, a self-creating, self-maintaining, and self-defining organism." It is also non-teleological: "There is no theory of a beginning time, no concept of a creator, no question of the purpose of it all. The universe is taken as a given." Such a universe has no hierarchy: "There is no center, or, perhaps if there is one, it is everywhere."[2]

That this textuality (literally, "that which is woven, web") extends beyond language means that right now you are reading more than the insights of Mahāyāna Buddhism, as interpreted by me: for in this page is nothing less than the entire universe. The Vietnamese Zen teacher (and poet) Thich Nhat Hanh makes this point well:

> If you are a poet, you will see clearly that there is a cloud floating in this sheet of paper. Without a cloud, there will be no rain; without rain, the trees cannot grow, and without trees we cannot make paper. The cloud is essential for the paper to exist. If the cloud is not here, the sheet of paper cannot be here either.[3]

The implications of such interpenetration and "mutual identity" were developed in the Huayan tradition of Chinese Buddhism, most notably by its third patriarch and true founder Fazang (643-712 A.D.). Indra's Net was only one, and evidently not the most important, of a number of similes used to demonstrate these difficult concepts. Within the *Avataṃsaka Sūtra* itself, Indra's jewels, although glittering like first-magnitude stars, are eclipsed by dust particles (Buddhas "perceive that the fields full of assemblies, the beings and aeons which are as many as all the dust particles, are all present in every particle of dust") and Sudhana's climactic vision of Vairocana's Tower ("...within the tower there are hundreds of thousands of towers, each one as exquisitely adorned . . . and each one, while preserving its individual existence, at the same time offering no obstruction to all the rest").[4] Huayan treatises employ several other images, including water and waves ("the entire ocean is in one wave, yet the ocean does not shrink; a small wave includes the great ocean, and yet the wave does not expand")[5] and the ocean-mirror *samādhi* (each thing in the universe is both a mirror, reflecting all, and an image, reflected by all). Fazang taught Empress Wu using a hall of mirrors and a golden lion ("in each of the lion's eyes, in its ears, limbs, and so forth, down to each and every single hair, there is a golden lion.... Furthermore, each and every hair containing infinite lions returns again to a single hair"[6]). These and other similes are used in Huayan to illustrate the central teachings of Mahāyāna.

D. T. Suzuki called Huayan the philosophy of Zen and Zen the practice of Huayan. Wing-tsit Chan has praised Huayan as the highest development of Chinese Buddhist thought.[7] Yet until the last century such claims made little sense to the more essentialist West. Recently, however, field theories have made the implications of Indra's Net more plausible and perhaps irresistible. For example, physics teaches that each electrically-charged particle exerts its charge everywhere in the universe and is affected by every other charged particle. In Berger and Luckmann's *The Social Construction of Reality*, the mutual determination of part and whole is used to understand the relationship between individuals and society. They summarize that interpenetration as follows: "Society is a human product. Society is an objective reality. Man is a social product."[8] Many scholars have noticed the similarities between Huayan and Whitehead's process philosophy.

Today the relevance of Huayan claims about such "cosmic ecology"[9] seems greater than ever. The environmental catastrophes which no longer merely threaten but are now happening reveal, more clearly than any postmodern arguments can, the bankruptcy of essentialist thinking, both individual (the Cartesian myth of autonomous self-consciousness) and species (the anthropocentric bias that privileges *homo sapiens* over all other life-forms). It is becoming obvious that we cannot discriminate ourselves from the interdependent web of life without damaging (and perhaps destroying) both it and ourselves. Awareness of mutual identity and interpenetration is rapidly developing into the only doctrine that makes sense anymore, perhaps the only one that can save us from ourselves.

Like Huayan philosophy, this paper will explicate the implications of Indra's Net, but a different historical context means we ponder different problems than the ones that engaged Fazang's school well over a millennium ago. What have not been noticed, as far as I know, are what might be called its "postmodern" implications because they parallel many of the major concerns of contemporary post-structuralist philosophy. These include similar critiques of self-existence/self-presence; a shared suspicion about the onto-theological quest for Being, and a corresponding emphasis on groundlessness; the deconstruction of such "transcendental signifieds" into ungraspable traces of traces; a rejection of Truth (with a capital T) as the intellectual attempt to fixate ourselves; and the questioning of both objectivist and subjectivist values. A particularly striking example of this parallelism is the reappearance of Fazang's hall of mirrors in Derrida's critique of Plato's myth of the cave:

> Imagine that mirrors would not be *in* the world, simply, included in the totality of all *onta* and their images, but that things "present," on the contrary, would be in them. Imagine that mirrors (shadows, reflections, phantasms, etc.) would no longer be *comprehended* within the structure of the ontology and myth of the cave . . . but would rather envelop it in its entirety, producing here or there a particular, extremely determinate effect.[10]

It is not only the metaphor that recurs, for Derrida draws the same conclusions as Huayan:

> In this play of representation, the point of origin becomes ungraspable. There are things like reflecting pools, and images, an infinite reference from one to the other, but no longer a source, a spring. There is no longer simple origin. Only mirrors reflecting mirrors: traces of traces. (*OG*, 36)

In this essay, a contemporary reference point for Huayan will be provided by citing other relevant passages from Derrida and reflecting on the juxtaposition. This will not provide a detailed evaluation of any particular issue, but it will demonstrate the relevance of Huayan, and Mahāyāna philosophy generally, to a cluster of themes which has recently become central in Western philosophy. My hope is that this paper will encourage a dialogue between the two parties.

The following discussion will first place Indra's Net within its context in the Buddhist tradition, which emphasizes *causality* in order to deconstruct self-existence. This deconstruction reveals our lack of ground and transforms our frustrated symbolic quest for such a ground into *non-abiding*. That in turn raises questions about our philosophical and religious search for *truth*, insofar as that search is an intellectual attempt to ground ourselves by grasping the concepts that grasp reality. The resulting "positionless position" seems vulnerable to accusations of relativism, but the nonduality of self and other escapes many of the problems usually associated with relativism. Although Indra's Net is non-teleological, that implies not the meaninglessness of life but its *meaningfreeness*. Meaning may not be fixed, but it is not lacking. Life becomes *play*, yet it has always been play: the issue is whether we suffer our games because they are the means whereby we hope to ground ourselves somewhere in Indra's Net, or whether we dance freely within the Net because we *are* it. The dangers of relativism in *ethics* are vitiated to the extent I realize my interdependence with other beings: I shall indeed love my neighbor as myself when I experience that I *am* him.

In discussing the above issues, we shall see how much Mahāyāna and post-modernism are mirrors facing each other; but we will also notice where they do not reflect. This summary already indicates how much the Buddhist perspective emphasizes the realization that self and world are nondual. This is an experience not to be gained from the study of texts alone, for it usually requires religious practice: that is, *meditation*, the "other" of philosophy, the repressed shadow of our rationality, dismissed and ignored because it challenges the only ground philosophy has. Derrida says that he has been trying to find a non-site, or a non-philosophical site, from which to question philosophy[11]— precisely what meditative practice provides. The postmodern realization that no resting-place can be found within language/thought is an important step towards the experience that there is no abiding-place for the mind anywhere within the Indra's Net of reflecting mirrors which constitutes our world. However, for Buddhism this further realization requires a "leap" that cannot be *thought*.

Causality

In order to appreciate the implications of Indra's Net, we must understand its role within the Buddhist tradition. Indra's Net, in which everything functions as a cause for everything else, is a more "positive" and metaphysical way to restate Nāgārjuna's denial that anything has self-existence. Indian emphasis on logic and epistemology is often contrasted with Chinese lack of interest in those areas, but Huayan continues the primary concern of the Indian (not only Buddhist) tradition with causality. This is apparent in the alternative name that Huayan gave itself: *dharmadhātu pratīitya-samutpāda*, "the dependent co-arising dharma-realm." Mādhyamika conclusions about nonsubstantiality and nonorigination are translated into the Huayan teachings of nonobstruction and non-impededness. The other crucial Huayan doctrine, the mutual identity of all phenomena (which Fazang explained using water/waves and Empress Wu's golden lion) repeats *prajñāpāramitā* claims about the identity of form (*rūpa*) and emptiness (*śūnyatā*).

Nāgārjuna's deconstruction of self-existence in the *Mūlamadhyamikakārikā* can be summarized into three stages. We begin with a naive understanding of the world as a collection of objectively-existing things (including *me*) causally interacting *in* objective space and time. We think as much as see these objects, for we project our notions of substantiality to objectify things. In the second stage, Nāgārjuna uses the causal interdependence of these objects to deconstruct their supposed self-existence; saying that everything is *śūnya*, "empty," is a shorthand way to express this absence of being. Yet this analysis of discrete objects into their interdependent relations is incomplete. Nāgārjuna emphasizes that the notion of dependence is also incoherent if there is no other self-existing thing to depend *upon*. The irony of his approach is that its use of causation also refutes causation: It is only because we superimpose our notions of substantiality to perceive the world as a collection of separate things that we must also superimpose causal relations to "glue" these things together. If things originate (change, cease, etc.), there are no self-existing things; but if there are no things, then there is nothing to originate and therefore no origination. This is the way to approach perhaps the most important verse in the *Mūlamadhyamikakārikā*: "That which, taken as causal or dependent, is the process of being born and passing on, is, taken non-causally and beyond all dependence, declared to be *nirvāṇa*."[12] Can Indra's Net help us understand this third stage?

There is a practical problem with Huayan: it casts its net too wide. To say that something is caused by everything else in the universe is so general that it is also useless; in daily life we need a more efficient causality which correlates one cause with one effect. Once that is granted, however, we should not overlook the corresponding difficulty with efficient causality: the infinite regress of a life that relates to everything as a means to something else.

To say that an event (e.g., Śakyamuni Buddha's twirling a flower) is caused by everything in the universe is *finally equivalent to saying that the event is caused by nothing*. It is not self-caused; rather, the category of causality is eliminated altogether. This is *tathatā*, the "thusness" or "just *this*!"-ness which describes the way an enlightened being lives. So the Buddha is the Tathāgata, the one who "thus comes" and "thus goes." The *Diamond Sūtra* concludes that "all phenomena are like a dream, an illusion, a bubble and a shadow, like dew and lightning"; and the *Gaṇḍavyūha Sūtra* (the last part of the *Avataṃsaka Sūtra*) relates this to what became Huayan's doctrine of nonobstruction: "Having realized that this world is like a dream, and that all Buddhas are like mere reflections, that all things are like an echo, you move unimpeded in the world."[13]

Nevertheless, if in this dream-like world my unimpeded body steps in front of a nonobstructed truck, a painful reminder of *pratītya-samutpāda* is predictable. Therefore the third stage of Mādhyamika deconstruction does not supersede the second stage but supplements it. We cannot ignore causality, yet neither should we overlook its limitations.

Non-abiding

Why do we experience life as *duḥkha*, frustrating? Can our problem be described in terms of Indra's Net? Buddhism relates our dis-ease to the delusive nature of the ego-self, which like everything else is a manifestation of Indra's Net *yet feels separate from it*. The basic difficulty is that insofar as I feel separate (i.e., an autonomous, self-existing consciousness) I also feel uncomfortable, because an illusory sense of separateness is inevitably insecure. The ineluctable trace of nothingness in my fictitious (because not really self-existing) sense-of-self is experienced as a sense-of-*lack*; in reaction, the sense-of-self becomes preoccupied with trying to make itself self-existing, in one or another symbolic fashion. The tragic irony is that the ways we attempt to do this cannot succeed, for a sense-of-self can never expel the trace of *lack* that "shadows" it insofar as it is illusory; while in the most important sense we are already self-existing, since *the infinite set of differential traces that constitutes each of us is the whole Net*. "The self-existence of a Buddha is the self-existence of this very cosmos. The Buddha is without a self-existent nature; the cosmos too is without a self-existent nature" (*MMK*, XXII: 16). What Nāgārjuna says here about the Buddha is equally true for each jewel in Indra's Net; the difference is that a Buddha knows it. I think this touches on the enduring attraction of what Heidegger calls onto-theology and Derrida calls logocentrism, not just in the West but everywhere: Being/being means security to us because it means a ground for the self, whether that is understood as experiencing something Transcendent or intellectually sublimated into a metaphysical principle underlying everything. We want to meet God face-to-face, or gain enlightenment, but the fact that everything is *śūnya* means we can never attain them.

The self-existence (*svabhāva*) that Mahāyāna refutes corresponds to the "self-presence" which Derrida criticizes in textual terms, by showing that every process of signification, including self-consciousness, is an economy of differences:

> The play of differences supposes, in effect, syntheses and referrals, which forbid at any moment, or in any sense, that a simple element be present in and of itself, referring only to itself. . . . There are only, everywhere, differences and traces of traces.[14]

Self-presence "has never been given but only dreamed of and always already split, incapable of appearing to itself except in its own disappearance." Discussions of this argument tend to focus on the *-presence* of self-presence, but the *self-* needs to be emphasized as much. It is "the hunger for/of self" that seeks fulfillment in "the absolute phantasm" of "absolute self-having" (*OG*, 112).[15]

As long as I am motivated by sense-of-*lack*, I will seek to real-ize myself by fixating on something that dissolves in my grasp, for not only texts but everything is an elusive trace of traces. Then the solution must have to do with not-catching, with no longer needing to bring these fleeting traces to self-presence. The *Aṣṭasāhasrikā*, perhaps the most important *Prajñāpāramitā-Sūtra*, begins by describing this:

> No wisdom can we get hold of, no highest perfection,
> No Bodhisattva, no thought of enlightenment either.
> When told of this, if not bewildered and in no way anxious,
> A Bodhisattva courses in the Tathāgata's wisdom.
> In form, in feeling, will, perception and awareness
> Nowhere in them they find a place to rest on.
> Without a home they wander, *dharmas* never hold them,
> Nor do they grasp at them . . . .
> But when he does not course in form, in feeling, or perception,
> In will or consciousness, but wanders without home,
> Remaining unaware of coursing firm in wisdom,
> His thoughts on non-production—then the best of all the calming trances cleaves to him.
> The Leader himself was not stationed in the realm which is free from conditions,
> Nor in the things which are under conditions, but freely he wandered without a home:
> Just so, without a support or a basis a Bodhisattva is standing.[16]

"How is prajñāpāramitā [the highest wisdom] characterized?" Subhūti asks later in the same sūtra. "It is characterized by non-attachment," replies the Buddha, who explains how defilement and purification are possible when there are no things to be defiled or purified:

> To the extent that beings take hold of things and settle down in them, to that extent there is defilement. But no one is thereby defiled. And to the extent that one does not take hold of things and does not settle down in them, to that extent can one conceive of the absence of I-making and mine-making. In that sense can one form the concept of the purification of beings, i.e., to the extent that they do not take hold of things and do not settle down in them, to that extent there is purification. But no one is therein purified. When a Bodhisattva courses thus, he courses in *prajñāpāramitā*.[17]

Nāgārjuna sees the implications of this for our concepts of being and nonbeing: "When there is clinging-perception (*upādāna*), the perceiver generates being. When there is no clinging perception, he will be freed and there will be no being" (*MMK*, XXVI: 7). The most-quoted line from the *Diamond Sūtra* encapsulates all this in one phrase: "Let your mind come forth without fixing it anywhere." This is believed to have precipitated the enlightenment of the sixth and greatest Chan patriarch Huineng, whose own *Platform Sūtra* emphasizes the same thing: "When our mind works freely without any hindrance, and is at liberty to 'come' or to 'go' we attain liberation." Such a mind "is everywhere present, yet it 'sticks' nowhere."[18]

It seems to me that this solution to the problem of self-existence is one that postmodern deconstruction has not yet realized, for the kind of liberation that Derrida achieves is textual—"the affirmation of a world of signs without fault, without truth, and without origin which is offered to an active interpretation" (*WD*, 292)—and therefore still logocentric from a Buddhist point of view. The danger is not only that we try to find a "fully meaningful" symbol to settle down with (the problem Derrida addresses), but that we will remain inscribed within an endless recirculation of concepts even if we do not grasp at the ones which are supposed to bring Being into our grasp (the situation Derrida ends up with). As long as we identify with language at all, even with language as a whole, we are still trying to retain a self-existing ground which reveals that we are still anxious about our feared lack-of-ground. Later we shall see how meditation—letting-go of all thought/language—is necessary if we are to resolve the problematical dualism between language and the objectified world we live "in." The non-abiding that Buddhism recommends applies as much to the way we live (in) that world as to the symbols we use to understand and organize it.

Is the Buddhist experience that of some spiritual ground (e.g., "Buddhanature"), or of groundlessness? If each jewel in Indra's Net mutually conditions and is conditioned by all the others, then to become completely groundless is to become completely grounded, not in some particular, but in the whole web of interdependent relations. The supreme irony of my struggle to ground myself is that it cannot succeed because I am already grounded—in the totality. I am groundless and ungroundable insofar as delusively feeling myself to be separate from the world; I have always been fully grounded insofar as I am the world.

This solves the problem of desire (the cause of our dis-ease) because, without the craving-for-being that compels me to take hold of something and try to fixate on it, I am free to become it. The Buddhist solution to the problem of life is thus very simple: the "bong!" of a temple bell, the "tock!" of pebble against bamboo, the flowers on a tree in springtime, to cite some Zen examples. Of course, becoming an object is precisely what we have been trying to do all along, yet in a self-defeating way, compulsively seizing on our own objectifications in order to stabilize ourselves. But I cannot become something by grasping at it. That merely reinforces a delusive sense of separation between that-which-is-grasped and that-which-grasps-at-it. The only way I can become a phenomenon is to realize I have always been it. When nothing is needed from it to make me real, the reverberating temple bell can be just what it is: the cause and effect of everything, therefore just as much the cause and effect of nothing; neither real nor unreal; and no longer frustrating because there is no longer anything lacking in me that I experience as something lacking in my world.

Such nondual experiences are serene, says Nāgārjuna, for "anything which exists by virtue of interdependent-origination is quiescence in itself" (*MMK*, VII: 16). Why? "When neither existence nor non existence is presented to the mind, then, through the lack of any other possibility, that which is without support becomes tranquil" (Śāntideva).[19] Without any self-being to protect, and without the impending threat of nonbeing to evade, *no jewel in Indra's Net has anything to gain or lose.* Such serenity is not a result of faith or the conviction of salvation, for that would make it contingent on the being of something else and liberation in Buddhism is not dependent on the self-existence of anything.

Truth

Dr. Johnson's definition of remarriage, "the triumph of hope over experience," also describes our truths: we soon find others to replace those we have become disillusioned with. If our final delusion is the belief that we have lost all delusions, and if there is no greater delusion than the one that eliminates all others, mustn't that delusion be . . . *the truth*? What does non-abiding imply about truth? The *prajñāpāramitā* verses quoted above began: "No wisdom can we get hold of," yet precisely that condition is recommended as leading to the highest wisdom. A non-dwelling mind is "free from delusion and reality alike"[20] because discriminating between them—rejecting the one, grasping the other—is one of the ways our mind seeks a secure dwelling-place.[21]

The Buddha compared his teachings to a raft that we may use to ferry ourselves across the river of birth-and-death (*saṃsāra*) to the "other shore" of *nirvāṇa*, but then to be abandoned, not carried around on one's back. He was also careful not to set up his teachings as the only truth. "It is not proper for a wise man...to come to the conclusion: 'This alone is Truth, and everything else is false'."[22] Nāgārjuna carried this to an extreme by declining to present any view of his own: "If I had a position, no doubt fault could be found with it. Since I have no position, that problem does not arise."[23] How could he avoid taking a position? "Ultimate serenity is the coming to rest of all ways of taking things, the repose of named things; *no Truth has been taught by a Buddha for anyone, anywhere*" (*MMK*, XXV: 24). If *nirvāṇa* is the end of all ways of "taking" things, the game of truth-and-delusion is turned upside-down. There is no truth to be taught because nothing needs to be attained; instead, delusion is something to be *un*learned. So Buddhism does not offer a metaphysical system to account for reality but shows how to deconstruct the socially-conditioned metaphysical system we know as everyday reality. It does not give us truths but shows how to become aware of and let go of the automatized truths we are normally not aware of holding.

Buddhism agrees with Nietzsche's insight that our truth consists of illusions which we have forgotten are illusions, but it encourages us to face the ones that cause us to suffer.

If truth is a matter of grasping the symbols that grasp reality, all truth is error on the Buddhist path. But notice the difference between this and Nāgārjuna's "the coming-to-rest of all ways of taking things." Nāgārjuna's recommendation may reinforce the deluded dualism we already make between words and things, thought and world. The danger is that we will "take" language/thought as a filter that should be eliminated in order to experience things/the world more immediately—an approach which reconstitutes the problem of dualism in the means chosen to overcome it. Here Dōgen is insightful: the point is not to avoid thought but to *liberate* it. "Metaphor in Dōgen's sense is not that which points to something other than itself, but that in which something realizes itself." For Dōgen symbols (and language generally) are not merely means of edification, for each can be experienced as an end in itself, like everything else. If a concept or symbol is somewhere the intellectual mind tries to ground itself, why blame the victim? If the symbol is not used to compensate for my lack of self-existence—which makes me try to get something *from* it—it can be a way my mind consummates itself. Then there is free interplay between mind and symbol: although symbols can be redeemed only by mind, the mind does not function in a vacuum but is activated by symbols.[24] Derrida makes a very similar point by distinguishing between "two interpretations of interpretation":

> The one . . . dreams of deciphering a truth or an origin which escapes play and the order of the sign, and which lives the necessity of interpretation as an exile. The other, which is no longer turned toward the origin, affirms play and tries to pass beyond man and humanism, the name of man being the name of that being who . . . throughout his entire history . . . has dreamed of full presence, the reassuring foundation, the origin and the end of play. (*WD*, 292)

When we no longer need a truth that restores self-presence, we can celebrate the interpretation that "disseminates."

The crucial issue is whether our search for truth is an attempt to fixate ourselves by fixating on certain concepts. When there is this compulsion, certain ideas can become seductive: i.e., *ideologies*. The difference between *saṃsāra* and *nirvāṇa* is that *saṃsāra* is Indra's Net experienced as a sticky web of attachments which attract us because they seem to offer something we feel the lack of: a grounding for the groundless sense-of-self. Intellectually, that seductive quality manifests as a battleground of conflicting ideologies competing for our allegiance. Ideologies provide the mind with a sure grasp on the world: now we know how the world is meaningful and what our role in that meaning is. "Ideology is . . . the assumption that since the beginning and end of history are known there is nothing more to say. History is therefore to be obediently lived out according to the ideology."[25] If "there is no specifiable difference whatever between *nirvāṇa* and the everyday world" (*MMK*, XXV: 19), then very different ideologies such as religions, philosophies, nationalisms, racisms, etc., are in the same dimension insofar as they serve the same function: trying to resolve the sense-of-self's sense-of-lack by identifying with a belief-system. The problem is that they tend to become computer-viruses of the mind; when we assent to them —let them in—they take it over and fill it up.

One of the more important issues in contemporary philosophy and critical theory is to what extent *rationality* itself may be such an ideology. Rather than myth being primitive reasoning, is our understanding of logic a literalized, one-dimensional myth? "Has reason constituted itself to be the ruler of philosophy?" asks Heidegger. "If so, by what right?"[26] From our usual perspective these questions may seem ridiculous, because self-refuting; but they also challenge that perspective. What has come to be known as post-modernism may be viewed as subverting this socially-constructed myth of rationality, and, just as in Nāgārjuna's painstaking refutation of all philosophical positions, it is reason that is deconstructing itself.

When sense of *lack* evaporates because sense-of-self evaporates, the seductive web of *saṃsāra* transforms into the polyvalence of Indra's Net, where each viewpoint is able to appreciate others because it no longer identifies with a Truth-project that is threatened by those others. This is not Nietzsche's perspectivism, each perspective trying to impress its own will-to-truth upon the world, but the non-abiding wisdom of a bodhisattva who can wander freely among truths without needing to fixate on any of them, for (as Huineng put it) non-dwelling mind does not stick on any of the six sense-objects, and that includes mind-objects.

Isn't this relativism, the bugaboo of all value-theory? If so, this approach to relativism defangs it of its poison in two ways. First, one of the main difficulties with relativism is the danger of destructive ideologies such as racism, sexism, etc. We want to be able to say that they are false. Buddhism meets this concern in a different way: when such ideologies lose their seductive quality they are exposed as collective examples of ignorance and stupidity to be *un*learned. They are attractive only because they offer an easy way to fill up our sense-of-*lack*.

Second, even if all ideologies are competing in the same intellectual arena, there are some important internal differences. Many ideologies are difficult to escape once you are committed. An old-style Marxist who began criticizing Marxism would be told to purge himself of his bourgeois tendencies; a psychoanalyst will tell the analysand that she is resisting. On the other side are what might be called *meta-ideologies* because they are designed to self-negate: to free us from all ideologies including themselves. Derrida speaks of the necessity to lodge oneself within traditional conceptuality in order to destroy it (*WD*, 111),[27] which expresses nicely why Nāgārjuna insists on *two* truths: the everyday transactional realm must be accepted in order to point to the higher truth that negates it (*MMK*, XXIV: 8-10). According to Mādhyamika, *śūnyatā* is like a poison-antidote that expels the poison from our bodies and then expels itself, for if the antidote stays inside to poison us we are no better off than before. The difference between ideologies and meta-ideologies rests on whether the sense-of-self's anxious groundlessness is to be resolved by providing something to identify with or by the sense-of-self letting-go of itself. Then the important issue is the liberating function of any truth or practice. The same thought that is liberating in one situation may be binding in another. Even the most valuable insights can lose their freshness and become "sticky" because they are now understood as something to cling to rather than a pointer to freedom; or rather, clinging to them is now misunderstood as the path to freedom. This suggests that we should distinguish between Buddhism as a path of liberation—a difficult path of dying to ourselves by letting-go of ourselves—and Buddhism as an institution providing cultural and psychological security, reassuring us of the meaningfulness of the Buddhist world-view and our place within it.

The particular danger with Buddhist meta-ideology is the version of dualistic thinking that motivates it: the distinction between *nirvāṇa* and *saṃsāra*, enlightenment and delusion. Enlightenment includes (although is not limited to) realizing how the distinction we come to make between enlightenment and delusion is itself delusive, that enlightenment does not liberate us in the fashion we look to be saved. What makes the game of enlightenment-versus-delusion a meta-ideology is that this realization is essential to the game:

> Those who delight in maintaining "without the grasping I will realize *nirvāṇa*; *nirvāṇa* is in me" are the ones with the greatest grasping. When *nirvāṇa* is not [subject to] establishment and *saṃsāra* not [subject to] disengagement, how will there be any concept of *nirvāṇa* and *saṃsāra*? (*MMK*, XVI: 9-10)

Play

For Derrida, the death of God unleashes limitless play; he goes so far as to call play "the absence of the transcendental signified."[28] But whether our God has died or not, we are already playing. The question is not whether we play but how. Do we suffer our games as if they were life-or-death struggles, because they are the means whereby we hope to ground ourselves, or do we dance with the light feet that Nietzsche called the first attribute of divinity? James Carse makes what amounts to the same distinction in his insightful *Finite and Infinite Games:*

> There are at least two kinds of games. One could be called finite, the other infinite. A finite game is played for the purpose of winning, an infinite game for the purpose of continuing the play.
> The rules of a finite game may not change; the rules of an infinite game must change.
> Finite players play within boundaries; infinite players play with boundaries.
> Finite players are serious; infinite players are playful.
> Finite players win titles; infinite players have nothing but their names.
> A finite player plays to be powerful; an infinite player plays with strength.
> A finite player consumes time; an infinite player generates time.
> The finite player aims to win eternal life; the infinite player aims for eternal birth.[29]

In terms of Indra's Net, the difference is between a player struggling to ground himself in the Net and a player who plays with the Net because she has realized that she is the Net. In Derrida's terms, it is the difference between dreaming of deciphering a truth which will end play by restoring self-presence, and affirming the play which no longer seeks to ground itself.

"So the grand destiny of humanity is . . . to play?" Does our incredulity reflect the absurdity of the proposal, or how far we have fallen from the Garden of Eden? Perhaps the predominantly negative connotations of the word reveal less about play than about us: our self-importance, our need to stand out from the rest of creation (and from the rest of our fellows) by accomplishing great things. We are to play not because there is nothing else to do, not because the lack of some higher meaning means we just while away our time, but because play is implied by the nature of meaning and time. This is not inconsistent with the selflessness of the Bodhisattva, for loss of self-preoccupation is what makes infinite play possible:

> To be playful is not to be trivial or frivolous, or to act as though nothing of consequence will happen. On the contrary, when we are playful with each other we relate as free persons, and the relationship is open to surprise; everything that happens is of consequence. It is, in fact, seriousness that closes itself to consequence, for seriousness is a dread of the unpredictable outcome of open possibility. To be serious is to press for a specified conclusion. To be playful is to allow for possibility whatever the cost to oneself.[30]

The Buddhist path of ego-death is not all fun-and-games. The very notion of a path to liberation seems to require distinguishing between means and ends and between different stages. Ironies abound as soon as we try to express this in terms of Indra's Net, which has no teleology and no hierarchy: "There is no center, or, perhaps if there is one, it is everywhere."[31] No jewel is apart from the Net; each is cause of the whole and effect of the whole; therefore each is the focus of the whole Net. But obviously some jewels realize and manifest this more than others. That is, a hierarchy is implied by the fact that some realize better than others that there is no hierarchy. The path is necessary in order to realize we are not going anywhere. We see again why Mahāyāna insists there are two truths. There is spiritual progress only from a phenomenal point of view, since progress involves realizing what has always been the case; therefore "on each stage, one is thus both a Bodhisattva and a Buddha," as Fazang says.[32] But this phenomenal viewpoint is necessary, for without a spiritual practice jewels do not realize their nonduality with the whole Net.

The inevitable clash between these absolute and phenomenal perspectives led to protracted debates in China about "intrinsic enlightenment" versus "acquired enlightenment," especially in the Tathāgatagarbha tradition, which posited an intrinsically pure matrix or embryo capable of developing into Buddhahood. If (as Huayan understood) Indra's Net extends temporally as well as spatially—i.e., is intrinsically dynamic—a philosophical synthesis between its nonteleology and the Tathāgatagarbha teleology of future Buddhahood may be possible. But that argument would take us beyond the scope of this paper.

Ethics

Derrida, like Heidegger (who has been a major influence on him) does not offer an ethics; commentators have developed in different directions the hints in his texts regarding the moral implications of deconstruction. However, another major influence on his thinking, and on the development of post-structuralism generally, has been the Jewish philosopher Emmanuel Levinas, who contrasts the demand for an ethical system with our face-to-face ethical relation to the Other.[33] The Buddhist approach also emphasizes how desire for a totalizing conceptual scheme interferes with our experience of the existential situation, but draws opposite conclusions about that existential situation: to experience the Other without such a conceptual scheme (*prapañca*) is to realize that he/she is *not* an other.

As long as we experience ourselves as alienated from the world and understand society as a collection of separate selves, the world is devalued into a field-of-play wherein we compete to full-fill ourselves. That is the origin of the ethical problem we struggle with today: without some transcendent ground such as God or Buddhanature, what will bind our atomized selves together? Again, there is an answer in Indra's Net. When my sense-of-self lets-go and disappears, I realize my interdependence with all other phenomena in that all-encompassing net. It is more than being dependent on them: When I discover that I am you, the trace of your traces, the ethical problem of how to relate to you is transformed. We don't need a moral code to tie us together if we are not separate from each other.

Just as Huayan causality is too general to be efficient, so this provides no simple yardstick to resolve knotty ethical dilemmas. Even as non-abiding implies that there is no one Truth to Grasp, there is also no single Right Way to Act. But more important is that this absolves the sense of separation between us which usually makes those dilemmas so difficult to resolve, including the belief that "I" have privileged access to the correct moral principles. Loss of self-preoccupation entails the ability to respond to others without an ulterior motive that needs to gain something, material or symbolic, from that encounter. The recent history of American Buddhism reminds us that the danger of abuse remains if my nondual experience is not deep enough to root out those dualistic tendencies which incline me to manipulate others. As long as there is sense-of-self, therefore, there will be need to inculcate morality—just as young children need training wheels on their bicycles. In Buddhism, ethical principles approximate the way of relating to others that nondual experience reveals; as in Christianity, I should love my neighbor as myself—because he/she *is* myself. But in contrast to the "Thou shalt not—or else!" of Mosaic law, the Buddhist precepts are not vows to anyone else but *undertakings*: "I undertake the course of training to perfect myself in the area of non-killing," and so forth. Even these precepts are eventually realized not to rest on any objectively-binding moral principle. In the Zen school of *kōan* practice that I am familiar with, the last ten *kōan* examine the ten Mahāyāna precepts from the enlightened point of view, to clarify what has by then become apparent: the precepts too are heuristic guidelines, spiritual training wheels. There are no limitations on my freedom—except the dualistic delusions which incline me to abuse that freedom in the first place.

Goethe saw the paradox: you have only to consider yourself free to feel yourself bound; you have only to consider yourself bound to feel free. Absolute freedom for an ego-self is impossible, for our lack of self-existence ensures that we never experience ourselves as free enough: *something* is always felt to constrain us. As important as it is, the myth of freedom has been correlative to the project of the self-grounding ego-self, which seeks to eliminate all the ties that limit it so it can be truly self-determined. Then what does the search for freedom mean if self-groundedness is not possible? When even the most absolute freedom does not end *duḥkha* but usually aggravates it (e.g., the last years of Howard Hughes), our struggle for freedom can be fulfilled only by transforming into a different quest. Then the ambiguity of the word "enlightenment" is fortuitous. The legacy of the eighteenth-century Enlightenment project—in social and scientific terms, that which liberates us from absolutism, dogmatism and superstition—must dovetail into the enlightenment that frees me from *me*. Goethe's statement implies that the greatest freedom comes from losing self-preoccupation and assuming responsibility for all things: not just for our family or our nation, but for the whole of Indra's Net. Present social and environmental conditions increasingly make such a commitment necessary.

For Buddhism such response-ability is neither the means to salvation nor the effect of liberation but natural to the expression of genuine enlightenment. Hee-Jin Kim explains Dōgen's view of the Buddhist precepts as nothing other than *tathatā* "thusness":

> *not-to-commit-any-evil* is neither the heteronomous "Thou shalt not" nor the autonomous "I will not," but is *non-contrivance*.... When morality becomes effortless, purposeless, and playful, it becomes a non-moral morality which is the culmination of Zen practice of the Way in which morality, art, and play merge together. When ought becomes is in the transparency of thusness, only then do we come to the highest morality. Moral excellence as such does not constitute absolute freedom and purity from the religious and metaphysical standpoint. Only when an ought becomes an expression of thusness, does it reach the highest morality. (Emphasis original.)[34]

This is the non-moral morality of the bodhisattva, who, having nothing to gain or lose, is devoted to the welfare of others. Contrary to popular belief, this is not a sacrifice. Indra's Net implies that, insofar as I am caused by the whole universe, it exists for my benefit; but insofar as I am the cause of the whole universe, I exist for it. This dilemma is resolved by realizing that there is no real distinction between the terms: when I am the universe, to help others is to help myself. The bodhisattva knows that no one is saved until we're all saved.

But then isn't the logical opposite (to help myself is to help others) also true? According to Buddhism, to become enlightened is to forget one's own suffering only to wake up in or rather *one with* a world of suffering. This experience is not sympathy or empathy but compassion, literally "suffering with." What will the meaning of life become for such a person, freed from the delusions of objective meaning and narcissistic self-preoccupation? What will that nondual freedom, which has nothing to gain or to lose, choose to do? The career of the bodhisattva is helping others: not because one ought to, for the bodhisattva is not bound by dogma or morality, but because one is the situation and through oneself that situation draws forth a response to meet its needs. Where does that response come from? Insofar as a bodhisattva is an effect of the whole universe—an effect no longer limited by the self-reflexive, mind-forg'd manacles of self-consciousness, because no ulterior motive is interfering—it can only be the whole universe that acts. As noticed earlier, however, such causation is so general that it ceases to have any meaning and becomes equivalent to no-cause at all. Therefore the bodhisattva experiences his/her nondual deed as arising uncaused: one simply wants to act in a certain way. There is, finally, a mystery that cannot be explained but perhaps does not need to be.

Meditation

In one way or another, all the previous sections have emphasized the nonduality of self and other. This claim, which is essential to the Mahāyāna understanding of enlightenment, distinguishes Buddhism from postmodern thought. Derrida's critique of "transcendental signifieds" includes doubts about the possibility of such "mystical" experiences. His skepticism is healthy insofar as the quest for such experiences is another version of our desire for self-presence. But there is another way to understand the nondual experience that Buddhism recommends. If the sense-of-self is shadowed by a sense-of-lack that continually motivates me to try to ground myself, the sense-of-self should be understood dynamically, as not a thing but a process: *the process that seeks self-presence.* If this is the source of our *duḥkha*, the ego-death that Buddhism encourages might lead not to the attainment of self-presence but to the opposite: the end of that usually-unconscious-and-automatized quest, an end which reveals something hitherto unnoticed about the world "I" am "in."

In his first book Derrida argues that "the establishment of a pure presence, without loss, is one with the occurrence of absolute loss, with death."[35] But can such absolute loss occur without physical death? If death is what the sense-of-self fears, the Buddhist solution is for the sense-of-self to die. If it is my nothing-ness I am afraid of, the best way to resolve that fear is to become nothing. A famous passage in the *Genjō-kōan* fascicle of Dōgen's *Shōbō-genzō* sums up this process:

> To study the buddha way is to study the self. To study the self is to forget the self. To forget the self is to be actualized by myriad things. When actualized by myriad things, your body and mind as well as the bodies and minds of others drop away. No trace of realization remains, and this no-trace continues endlessly.[36]

"Forgetting" itself is how a jewel in Indra's Net loses its sense of separation and realizes that it is the Net. Meditation is learning how to die by learning to "forget" the sense-of-self, which happens by becoming absorbed into one's meditation-exercise. Since the sense-of-self is a result of consciousness attempting to reflect back upon itself in order to grasp itself, such meditation practice is an exercise in *de-reflection.* Consciousness unlearns trying to grasp itself, realize itself, objectify itself. Enlightenment occurs when the usually-automatized reflexivity of consciousness ceases, which is experienced as a letting-go and falling into the void and being wiped out of existence. "Men are afraid to forget their minds, fearing to fall through the Void with nothing to stay their fall. They do not know that the Void is not really void, but the realm of the real Dharma."[37] Then, when I no longer strive to make myself real through things, I find myself "actualized" by them, says Dōgen. What we fear as nothingness is not really nothingness, for that is the perspective of a sense-of-self anxious about losing its grip on itself. Letting-go of myself and merging with that nothingness leads to

something else: when consciousness stops trying to catch its own tail, I become nothing, and discover that I am everything—or, more precisely, that I can be anything.

If I let-go and become a nondual sound, what happens to "my" mind? Indra's Net implies that when a jewel has no inside, the outside is not outside. Dōgen described his own experience by saying that he realized mind is nothing other than rivers, mountains and trees, the sun and the moon and the stars.

> All the Buddhas and all sentient beings are nothing but the one mind, beside which nothing exists. This mind, which is without beginning, is unborn and indestructible. It is not green nor yellow, and has neither form nor appearance. It does not belong to the categories of things which exist or do not exist, nor can it be thought about in terms of new or old. It is neither long nor short, big nor small, for it transcends all limits, measures, names, traces and comparisons. It is that which you see before you—begin to reason about it and you at once fall into error.[38]

The mind that Dōgen and Huangbo refer to is not some transcendent Absolute. It is nothing other than your mind and my mind, which is not green or yellow or big or small because it is not bound to any particular form, which is why it can become green or yellow or big or small or.... Our minds need to realize that they are *ab-solute* in the original sense: "unconditioned." Meditative techniques decondition the mind from its tendency to secure itself by circling in familiar ruts, thereby freeing it to become anything.

Yungming, a Sung dynasty Chan and Pure Land master, summarizes this process: "The One Mind can take in all minds and return them to the One Mind, this is the meaning of Indra's Net."[39] Garma C. C. Chang has argued that the Mind-only teaching of Yogācāra is not as important to Huayan as Mādhyamika nonsubstantiality,[40] but the above account shows the integral relationship between them. Rather than being a metaphysical idealism, the Mind-only doctrine attempts to describe meditative experience. It is rather our "commonsense" subject-object dualism which is metaphysical, for it presupposes both idealism (that there are subjective minds) and materialism (that there is objective matter)

Conclusion

This paper originated in my wonder at these parallels between an ancient Asian philosophical system/religious way and one of the most provocative developments in contemporary Western thought. That there are also major differences is not an impasse but an opportunity: the place where fruitful dialogue can occur. I think such a conversation has much to offer both parties. Historically, Buddhism has been a flexible religion, adapting its own message and practices to different cultural contexts; but dogmatism and institutionalization overtake all such movements. Today it faces its greatest challenge, as we ask what Buddhism has to offer a rationalized, technological world which is rapidly devouring what remains of its own spiritual roots.

From a Buddhist perspective, the post-structural realization that the meaning of a text cannot be totalized—that language/thought never attains a self-presence which escapes differences—is an important step towards the realization that there is no abiding-place for the mind anywhere within Indra's Net. But the textual dissemination liberated by Derrida's deconstruction will not be satisfactory unless the dualistic sense-of-self—not just its discourse—has been deconstructed. Without dying to itself and experiencing that it *is* Indra's Net, even a postmodern, disseminating self will continue to be haunted by a sense of *lack* which seeks to ground itself in one or another symbolic fashion. This "bad infinity" is only a parody of true liberation, rather than the "good infinity" that can become anything because it needs to become nothing.

Notes

The longer original version of this paper appeared in *Philosophy East and West* (*PEW*) 43, no. 3 (July 1993): 481-510.

1. Francis H. Cook, *Hua-yen Buddhism: The Jewel Net of Indra* (University Park: The Pennsylvania State University Press, 1977), 2. Huayan is the Chinese translation of *Avataṃsaka*, "Flower Garland."

2. Cook, *Hua-yen Buddhism*, 2.

3. Thich Nhat Hanh, *The Heart of Understanding* (Berkeley, CA: Parallax Press, 1988), 3.

4. In Paul Williams, *Mahāyāna Buddhism:The Doctrinal Foundations* (London: Routledge, 1989), 124, 125.

5. Fazang, quoted in Garma C. C. Chang, *The Buddhist Teaching of Totality: The Philosophy of Hua-yen Buddhism* (London: Allen and Unwin, 1972), 146.

6. Chang, *The Buddhist Teaching of Totality*, 229.

7. D. T. Suzuki, introduction to Beatrice L. Suzuki, *Mahayana Buddhism* (London: Allen and Unwin, 1981), 12; Wing-tsit Chan, *A Source Book in Chinese Philosophy* (Princeton: Princeton University Press, 1963), 406.

8. Peter Berger and Thomas Luckmann, *The Social Construction of Reality* (Harmondsworth: Penguin, 1966), 79.

9. Cook's phrase, *Hua-yen Buddhism*, 2.

10. Jacques Derrida, *Dissemination*, trans. Barbara Johnson (London: Athlone Press, 1981), 324. The following abbreviations will be used for the works by Jacques Derrida:

OG: *Of Grammatology*, trans. Gayatri Spivak (Baltimore: Johns Hopkins University Press, 1978).

WD: *Writing and Difference*, trans. Alan Bass (Chicago: University of Chicago Press, 1978).

11. Interview with Richard Kearney in *Dialogues with Contemporary Continental Thinkers*, ed. Richard Kearney (Manchester, UK; Dover, NH, USA: Manchester University Press, 1984), 98.

12. *Mūlamādhyamikakārikā* XXV. 9, Mervyn Sprung's translation in his edition of Chandrakīrti's *Lucid Exposition of the Middle Way* (Boulder: Prajna Press, 1979), 225. Hereafter *MMK*. Sprung translates *śūnyatā* as "the absence of being in things." These three stages also correspond to the *trisvabhava*, "three natures," of Yogācāra.

13. Williams, *Mahāyāna Buddhism*, 121. Also see *MMK* VII: 24.

14. Jacques Derrida, *Positions*, trans. Alan Bass (Chicago: University of Chicago Press, 1981), 26. The Buddhist doctrine of *pratītya-samutpāda* makes the same point about consciousness.

15. For more on the sense-of-lack as "shadow" of the sense-of-self, see David Loy, *Lack and Transcendence: Death and Life in Psychotherapy, Existentialism, and Buddhism* (Atlantic Highlands, New Jersey: Humanities Press, 1996).

16. Edward Conze, trans. & ed., *The Perfection of Wisdom in Eight Thousand Lines and Its Verse Summary* (Bolinas, California: Four Seasons Foundation, 1973), 9-10.

17. Conze, trans. & ed., *The Perfection of Wisdom in Eight Thousand Lines and Its Verse Summary*, 237-238.

18. Wong Mou-lam, trans., *The Sutra of Hui-Neng* [*the Platform Sutra*] (Boston: Shambhala, 1990), 80-81.

19. Śāntideva, *Bodhicaryavatara* IX, 35, in *Entering the Path of Enlightenment*, trans. Marion L. Matics (London: Macmillan, 1970), 214.

20. Hui Hai, *The Zen Teaching of Hui-Hai*, trans. & ed. John Blofeld (London: Rider, 1969), 56.

21. Nietzsche also suspected how the search for truth is an intellectual attempt to fixate ourselves by grasping the concepts that grasp reality: "Look, isn't our need for knowledge precisely this need for the familiar, the will to uncover under everything strange, unusual, and questionable, something that no longer disturbs us? Is it not the instinct of fear that bids us to know? And is the jubilation of those who attain knowledge not the jubilation over the restoration of a sense of security?" (Friedrich Nietzsche, *The Gay Science*, trans. Walter Kaufmann [New York: Vintage, 1974], pp. 300-301, no. 355.)

22. Canki-sutta, *Majjhima Nikāya* no. 95.

23. Vigraha-vyavartanī, 29.

24. Hee-jin Kim, *Dogen Kigen—Mystical Realist* (Tucson: University of Arizona Press, 1975), 259. "Words are no longer just something that the intellect manipulates abstractly and impersonally but something that works intimately in the existential metabolism of one who uses them philosophically and religiously in a special manner and with a special attitude. They are no longer mere means or symbols that point to realities other than themselves but are themselves the realities of original enlightenment and the Buddha-nature" (Kim, *Dogen Kigen—Mystical Realist*, 110).

25. James P. Carse, *Finite and Infinite Games* (New York: Free Press, 1986), 72-73.

26. Martin Heidegger, *What is Philosophy*?, trans. W. Kuback and J. T. Wilde (New York: Twayne Publishers, 1958), 25.

27. Derrida declares a double strategy: on the one hand, "to attempt an exit and a deconstruction without changing terrain . . . by using against the edifice the instruments or stones available in the house," at the risk of thereby reconfirming what one allegedly deconstructs; on the other hand, "to decide to change ground in a discontinuous and irruptive fashion...by affirming an absolute break and difference," with the risk of reinstating that new terrain on the old ground. The way to reduce these risks is "to speak several languages and produce several texts at once" (*Margins of Philosophy*, trans. Alan Bass [Chicago: University of Chicago Press, 1982], 135).

28. Jacques Derrida, *The Archaeology of the Frivolous*, trans. J. P. Leavey (Pittsburg: Duquesne University Press, 1980), 118.

29. Carse, *Finite and Infinite Games*, pt. 1.

30. Carse, *Finite and Infinite Games*, 15.

31. Cook, *Hua-yen Buddhism*, 2.

32. Quoted in Cook, *Hua-yen Buddhism*, 112.

33. See, Emmanuel Levinas, *Totality and Infinity*, trans. A. Lingis (Pittsburg: Duquesne University Press, 1979). Derrida's appreciative essay on Levinas appears in "Violence and Metaphysics," in *WD*, 79-153.

34. Kim, *Dogen Kigen—Mystical Realist*, 294.

35. Jacques Derrida, *Speech and Phenomena and other Essays on Husserl's Theory of Signs*, trans. David B. Allison (Evanston, IL: Northwestern University Press, 1973), 151.

36. Kazuaki Tanahashi, ed. *Moon in a Dewdrop: Writings of Zen Master Dogen* (San Francisco: North Point Press, 1985), 70.

37. John Blofeld, trans. *The Zen Teaching of Huang Po* (London: Buddhist Society, 1958), 41.

38. Blofeld, trans. *The Zen Teaching of Huang Po*, 29.

39. Yung-ming, *On the Zen Mirror*, quoted in Chang, *The Buddhist Teaching of Totality*, 157.

40. Chang, *The Buddhist Teaching of Totality*, 172.

Part Three

Deconstructing Buddhism

Introduction

The essays in Part Three breach an important issue in understanding not only the relationship between Buddhism and deconstruction but what can be generally categorized as non-substantialist philosophy. As a philosophical system (and religious tradition), the non-substantialist mode of thinking carries a risk within itself in that the claim of non-substantialism is being articulated and maintained through a medium (language) that has a basically substantailizing tendency. One way Buddhist tradition deals with this issue is through the device of the two-levels of truth. Ian Mabbett applies this idea to deconstruction in the "life-world" and thus tries to resolve the possible conflict between the deconstructive operation—movements of *différance* and trace—and its institutionalized reality such as books or courses on deconstruction in academia. The idea of two levels of truth, both in the Buddhist tradition and its application to the non-substantialist mode of thinking, does not endorse institutionalization as an inevitable reality in human society. Instead, it constantly reminds us of its problems and limitations, keeping non-substantialism from falling into nihilism or annihilationism.

Roger Jackson sees the two-levels of truth in the broader spectrum of Buddhist tradition. In his essay, Jackson interprets Mahāyāna Buddhisms in India and Tibet by employing what he calls the two poles in Buddhist philosophy: namely, deconstruction and foundationalism. Foundationalism is to be distinguished from essentialism in that it does not have to advocate an Absolute. Jackson reminds us that the most deconstructive philosophy contains foundationalist elements and *vice versa*. Applying this idea to Buddhism, Jackson places Nāgārjuna at the most deconstructive pole, Dharmakīrti at the foundationalist pole, while the middle is occupied by Early Buddhism, Svātantrika-Mādhyamika and the Tibetan dGe lungs. All of these, however, are not exclusively either deconstructive or foundationalist but mixtures of the two. The deconstructive ontology of "no-self" coexists in early Buddhism together with foundationalist doctrines such as *nirvāṇa*, the principle of dependent origination, and the Four Noble Truths. The Mādhyamika Buddhism of Nāgārjuna, the most relentless deconstructionist in Buddhist history, is also anchored within the foundational frame of "a real enlightenment through real knowledge of what is really true about the world." Dharmakīrti's foundationalist Buddhism (the Pramāṇa School) still remains faithful to the deconstructive non-substantialistic ontology and worldview of Buddhism. Jackson tells us that the Buddhist teaching of the Middle Path can be understood as a balance between deconstructive and foundationalist tendencies. Buddhist philosophy, he concludes, can be understood as multi-layer frames in which foundationalist and deconstructive tendencies alternately overlap. Jackson cautions us that an attempt to find a resolution between these polarities may as well be suggestive of a failure of a philosophy, and the Buddhist Middle Path teaches exactly the opposite of such an endeavor. The middle between "hedonism and asceticism, eternalism and annihilationism, or simply, 'is' and 'is not'" is the very logic of the Buddhist middle path. I read this as the meaning of the tetralemma in which A and ~A are the same and at the same time are not. This is also the idea of living the inconceivable in the Huayan Buddhist world, the mental exercise of the "middle path" or "middle voice." And this is the play without recourse to the center, as Derrida describes it.

Ellen Zhang also notes a coexistence of deconstructive and "un-deconstructive" elements in Buddhism as she explores the Chinese Sanlun school's employment of the theory of emptiness. Zhang's interpretation of the meaning of this "un-deconstructive" instance in Sanlun Buddhism, however, is different from Jackson's, proposing that we think about, once again, the relationship between philosophy and religion as discussed in Cai and Loy.

Focusing on Ji Zang's negativity in his *śūnyatā* (emptiness)-speech and Derrida's *dénégation* (denial), Zhang argues that both Buddhist *śūnyatā* and Derridean *dénégation* are to be understood as "a movement of thought," which should be viewed as a way to emancipate meaning and not as a nihilistic play of "reducing meaning into non-meaning." Ji Zang employed the "negative play" of the *śūnyatā*-speech in order to criticize both the Satya-siddhi Hīnayānists and the Original Non-being Mahāyānists, as Derrida works with the idea of *dénégation* in his deconstruction of the metaphysics of presence. Here Zhang addresses a critical difference in the concept of negativity and the meaning of "being" and "nonbeing/nothing" in the East and the West.

The traditional Western understanding takes negativity as an "absence" of affirmation. By the same token, nonbeing is understood as the absence of being. The privilege of presence, essence and logos in the metaphysical tradition anchors itself on the privileged position of "being" over non-being. Emptiness or negativity in the Sanlun Buddhist *śūnyatā*-speech, however, does not indicate a simple negation of being. As Zhang points out, it is "self-negating and self-deconstructing." When negativity is identified with the negation of being and the absence of the present, philosophy is bound by the closed system of being, which further reifies its own system. Within that structure, a thought system based on negativity is viewed as nothing but annihilating. Negativity, however, cannot be a mere opposite of affirmativity, nor can non-being be a lack of being. Negativity points to the limits of our affirmation, as non-being reminds us of the limits of being. When negativity is understood as self-deconstructive movements, it opens up the limitation of self-closure of the philosophy of being and presence by delimiting its own boundary. Negativity in this sense is another instance of "the unnameable," which Sanlun Buddhism exercises in the name of "emptiness" (*śūnyatā*). Negativity and *śūnyatā* cannot set up their own system, for they are empty themselves (*śūnyatā-śūnyatā*): they are operators, not entities. Likewise, Derrida's *dénégation* is a "double movement . . . that sustains no closure of the final truth or principle." It implies the "excess of meaning," rather than either a negation or the opposite of negation (affirmation). To Derrida, presence is always deferred and differed, and thus always under erasure. Derridean "denial" is a motion pointing toward this always-deferred presence: presence as *différance*.

This negativity is to be distinguished from that in negative theology. As Derrida points out, negative theology is another name for "hyper-essentiality," "an affirmation *qua* negation." Ji Zang and Derrida in this sense show us "the limit of metaphysics and metaphysical language." (JYP)

Five

Deconstructive and Foundationalist Tendencies in Indian and Tibetan Buddhism[1]

Roger R. Jackson

The article employs two opposed concepts much under discussion by late twentieth century Western philosophers, foundationalism and deconstruction, and examines the degree to which (with suitable comparative caution) their opposition may serve as a useful conceptual tool for understanding Indian and Tibetan Buddhist thought—which often has been likened to deconstruction, but seldom regarded as foundationalist. I survey, in turn, the Buddhist ideology of the Pāli canon (1st century B.C.E.), which is found to contain a roughly equal measure of deconstructive and foundationalist tendencies; the main Mādhyamika writings of Nāgārjuna (1st century C.E.), whose rhetoric is primarily deconstructive, yet who also displays traces of, and is motivated by, foundationalist assumptions; the logical and epistemological works of Dharmakīrti (7th century C.E.), which appear to be strongly foundationalist, yet also contain important deconstructive elements; and the attempts by later Mādhyamika thinkers, from Jñānagarbha (8th century C.E.) to Tsong kha pa (15th century C.E.), to develop a systematic philosophy that includes both the deconstruction of Nāgārjuna and the foundationalism of Dharmakīrti. As a result of my survey, I assert that the Buddhist philosophers I have examined all display both deconstructive and foundationalist tendencies: even the most thoroughgoing deconstructionist (e.g., Nāgārjuna) leaves room for the conventional world, and is motivated by Buddhist soteriological concerns that presuppose a "way things are," while even the most positive and foundationalist approach to the world (e.g., that of Dharmakīrti) also will include the recognition that the way things are is, at least to some degree, a result of our own mental construction, hence unfounded. The Buddhist philosophical ideal, I conclude, is like a high wire act, in which one walks a thin line, holding a balance pole weighted at one end by deconstruction, at the other by foundationalism, and that the goal only will be reached to the degree that both tendencies are kept in balance.

Deconstruction and Foundationalism

Two concepts have been much discussed of late in both Anglo-American and continental philosophy: deconstruction and foundationalism.[2] Deconstruction, best known through the writings of Jacques Derrida (who himself cites Nietzsche and Heidegger as prime influences), begins as a critique of the idea that there is a privileged authorial point of view to be found in literary texts and ends as an attack on the essentialist, substantialist "logocentrism" of all Western philosophies of "presence." Throughout his or her critique, the deconstructionist generally is careful not to propound any privileged point of view that might itself be regarded as logocentric and hence ripe for deconstruction.

> Theories grounded on presence—whether of meaning as a signifying intention present to consciousness at the moment of utterance or of an ideal norm that subsists behind all appearances—undo themselves, as the supposed foundation or ground proves to be the product of a differential [i.e., self-contradictory] system.... But the operation of deconstruction or the self-deconstruction of logocentric theories does not lead to a new theory that sets everything straight.
>
> Even [traditional] theories [that criticize] logocentrism . . . do not escape the logocentric premises they undermine; and there is no reason to believe that a theoretical enterprise could ever free itself from those premises. Theory may well be condemned to a structural inconsistency.[3]

Indeed, deconstruction is more a technique than an ideology. It seeks, through a "strategic nimbleness" (*OD*, 155) that often resembles word-play, to expose the ideological underpinnings, the limitations, the illogic of all thought and interpretation. It comes, thus, to serve a primarily *critical* purpose in the ongoing conversation of philosophy, to deflate the certainties to which human thought—ever hopeful and ever self-deluding—is prone.

Foundationalism is not, strictly speaking, the "target" of deconstruction; it is a term (coined, it would seem, by its opponents) that has emerged from recent discussions in the Anglo-American tradition.[4] Nevertheless, it does seem to form a kind of natural polarity with deconstruction, to which its assumptions are diametrically opposed. It is that approach to philosophy—rooted in Plato and revived by Descartes—that presupposes that it is both necessary and possible to establish firm ontological or epistemological foundations for the construction of human knowledge.

> Foundationalism . . . refers to the conviction that knowledge as a true and justified belief is based on foundations. Humans have beliefs and opinions that they need to justify if these beliefs and opinions are to become knowledge. A foundation, however, is neither justified by other beliefs nor based upon other beliefs, but rather provides the support for all other beliefs, itself needing no such support. Foundationalism presupposes certain basic truths that can be described either as self-justified (that is, not as justified through something else) or as irrefutable. All other truths are either justified by these basic foundational truths or are foundational in that they are self justified, irrefutable and justify others.[5]

Without these foundations, whether they be Platonic "forms" or a Thomistic God or Cartesian "clear and distinct ideas," knowledge cannot be certain, and the ensuing skepticism and relativism will insidiously erode the meaning of "truth." With these foundations, knowledge is possible, communication can proceed, and the world can be ordered in a meaningful way. Foundationalism tends to be tied historically to a "correspondence" theory of truth, to the belief that true statements are those that correspond to a "way things are" extrinsic to the statements themselves. This, in turn, presupposes that there *is* a discernible "way things are," and that it can be known and expressed propositionally. Thus, foundationalism is a quest for and a confidence in precisely that kind of certainty that deconstruction seeks to subvert.

The overall project of Western thought, as reflected in such seminal figures as Plato, Aristotle, Aquinas, Descartes and Kant, has tended to be foundationalist, though this foundationalism has periodically been subjected to skeptical or deconstructive attack. In recent times, the attacks have increased, and the history of the last three centuries is one of the steady erosion of foundationalism and its replacement by one or another approach with deconstructive techniques or implications. Certainly today, foundationalism of the traditional variety is in considerable disrepute, and the anti-foundationalist successors of Heidegger and Wittgenstein dominate philosophical discussion. Still, the tension between the two tendencies hardly has been resolved for good, as evidenced by the ongoing and very important debate over "rationality and relativism," i.e., whether cross-cultural understanding is possible without some common fund of human knowledge to serve as a basis for communication, and whether, thus, some form of foundationalism must not, finally, be required. This debate, in turn, lays bare the inherent strengths and weaknesses of each approach. Foundationalism has the advantage of providing secure grounding for communication and "the world," along with the disadvantage that such secure grounding is notoriously difficult to establish—perhaps because of the paradoxes inherent in knowledge itself. Deconstruction has the advantage of dispensing with the ancient but dubious quest for certainty and embracing the limited, interpretive nature of all knowledge, along with the disadvantage of leaving us in doubt as to how any judgments are to be formed on matters of knowledge and morals.

If Western thought is a foundationalist project that no longer has the confidence of its convictions, Buddhism—with its strongly if not unequivocally anti-substantialist tenor—might seem at first glance to be precisely the opposite: an essentially deconstructive movement that occasionally has been infected by foundationalism. This is the view of Robert Magliola, who explicitly links Buddhism with deconstruction, primarily through an analysis of Madhyamaka and Zen.[6]

The deconstruction-foundationalism polarity is useful for interpreting Buddhist philosophy; the terms may not be Buddhist, but the tendencies they describe are very much present in Buddhist thought. However, Buddhism is not so clearly "deconstructive" a tradition as Magliola and others have suggested. There are both individuals and movements within Buddhism that are more foundationalist than deconstructive and thinkers and traditions that would be classed as deconstructive have in them strong, unavoidable, elements of foundationalism.

This assertion requires qualification in two ways. First, it is important to note that foundationalism (and, for that matter, philosophies of "presence") in the West generally have been grounded in some ontological or epistemological absolute, such as Being or the Cogito or some transcendental subject. If such grounding is definitive of foundationalism, and if we accept the common, though controversial, assumption that Buddhism denies the existence of any such absolute, then Buddhism cannot be considered foundationalist.[7] If, on the other hand, foundationalism can be described and defended without recourse to such absolutes, then we still can apply the term to Buddhism. The sort of non-absolutist foundationalism I am describing would be marked by its willingness to assert that, e.g., perception and inference can be the "foundations" of objective though not absolute certainty regarding important features of the world. Its denial of *absolute* certainty would distinguish it from classical Western foundationalism, while its assertion of *objective* certainty would distinguish it from either coherentism or pragmatism, which regard "objectivity" far more suspiciously, considering it relative either to particular conceptual schemes or particular human purposes.

Second, even if we admit that "foundationalism" is a term that may be applied to a non-absolutist tradition like Buddhism, we must specify that there are different *types* of foundationalism that may be encountered at different levels of discourse. Specifically, it is useful to distinguish between a "strong" foundationalism (whether "absolutist" or not) that claims that our knowledge *can* be certain, because it is grounded in objectively valid judgments about "the way things are," and a "weak" foundationalism that, while explicitly rejecting any such foundations, turns out to involve unstated (or understated) certainties about the way things are, hence the implicit presupposition of certain foundational facts about the world. It might be objected that such a "weak" foundationalism would be so all-embracing that both our everyday activities and the process of deconstruction itself would turn out to be foundationalist. At the risk of trivializing the meaning of "foundationalism," it is important to observe that there is, in fact, a kind of foundationalism at work in such areas—though it must be remembered that these foundations are not metaphysical absolutes but relatively adequate versions of the world that can in principle be defended by recourse to rational arguments based on some consensus about "the way things are."

The Buddhist tradition includes both deconstruction and foundationalism, and one way of understanding the Buddhist "middle way" is as a dialogue between and balance of the deconstructive and foundationalist poles. I will generally employ this metaphor of "poles" in speaking of the tradition as a whole. When I explore particular positions within Buddhism, the metaphor I will employ is that of "frames." In other words, a particular thinker or school can be located along a generalized continuum that runs from the pole of deconstruction to that of foundationalism, and that thinker or school then may be described more specifically in terms of, e.g., whether it is a primarily deconstructive enterprise that is framed by foundationalism, or a foundationalist enterprise framed by deconstruction.[8]

In what follows, we will look briefly at deconstructive and foundationalist tendencies in the Pāli canon—so-called "early Buddhism"— then examine, in turn, one classically "deconstructionist" Buddhist thinker, Nāgārjuna, and one classic "foundationalist," Dharmakīrti. We also will examine some later Indian and Tibetan attempts to synthesize these two apparently incompatible tendencies. Having seen that Buddhist thinkers, on whichever side of the divide we may place them, in fact combine elements of *both* deconstruction and foundationalism, we may be able to make some concluding observations about the "middle way" in Buddhist thought.

Deconstruction and Foundationalism in the Pāli Canon

If we see deconstruction as an approach to philosophy that is epistemologically skeptical and ontologically anti-essentialist, there is much in the tradition of so-called "early Buddhism" to justify the claim that Buddhism is a fundamentally deconstructive tradition. This is especially true when we compare Buddhism's ideas not with those of the contemporary West, but with those of the other Indian traditions that co-existed with it and from which, to a degree, it emerged. Buddhism was, to begin with, a *śramaṇic* movement, one of that minority of groups—the Jainas and Materialists were others—that rejected the authority of the Vedas. Buddhists did, of course, accept the validity of their own scriptures, but they did not regard them as "divine," i.e., the eternal in verbal form, in the way that most Hindus regarded the Vedas.

Furthermore, there are a good many places in the Pāli canon where the Buddha severely restricts the number of avenues through which valid knowledge may be acquired. The most famous of these, perhaps, is in his advice to the Kālāmas (*Anguttara-nikāya* I, 89) not to be certain in doubtful matters on the basis of report, tradition, hearsay, "proficiency in the collections," logic, inference, considering reasons, reflecting on and approving some theory, concern for propriety, or respect for a recluse. Virtually every socially- or intellectually-based foundation for knowledge is rejected: socially-based foundations would be any that are derived in any way from the testimony of others, whether because the tradition itself must be accepted or because the teacher is regarded as uniquely authoritative; intellectually-based foundations would be those that are derived through rational processes. Examples could be multiplied, but it is safe to say that there is a strong element of caution—if not outright skepticism—running through early Buddhist epistemology.

By the same token, early Buddhist ontology is clearly anti-essentialist or, in deconstructionist terminology, non-logocentric. There is no enduring substance to be found anywhere in the phenomenal world through any method of investigation. Thus, the cosmos itself has as neither its source nor its substance any kind of immutable principle, whether it be considered Brahman or Brahmā; on the contrary, it proceeds beginninglessly on the basis of material forces and the karma of sentient beings—all of which are transient conditions.[9] Similarly, and even more important, the individual neither has nor is at his or her core any kind of eternal soul-substance, such as the *ātman* of Hinduism or the *jīva* of the Jainas. Indeed, what we conventionally call a "person" is merely a constellation of five ever-changing aggregates, of matter, sensation, recognition, dispositions and consciousness. These aggregates are exhaustive of the "person." Hence, in an ultimate sense, search as we may for an objective correlative for our term, "I," we only will discover—as when we peel an onion—that at the core there simply is nothing. This point about the absence of enduring self may or may not be—as later tradition claimed—the "central doctrine" of early Buddhism. There can be no doubt, however, that it has been an important idea from the very earliest times, one that is expounded in countless passages in the Pāli canon. To cite just one important example: in the *Milindapañhā* (section 25), the Buddhist monk Nāgasena argues in detail to the Indo-Greek king Milinda that there exists no "self" apart from the aggregates any more than there exists a chariot apart from the pole, axle, wheels, chariot-body, and banner-staff; indeed, the "self," like a "chariot," is merely "a way of counting, a term, an appellation, a convenient designation, a name."[10]

There is, thus, a sense in which both knowledge and reality are "deconstructed" by the early Buddhist tradition. At the same time, however, early Buddhism is not utterly deconstructionist; indeed, there are important, if subtle, ways in which it is foundationalist. This latent foundationalism begins to emerge when we recall the overall context and purpose of the Buddhist movement: the achievement of *nirvāṇa.* The achievement of *nirvāṇa* is, of course, the "gospel," the "good news," of Buddhism, and it is an important assumption of many—if not all—early Buddhist texts that our success or failure in achieving *nirvāṇa* results from our apprehension or misapprehension of certain crucial features of the cosmos, e.g., the existence or non-existence of a substantial self. *Nirvāṇa* depends, in short, on knowledge. If *nirvāṇa* is possible, and depends at least in part on knowledge of the way things are (*yathābhūtam*), then there must be a clearly identifiable and knowable way that things are. There must, as a result, exist *some* type of knowledge that has universal validity, that can serve as a foundation for our apprehension of the truth. This is where the second part of the Buddha's discourse to the Kālāmas is pertinent. For all his distrust of testimony and reason as sources of knowledge, the Buddha does assure the Kālāmas that one's own experience is a source of knowledge on which one may rely. Thus,

> . . . when you know for yourselves: These things are unprofitable, these things are blameworthy, these things are censured by the intelligent; these things, when performed and undertaken, conduce to loss and sorrow—then indeed do ye reject them, Kālāmas. . . . If at any time ye know of yourselves: These things are profitable, they are blameless, they are praised by the intelligent; these things, when performed and undertaken, conduce to profit and happiness—then, Kālāmas, do ye, having undertaken them, abide therein.[11]

There are any number of philosophical questions that this approach may beg, and I will not enter here into the debate as to whether this outlook reflects an early Buddhist "empiricism thesis." It is sufficient for our purposes to indicate that knowledge is an important and necessary element of the path to *nirvāṇa*, and that correct knowledge, based above all on one's own experience, is possible. It may be that the "experience" invoked is of an extraordinary rather than the ordinary kind, perhaps achievable only through meditation. Nevertheless, in early Buddhism there does exist a foundation for correct human knowledge.

Similarly, although early Buddhist ontology has a strongly deconstructive element, not every object of ontological knowledge is regarded with the same suspicion as is the self. Indeed, the Buddha himself makes it clear on a number of occasions that there are objects that he rejects categorically, objects that he rejects or asserts provisionally, and objects that he asserts categorically. It is, for instance, arguable that the general formula of dependent origination (expressed abstractly as "if *x*, then *y*; if no *x*, then no *y*") though of course asserted to be true *a posteriori* on the basis of the Buddha's experience, functions for many Buddhists very much like an *a priori* ontological principle, serving as it does as the virtually unquestioned basis for explaining all the processes of both *saṃsāra* and the path to *nirvāṇa*.[12] Dependent origination may not involve any kind of essentialism or logocentrism, but it does serve as a principle more fundamentally "true" than other principles. Similarly, the four noble truths are regarded as being among those objects that the Buddha categorically asserted. In other words, they are true for all people in all times and places. Thus, like the principle of dependent origination, they are foundational t uths, not subject to the same type of "deconstruction" as, e.g., Brahmā or the *ātman*. Not only is there in early Buddhism a foundation for knowledge on the subjective side—one's own experience—but there also are objects of knowledge, "truths," that are themselves considered universal and foundational.

Early Buddhism, despite a certain deconstructive tone, turns out on closer examination to have foundationalist elements as well. Indeed, precisely to the degree that the Buddha claimed to have discovered a *dharma* that was universal, he assumed (a) that there were certain vital truths that had to be known by every sentient being, and (b) that there must exist an epistemological basis for their apprehension. Thus, he could not help but invoke some form of foundationalism. Still, on balance, I think we have to regard early Buddhism as a middle way between deconstruction and foundationalism. There do exist foundational truths and a way of knowing them aright, but the very truths that are known have as an important—if not exclusive—part of their content an understanding that "foundations"—if they are taken as ontologically substantial—are nowhere to be found. There is little evidence that the early Buddhist tradition drew out all the implications of its exercise in deconstruction, but such implications certainly could be drawn in principle. They were, in fact, explicitly drawn by the radical thinkers of the early Mahāyāna, especially the authors of the Perfection of Wisdom *sūtras* and the great philosopher, Nāgārjuna.

Deconstruction and Foundationalism in Nāgārjuna

If the early Buddhist tradition contains clearly deconstructive elements, but does not follow the deconstructive tendency to its logical conclusion, there would appear to be many instances in Mahāyāna thought where deconstruction is undertaken relentlessly and thoroughly, even to the point where the cosmology and sotereology explicated in the Pāli canon seems to be called into question. Here we cannot consider all the deconstructive trends in the Mahāyāna but will examine just one, the Madhyamaka philosophy of Nāgārjuna.[13]

There is much dispute over precisely which works attributed to Nāgārjuna actually were written by him, but almost all scholars agree that, at the very least, he can be credited with two philosophical treatises in verse, the *Madhyamakakārikā* ("Stanzas on the Middle Way")[14] and the *Vigrahavyāvartanī* ("Averting the Arguments").[15] In these two texts are found probably the most relentlessly deconstructive arguments ever framed by a Buddhist. In the twenty-seven chapters of the *Madhyamakakārikā*, Nāgārjuna demonstrates through a variety of dialectical strategies (most famously the "tetralemma" known as the *catuṣkoṭi*) that concept after concept employed by philosophers in general and Buddhists in particular simply does not stand up to a rigorous analysis, is "empty" (*śūnya*), and therefore must be discarded by the wise.

For instance, in the first chapter, Nāgārjuna analyzes causation and establishes that absurd consequences ensue no matter how the process is described. If entities arise from themselves, then we sacrifice the meaningfulness of the distinction between cause and effect, for they would be identical. If they arise from something other, then we are hard pressed to explain how particular effects may be "connected" to particular causes. If they arise from both themselves *and* from something other, then contradictory properties are being illegitimately asserted of one and the same entity. If they arise from neither themselves nor something other, then nihilistic chaos may be entailed. Thus, all possible explanations of causation entail absurdity.

In the twenty-fifth chapter, Nāgārjuna subjects the *summum bonum* of Buddhism, *nirvāṇa,* to a similar analysis. If *nirvāṇa* is said to exist, then it must be an entity subject to production and destruction, but this contradicts the definition of *nirvāṇa* as unconditioned. If it is said not to exist, then its very possibility as a human attainment is being denied, and this is contrary to the "gospel" of Buddhism to the effect that enlightenment is possible. If it both exists and does not exist, then contradictory properties are being asserted of the same concept. If it neither exists nor does not exist, then no meaningful statement is being offered. Thus, *nirvāṇa*, like causation, cannot stand up to analysis. Other concepts are negated because they are relative to one another, like the different aspects of time, motion, or quantity, while still others are denied because they are made up of parts, or are dependent on causes and conditions that are extrinsic to them. By the time one has worked one's way through the major part of the *Madhyamakakārikā*, there seems little of the world left to stand on—the ontological foundations seem to have been utterly deconstructed.

If the *Madhyamakakārikā* is Nāgārjuna's great exercise in ontological deconstruction, then his great critique of epistemology is found in the *Vigrahavyāvartanī*. There, in verses 31-51, he analyzes the concept of epistemological authority (*pramāṇa*), those sources of knowledge such as perception or inference that were taken by virtually all Indian philosophical schools of his time to be the foundations of our understanding of the world. Using a dialectic similar to that employed in the *Madhyamakakārikā*, he demonstrates that if authority is derived from itself, then it will be self-referential and tautologous, whereas if it requires another authority for its validation, then that authority will require a further validating authority, and so on, in infinite regress. Similarly, if an authority is said to prove something that has not already been proved—a standard requirement for a formal inference—then it must forever be separated from the provable, and thus will prove nothing, whereas if an authority proves something that already has been proved, then it will be redundant, and will not prove anything, either. Thus, Nāgārjuna concludes, "[a]uthorities are not proven by themselves, by each other, or by other [sources]; there is no existence of authorities through authority objects or accidentally" (*VV*, verse 51). Thus, the means of knowing the world, the *pramāṇas*, are vitiated by Nāgārjuna as surely as are the ontological constituents of the world.

It would seem that we have arrived at a deconstructive impasse, where no object or means of knowledge has any foundation, and knowledge itself—including knowledge of the Buddhist path—thus becomes impossible. This, in fact, is precisely the criticism directed at Nāgārjuna by an unidentified opponent at the beginning of the twenty-fourth chapter of the *Madhyamakakārikā*, and it is Nāgārjuna's response to this criticism that makes it clear that his enterprise is not a purely deconstructive one. It must be understood, Nāgārjuna says, that in teaching the *dharma*, the Buddhas have recourse to two levels of truth, or the utterance of truths from two perspectives: the concealing, or conventional, truth (*samvṛisatya*) and the highest, or ultimate, truth (*paramārtha satya*) (*MMK*, 24: 8). The ontological and epistemological deconstruction to which Nāgārjuna has devoted so much effort is his attempt to understand things from the ultimate point of view, i.e., to demonstrate that no entity, concept, or authority can hold up to ultimate analysis, because it cannot be shown to exist *svabhāveṇa*, that is, intrinsically, by its own nature, independently, substantially. Conventionally, all the concepts that Nāgārjuna has analyzed are perfectly valid; they only are negated in terms of *svabhāva*. Indeed, Nāgārjuna points out (*MMK*, 24: 14), it is only because entities and concepts are empty of *svabhāva* that there even can be a conventional world, for a world in which entities did have *svabhāva* would be a world in which change was impossible, and the world is only comprehensible on the basis of its changes, its differences. Thus, Nāgārjuna not only affirms the conventional world, but actually establishes it through his ultimate-level deconstruction of it! He is quite explicit about this in his own commentary to the final verse of the *Vigrahavyāvartanī*, where he insists that "[a]ll things obtain for him in whom emptiness obtains, while nothing obtains for him in whom emptiness does not obtain." What, specifically, obtains is dependent origination (*pratītya samutpāda*), which Nāgārjuna already has established (at *MMK*, 24: 18, and *VV*, verse 22) as both a basis for and a positive counterpart to the concept of emptiness. Dependent origination, in turn, entails not only the basic principle of causality, but the specific validity of the various conventions of the Buddhist path.[16] That Buddhist path, it is evident, can be completed; there is a *nirvāṇa* at its end. Indeed, *nirvāṇa* is to be achieved precisely through the wisdom, *prajñā*, that comprehends that entities and concepts are empty of inherent existence. Emptiness, it ought to be noted, is an extension of, but by no means a radical reformulation of, the concept of no-self, comprehension of which, we may recall, is an important requisite for the achievement of *nirvāṇa* in the early Buddhist tradition.

Thus, for all his deconstructive rhetoric, Nāgārjuna turns out to be a foundationalist, too, for his entire critical enterprise can only finally be understood within the still larger frame of a conventional Buddhist pursuit of enlightenment. In that pursuit, which motivates and shapes Nāgārjuna's entire project, it is assumed that (a) there is an enlightenment to be achieved by sentient beings, (b) there is a way the world is—empty—that must be known if enlightenment is to be achieved, and (c) there is a way—intellectual and intuitive *prajñā*—that the way the world is can be known. Granted, the content that is cognized by one who knows the world as it actually is—emptiness—is the sort of "object" that, comprehended, may vitiate many of our assumptions about the world and thus lead us to deconstruct it. But if we deconstruct the world utterly, rob it of all its foundations, then we will have misunderstood the Buddha's purpose in teaching emptiness and will have abandoned precisely those cosmological, ontological and epistemological assumptions that are the foundation for our exercise in deconstruction.[17]

Though there is not the space to analyze them separately here, it should be evident, *mutatis mutandis*, that the negative rhetoric of the Perfection of Wisdom *sūtras*, the radical perspectivism of the Yogācāra, and the endless rug-pulling favored by tantric and Zen masters are not any more exclusively deconstructive than Nāgārjuna's analyses, for they, too, must be seen within the larger frame of a quest for a real enlightenment through real knowledge of what is really true about the world. This only can be achieved if there are ontological and epistemological foundations on which we may securely rest; thus, these movements, too, however deconstructive they may appear, presuppose at least a "weak" version of foundationalism.[18]

Foundationalism and Deconstruction in Dharmakīrti

The "deconstruction" that is so important a part of the project of Nāgārjuna and other Buddhist thinkers masks an element of foundationalism that implicitly motivates and helps to shape that project. It still may appear, however, that Buddhist philosophy is a fundamentally deconstructive enterprise, in which foundationalism serves as a problematic but peripheral element. But, for a significant number of Indian Buddhist thinkers the establishment of epistemological foundations is a central rather than a peripheral concern. Such foundations arguably are the concern of the architects of the *abhidharma*, from the authors of the Pāli *Abhidhamma Piṭaka*, to the compilers of the *Mahāvibhāṣa*, to Saṅghabhadra and Vasubandhu, to Asaṅga—for what is the *abhidharma* but a foundational description of the elements and categories of existence acceptable to Buddhists? If the point is debatable in regard to the *abhidharma*, it cannot seriously be questioned when we look to the representatives of what sometimes has been called the "Pramāṇa School"—the tradition of Buddhist thought that focused above all on the establishment and delineation of the sources of epistemic authority (*pramāṇa*), without which our knowledge of neither the conventional world nor the salvific truths of Buddhism ever could be established. Although they do not always receive detailed attention in intellectual—let alone popular—histories of Buddhism, such figures as Dignāga, Dharmakīrti, Dharmottara, Jñānaśrīmitra, and Ratnakīrti provided both the tools and a major part of the agenda for Buddhist philosophy from 500 C.E. onward, first in the Indian tradition, and then in the Tibetan, where their influence is felt to this day.

From among these figures, Dharmakīrti (6th-7th centuries C.E.) stands out as especially interesting for our present discussion.[19] Dharmakīrti begins one of his last and most important works, the *Nyāyabindu*, with the ringing affirmation that "[a]ll successful human action is preceded by correct cognition."[20] The indispensability of knowledge for the successful completion of human projects, whether secular or religious, entails the necessity of establishing what, in fact, knowledge is, what its types are, and how we can determine whether it is delusive or veridical. Thus, Dharmakīrti seeks, in his various works, to determine the nature and possible applications of the sources of epistemic authority, the *pramāṇas*. Indeed, the work considered his masterpiece by later generations makes this evident with its title: *Pramāṇavārttika*, the "Commentary on Authority."[21]

We may recall that the *pramāṇas* were—at least from an ultimate standpoint—rejected by Nāgārjuna in his *Vigrahavyāvartanī*; Dharmakīrti, on the other hand, seems to have entertained no such doubts about the possibility of establishing the foundations of epistemic authority. Indeed, the entire *pramāṇa* tradition exudes confidence that we can know how it is we know, and that once this is established, there are few areas that our knowledge cannot confidently approach. For Dharmakīrti, as for Dignāga before him, there are two, and only two, epistemic authorities, namely, perception, and inference. Of these, perception, which is direct and nonconceptual, is the more basic. There are four different types of perception that are accepted: sense perception, which is the direct, nonconceptual apprehension of a sensory object; mental perception, which is the direct apprehension of a mental moment following on a sense perception; apperception (*svasaṃvedanā*), which is a simultaneous cognition that directly apprehends any sensory or inferential cognition; and yogic perception, which is a direct apprehension of ultimate reality, as, for instance, the four noble truths, or no-self.[22] Just as the subjective side of perceptual knowledge is securely grounded, so is the objective: that which perceptions apprehend are the real "own-marks," or "specific characteristics" (*svalakṣaṇa*) of entities. What is important here is not what these own-marks may be, but the fact that Dharmakīrti assumes that such things exist. This implies that there are actual ontological foundations of the world that can serve as the objects of actual, founded epistemic authorities.

Because it is direct and nonconceptual, perception may be the more fundamental of the two authorities; inference is indirect and conceptual, but it is securely founded knowledge, for it is rooted in the positive and negative concomitance between a reason, or sign (*hetu, liṅga*) and the subject (*dharmin*) and predicate (*pakṣa*) of a proposition (*pratjñā*). This concomitance is not merely an arbitrary or purely logical relationship, as it might be in some forms of Western symbolic logic. Rather, it is assured by the fact that it has invariably been *observed* to obtain. The importance of observation for inference is shown by the fact that built into the essential structure of what is sometimes called the Buddhist "syllogism" is the requirement that positive and negative instantiations of the probative concomitance be cited. Thus, it is not sufficient merely to assert that "on that hill (subject), there is fire (predicate), because there is smoke (reason)." The probative concomitance between smoke and fire must be exemplified by adding, "like in a kitchen"—where there is fire—and "unlike in a lake"—where there is none. Thus, inference explicitly invokes and is grounded in perception, and ultimately in the direct apprehension of the actual own-marks of real entities. It is for this reason that Dharmakīrti specifies on a number of occasions that valid inferences must be "effected by the force of actual entities" (*vastubalapravṛtta*).[23]

On the basis of such valid inferences, Dharmakīrti believes, we may come conceptually to know truths not only about the everyday world, but also about such great matters as the existence or non-existence of the self, the reality or unreality of past and future lives, and the comparative validity of the systems of the great philosophers and religious teachers. Indeed, Dharmakīrti devotes an entire chapter of his *Pramāṇavārttika*, that on the "Establishment of Authority" (*Pramāṇasiddhi*), to a systematic attempt to demonstrate that the Buddha is uniquely authoritative for those intent on spiritual liberation. He seeks to do this by proving logically (a) the possibility of the Buddha's having achieved an enlightened state and (b) the validity of what he teaches on the basis of his enlightenment, the four noble truths. This, in turn, entails various subsidiary proofs of, e.g., the non-existence of God, the mind's independence of the body, the limitless expandability of mental qualities, and the unique stereological value of the insight into no-self.[24] Whether or not Dharmakīrti succeeds in his demonstration is not the issue here; what is important is that he believes that such a demonstration is possible, and it is possible because it ultimately is rooted in common, securely-grounded *observations* about the way the world actually is.

Dharmakīrti's project seems almost diametrically opposed to Nāgārjuna's: there *is* a way entities actually exist, and it is given to us directly and vertically in the various modes of perception, which are, in turn, the basis for legitimate conceptual knowledge about the world, both the everyday world that is closely related to the senses and the metaphysical world that lies beyond them. Dharmakīrti seems overtly and thoroughly a foundationalist, who could gladden the heart of an Aquinas or Descartes.

It hardly should surprise us, however, that matters are not so simple. Just as there turned out to be elements of foundationalism in Nāgārjuna's enterprise, so, too, are Dharmakīrti's writings—foundationalist as they may seem—shot through with deconstructive elements. To begin with, Dharmakīrti's ontology is fundamentally that of classical *abhidharma* Buddhism and therefore is based on the assumption that nowhere in the cosmos is there to be found an entity that is or has abiding substance (*ātman*). In Dharmakīrti, this assumption is expressed in a number of important ways, e.g., through his defense of a soteriology based on no-self; his insistence that those real, efficient entities that are possessed of own-marks abide only for the shortest conceivable instant (*kṣaṇa*), and then are destroyed; and his assertion that we comprehend classes of objects not through apprehending some inherent universal—for the permanence usually predicated of universals is an impossibility—but through the exclusion (*apoha*) of what is *not* an appropriate classification. All these notions, whatever their philosophical strengths or weaknesses, serve to undermine a substance ontology, and to the degree that they do so, they tend to undermine the absolute certainty with which anything may be said to exist in a particular, definite manner—for such specification often results from conceptual misapprehensions rooted in substantialist assumptions. This last point is certainly arguable, for Dharmakīrti would appear to believe that his non-substantialist ontology does not vitiate his epistemological foundationalism. Indeed, he goes to considerable lengths to demonstrate that it is perfectly compatible with it, and, in fact, the only ontology on the basis of which knowledge actually can be explained.

Even if the deconstructive effect of Dharmakīrti's non-substantialist ontology is questioned, one finds that another, still more basic tendency toward deconstruction informs his thought: his adherence to the Yogācāra view that all the three worlds are "only a percept" (*vijñaptimātra*).[25] The corollary of this view is the assumption that the mistaken belief in an ultimate duality of subject and object is the basis of our circling in *saṃsāra*, and that the direct realization of their non-duality is the essential point to be realized in yogic perception, which is the experience of an *ārya*, who has cut the roots of ignorance and is assured of enlightenment. If the non-duality of subject and object is what must ultimately be realized on the Buddhist path, there is a sense in which ordinary perceptual and inferential knowledge is sublated and relativized, for ordinary knowledge is necessarily dualistic, and such dualism turns out to be without any foundation in ultimate reality. Like Nāgārjuna, Dharmakīrti claims that conventional knowledge has a conventional validity, but is negated by the higher perspective of one who sees things as they ultimately really are. There is a more than incidental element of deconstruction involved in Dharmakīrti's thought.

Our discussion cannot end here, however, for just as the outermost frame of Nāgārjuna's deconstructive project was a type of foundationalism that assumed that there is a knowable way things really exist, i.e., as empty; so, too, the outermost frame of Dharmakīrti's project involves a similar perspective. Just as the foundationalism that seems so basic to Dharmakīrti turns out to be sublated in important ways by an ultimate standpoint in which all dualistic knowledge is delusive, so, too, that ultimate standpoint turns out to be sublated by a further foundationalism that structures the entire project. As with Nāgārjuna, this foundationalism assumes that there is a way the world is in the ultimate sense, i.e., only as a percept, and that this way that the world is, can be known authoritatively, e.g., by yogic perception. Thus, both ontology and epistemology, in the final analysis, have foundations, even if the foundational object (non-duality) and subject (yogic perception) represent a radical departure from and perhaps an implicit undermining of the conventional ontological and epistemological foundations that we require in the everyday world.

The Meeting of Nāgārjuna and Dharmakīrti: Indian Svātantrika and Tibetan Prāsaṅgika

Our selection of Nāgārjuna and Dharmakīrti to represent, respectively, the tendencies toward deconstruction and foundationalism in Buddhist thought is not entirely arbitrary. Although they never used the terms deconstruction and foundationalism, Buddhist philosophers of the later first millennium C.E. recognized instinctively that the two tendencies represented by Nāgārjuna and Dharmakīrti were in some way of fundamental importance, that neither could be entirely ignored, and that, consequently, both had to be elements of a serious philosophical enterprise. As a consequence, some of the most important thinkers of late Indian Buddhism were explicitly engaged in the attempt to harmonize the deconstruction of Nāgārjuna and the foundationalism of Dharmakīrti. This tendency in turn was adopted by the Tibetan philosophical tradition and has continued as one of the notable features of Tibetan Buddhism until this day.

Nāgārjuna was very suspicious of attempts to establish the traditional foundations of knowledge. Despite his implicit acceptance of some canons of rationality, such as the tetralemma (which itself implied an Indian equivalent of the law of the excluded middle), he avoided argumentation in syllogistic modes and devoted himself primarily to applying a critical, deconstructive dialectic to the propositions of other schools. This approach was adopted and defended by one of the two Mādhyamika traditions that developed in the centuries after Nāgārjuna, the Prāsaṅgika, whose most important representatives were Buddhapālita and Candrakīrti. A second group of Mādhyamikas, however, the Svātantrikas, saw the value (and perhaps the necessity) of arguing more constructively, and thus concerned themselves not only with the dialectics of emptiness, but with the attempt to establish and build upon epistemological foundations—perhaps in an attempt to secure a solid and specific grounding for conventional truth. After all, Nāgārjuna himself had said (*MMK*, 24: 10) that conventional truth was a necessary prerequisite to ultimate truth, but he had said little about the particulars of that conventional truth. If the conventional truth was so important, it needed to be established firmly, and the writings of the members of the *pramāṇa* tradition provided the most promising grounds for such establishment.

Thus, beginning with Bhāvaviveka in the sixth century, and continuing down through such figures and Jñānagarbha, Śāntarakṣita and Kamalaśīla, Svātantrika Mādhyamikas deliberately attempted to combine, on the one hand, the Mādhyamika concern to establish emptiness as the ultimate mode of existence of all phenomena and, on the other hand, the *pramāṇa* tradition's concern with epistemic authority and its extension into rational argumentation and philosophical construction. The Svātantrikas themselves evinced at least two different tendencies in their analysis of conventional reality, leading to a later Tibetan division of the tradition into "Yogācāra" and "Sautrāntika" sub-schools,[26] but the main lines of the Svātantrika approach are common to both, and involve "a tendency to reconceive traditional ontological questions in the epistemological form made popular by Dignāga and his successors."[27] Thus, not only might formal inference be applied to the demonstration of the ultimate truth that all entities are empty of substantial existence, but questions of conventional truth would be framed primarily in terms of concepts and issues that had come to the fore in the *pramāṇa* tradition, such as the nature and types of authority, momentariness, causal efficiency, universals and particulars, etc. Further, many Svātantrikas applied themselves not only to the critique of other schools, but also—very much in the spirit of Dharmakīrti—to the positive establishment of a variety of Buddhist philosophical and religious ideas, i.e., to proving Buddhism true through rational argumentation.[28] Whatever their success or failure in balancing two such fundamentally contrasting trends in Buddhist thought, the important point remains that the Svātantrikas attempted to do so, and thus, implicitly, accepted that deconstruction and foundationalism were approaches to knowledge and the world that were not fundamentally at odds.

Buddhism died out in most of India during the thirteenth and fourteenth centuries, but not before the majority of its latter-day systems of theory and praxis had been transplanted to Tibet. Svātantrika Madhyamaka was very influential in the formation of Tibetan philosophical attitudes, especially in the early period of Buddhism's spread, during the eighth and ninth centuries. During the later period of Buddhism's spread, from the eleventh century onward, Tibetans increasingly—though not exclusively—tended to consider themselves Prāsaṅgika rather than Svātantrika Mādhyamika. However, this did not mean an abandonment of the Svātantrikas' epistemological concerns. The study of Madhyamaka and *pramāṇa* developed simultaneously in the Tibetan lineages, and their lines of development tended to converge,[29] to the point where, in the fifteenth-century founder of the dGe lugs, Tsong kha pa, they have become fused into a single intellectual enterprise. That enterprise is nominally Prāsaṅgika, and therefore technically avoids defining conventional truth in terms derived from the *pramāṇa* tradition. In fact, however, the dGe lugs account of conventional reality is rooted precisely in that tradition. Study of the works of Dignāga and, especially, Dharmakīrti is a cornerstone of dGe lugs philosophical training, nearly as important as the study of Madhyamaka itself. This, in fact, is the case for all of the major Tibetan schools. They may disagree among themselves over the strength of the connection between conventional and ultimate cognitions, and thus over the importance of rationality for soteriology—to this extent they may be characterized as more or less deconstructive or foundationalist[30]—but they all agree that any substance ontology ultimately must be deconstructed and that secure foundations are available for the establishment of conventional objects and modes of knowledge.[31] Thus, their monastic curricula all include the study of both Nāgārjuna and Dharmakīrti.

Thus, at least one very important line of Buddhist thought, beginning in India and extending into Tibet, explicitly attempted to balance the tradition's contrary tendencies toward deconstruction and foundationalism. Whether this resulted in a sublime harmony of the fundamental poles of philosophical thought or was an ill-conceived attempt to eat one's cake and have it too, is not for us to determine here; what is important is simply the fact that a major segment of the Buddhist philosophical tradition saw the indispensability of both deconstruction and foundationalism, and the consequent necessity to include *both* in any serious intellectual enterprise.

Deconstruction, Foundationalism and the Middle Way

Deconstruction and foundationalism form an important, if implicit, polarity in Buddhist thought, and almost any Buddhist system of philosophy or meditation may be placed at some point on the spectrum that runs between the two poles. Of the thinkers and schools that we have examined in detail, Nāgārjuna would be found very close to the deconstructive pole, Dharmakīrti very close to the foundationalist pole, and such traditions as early Buddhism, Svātantrika Madhyamaka and the Tibetan dGe lugs somewhere in the middle. The close identification of a thinker or movement with one or another of the poles does not mean the exclusion of the other pole. Even predominantly deconstructive enterprises like Nāgārjuna's have foundationalist elements, and foundationalisms as apparently thoroughgoing as Dharmakīrti's have important deconstructive tendencies built into them. There is no system that does not include both poles. It might well be argued that the Buddhist "middle way" is to be found precisely in any given system's negotiation between deconstruction and foundationalism.[32]

In terms of our other metaphor, that of frames, the innermost frame in a Buddhist system tends to be the "strong foundationalist" assertion of worldly and religious conventionalities. (In the case of, e.g., Dharmakīrti, this is the frame on which our attention focuses.) That frame is surrounded and sublated by a wider frame that involves, in one way or another, the ultimate deconstruction of those conventionalities. (In the case of, e.g., Nāgārjuna, this is our focus.) That deconstructive frame, however, is in turn surrounded by the still wider "weak foundationalist" frame of the essential Buddhist values, which structure the very enterprise of distinguishing between the conventional and the ultimate. The frame metaphor might seem to imply that Buddhism is in the final analysis a type of foundationalism, albeit a "weak" one, but that "outermost" foundationalist frame is itself still subject to further deconstruction. We may imagine that outermost frame corroded by the deconstructive element within it, or we may imagine its being surrounded by still another deconstructive frame.

Regardless of which metaphor we employ, the relationship between deconstruction and foundationalism in Buddhism is not static, and neither one can finally seal off or exclude the other. Any foundationalist assertion is subject to ultimate deconstruction from a variety of viewpoints: no-self, emptiness, mind-only, and so on. Conversely, any deconstruction presupposes that some conventionalities have enough of a foundation in reality that both the ordinary world and the deconstructive enterprise itself can make some sense. Those foundations are themselves open to further deconstruction, but the deconstruction of them, in turn, involves certain conventional foundations that may themselves be deconstructed, and so on, *ad infinitum*. It would seem that Buddhism issues an aporeitic dialectic of endless sublation that only will lead to philosophical and spiritual frustration. However, it may well be that the real source of philosophical and spiritual failure is precisely the attitude that would seek finally to resolve the deconstruction-foundationalism polarity in favor of one or the other. From the Buddhist point of view, this would be a fall to one extreme or the other—and we must recall that one of Buddhism's most basic metaphors is that of holding to a middle between extremes, whether of hedonism and asceticism, eternalism and annihilationism, or, simply, "is" and "is not." The spiritually agile Buddhist walks a difficult tightrope, balancing two truths, holding a pole weighted deconstructively on one end and foundationally on the other, knowing that if equilibrium is lost, the fall will be a long one.[33] As long as both are under control, however, passage will be possible and the goal—which is no goal, but a goal nevertheless—will be attainable.

Notes

1. This is a somewhat abridged and updated version of my article, "Matching Concepts: Deconstructive and Foundationalist Tendencies in Buddhist Thought," which appeared in *The Journal of the American Academy of Religion* (57: 3, 1989, 561–589), with whose kind permission it is reprinted. The paper on which the article is based originally was presented at a symposium on Buddhist Thought and Culture graciously organized in April, 1988, at the University of Montevallo, Montevallo, Alabama, by Prof. Frank Hoffman. I would like to thank Mr. Patrick Pranke of the University of Michigan for first articulating for me the tension in Buddhist thought explored here; Drs. John E. Thiel, Janet Gyatso, and Lynn Stephens for their helpful comments and criticism of that earlier version; and Dr. Nancy McCagney and *JAAR*'s anonymous reader for suggestions regarding a later draft. Thanks, too, to Prof. Jin Y. Park for her skill and patience in helping bring the article to rebirth in its present form.

2. Many of the ideas in the next several paragraphs are indebted to Richard Rorty's *Philosophy and the Mirror of Nature* (Princeton: Princeton University Press, 1979), which first suggested the deconstruction-foundationalism polarity to me. For concise, recent discussions of related issues, see works by John E. Thiel, *Nonfoundationalism* (Minneapolis, MN: Fortress Press, 1994) and Paul Lakeland, *Postmodernity: Christian Identity in a Fragmented Age* (Minneapolis: Fortress Press, 1997).

3. Jonathan Culler, *On Deconstruction: Theory and Criticism after Structuralism* (Ithaca, NY: Cornell University Press, 1982), 109. Henceforth *OD*.

4. In those discussions, foundationalism most often is contrasted with coherentism; see Ernest Sosa's "The Foundations of Foundationalism," *Nous*, vol. 14 (1980): 547-564, and "The Raft and the Pyramid: Coherence and Foundations in the Theory of Knowledge," *Midwest Studies in Philosophy* 5 (1980), 325ff. Alternatively, foundationalism may be contrasted with pragmatism, as in Richard Rorty, *Consequences of Pragmatism: Essays 1972-1980* (Minneapolis: University of Minnesota Press, 1982)—though Jonathan Culler (*OD*, 153-156) insists that deconstruction should not be identified with pragmatism.

5. Francis Schüssler Fiorenza, *Foundational Theology: Jesus and the Church* (New York: Crossroad, 1985), 285.

6. Robert Magliola, *Derrida on the Mend* (West Lafayette, IN: Purdue University Press, 1984), part 3. It ought to be noted that Magliola (89) agrees that "the dominant forms of . . . Buddhism . . . *are* logocentric in the Derridean sense"—it is primarily in Nāgārjuna and Zen that he finds a "Middle Path, [a] Way of the Between [that] tracks the Derridean trace, and goes 'beyond Derrida' in that it frequents the 'unheard-of-thought', and . . . allows the reinstatement of the logocentric too" (87). As will become evident below, I believe that Magliola both overstates *and* underestimates Nāgārjuna's affinity with Derrida. Other works that have addressed the Nāgārjuna-Derrida connection include Harold Coward, *Derrida and Indian Philosophy* (Albany: State University of New York Press, 1990), David Loy, *Nonduality: A Study in Comparative Philosophy* (Atlantic Highlands, N.J.: Humanities Press, 1997), and Newman Robert Glass, *Working Emptiness: Toward a Third Reading of Emptiness in Buddhism and Postmodern Thought* (Atlanta: Scholars Press, 1995).

7. The question whether Buddhism admits an "absolute" has, of course, been much discussed. It ought to be recalled that "absolute" is a Western term, and that its presence or absence in Buddhism will depend in part on the way it is defined. Is an "absolute" a metaphysical entity, an immutable essence? Or is it simply a "limiting principle" of some sort? If it is the latter, then probably no Buddhist tradition lacks an absolute. If it is the former, I think it can be argued that a significant, if not overwhelming, majority of Buddhist traditions are committed, at the very least on a rhetorical level, to non-absolutism.

8. It might seem that to imagine deconstruction as a "pole" or a "frame" is to misconstrue it as merely one among many philosophical positions, whereas we have seen above that deconstruction is not simply another position, but a technique for exposing the incongruities inherent in any position. It is, thus, a sort of meta-position, not "locatable" in the ways that my metaphors would suggest. Granted, we must be as cautious in applying metaphors as in "translating" philosophical terminology, but I believe that (a) an approach that "deconstructs" all philosophical positions must itself engage in deconstruction from a particular "perspective," and a perspective—even if temporary and itself subject to subsequent deconstruction—is, at least in *some* meaningful sense, a "position"; and (b) even if deconstruction is not described as a "position," it does, at least conventionally, reflect an attitude toward the possibility of grounded knowledge that can meaningfully be contrasted with other attitudes, such as foundationalism. Where a meaningful contrast is appropriate, metaphors such as those I will employ may prove of some value.

This same problem often arises in discussions of whether the thought of Nāgārjuna really can be called "philosophy"—especially since Nāgārjuna himself insists (at *Vighrahavyāvartanī*, 29) that he has no "thesis" (*pratijñā*) to propose. Nāgārjuna's commentators disagree on how literally this is to be taken. As with deconstruction, it is at least arguable that the "position of no position" still requires a certain perspective and set of assumptions, and so in some sense still is a position. For an interesting discussion of this issue see Robert A. F. Thurman, *Tsong Khapa's Speech of Gold in the Essence of True Eloquence: Reason and Enlightenment in the Central Philosophy of Tibet.* Princeton Library of Asian Translation (Princeton, NJ: Princeton University Press, 1984), 161ff; and, more recently, Dan Arnold, *Buddhists, Brahmins, and Belief: Epistemology in South Asian Philosophy of Religion* (New York: Columbia University Press, 2005), part III.

9. *Nirvāṇa* is—arguably—immutable, hence a candidate for an early Buddhist "absolute"—but it does not serve as the source or substance of the phenomenal world; it is, rather, the radical alternative to the phenomenal world, qualified by characteristics that the phenomenal world lacks—hence immensely difficult to conceptualize or describe for those of us whose knowledge is exclusively phenomenal. For a discussion, see K. N. Jayatilleke, *Early Buddhist Theory of Knowledge* (Delhi, Varanasi, Patna: Motilal Banarsidass, 1963), chapter VI.

10. Henry Clarke Warren, *Buddhism in Translations* (New York: Atheneun, 1984), 132.

11. Sarvepalli Radhakrishnan and Charles A. Moore, eds., *A Sourcebook in Indian Philosophy* (Princeton: Princeton University Press, 1957), 346.

12. And coming too to serve as what has been called a Buddhist "creed," found in inscriptions throughout India: *ye dharmā hetuprabhāvā hetūṃ teṣāṃ tathagato hyavadat teṣāṃ ca yo nirodho evaṃ vadī mahāśramaṇa* ("Whatever *dharmas* are generated from causes, the Tathāgata has described their [causes], and whatever is their cessation [he also has described]; thus speaks the great recluse").

13. There is, in fact, some dispute among scholars as to whether Nāgārjuna ought to be counted as a Mahāyānist—A. K. Warder (*Indian Buddhism*, second revised edition; Delhi, Varanasi, Patna: Motilal Banarsidass, 1980) and David Kalupahana (*Nāgārjuna: The Philosophy of the Middle Way* [Albany: State University of New York Press, 1986]) are both conspicuous in arguing that he should not—but this raises hermeneutical and textual issues beyond the scope of this paper, and does not affect the direction of our discussion. The best recent work on Nāgārjuna's historical and institutional context is Joseph Walser, *Nāgārjuna in Context: Mahāyāna Buddhism and Early Indian Culture* (New York: Columbia University Press, 2005).

14. For an edition and translation of the Sanskrit text of the *Madhyamakakārikā* (hereafter *MMK*) see, e.g., Kenneth K. Inada, *Nāgārjuna: A Translation of his Mūlamadhyamakakārikā with an Introductory Essay* (Tokyo: The Hokuseido Press, 1970). For a translation of the Tibetan version, with an extremely helpful philosophical com-

mentary, see Jay Garfield, *The Fundamental Wisdom of the Middle Way: Nāgārjuna's Mūlamadhyamakakārikā* (New York: Oxford University Press, 1995).

15. For an edition and translation of the *Vigrahavyāvartanī* (henceforth, *VV*) , see, e.g., Kamaleshwar Bhattacharya (trans.), *The Dialectical Method of Nāgārjuna (Vigrahavyāvartanī)*; text critically edited by E. H. Johnston and Arnold Kunst (Delhi, Varanasi, Patna: Motilal Banarsidass, 1978).

16. For a discussion of some of the implications of this verse, see Roger Jackson, "For Whom Emptiness Prevails: An Analysis of the Religious Implications of Nāgārjuna's *Vigrahavyāvartanī* 70," *Religious Studies*, vol. 21 (1985): 407–414.

17. It must be noted that, while Nāgārjuna is in certain senses a foundationalist, he does not—*contra* Magliola (above, note 6)—"reinstate the logocentric," for the conventions that are "founded" by the equivalency of emptiness and dependent origination only are possible in the absence of any *svabhāva* or *logos*; in other words, they are founded on a de-essentialized foundation of causal interdependence.

18. For further discussion, see Roger R. Jackson, *Is Enlightenment Possible?: Dharmakīrti and rGyal tshab rje on Knowledge, Rebirth, No-Self and Liberation* (Ithaca, NY: Snow Lion Publications, 1993), 55–63.

19. Dharmakīrti's position in the *pramāṇa* tradition is not precisely analogous to Nāgārjuna's founding role in Madhyamaka, for much of the intellectual groundwork was laid for Dharmakīrti by his great predecessor, Dignāga. Nevertheless, Dharmakīrti has been considered by later tradition to be at least as important a figure as Dignāga; indeed, for the Tibetans, he is more important. More to the point for our concerns, it was Dharmakīrti who pursued the implications of his foundationalism the farthest, seeking not only to establish secure bases of epistemic authority, but to apply those authorities toward the solution of traditional problems in ontology and religious metaphysics.

20. For a translation of the verse that includes Dharmottara's important commentary, see F. Th. Stcherbatsky, *Buddhist Logic*, 2 vols. (New York: Dover Publications, 1962), vol. II, 1.

21. The title generally is glossed by Dharmakīrti's commentators as the "Commentary on [Dignāga's 'Compendium on] Authority'." The *Pramāṇavārttika* has not yet been translated *in toto* into a Western language. The most useful edition presently available is Y. Miyasaka, (ed.) *Pramāṇavārttika-kārikā Sanskrit and Tibetan* (*Acta Indologica* 2, 3, 4 1972-1977), which includes the Sanskrit and Tibetan on facing pages. The two most interesting general works on Dharmakīrti in recent years are Georges Dreyfus, *Recognizing Reality: Dharmakīrti's Philosophy and Its Tibetan Interpretations* (Albany: State University of New York Press, 1997) and John D. Dunne, *Foundations of Dharmakīrti's Philosophy* (Boston: Wisdom, 2004).

22. See, e.g., Stcherbatsky, *Buddhist Logic*, vol. II, pp. 25-33. No-self, in fact, is regarded as one of the "sixteen aspects of the four noble truths" that must be realized according to several *abhidharma* traditions. Specifically, it is one of the four aspects of suffering, the other three being suffering, impermanence, and emptiness.

23. A discussion of this is found in, e.g., *Parārthānumāna* chapter, verses 48-71 in Dharmakīrti's *Pramāṇavārttika*. See Tom J. F. Tillemans, "*Pramāṇavārttika* IV (1)" *Wiener Zeitschrift für die Kunde Südasiens und Archiv für Indische Philosophie*, Band XXX (1986), 147, note 17.

24. The Sanskrit original of the *Pramāṇasiddhi* chapter of the *Pramāṇavārttika* has been translated *in toto*, but not published, by Masatoshi Nagatomi ("A Study of Dharmakīrti's *Pramāṇavārttika*: An English Translation and Annotation of the *Pramāṇavārttika*, Book I"; unpublished dissertation, Harvard University, 1957), and partially translated by Tillman Vetter (*Der Buddha und Seine Lehre in Dharmakīrtis Pramāṇavārttika* (Wien, 1984) and Eli Franco (*Dharmakīrti on Compassion and Rebirth.* (Wien: Arbeitskreis für Tibetische und Buddhistische Studien Universität Wien, 1997). A

full translation of the Tibetan translation, keyed to rGyal tshab rje's fifteenth-century commentary, appears in Jackson, *Is Enlightenment Possible?*.

25. See, e.g., Dharmakīrti's *Pramāṇavārttika*, *Pratyakṣa* chapter, verses 320ff.

26. See, e.g., Geshe Lhundup Sopa and Jeffrey Hopkins (trans.), *Practice and Theory of Tibetan Buddhism* (New York: Grove Press, 1976), 122–145, and Donald S. Lopez, Jr., *A Study of Svātantrika* (Ithaca, NY: Snow Lion Publications, 1987), 299–386.

27. Malcolm David Eckel, *Jñānagarbha's Commentary on the Distinction Between the Two Truths: An Eighth Century Handbook of Madhyamaka Philosophy* (Albany: State University of New York Press, 1987), 51.

28. Especially notable in this regard was Śāntarakṣita, in his *Tattvasaṃgraha*; this has been translated, along with Kamalaśīla's commentary, in Ganganatha Jha (trans.), *The Tattvasaṃgraha of Śāntarakṣita with the Commentary of Kamalśīla* (2 vols.; Delhi: Motilal Banarsidass, 1986).

29. On this, see, e.g., Leonard W. J. van der Kuijp, *Contributions to the Development of Tibetan Buddhist Epistemology* (Alt- und Neu-lndische Studien, no. 26, Wiesbaden, 1983).

30. From this perspective, the dGe lugs pas would be the most strongly foundationalist, and the rNying ma pas the most deconstructive, with the Sa skya pas and bKa' brgyud pas somewhere in between. All, however, contain elements of both. For another way of thinking about the spectrum of Tibetan schools, in which they are ranged between "shamanic" (more deconstructive) and "clerical" (more foundationalist) poles, see Geoffrey Samuel, *Civilized Shamans: Buddhism in Tibetan Societies* (Washington, DC: Smithsonian, 1993).

31. There is some question whether Tibetan thinkers who adhere to the so-called "Extrinsic Emptiness" (*gzhan stong*) interpretation of Madhyamaka have a "substance ontology." These thinkers, who have included influential members of every tradition but the dGe lugs, assert that, while conventionalities are intrinsically empty of inherent existence, *buddha* is empty of *saṃsāric* properties that are extrinsic to its inherent purity. Opponents of this view argue that it is a substantialism as noxious as that of Hinduism; its proponents argue that it goes beyond mere philosophy to express an experiential truth about enlightenment. See S. K. Hookham, *The Buddha Within: Tathagtagarbha Doctrine According to the Shentong Interpretation of the Ratnagotravibhaga* (Albany: State University of New York Press, 1991) and Cyrus Stearns, *The Buddha from Dolpo: A Study of the Life and Thought of the Tibetan Master Dolpopa Sherab Gyaltsen* (Albany: State University of New York Press, 1999).

32. For further reflections on Buddhism as a middle way, see Roger R. Jackson, "Buddhism in India," in *Companion Encyclopedia of Asian Philosophy*, ed. I. Mahalingam and B. Carr (London: Routledge, 1997), 318–348, and "In Search of a Postmodern Middle," in *Buddhist Theology: Critical Reflections by Contemporary Buddhist Scholars*, ed. Roger R. Jackson and John Makransky (Richmond, Surrey, UK: Curzon Press, 1999), 215-246.

33. It might he noted that in many Mahāyāna traditions, a *buddha* is defined cognitively by his/her/its ability to know simultaneously all conventional and ultimate phenomena, i.e., the two truths; this is an ability that sentient beings, even high-level *bodhisattvas*, lack: they are capable of cognizing only one or the other. On buddhahood, see e.g., Paul J. Griffiths, *On Being Buddha: The Classical Doctrine of Buddhahood* (Albany: State University of New York Press, 1994) and John J. Makransky, *Buddhahood Embodied: Sources of Controversy in India and Tibet* (Albany: State University of New York Press, 1997).

Six

Ji Zang's *Śūnyatā*-Speech: A Derridean *Dénégation* with Buddhist Negations

Ellen Y. Zhang

1.

The doctrine of the "twofold truth (*erdi*)" explored by Ji Zang (549-623), the systematizer of the Sanlun School (or, the Three Treaties School) of Chinese Buddhism, has often been viewed as a sinicized version of Nāgārjuna's Mādhyamika position on "non-substantiality, or emptiness of all dharmas." In this article, I shall focus on the rhetorical dimensions of *śūnyatā*-speech (*kon-glun*) in Ji Zang's interpretation of the twofold truth, and explicate how the middle path in terms of *śūnya* (the emptiness of the conventional) and *aśūnya* (the functionality of the conventional) is played out by Sanlun Buddhist philosophers. My argument is that Ji Zang's thematization of the "four levels of the twofold truth (*sichong erdi*)" is neither purely "apophatic" nor purely "kataphatic," but a form of linguistic twist, carried out by a double-speech. Namely, it is a negation within the logic of negation. *Śūnyatā*-speech is, then, a gesture neither "of itself" nor "from itself," a kind of practice that is reminiscent of Derrida's *dénégation*. The double-speech is employed by Ji Zang to avoid every possible polarity and, ultimately, it points to a non-dual, non-exclusive relation between the ultimate truth and the conventional reality. I use the word "rhetorical" here to suggest that Ji Zang's argument of *śūnyatā* in most cases tends to be methodological rather than (anti)metaphysical. Despite a significant difference in philosophical motivation between Chinese Buddhism and deconstruction, there are some remarkable similarities in terms of argumentative strategies and methods by which both attempt to show the limits of metaphysics and metaphysical language.

I shall attempt to encapsulate Ji Zang's *śūnyatā*-speech as follows: First, it postulates a non-dual relationship between emptiness (*wu*) and non-emptiness (*feiwu*) by denying the existence of both self-nature (*zixing*) and a lack of self-nature (*wuxing*); secondly, it plays with the limit of language by using constant negations within a negative scheme. As a philosophical method of negation, Ji Zang's argument on emptiness intends to invalidate all metaphysical arguments, including the format of the four alternatives (*sijü*), i.e., the tetralemmic scheme, which is viewed as part of the "language-game" or the "conceptual play (*xilun*)"; thirdly, *śūnyatā*-speech is deconstructive in its methodological negation yet un-Derridean in that *śūnyatā* "points to" an experiential dimension that is not confined to language, or even thought.

2.

The Chinese Sanlun School is centered around the concept of emptiness. The "ground theory" upon which the entire school tradition is based is the argument of "non-substantiality," or the "Non-being" of all dharmas. Namely, Sanlun Buddhism maintains that there is a lack of self-existence or essence of all entities in reality. "Essence" here refers to what is immutable, eternal, and of independent origin; and this is, according to Buddhism, exactly what things in the phenomenal world lack. "Suffering" arises because of the very fact that people perceptually "cling" or "attach" to objects or ideas as if they were essential. Following the basic line of Buddhist causality, Ji Zang speaks of the emptiness of both production (*sheng*) and existence (*cun*), and the relationship of emptiness to dependent-origination, or causal conditioning:

> The conventional truth is that all dharmas arise via causal conditioning, therefore have self-nature. The ultimate truth, however, is to analyze conditions and realize that there is no essence.[1]

To put it differently, the reason that things in reality are empty is twofold: 1. They are dependent in their production and creation; 2. They are dependent in their existence. This, in Buddhism, is called "dependent-origination" (*yuansheng*; Sk. *pratītya-samupāda*). As implied in the Sanskrit term, which is a compound of the two words, *pratītya* ("dependent") and *samutpāda* ("originating," dependent-origination means that all things arise conditionally (literally, "coming together in connection"). Ji Zang takes the position that all dharmas, though they have empirical validity, are devoid of self-nature and self-identity since anything that comes to be is dependent on another and so is not in essence actually coming into being.[2]

Though such concepts as "voidness (*xu*)," "mutual productions (*xiangsheng*)," "carrying *yin* and embracing *yang* (*fuyin baoyang*)" had been existent in Chinese Daoism long before the influence of Indian Buddhism, Ji Zang's argument on *śūnyatā* in terms of "no self-nature" or "no constant identity" still proposes a radical challenge to the Chinese intellectual tradition that has been embraced by both Daoists and Buddhists since the Wei-Jin period. On the other hand, Ji Zang attempts to avoid treating *śūnyatā* only as part of the *wu-you* debates initiated by Daoism and other Buddhist schools in China because he sees the risk in identifying *śūnyatā* with nothingness (*wu*) or no self-nature (*wuxing*). Thus Ji Zang says:

> All dharmas have differences,
> Therefore, they are all devoid of self-nature.
> The dharma of no self-nature also lacks self-nature
> Because all dharmas are empty.[3]

Here Ji Zang insists on a non-dual relationship between emptiness and non-emptiness by denying the existence of both self-nature and a lack of self-nature. For Ji Zang, this non-dual view of self-nature and absence of self-nature is crucial because it ultimately determines a non-dual view of the twofold truth. Then, how can we reconcile a model of *śūnyatā* which involves both a present infinity in discursive process with a rigorous notion of the transcendent mind which goes beyond all concepts? Ji Zang's reluctance to ascribe *śūnyatā* to another conceptual expression shows his concern that *śūnyatā* itself is a concept functioning only as a provisional or methodological principle, instead of a metaphysical or cognitive description. The connection between *śūnyatā* itself and *śūnyatā*-speech is a dialectical one. For Ji Zang, most discursive statements about emptiness (i.e., emptiness as an absence) addressed to his implied audience aim to have a rhetorical or perlocutionary force. That is to say, Ji Zang's *śūnyatā*-speech depends crucially upon the response of the audience, specifically one who tends to "cling" to phenomenal entities. Thus *śūnyatā*-speech is used as a "thought-provoking" method to capture the attention of the audience as well as to address the controversy on the *you/wu* debate existent in Chinese Buddhism.

Quite obviously, Ji Zang is conscious of the risk of using the concept of emptiness, for people would equate emptiness with nothingness. Ji Zang therefore maintains that his teaching on "the negative play" of *śūnyatā* is given as "medicine" to cure the "symptoms" presented in the Chinese Buddhist tradition, specifically the two views with regard to the middle path represented by Satyasiddhi Hīnayānists and the Original Non-Being Mahāyānist, and, as such, the negativity itself has no definite meaning by itself. In other words, negativity is not simply a negation, nor is it another way of affirmation. Instead, it is open to self-negating and self-deconstructing, and is "always in correspondence with" whatever happens in a specific situation. It is in this sense I argue that Ji Zang's teaching on *śūnyatā* is meant to be "practical" in nature. To put it differently, no conceptual truth, including *śūnyatā*, is "true" by itself, but is recognized as "truth" only in the light of a certain linguistic context, and in the case of Sanlun Buddhism, as a rhetorical way to "entrap the opponents." Since there is no substantiality of all dharmas, nothing experienced in the phenomenal world has a fixed, determinate nature. Accordingly, no description of any phenomenon can be said to be the final truth, not even such ideas as emptiness and impermanence. Hence Ji Zang repeatedly argues that "'emptiness' is used only as medicine. If the disease has been cured, the medicine of emptiness is no longer needed" (*SLXY* in *SLXYJS*, 132).

However, at the same time, a description of phenomena cannot be completely crossed out since no ultimate truth can be attained without the conventional truth in the empirical world. As we read in Nāgārjuna, "Without dependence on everyday practice, the ultimate is not taught."[4] Here "everyday practice" refers to the conventional world (including everyday language) which forms the basis for Buddhist religious activities. According to Ji Zang's reading of Nāgārjuna, the notion of "the conventional truth" (*sudi*, *shidi*, or *youdi*) embraces three meanings. First, it means "illusory existence of things (*huanyou*)," or "falsifiable illusions (*wangyou*)." The term "illusory" in Sanskrit also means "clouding." Second, it denotes the "provisional truth," or the "temporary truth" (*duanjian*). Third, it indicates "social conventions," or the "secular etiquette" (*fengsu*). The first two are discussed to a great extent by Nāgārjuna, who negates the illusory truth and the provisional truth respectively from the perspective of the ultimate truth. Ji Zang speaks of the same idea when he maintains that there is no self-nature in myriad things. Yet at the same time Ji Zang does not completely cancel out the provisional validity of social conventions, contending that it is fine for a gentleman to follow the established etiquette and social custom. Though we may argue that Ji Zang's maintenance of social conventions shows a Chinese way of immanentizing/samsarizing the transcendent/*nirvāṇa*, we can also argue that this recognition of the conventional world as non-obstruction to the ultimate truth is in agreement with the Buddhist dialectic of interplay of the two truths, and of the non-dual relationship between *nirvāṇa* and *saṃsāra*. As Ji Zang puts it, "The conventional truth is not a fixed concept, for the conventional names must be posited against the ultimate truth; The ultimate truth is not a fixed concept, for the ultimate names must be posited against the conventional truth" (*EDY* in *SLXYJS* 25). It means that the teaching of the true reality cannot be taught by erasing all conventional names. In his commentaries on the doctrine of emptiness, Ji Zang makes the following observations: (1) the argument of causal production is used to disprove the coming into being of anything in virtue of its own nature; (2) the assertion of *śūnyatā* is to negate the supposed fact or superficial causal efficacy; (3) emptiness does not mean no-thing (voidness); (4) the middle path is maintained in order to avoid falling into a dualistic trap (a false disparity) one posits between the conventional and the ultimate.

On the other hand, Ji Zang attempts to avoid a nihilistic interpretation of *śūnyatā* by negating the existence of both self-nature and a lack of self-nature. For Ji Zang, those who see "no self-nature" simply as "no reality," or "non-existence," fail to apprehend the profound significance of the dialectical relationship between the two levels in the twofold truth. What Ji Zang's negation tries to accentuate are the limitations of all metaphysical views associated with the problem of logical/conceptual attachment. *Śūnyatā* then means "absolutely non-abiding (*wusuoyi*)" of all discursive and conceptual claims. Accordingly, *śūnyatā* is not a cognitive concept referring to any reality, but simply a convenient/skillful device to teach one to free oneself from all clinging and attachments. As Richard Robinson rightly points out, "Emptiness is not a term in the primary system referring to the world, but a term in descriptive system (meta-system) referring to the primary system. Thus it has no status as an entity, nor as the property of an existent nor an inexistent. If anyone considers it so, he turns the key term in the descriptive system into the root of all delusions."[5] In a similar manner, Francis Cook also contends that "Emptiness is not a term outside the expressional system, but simply the key term within it. Those who would hypostatize emptiness are confusing the symbol system with the fact system."[6] Since *śūnyatā* functions only as a meta-system or symbol-system, Ji Zang maintains the importance of one's understanding of "*śūnyatā-śūnyatā* (*kongkong*)," which means *śūnyatā* itself has no inherent existence, either. What Ji Zang tries to argue here is not emptiness as truth but a negation of the concepts of both "*śūnyatā*" and "*aśūnyatā*," as conceived by other Buddhist schools, in order to destroy all closures (*feng*), and "delusive knowledge (*yu*)," that is, a "fixed interpretation (*dingjie*)," that is cut off from all attachments (*zhuo*) and bondages (*fu*). After all attachments and bondages are banished from the mind, there is no need for any truth, including the twofold truth.

Here, we find a similar situation in the Derridean deconstructive project where Derrida radically negates what he calls a "metaphysics of presence," namely, the illusory "order of things" (Being) that is seen to be the foundation of everything else. On the one hand, Derrida attempts to reverse the priority of a "presence-being" or a "transcendental signified" by introducing a new term, *différance*, to indicate a "different/deferred meaning." Derrida repeatedly contends that " . . . différance is not, does not exist, is not a present-being in any form . . . . It derives from no category of being, whether present or absent . . . Différance is not only irreducible to any ontological or theological-ontotheological-reappropriation, but as the very opening of the space in which ontotheology-philosophy produces its system and its history..."[7] If *śūnyatā* of Buddhism refers to a meta-system or symbol-system, then Derrida's negation of the presence also indicates that what is often perceived as the "presence" is simply a signified that is "always already" a sign, inevitably inscribed and mediated. What has been valued as "truth" in the conventional world in fact is appropriation and reappropriation, and as such it is always relative, provisional, and dependent-originating. In Buddhist terms, Derrida's "different/deferred meaning" implies a causal relationship among texts and meanings of text, which Derrida calls "intertextuality." The meaning of a text is always related to another text, and is conditioned by the interaction of different signifiers. Therefore, there is no "self-present meaning" which stands outside as self-containing and self-existing. It turns out that all meanings are the result of *pratītya-samutpāda*, and therefore, are empty in terms of their self-origination and self-identity.

In his deconstructive project, Derrida also poses the negation of the presence as something that points beyond "the field of episteme" and "the order of understanding." What Derrida seems to be suggesting is that our thought, knowledge, understanding, and etc., *via* conceptual language is always incomplete and thus requires "a blank text," a trace of "unheard-of thoughts," or "a necessarily indeterminate index."[8] Like Derrida's critique of the conceptual truth, Ji Zang's interpretation of the twofold truth represents a logical extension of the Buddhist idea of an ultimately non-conceptualized approach to truth; according to which, the twofold truth, the truth of the phenomenal world (the conventional truth) and that of the ultimate, should not be taken as two fixed truths, polarized by their very nature but to be rather a methodological construct that leads one to a "gradual negation" of all dualistic polarities and all conceptualized schema, including the distinction between the two truths. In *SLXY* and *Dacheng xuan lun* (*Metaphysical Inquiries into Mahāyāna*), Ji Zang formulates the four levels of the twofold truth in terms of the "four-step process" which can be rendered as follows:

the conventional truth		the ultimate truth
1. affirmation of *you* (Y)	<------------- ------------->	1. negation of *you* (~Y)
2. affirmation of both *you* and not-*you* (Y.~Y)	<------------- ------------->	2. neither *you* nor not-*you* ~ (Y . ~Y)
3. either affirmation or negation of both *you* and not-*you* (Y . ~Y) v ~ (Y ~Y)	<------------- ------------->	3. Neither affirmation of *you* and not-*you* nor negation of *you* and not-*you* ~ [(Y . ~Y) v ~ (Y . ~Y)]
	4. beyond verbalization and conceptualization O	

Ji Zang's formula is based upon the previous model of the "three levels of twofold truth" that can be found in previous Buddhist texts. As the "tetralemmatic ladder" indicates above, at the first level, *you* is seen as the conventional, and *wu* as the ultimate; at the second level, both *you* and *wu* are seen as the conventional and negation of both as the ultimate; at the third level, either affirmation or negation is seen as the conventional and neither affirmation nor negation is as the ultimate. The notion of "neither-nor (*liangfei*)" as the ultimate also indicate the cessation of two extremes; at the fourth level, it indicates that *śūnyatā/kong* is "beyond verbalization and conceptualization (*wangyan juelü*)." That is to say, it is "beyond tetralemmatic expressions (*lichao siju*)," and beyond the discursive discourse (*chaoyanyu*) of *you* and *wu*. Ji Zang calls this trans-tetralemmatic space as a realm of "no-sounded word (*wushengzi*)," one that Buddhists often refer to as the realm of "neither thinking nor not-thinking (*feixiang feifeixiang*)." The ultimate Dao/Path is "inconceivable (*buke siyi*)" and "inexpressible (*bukeshuo*)" and because of this very character of inconceivability and inexpressibility, the ultimate truth cannot be taken as "the object of knowledge (*suozhi*)." Even the distinction between the conventional and the ultimate is only a relative and provisional one. Again, Ji Zang remarks that the ultimate Dao/Path

> transcends tetralemmatic expressions and limitations of all falsifications. Verbal language fails to characterize its true meaning, and defiled consciousness fails to attain its insight. The *you* person holds on its "essence," and the *wu* person cannot see its functionality. (*SLXYJS*, 48)

For Ji Zang all views, expressed by our conventional language, are in one way or another associated with verbalization, conceptualization, discriminations, and differentiation, and thus are partial and relative. In the end, both the conventional and the ultimate should be erased, if one is to experience the infinite flux of *śūnyatā*, and comprehend "the ultimate wonder" of "things-as-they-are (*shixiang*)."

Thus Ji Zang reaches, through a series of negations, the level where nothing is affirmed and nothing negated; this is also the highest level of the middle path. In *SLXY*, Ji Zang discusses three kinds of "middle path," which include the middle path of the conventional, the middle path of the ultimate, and the middle path of neither the conventional nor the ultimate. Among these three middle paths, the last one, which is also identified with the twofold truth, is considered as being at the highest level (*SLXYJS*, 214). It is important to note that for Ji Zang the highest level of the "middle path" is not simply a "mean between the two" (that is, between the conventional truth and the ultimate truth, or between existence and non-existence). Rather, the middle path indicates an effort to avoid the binary categories of existence and non-existence, annihilation and permanence, identity, and difference. Ji Zang sees this "not-one-and-not-two," or "non-identity-and-non-difference" position as one that is "far away from the two extremes (*yuanli liangbian*)." The middle path, as such, is the negation of the two extremes (*bupian buyi*). Ji Zang insists that the acceptance of the middle path requires the "non-acceptance of either affirmative or negative views, of all (conceptual) views." Any attachment to conceptual views, including negation, is "like a snake incorrectly seized, or like a spell incorrectly cast."[9]

The tetralemmatic formula was also adopted by Zhi Yi (538-597), one of the most influential masters of the Tiantai School, particularly when the latter speaks of the threefold truth in the scheme of the ultimate (*kong*), the conventional (*jia*), and the middle (*zhong*). Meanwhile, Zhi Yi has developed the tetralemmatic formula further by combining *siju* with specific meditative techniques for practitioners with different levels of understanding. Zhi Yi's concept of "penetrating the Dao/Path via four doors (*simen rudao*)" resembles Sanlun philosophy at its theoretical level. Like Ji Zang, Zhi Yi also employs the concept of the middle path to denote the idea of "ending (*zhi*)" the two extremes. "That which goes beyond annihilation and permanence (*liduanchang*) is called the middle path."[10] Meanwhile, Zhi Yi relates the middle path to the final understanding of what he calls "Buddha-nature," and thus creates the Tiantai concepts of "the middle-path Buddha-nature (*zhongdao fuxing*)," the threefold truth of *kongjiazhong*, and threefold contemplation. For Zhi Yi, the middle path in terms of Buddha-nature not only incorporates the idea of emptiness into the conventional existence of things, but also embraces a soteriological dimension which, he believes, is lacking in the Sanlun system.[11] Here we see a clear linguistic shift from Ji Zang's "negative" middle path *qua* emptiness to Zhi Yi's "affirmative" middle path *qua* Buddha-nature. The idea of "avoiding all sorts of extremes" however, is similar in these two schools, although Ji Zang is more interested in the functionality of the language of negation and thus represents more the deconstructive aspect (i.e., the negative play) of Buddhism.

3

Robert Magliola, one of the leading scholars who first acknowledged the remarkable parallel between the Derridean notion of "between-ness" and the Buddhist "middle path" in terms of the tetralemmatic argument, contends that the Buddhist way of the between "tracks the Derridean trace, and goes 'beyond Derrida' in that it frequents the 'unheard-of thought,' and also, 'with one and the same stroke,' allows the reinstatement of the logocentric too."[12] The interesting question here is whether the Buddhist effort of "having it both ways" leads to a logocentric affirmation, or whether *śūnyatā* is a "divine name," one which Derrida calls a form of "hyper-essentiality" in an apophatic fashion. As I argued earlier, *śūnyatā* goes beyond affirming and negating the proper names of being, or even goes beyond the negative way that is seen to supplement the positive way of approaching the truth (such as Zhi Yi's concept of Buddha-nature). The Sanlun middle path allows the reinstatement of the logocentric as well as the deconstruction of the logocentric.

In his essay "How to Avoid Speaking: Denials," Derrida insists that deconstruction should not be understood as a simple form of reversal or negation, nor a form of "affirmation-*qua*-negation." By creating a new term, "dénégation," Derrida attempts to separate his negativity from the traditional form of negation in negative theology in the West which is, as Derrida sees it, still confined to a closed system of onto-theological presence. Negative theology is, says Derrida, a mode of affirmation *via* negation, despite the fact that negative theology shares certain deconstructive characteristics in "the detours, locutions, and syntax." Then what distinguishes deconstruction from negative theology in terms of negation and negativity? Derrida maintains that the concept of the negativity of deconstruction does not mean anything, it is "'before' the concept, the name and the word," and "before" "'something' that would be nothing, that no longer arises from Being, from presence or from the presence of the present, nor even from absence...."[13] *Dénégation* is, then, a "double movement" or a "double event" that sustains no closure of the final truth or principle. Therefore, negation will not be recuperated by affirmation, since there is always a transgressive overflow (excess) that will remain negative. For Derrida, *dénégation* is neither a negation nor the opposite of negation (affirmation). *Dénégation* is irreducible because it implies the excess of meaning.

Likewise, the Sanlun notion of the "middle path" is not operated by identity or from the view of identity of a reconciliatory unity, or one term over another.

Instead it is operated by the process of negation by which it adds itself to something that is a plus. As Ji Zang understands it, the use of *śūnyatā*-speech is an attempt to avoid replaying one kind of conceptual certainty with another, and as such it does not assert itself as a principle. Like other Buddhist terms such as no-mind, no-word, no-origination, and etc., *śūnyatā* indicates that everything "deconstructs" itself, and in doing so, Buddhism avoids seeking for another kind of self-identical "presence" questioned by Derrida. When arguing that deconstruction does not, by simple inversion, mean that the signifier is fundamental or primary, Derrida has realized that a simple reversal is a new form of dogmatism, and as such a new form of logocentrism. Like Buddhists, Derrida believes that it is the process of conceptualization, including the structure of reversal, that must be deconstructed. Derrida insists that *différance* is a "middle way" or "middle voice," a space between limits and no-limits rather than a transcendental principle which could be theoretically articulated. Deconstruction has, says Derrida,

> set up a pharmacy in which it is no longer possible to count by one, by two, by three; in which everything starts with the dyad. The dual opposition (remedy/poison, good/evil, intelligible/sensible, high/low, mind/matter, life/death, inside/outside, speech/writing, etc.) organizes a conflictual, hierarchically structured field which can neither be reduced to unity, nor derived from a primary simplicity, nor dialectically sublimated or internalized into a third term.[14]

Derrida's language of the "middle path," the "middle voice," and the "third term" is close to the Buddhist formula of neither "this" nor "that," according to which one should give up the dualistic thinking of the reality in terms of the "either/or" logic. This negative dialectic of differ/defer parallels Ji Zang's notion that *śūnyatā* exceeds any ontological binary system of *you* and *wu*, existence and non-existence.

Another question one may ask: Is Ji Zang or Derrida "riding a horse and claiming that there is no horse"? My argument is that what is being questioned here is the very self-nature of the "horse"(language), but not the act of "riding" (the use of language). The biggest problem, for Sanlun Buddhists as well as for Derrida, is not the fact that we use language, but that we substantialize language by looking for a fixed or closed meaning. The ultimate truth, however, as Ji Zang sees it, remains irreducible because it is not a "form," not even a form of *śūnyatā*, emptiness, or zero, but is always in the process of trans-formation. In other words, the "*śūnyatā*-experience" should be better represented by a "marked field" of no-thing-ness, or "things-deconstructed."[15] Here, "things-deconstructed" is always an open entity, a concept *sous rature*. As such, the *śūnyatā*-speech does not assert itself as a principle as to what it has said, but what kind of effects it may evoke by saying or not saying something. Meanwhile, *śūnyatā*-speech requires that every discourse "deconstructs" itself, and in doing so it opens up the possibility of de-inscribing and re-inscribing our language pertinent to the questions of knowing and understanding while fully realizing all linguistic articulations are "limited views (*duanjian*)." This is quite similar to Derrida's understanding of philosophy when he says that "philosophy always reappropriates for itself the discourse that delimits it." To borrow Derrida's words, *śūnyatā* takes place, rather than a place; it is not a place in that it points to no origin, nor a destination, a home, a center, a site, a realm, a totality of the transcendental signified. For Ji Zang, the middle path is one both in-between and beyond names and concepts; it recognizes them, even acknowledges their values and multiple functions, yet sees them as being "empty." Like most other Buddhist philosophers, Ji Zang holds that names and concepts are provisional as a pedagogical means, or expedients (*upāya, jiaming*), and thus they are devoid of any fixed meaning.

As Robert Magliola has observed, *śūnyatā*, as a provisional name, has to be "crossed out" since "*śūnyatā*, like Derridean différance, should not be hypostatized and cannot be framed by ratiocination . . . *śūnyatā* is not voidness but devoidness."[16] The choice of the word "devoidness" is significant here because devoidness casts off the conceptual opposition of voidness and fullness as proposed by any entitative theory. Magliola further connects *śūnyatā* with the notion of "work," pointing out that *śūnyatā* implies the process of "happening," and that it "always is 'in correspondence with' happenings." The notion of "working" and "happenings" with regard to *śūnyatā* reminds us of Derrida's argument on the deconstructive concept of "trace" or "non-place." From a Derridean perspective, the God of negative theology is still operative within the framework of a self-contained presence, a "transcendental signifier," or a "place" with "hyperessentiality" that represses and excludes. Derrida maintains that the meaning and the signified (God or otherwise) is never a transcendental, self-contained presence, but, like the signifier, is always a "trace," a mark of the absence of a presence, and therefore a presence is always under erasure. Upon Derrida's understanding, negative theology does not stand outside metaphysical thinking because of its privileged view on presence. Derrida is particularly troubled by such language as the mystic union, the act of unknowing, the darkness beyond intellect, the "secret of no, not, without, getting rid of, neither...nor, beyond." For Derrida, behind the unnamable laments, there is a divine name and "[T])here is a secret of denial and denial of a secret"[17] (*DNT*, 95). As I suggested earlier, Derrida rejects such ideas as being "enigmatic," "mystical," and "hyperessential" because he is particularly troubled with the notion of "an affirmation *qua* negation" by the language of "beyond being" which is, for Derrida, a purest form of affirmation in a negative gesture. However, the Buddhist notion of *śūnyatā* as a method of negativity is not directed toward an affirmative place, or called "a silent intuition of God"; instead it takes place, it works, it happens. Thus the arguments for the non-cognitive "essence" of *śūnyatā* and the "on the move" spirit of Buddhism resemble the Derridean idea of *dénégation* that points to the "always-deferred nature of the Messiah."

As I have said repeatedly, we need to emphasize that Buddhist philosophy does not deny the use of language and the functional capacities of language. In fact, Ji Zang is fully aware of the power and efficacy of names and naming/unnaming as a means to deconstruct what he calls "fallacious views." Thus, Ji Zang's *śūnyatā*-speech *via* negations aims at a twofold task: 1. to reverse "fallacious views;" and 2. to put all discriminatory extremes under erasure, including essentialist interpretations of *aśūnyatā* (*feiwuyi*) and nihilistic interpretations of *śūnyatā* (*feiyouyi*), the two major arguments held by both Chinese Buddhists and Daoists in Ji Zang's time. The paradoxicality of Ji Zang's twofold truth played out by *you*/*wu* is a result not only of the paradoxical nature of conceptualization itself, but also the paradoxical nature of language as a whole. Meanwhile, by turning to the "four alternatives" as a paradoxical movement of repetition, Ji Zang shows how we can "skillfully" employ language to play against language, and how conceptual argument can lose its "immediate signification" through each execution of negative references. Ji Zang's "emptiness" is not to deny the conventional or linguistic necessity, or even the empirical validity of knowledge—which has been in fact well studied by Buddhism as a pedagogical means—but to deny the existence of intrinsic reality as well as substantiality of truth-claims that can become attached through our philosophical language. As a thing-deconstructed, emptiness is parasitic in that negation presupposes a self-created affirmation that very often determines the form and content of negation. On the other hand, emptiness is self-negating, it attempts to put an end to its self-created structure. This is the double-binds nature of *śūnyatā*: a deconstruction of the logocentric yet functions within a schematic (quasi-logocentric) circle at the same time.

For Ji Zang, the negation of other views cannot be recuperated by a pure affirmation in its absolute sense, since there is always an overflow (excess) that remains undefined. Therefore, the Buddhist middle path *qua śūnyatā* is neither an affirmation nor the opposite of affirmation since it keeps adding itself to something that is a plus. Yet the language of this "excess" or "plus" (e.g., neither *śūnyatā* nor *aśūnyatā*, neither dual nor nondual) is still confined to the realm of the conventional. We may say that the irony for both Ji Zang and Derrida is that one has to rely on conceptual language to show that conceptual language does not always work, at least, not the way we want it to work. However, it is just this self-contradiction that allows us to de-center the "logocentric circle," and "speak of" philosophy "differently." This means we should no longer try to justify an argument or viewpoint through reference to a set of a priori theories as objective truth, nor cling to the possibility that any conceptual doubt, uncertainty, and confusion can be resolved through philosophical language once and for all. Therefore, *śūnyatā* is an argumentative maneuver neither purely "from the above" (as shown in negative theology), nor purely "from the below" (as shown in deconstruction); it is an "in-between" play that delimits the dichotomy between words and non-words, existence and nonexistence, conventional truth and ultimate truth, *you* and *wu*.

The middle path also allows Sanlun Buddhism to avoid a nihilistic interpretation of *śūnyatā*, and the same argument can be applied to deconstruction. When speaking of deconstruction as "religion without religion," John Caputo remarks, deconstruction is "a movement of transcendence," (yet not "transcendence" in a traditional sense). It "means excess, the exceeding of the stable borders of the presently possible."[18] Deconstruction also implies a gesture of undecidability (between theism and atheism) and that the acceptance of this undecidability requires "faith-passion" with "prayers and tears." According to Caputo, deconstruction is a passion for transgression, a "passion for trespassing the horizons of possibility."[19] I think the same thing can be said of Sanlun Buddhism: *śūnyatā* is *passion* of the *pas*; by erasing the possibility of the objective (conceptual) truth, Buddhism leads us to the sphere of the impossible and the unrepresentable. In Buddhist terminology, this is a transformative process from the limited view (*duanjian*) to the unlimited view (*wuliangjian*). It is not a mere form of skepticism; instead it is a way towards liberation, freedom, enlightenment (i.e., spiritual transformation), and the "Buddhist paths of no boundaries (*wuliang zhufodao*)."

4

I fully realize that there is in fact a profound difference between negations in Ji Zang's *śūnyatā*-speech on the one hand and *dénégation* in Derrida's deconstruction on the other. One of the major differences between these two traditions is that *différance* and *dénégation* are rooted in language (i.e., the Western language in terms of its fundamental distinction between *langue* and *parole*), along with a particularly historical and philosophical critique that deconstruction entails, namely the language of a logocentric "self-presence" in the Western tradition. For Derrida, *dénégation* is "in writing," though it also implies "the unspeakable trace" that is "before writing," and "older" than writing. *Śūnyatā*, on the other hand, deals with, yet by no means confines itself, to writing or speech, which is, after all, part of the "conceptual play." As Ji Zang's twofold truth indicates, *śūnyatā* is the result of calming the categorizing and conceptualizing mind, so any tendency to conceptualize *śūnyatā* should be refuted. After all *śūnyatā* is all beyond any linguistic and intellectual affirmation/negation. Ji Zang's negation suggests an objection to logical reasoning which is, for him, based on the ontological as well as linguistic differentiation of *you* and *wu*, subject and object. The true nature of reality is, according to Buddhism, free from conceptualization and representation. *Śūnyatā* is transcendent but does not constitute a transcendental ground, for it is the self-emancipation of ontology from its foundation. Thus the Sanlun Buddhist way of looking at the world involves a rejection of the philosopher's reductionism and conceptualism.

Śūnyatā is ineffable not merely because it negates any linguistic articulation, but because it negates all dualistic thinking modes associated with mental activities. And according to Buddhism, a quiescent mind, or the no-mind, (*xinwu*) is elicited from meditative practice. C. W. Huntington rightly observed: "A solid intellectual grasp of the symbolic structure of the Mādhyamika philosophy must be cultivated through practice. In order to proceed, the Bodhisattva must learn how to cease clinging to every concept of 'truth' and 'reality'—including emptiness. . . through meditation."[20] The Buddhist meditative practice thus points to, if not a mere "supplement" to, another possible dimension that could be a "trace" of the un-thought; a trace of "the impossible" (and it is impossible from the perspective of the conventional world). This very trace of the un-thought cannot be reduced to what Derrida sees as a "form of hyperessentialism," "a transcendental-signified," or "the homology of hierarchy which leads to that which situates itself beyond all positions," or any other characteristics Derrida has attributed to theology's *via negativa*.

In sum, the middle-path (in-between-ness) does not suggest a specific locality, a specific point of in-between-ness; rather it suggests the infinite flux, the on-going process of signification in that it always adds itself to something that is a plus: A thing always becomes something that is more than itself, or even other than itself. *Śūnyatā* as a trans-tetralemmatic space is not a space, or a site marked by *you* or *wu*, presence or absence. Rather it indicates a complex interplay between the conventional and the ultimate in the infinite process of happenings. The play of *śūnyatā/dénégation* implies a movement of thought that sees the surplus of thought, and understanding this surplus sometimes requires the un-thought. The moment of negativity is, therefore, also the moment of construction and creativity. *Śūnyatā/dénégation* is not simply a nihilistic play of reducing meaning to non-meaning, reality to non-reality. On the contrary, it is the moment of emancipation of meanings, we find in the Chinese traditions from Zhuangzi to Buddhist philosophers and Chan masters. Meanwhile, the experiential dimensions in the process of transforming our thought and consciousness explored by Daoism and Buddhism also offer a possible critique of postmodern discourse.

Notes

1. *Dacheng xuanlun* in *Sanlun xuanyi jiasohi* [hereafter *SLXYJS*] ed. Han Yan-jie (Beijing: Zhonghua Shuju, 1989), 42.

2. According to Dazhengzang and Xuang, Ji Zang has written more than twenty essays on Mādhyamika and other Buddhist theories, among which the most well-known works are *Sanlun xuanyi* (*Metaphysical inquiries into the three treaties* [hereafter *SLXY*]), *Zhongguan lun shu* (*Commentary on Mādhyamika*), *Dacheng xuan lun* (*Metaphysical inquiries into the Mahāyāna*) and *Erdi yi* (*On the Twofold Truth*, hereafter [*EDY*]). All quotations from these works are from *SLXYJS* and all translations are mine unless otherwise noted. Regarding Nāgārjuna's position, see Jay L. Garfield. *The Fundamental Wisdom of the Middle Way* (London: Oxford University Press, 1995).

3. A quotation from *Kumarajiva's Treaties on Mādhyamika* (*Zhongguan lun*). *Taishōshihshū daizōkyō* 30.18a.27-28. Also see *SLXYJX*, 36.

4. Nāgārjuna, *Mūlamadhyamakakārikā*, XXIV.

5. Richard Robinson, *Early Madhyamika in India and China* (Madison: University of Wisconsin Press, 1967), 43.

6. Francis F. Cook, *Hua-yen Buddhism: The Jewel Net of Indra* (University Park and London: The Pennsylvania State University Press, 1977), 40.

7. Jacques Derrida, *Margins of Philosophy*, trans. Alan Bass (Chicago: University of Chicago Press, 1982), 6.

8. See Robert Magliola, *Derrida on the Mend* (Lafayette, Indiana: Purdue University Press, 1984), 87-98. Also for detailed discussion on the notion of double-binds implied in Derrida's deconstruction, see Magliola, *On Deconstructing Life-worlds* (Atlanta: Scholars Press, 1997), Part Two, Section ii. 157-166.

9. See Nāgārjuna, *Mūlamadhyamakakārikā*, XXIV.

10. For discussion on Zhi Yi's position on the twofold truth, see Paul L. Swanson's *Foundations of T'ien-T'ai Philosophy: The Flowing of the Two Truth Theory in Chinese Buddhism* (Berkeley: Asian Humanities Press, 1989).

11. Due to the scope of this paper, I cannot elaborate this point. See Ng Yu-Kwan's *Tien-T'ai Buddhism and Early Mādhyamika* (Honolulu: University of Hawaii, 1993) for a comprehensive study of similarities and differences between the two traditions.

12. Magliola, *Derrida on the Mend*, 87.

13. Jacques Derrida, "How to Avoid Speaking: Denials," in *Derrida and Negative Theology*, eds. Coward, H. and T. Foshay (Albany: State University of New York Press, 1992), 79.

14. Derrida, *Margins of Philosophy*, 73.

15. A term borrowed from *Magliola's On Deconstructing Life-Worlds*.

16. Magliola, *Derrida on the Mend*, 116.

17. Derrida, "How to Avoid Speaking: Denials," 95.

18. John Caputo, *The Prayers and Tears of Jacques Derrida* (Bloomington: Indiana University Press, 1997), xix.

19. Caputo, *The Prayers and Tears of Jacques Derrida*, xix.

20. Huntington, C. W. and Gesh N. Wangchen, *The Emptiness of Emptiness: An Introduction to Early Indian Mādhyamika* (Honolulu: University of Hawaii Press, 1989), 112.

Part Four

Chan/Zen Buddhist Deconstruction

Introduction

The coexistence of deconstructive and "un"-deconstructive aspects in our mode of thinking has been a concern of Chan Buddhism, the history of which reveals the process of the school's constant self-examination in the face of the substantializing and essentializing tendency of the human mind. The essays in Part Four discuss two such instances in Chan Buddhism: the establishment of the Southern/sudden school of Chan during the formative period of Chan Buddhism, and the use of a question and answer technique known as *gong'an*.

Youru Wang asserts deconstructive operation as an essential motive in the development of early Chan Buddhism. Bringing attention to two occasions, Huineng versus Shenxiu and the Hongzhou school versus Shenhui, Wang interprets Chan Buddhism as crossroad of the emptiness-orientation found in the *Prajñāpāramitā* and the Mādhyamika traditions on the one hand and the Buddha-nature orientation of the Yogācāra school and some of the *tathāgatagarbha* texts on the other. Wang argues that each time either one of the two tendencies tries to dominate the other party, a deconstructive operation becomes active, failing the reifying tendency of the ruling power. Huineng's "no-thought" (*wunian*) attacks Shenxiu's dualistic concept of "freeing from thought" (*linian*), and the Hongzhou school's "moving along the things and circumstances" (*renyun zizai*) aptly problematizes the favoritism and dualism in Shenhui's "empty and tranquil awareness" (*kongji zhi zhi*). In order to meet the requirements of the constantly changing situations and at the same time prevent the reification of any given concept or situation, Wang argues, Hongzhou masters alternately employ positive and negative discourses, thereby keeping the deconstructive operation rolling.

One might ask in what sense these movements in early Chan Buddhism can be identified as deconstructive, instead of as critical, oppositional, or simply expressing different positions as in any event that occurs in the history of ideas. As Derrida explains it, any attempt to define deconstruction as "X" or "Y" would be misleading. But at the same time, it is true that the deconstructive operation distinguishes itself from those schools I listed above, in the sense that deconstructive operation does not establish its own identity as opposed to the context upon which deconstruction is executed. Rather, deconstruction points out the gaps and fissures in the existing theory/thought/text and thus reveals its limitations.

According to Wang, what distinguishes Chan deconstructive operation in early Chan from critical reaction lies in the way Chan deals with the material. Huineng's "no-thought" is not just a criticism of Shenxiu's "freeing from thought"; it does not establish itself at the other end of Shenxiu's idea. From Huineng's (and the Southern School's) perspective, Shenxiu's "freeing from thought" substantializes and entitifies the "thought" itself, reifying the "purity" as the "original" position. The purity, however, does not and cannot exist by itself if the world is based on dependent-nature which is emptiness. The thought itself is transparent, and thus empty. There is no way to free oneself from any thought and go back to the pure origin. Huineng's "no-thought" therefore does not imply the lack of thought, but a non-dualistic mode of thinking. Thus Wang contends that the deconstructive operation of Chan does not aim to "replace . . . old binary distinctions or logocentric hierarchies with new ones" but to "detach from any dualistic oppositions."

Frank W. Stevenson explores the Chan technique of question-answer (*gong'an*) in relation to Derridean-Magliolan deconstruction in the context of un-thought/thought and silence/language. One basis of the *gong'an* technique, states Stevenson, lies in suspending the mind in a state of doubt, the moment of pre-thought, pre-voice before the question emerges into a thought. Stevenson views this pattern of the imminence of between-ness in *huatou* not only as prolongation but also as repetition. He states that Magliola's readings, which tend to foreground the (off-) logical-dialectical side of the paradoxes, assume a temporal-dynamic view of the dialogue in which the question is taken as self-repeating. This self-repetition, Stevenson concludes, can be a pattern of the "return" of contingent, asymmetric possibilities, where the pure contingency or a random free play of the merely possible is qualified by the dynamics of the return (reversal and repetition).

The *gong'an* (J. *kōan*; K. *kongan*) tradition has been one of the most distinguished features in Chan Buddhist efforts to work with the reifying tendency of one's mode of thinking. A typical *gong'an* case consists of a dialogue between a Chan master and a student, usually in the format of a question and an answer. The key here is a seeming gap between the question and the answer, which frequently violates the logic of daily conversation. The insight of the Chan device of *gong'an* reveals the hidden rule in our habit of a question and answer. Questioning by definition is to be an open-action. When a person asks a question, the assumption is that the questioner opens her/himself up and prepares a space for answers regardless of their nature. This, however, is not exactly what happens in our experience of question-answer, in which the questioner already has a frame for the answer, if not the answer itself. The fact that *gong'an* has been working as *gong'an* is in itself evidence that in our use of language, and our way of thinking as well, a dialogue has in fact been a monologue. Derrida explains such a situation as the logocentric desire to possess the essence of things. The desire is embodied in the format of our question: "what is…?" The what-ness of things, as inscribed in our minds, keeps us from conversing with objects, without first domesticating them. Maintaining the self-closure of this "what-ness" of being, we remain in the abyss of monologue.

Stevenson reads Magliola's reading of *gong'an* as the between-ness "between" thought and un-thought, language, and silence. If we are to take this as a deconstructive operation, one must be cautious in understanding the moment of "un-thought." Derridean deconstruction would ask about the possibility of the moment of the "pre-thought" and "pre-voice" and further ask whether this is another occasion of creating the pure origin. Stevenson thus emphasizes the "differentialism" between thought and un-thought, language and silence. How does one define the un-thought? Is it the same as Huineng's "no-thought"? Or is it still possible to think about between-ness without identifying the "between" where this between-ness locates itself? How do we keep silence? Is silence a lack of language or the state of non-language? Clarifying these issues will be crucial for the investigation of *gong'an* in Chan Buddhism as a deconstructive operation. (JYP)

Seven

The Chan Deconstruction of Buddha Nature

Youru Wang

Although much has been said about deconstruction in Mādhyamika Buddhism, very little has been done in the study of deconstructive strategy in Chan Buddhism. Robert Magliola, for example, makes a distinction between logocentric and differential trends in Chan/Zen Buddhism in his study on deconstruction and Nāgārjuna.[1] This distinction allows us to take a fresh look at the inner struggle in the evolution of Chan Buddhist thought. Magliola's study leaves the impression that the deconstructive or differential trend is connected with Southern Chan but does not follow up on the issue with further doctrinal and textual investigation.

Bernard Faure also touches upon the issue of logocentric and differential trends in Chan in his comprehensive critique of the Chan tradition. Faure criticizes Magliola for making a connection between his logocentric/differential distinction and the historically well-defined distinction between Northern and Southern Chan, and claims that such a hasty connection is "counterproductive."[2] As opposed to Magliola's approach, Faure suggests that it is impossible to identify one school or one figure in the Chan tradition as either logocentric or deconstructive. He asserts that there are "only combinations" of these two types in the Chan tradition.[3] It appears that this position of "combination only" avoids a one-sided view and the error of jumping-to-a-conclusion. However, by concluding that there are only combinations, Faure turns away from the possibility and necessity of identifying different deconstructive trends within Chan Buddhism and from the possibility of providing a coherent interpretation regarding different schools within the Chan tradition.

This paper is an attempt to investigate a major deconstructive trend in Chan Buddhism, namely, that of the Huineng and the Hongzhou Chan. For that purpose, this article will take up the issue in three aspects. First, based on a distinction between the historical orthodox form of Chan and the modern orthodox interpretation of Chan, I will provide a reinterpretation of the historical orthodox form of Chan, which will be very different from the modern orthodox interpretation of Chan. Second, I will investigate the deconstruction of Buddha nature in Chan Buddhism. The notion of Buddha nature originates from the doctrine of *Tathāgatagarbha* and is nurtured by the Chinese transformation of Buddhist thought. Like all other Buddhist soteriological terms, the word "Buddha nature" can be easily reified or sedimented into a logocentric term, since the word, after all, comes out of the conventional vocabularies of binary discrimination. Upon closer examination, we will find that the main stream of Chan Buddhism does not engage so much in developing a theory of Buddha nature as in deconstructing the concept of Buddha nature. In deconstructing Buddha nature, Chan Buddhists, to some extent, restore the spirit of the *Prajñāpāramitā* and Mādhyamika while transcending their limits in echoing the call of practice. Thirdly, this essay will explore the context of inner struggles within the evolution of Chan Buddhist thought. By analyzing the inner struggles between the reification of soteriological terms and the deconstructive operation, I will clarify *specific contexts* of Chan deconstructive operation on the one hand, and reifying tendency—the target of that deconstruction, on the other.[4]

The Deconstruction of Buddha Nature in the *Platform Sutra*

Huineng's deconstructive operation and its target—Shenxiu's doctrine of *linian*—in the terms of the *Platform Sutra* concern the understanding of Buddha nature. Huineng's famous verse about enlightenment most clearly subverts the reifying tendency in Shenxiu's understanding of enlightenment and the Buddha nature.[5] The verse radically cancels the concept of the Buddha nature as something entitative or substantial by undermining the dichotomy that Shenxiu's verse maintains between the Buddha nature and the deluded mind in the metaphor of mirror and dust. In order to better understand Huineng's deconstructive endeavor, we need to examine the details of Huineng's and Shenxiu's doctrines.

Shenxiu draws his idea of *linian* from the text of the *Dacheng qixin lun* (*The treatise on the awakening of Mahāyāna faith*). In a treatise on the five expedient means of the Mahāyāna, Shenxiu quotes passages directly from the *Dacheng qixin lun*. For example, "What is called enlightenment means that the whole of the mind frees from [deluded] thoughts. . . ."[6] The use of the term *linian* (freeing from thoughts) thus here appears to be the starting point of Shenxiu's own interpretation of *linian*. The *Dacheng qixin lun* identifies the Buddha nature, or the mind of suchness, with emptiness in an effort of desubstantialization. By emphasizing *yinian xiangying* (one instant of thought corresponds to suchness) or *linian*, and by identifying suchness with the minds of sentient beings, it also suggests a way of existentializing the issue of Buddha nature as the transformation of the ordinary mind. This, however, is only suggested in the text, which leaves plenty of room for different interpretations. Moreover, despite its identification between the mind of suchness and the mind in *saṃsāra*, the text obviously emphasizes the mind of suchness and its purity.[7] As a result, the idea of *linian* could entail very different understandings.

Shenxiu's interpretation is a quasi-reifying one. It is not utterly reifying mainly because the general context of his doctrine is soteriological-practical and he maintains certain nondualistic clarifications, though not always clearly, as some critical historians have tried to reveal (See *NS*, 213, 225; *WO*, 43-44). Nevertheless, the criticisms from other Chan Buddhists should not be seen as merely polemic and sectarian. There are obvious doctrinal and practical reasons that call forth the deconstruction of Shenxiu's interpretation. Let us first look at how Shenxiu interprets *linian*:

> If the body and the mind are not aroused, one constantly maintains the true mind. What is suchness? When the mind does not move, that is suchness; when the form is not in motion, that is also suchness. (*T* 85. 2834.1273c; trans. in *WO*, 43 with minor modifications; *NS*, 174)

> The whole [or essence] and the function are clearly distinguishable: freeing from thoughts is the whole; seeing, hearing, feeling and knowing are the function. (*T* 85. 2834.1274b; *NS*, 178)

> Question: By what means can one achieve Buddhahood?
> Answer: One achieves Buddhahood with the whole [or essence] of the pure mind.[8]

Shenxiu's interpretation clearly leaves room for a logocentric hierarchy that privileges pure over impure, motionlessness over motion, the true mind over the ordinary mind, the whole (*ti*) over the function (*yong*), even transcendence over immanence. Although the Buddha nature or the mind of suchness in the *Dacheng qixin lun* involves the aspects of pure and impure, true and deluded, *ti* and *yong*, Shenxiu places his notion of *linian* solely on the side of pure, true, and *ti*. Thus "freeing from thoughts" not only means freeing from deluded thoughts but also from motions and actions, including seeing, hearing, feeling, knowing and thinking. By entering into this "pure" and "quiet" state, Shenxiu and his followers believe that they can attain liberation. What kind of liberation are they searching for? Does it not reflect a sort of Chan escapism?[9] Related to this escapism is inevitably a tendency towards reification, pointing to an enchanted place, which is a foundation. Although Shenxiu does talk about the identification of *ti* and *yong*, *ti* is something from which *yong* flows and to which it also returns. This dialectic of *ti* and *yong* looks somewhat analogous to a Hegelian dialectic, insofar as it privileges *ti*.

Such a notion of *linian* becomes the target of Huineng's deconstructive operation. It is true that Huineng's idea of *wunian* (no-thought or no-thinking) also comes from the *Dacheng qixin lun* in which the two terms, *linian* and *wunian*, are almost synonyms. However, if we look at Huineng's creative interpretation of *wunian*, we must admit the great difference between Shenxiu's *linian* and

Huineng's *wunian*. To subvert Shenxiu's *linian*, Huineng does not simply fall back on the opposite of Shenxiu's abandonment of all thoughts, such as an emphasis on the importance of thoughts. Rather, Huineng proposes something that is neither Shenxiu's nor of its opposite. Huineng's endeavor is a typically deconstructive one. He interprets *wunian* as follows.

> No-thought means not to be carried away by thought in the process of thought.[10] . . . Successive thoughts do not stop; prior thoughts, present thoughts, and future thoughts follow one after the other without cessation. . . . If one instant of thought clings, then successive thoughts cling; this is known as being fettered. If in all things successive thoughts do not cling, then you are unfettered. Therefore, we consider this non-abiding essential.[11] ... But do not stop thinking about everything and eliminate all thoughts. As soon as thought stops, one dies and is reborn elsewhere. (*PS*, 51)

Huineng does several things to dismantle Shenxiu's misleading ideas. First, as we may note, Huineng appeals to the causal chain of thoughts and things. All thoughts and things are interrelated and one causes another. We all live with this flow of thoughts and things, and no one can stop it. Huineng regards this unceasing flow, this non-abiding, as something of the essential condition for human existence or of human nature (*weiren benxing*) (*PS*, 50).

Both being free from thoughts (here referring to Shenxiu's idea) and attachment to thoughts (a common illness addressed in Buddhist soteriological discourses) are, for Huineng, two extremes that run counter to this essential condition or nature. For this reason, they are the hindrance to the way of liberation. Huineng's solution to this problem is to maintain the Middle Way; though a difficult way, the advice is not to stop something that you will never be able to stop but to detach yourself from it. This is none other than *flowing together* with thoughts and things. To some extent, to practice this (as a soteriological expedient) is to return to your own nature.

Next, in relation to this advice, Huineng proposes his thesis that *dao* must flow freely (*dao xu tongliu*) (*PSSP*, 136; *PS*, 46). He asks: "Why should *dao* be impeded instead? (*PS*, 49). If the mind does not abide in things, the *dao* circulates freely; if the mind abides in things, it becomes entangled" (*PSSP*, 136, with minor modifications). He also names this mind of *dao* the "straightforward mind (*zhixin*)" and teaches his disciples "only practicing straightforward mind, and in all things having no attachments whatsoever" (*PSSP*, 136). In other words, they should "practice the straightforward mind at all times, whether walking, standing, sitting, or reclining" (*PS*, 47). These statements, tinged with Daoist spirit, make it clear that for Huineng, enlightenment or the realization of the Buddha nature is not to impede the living flux of the everyday world. Enlightenment or *dao* is rather the unimpeded or straightforward flowing together with thoughts and things in all everyday circumstances. Huineng's deconstructive operation upon Shenxiu's idea apparently serves this soteriological motif. It is from this perspective of free flowing together with all thoughts and things that Huineng strongly opposes Shenxiu's way of "contemplating the mind and contemplating purity, not moving and not activating the mind" (*PSSP*, 137). Huineng's thesis foreshadows, or is echoed by, the Hongzhou notion of *renyun* (following along with the movement of all things or circumstances), a thesis central to mainstream Chan, though not always properly understood.

The consequence of Huineng's interpretation of *wunian* is significant. For instance, the affirmation of the causal chain and unimpeded flux of thoughts and things provide the legitimacy for the emphasis on the existential awakening of the human mind. According to Huineng, the imagined cessation of this causal chain and flux leads nowhere but to continuous sufferings. Only by practicing non-attachment within this chain or flux of thoughts and things can we hope to attain liberation.[12] This chain or flux also makes possible the transformation of the human mind from delusion to enlightenment. The reason is obvious: this flux (or the change of all individual thoughts or objects) brings about passion, craving, impermanence, disillusionment, as well as enlightenment. Although one instance of suffering does not necessarily entail enlightenment, how could there be enlightenment without the affliction resulting from passion? They are not only interrelated but also mutually involved. Therefore, Huineng stresses: "[T]he very passions are themselves enlightenment (*ji fannao shi puti*)" (*PSSP*, 148).

On the other hand, since the existence of a person is the flow of thoughts and feelings, the existential difference of the mind and thought is always possible. In this sense Huineng underscores: "[U]nawakened, even a Buddha is a sentient being," and "even a sentient being, if he is awakened in an instant of thought, is a Buddha" (*PSSP*, 151). In other words, "[E]ven these sentient beings, filled with passions and troubles," are able to "gain enlightenment" through the change of one instant of thought (*PSSP*, 150). This accent on the existential transformation of the human mind and thought has, without doubt, the consequence of excluding any substance, essence or foundation outside the function of the human mind. Nor does it tend to reify the human mind or subjectivity itself, since the goal of this transformation is to flow together with all things through an empty mind, the mind devoid of self-attachment. Thus Huineng's teaching develops the existentializing point of the *Dacheng qixin lun* concerning the realization of the Buddha nature, without relying too much on a "true mind" distinguishable from the mind of the sentient being.

Huineng's use of the term *zixing* (self nature) can also be correctly understood in this context. Throughout the *Platform Sutra*, Huineng seldom uses the term "Buddha nature." He substitutes "self nature" for "Buddha nature." At first sight, this seems no different from the use of the term in *tathāgatagarbha* texts which refer to the *tathāgatagarbha* as the mind of self nature and purity as well. It is true that there are linguistic and phrasal links between the *Platform Sutra* and those texts of *tathāgatagarbha* thought, especially the *Dacheng qixin lun*. However, upon closer inspection, one can find that Huineng's use of "self nature" is very unique. Huineng's "self nature" emphasizes more plainly the possibility of existential awakening *within* the living body and mind of every sentient being. It underlines that every human being can actualize this possibility through the practice of non-attachment in all everyday circumstances. As we have indicated, it does not stress the need to establish a Buddha nature or true mind clearly distinguishable from the living mind of every sentient being, namely, the mind in *saṃsāra*. Attaining Buddhahood is none other than the existential transformation of the mind which is the same as that in every human being in everyday life. Huineng makes this point far clearer in his *Platform Sutra* if we compare it with the *Dacheng qixin lun*. The meaning of this term, therefore, is soteriological, functional, and non-substantialist.

"Self nature" here does not indicate anything that exists in and by itself, or self-identity. There is no such meaning involved in the use of this term at all. Rather, Huineng points out: "Human nature is empty (*shiren xingkong*)" (*PSSP*, 146; *PS*, 68). Here emptiness is used, first of all, in the same sense as the *Prajñāpāramitā* and Mādhyamika would maintain, namely, devoid of self existence or self nature. Secondly, it is used in the Post-Mādhyamika sense as the Yogācāra school and some *tathāgatagarbha* texts would maintain, namely, that emptiness, or being devoid of self existence, is the nature of all things. This understanding of the empty nature of all things, in its best form, is maintained as something like the condition of the possibilities of all things. It is not an origin or essence of all things but nonetheless involves everything. Everything becomes possible because of this emptiness, this web of relativity. Huineng's saying that the self nature involves the ten thousand things should be understood in terms of this meaning (*PSSP*, 146; *PS*, 68). It is clear that this view involves an objective or cognitive element, insofar as it describes the condition of the possibilities of all things. We may call it quasi-transcendental or ontologically neutral, since it can be led to a reified view by substantializing this condition or to a desubstantialized view by stressing its pragmatic function as expedient. However, when Huineng states that emptiness is human nature or human nature is empty, he does not end with this second usage but gives the term new meanings. His use of the term involves the meanings of relationality, the existential changeability of personhood, and the accomplishment of action.

To make this point clearer, I must clarify the linguistic-cultural background of Huineng's use of the term *xing* (nature) or *renxing* (human nature) in relation to the term *zixing*. Scholars have commonly accepted that the Confucian, especially Mencian, emphasis on the innate goodness of human nature had great impact on the Chinese Buddhist acceptance of *tathāgatagarbha* thought. However, scholars have recently revealed that the notion of human nature in Chinese philosophy is different from the Western notion of human nature as a changeless essence contained in all individual human beings. For instance, Tang Junyi, in his extensive study on *renxing*, explicates that the classical Confucian conception of *xing* is concerned primarily with the existential changeability and growth of each living human being. The *xing* is discussed from a practical and dynamic perspective. The meaning of *xing* involves directionality, relationality, and existential-practical development.[13] In the Mencian theory of mind-nature, the *xing* is explained in terms of the growth of each individual mind. "It should not be termed an essence or principle deeply rooted in the mind."[14] In a similar vein, Roger Ames radically questions the adequacy of the translation of the Chinese term *renxing* as "human nature" in its Western sense.[15] Ames clarifies the Chinese meaning of *xing* as "a creative act."[16] "[*X*]*ing* denotes the entire process of being a person. . . . [A] person is not a sort of *being*, but first and foremost a *doing* and *making* . . . [*X*]*ing* is not reducible to what is innate or *a priori*."[17] These expositions have, to some extent, clarified the linguistic-cultural background of Huineng's use of *xing* as well. Let us now look at one example of Huineng's use of *xing* in the *Platform Sutra*:

> . . . immediately awakened. It is like the great sea which gathers all the flowing streams, and harmonizes the small waters with the large waters as a whole. This is realizing your own nature. [Such a person] does not abide either inside or outside; he is free to come or go. Readily he casts aside the mind that clings [to things], and there is no obstruction to his passage. (*PSSP*, 150, translation modified)

Realizing one's own nature here is not explained with what one recognizes but how one acts, how one achieves the existential transformation of the mind, and how one practices the free flowing together (or being harmonized) with all things. The focus is not on the cognitive element contained in the second usage, but on the existential function of the mind and pragmatic wisdom (*zhi*), on the practical-behavioral carrying out of non-attachment. The usage of *xing* here is plainly operational. We have no difficulty in detecting the underlying accord of Huineng's usage with the Confucian one, despite its Buddhist context. The understanding of this unique usage is crucial to the avoidance of any accusation that Huineng's, or his followers', "self nature" is a substantialist view. The usage is also a good example to show the Chinese transformation of the original Buddhist usage.

Deconstruction in Hongzhou Chan

A main target of the Hongzhou school's deconstruction is Shenhui's teaching of "establishing awareness and cognition (*li zhijian*)" (*Shoki*, 154) in relation to his understanding of the Buddha nature. Although Shenhui is on the side of Huineng and makes a significant contribution to the criticism of Shenxiu's idea of *linian*, scholars have indicated that Shenhui's thought deviates from Huineng's in some important aspects.[18] Shenhui's own interpretation of *wunian* becomes problematic when we compare it with Huineng's *wunian*. And this is where the Hongzhou school's deconstructive operation comes in. The Hongzhou school should be rather considered the true inheritor of Huineng's thought in those essential aspects. We do not deny that Shenhui's teaching is to be read in a soteriological context, and in some respects he does stand in line with Huineng and with Hongzhou. Hence one might want to see only some elements of his thought as quasi-reifying or quasi-logocentric. However, it is these elements that make the difference between the Hongzhou and Shenhui's teachings and make a deconstructive operation indispensable.

These are two major interrelated problems in Shenhui's teaching. First, he privileges "awareness" or "intuitive knowledge" over ordinary, discriminative cognition. The former is called "empty tranquil awareness" ("*kongji zhi zhi*").[19] The latter refers to all ordinary activities of seeing, hearing, feeling, and knowing (*jian wen jue zhi*) with respect to discriminative consciousness. Shenhui claims that all ordinary activities of seeing, hearing, feeling, and knowing must be emptied or transcended in the state of *wunian.*[20] This disruption from ordinary cognitive activity is overemphasized by his interpretation of awareness. As he states, "This awareness does not have any causal link, since it is the *prajñā* wisdom of the original whole [or essence] of emptiness and tranquility itself that is aware."[21] By cutting off its causal link, Shenhui comes to isolate this "awareness" from all everyday activities. He equates the achievement of this awareness with the attainment of Buddhahood. In Zongmi's (780-841) terms, he considers "the one word 'awareness' [or intuitive knowledge] the gate to all wonders."[22]

Second, in using the category of *ti* and *yong* to explain awareness, Shenhui favors the *ti* and sees "awareness" as the *benzhi zhiyong*, the function of the wisdom of the *ti* itself that relies on no other conditions. For instance, he states: "In the whole (*ti*) of emptiness and tranquility, there is the original wisdom, the illuminating function (*yong*) of which is called awareness."[23] It is true that this view involves the identification of the *ti* and the *yong*, since the *yong* is only the *yong* of the *ti* and the *ti* is that which functions (*yong*). However, upon closer examination, we find that he cancels, in fact, the *yong* in favor of the *ti.* Zongmi's explanation is revealing at this point. He indicates: "[Shenhui's notion of] the awareness of tranquility points to the *ti.*"[24] It is the *ti* that is aware of itself and of all things. This *ti* is also equivalent to the mind of non-abiding, the Buddha nature or self nature. Since this *ti* does not rely on any causal link or causal condition, it is clearly distinguishable from the mind in *saṃsāra*. This is an apparent departure from Huineng's notion of self nature or the mind of non-abiding that is identified with the mind at one instant of thought, namely, the mind of the sentient being. As we have noted, the mind of non-abiding, in Huineng, is the existential awakening of the same mind of the sentient being. It does not presuppose a foundation-like "whole of mind" (*xinti*). Shenhui's privilege of the *ti*, it seems to me, falls back on Shenxiu's notion of true mind (*zhenxin*) and that of the *Dacheng qixin lun*. There seems no fundamental difference between Shenhui's *xinti* and Shenxiu's *zhenxin* in their quasi-reifying aspect. Although Shenhui shows the non-objectified feature of this "mind of emptiness and tranquility" by relating it to wisdom and to the function of awareness, it is not clearly distinguishable from an absolutized subjectivity—an inverted substance.

The Hongzhou school overturns Shenhui's position in both aspects. First, the Hongzhou school strongly opposes any characterization of the realization of the Buddha nature or of enlightenment as *zhijian* or *zhijie*. It challenges each pair of opposites: that is the equation of enlightenment with ordinary cognition on the one hand and that of enlightenment with awareness or intuitive knowledge isolatable from ordinary cognitive activities on the other. The second position is Shenhui's. The Hongzhou position is best represented by the following exposition found in the sayings of Huangbo Xiyun (?-850):

> [Y]ou students of the *dao* . . . will realize your original mind only in the realm of seeing, hearing, feeling and knowing. Although the original mind does not belong to seeing, hearing, feeling and knowing, this mind cannot be separated

> from them. You should not simply start your cognitive maneuver from them, nor allow them to give rise to any conceptual thought; yet nor should you seek the mind apart from them or abandon them in your pursuit of the *dharma*. Do not let your mind be identical with them nor separated from them . . . be free everywhere, and nowhere is a place where the *dao* cannot be practiced.[25]

The point of Hongzhou expressed here by Huangbo is evident: although enlightenment cannot be pursued through mere cognition, it cannot be isolated from all activities that may be related to a further cognitive maneuver. What is important for enlightenment is the cessation of one's cognitive maneuver—the illusory grasping of the object of self-identity. However, what is of equal importance is not to separate oneself from everyday activities. Everyday activities are opportunities or necessary conditions for the realization of enlightenment. This understanding is due to the Hongzhou belief in the Mahāyāna dictum that without *saṃsāra* or *saṃvṛti* there is no *nirvāṇa* or *paramārtha*, a strictly relational perspective. Enlightenment is only the establishment and function of the attitude of non-clinging within ordinary activities. The Hongzhou masters often ask where one can go or how one can be enlightened if apart from this conventional world and everyday activities. As authentic followers of the Middle Way, the Hongzhou masters see Shenhui's isolation of awareness from ordinary activities as another kind of attachment or fixation. From a relational perspective, it must be overturned.

Second, the Hongzhou school makes invalid Shenhui's logocentric hierarchy of *ti* and *yong*. Shenghui's ti is independent of all conditions (*yuan*). Zongmi defines Shenhui's hierarchy as "the original [or self] function of the self nature" (*zixing benyong*), while the Hongzhou position is criticized by him as "the application [of the self nature] in various conditions" (*suiyuan yingyong*).[26] Since Shenhui's *ti* or self nature is independent of all conditions, its own *yong* is abstracted from everyday activities and all circumstances. Shenhui and Zongmi prefer this kind of self function. However, without that "application in conditions," how can there be any real function at all? There is no doubt that Shenhui's view results in the cancellation of the *yong* in favor of the *ti*. From the contrary perspective of Hongzhou, there is only "application in conditions," and there is no such thing as the "self function of the self nature." The Hongzhou position, as formulated by Zongmi, goes as follows:

> If one examines the nature of this whole [or essence], he will find that ultimately it can neither be perceived nor realized just as the eye cannot see itself, and so forth. If one considers its application, he will see that every move and every action that he takes is the Buddha nature, and that there is nothing else that can either realize it or be realized.[27]

The stance of the Hongzhou Chan here is to restore more completely the existential-soteriological and pragmatic-behavioral concern of Buddhism in the Chinese context. It strives against any quasi-metaphysical or quasi-reifying use of the Chinese category of *ti* and *yong*, including Shenhui's. The Hongzhou Chan does not oppose the use of the term *ti* itself. What the Hongzhou masters are concerned with is how one should use it. It is all right for them to use the *ti* as an equivalent to the realization of the Buddha nature or enlightenment. However, it must be used in the perspectival, relational, dynamic, pragmatic-behavioral sense and as temporary expedient only, just as *xing* is used in the *Platform Sutra* that we have discussed above. Since the *ti* or the Buddha nature or enlightenment is not any kind of substance or entity, we can neither perceive nor grasp it. But if we consider the *ti* as a dynamic whole or a web of relativity in which we live and act every day and with which we attempt to live and act in harmony, then every movement or action is connected to, or a part of, it. Precisely in this sense the Hongzhou masters emphasize that all daily activities are nothing but the function of the Buddha nature. The *ti* (or the Buddha nature), the *yong* (function or application) and the *yuan* (temporal conditions) cannot be separated. This identical relation is in favor of the *yong*. It is the subversion of Shenhui's privilege of the *ti*. One may have the objection that this seems to be the cancellation of the *ti*. However, if the *ti* is only a temporary expedient and is understood in the sense of action, application and relation, there is no need to cancel it. The *ti* cannot exist in and of itself, and cannot be independent of this practical-behavioral context.

Although Zongmi's formulation of the position of the Hongzhou school is fair, his interpretation of it is definitely wrong. For example, Zongmi explains the position of Hongzhou as follows: "[T]he blackness itself is the bright pearl, and the substance of the bright pearl is ever invisible. If one wants to know the pearl, blackness itself is brightness."[28] In this metaphorical expression, Zongmi suggests that the Hongzhou school mixes the ordinary activities of the unenlightened person with the activities of the enlightened person. In that case, the Hongzhou Chan runs the risk of canceling the necessity of Buddhist practice. This is a complete misunderstanding of Hongzhou. The central point of the Hongzhou teaching is, of course, not to cancel Buddhist practice, but to further remove all hindrance to Buddhist practice. One more hindrance is the tendency of reification. As is indicated in Zongmi's own description, the Hongzhou Chan advocates the motto "let the mind be free (*renxin*)":

> *Dao* is the [ordinary] mind itself, and one cannot use the [Buddha] mind to cultivate the [ordinary] mind; evil is also the mind itself, and one cannot cut off the [evil] mind by means of the [other] mind. Do not cut and do not produce; letting the mind follow along with all circumstances and letting it be free, this is called liberation.[29]

In this account, the Hongzhou identification of all activities of the ordinary mind with the Buddha nature deconstructs the dualistic distinction of the ordinary mind and the Buddha nature. It is to recover enlightenment as the existential-practical transformation of the ordinary mind. The Hongzhou view is not to demolish the existential changeability of the sentient being but to reaffirm it through its overturning of the original hierarchy of the Buddha nature and the ordinary mind. It echoes and develops Huineng's teaching by placing more weight on the relation between all activities of the ordinary mind and the realization of the Buddha nature. The Hongzhou view must be understood in terms of this relational perspective. As we have mentioned, everyday activities, for Hongzhou, are the necessary condition for enlightenment in the first place. Without *saṃsāra*, there is no *nirvāṇa*; therefore, the ordinary mind is *dao*. I call this the pre-enlightenment aspect.

The Hongzhou view also involves a post-enlightenment aspect. It underscores that you must verify your own enlightenment in everyday activities. After attaining enlightenment, you are still an ordinary person doing ordinary tasks. The only difference, as pointed out by many Chan masters, is that you now have an attitude of non-attachment and that attitude always works in everyday activities. In an enlightened eye, then, every action is and can be seen as the function of the Buddha nature. The relational perspective, therefore, is an enlightened perspective, not an unenlightened one. But the disclosure and stress of this enlightened perspective are extremely important for unenlightened practitioners. It leads them in a right direction—to resist any separation of enlightenment from everyday activities. Here our distinction of pre- and post-enlightenment aspects is only for the purpose of analysis. Generally speaking, the Hongzhou view advises students to see the mutual conditioning and mutual involvement of the enlightened and the unenlightened. This is not to mix them up but to see them in the living reality of change and flux. The promotion of Buddhist practice is possible only within this living reality of change and flux.

No Root, no Foundation, no Mind and no Buddha: Hongzhou Chan Masters

To flow together with this ever-changing reality is called *renyun* in the Hongzhou school. The result of the deconstructive maneuver of Hongzhou is not to replace all old binary distinctions or logocentric hierarchies with new ones. Its standpoint or its strategy is rather to eschew or detach from any dualistic oppositions. In other words, the Hongzhou masters keep themselves busy moving with all things and circumstances, staying with neither the Buddha nor the sentient being, neither extraordinary nor ordinary, neither grasping nor rejecting, neither terminable nor permanent, neither knowledge nor non-knowledge, and so on. This elusive position is called and explained by the Chinese words *renyun zizai*, meaning "following along with the movement of all things or circumstances and being free" ("Tsung-mi," 47). It constitutes both part of the deconstructive strategy of Hongzhou and the underlying thesis that this deconstructive strategy ultimately serves. In the recorded sayings of those famous Hongzhou masters, we find the frequent use of these words and similar expressions.

> . . . following along with the movement of all things and in this way living out your time.[30]

> At all times . . . never attach yourself to one thing; just follow along with the movement of all things the whole day long.[31]

> Merely according to circumstances as they are, use up your past *karma*; following along with [the change of] circumstances, put on your [different] clothes.[32]

A similar expression is found in Master Linji's (?-867) quotations: "The mind changes in accordance with the myriad circumstances;/the way it changes is truly profound./If you can realize its nature through this flow,/you will have neither joy nor sorrow."[33] In view of these understandings, the soteriological goal of Buddhist practice, for the Hongzhou Chan, should by no means be static or isolatable. The goal is to let us keep moving or flowing with all things or circumstances. The masters know very well that the living process of change and flux will ruthlessly undercut every fixed position and every attachment to self or self-identity without ever stopping. Reality itself is deconstructive. Enlightenment cannot occur *outside* this flow. Enlightenment is nothing but being harmonious with change and flux. An enlightened person would find inexhaustible wonders by living a life in harmony with change and flux. This is the exact content and context of the Hongzhou teaching of realizing the "self nature" or "self mind," insofar as the Hongzhou masters usually do use these words. However, the profundity of this soteriological motif pushes their deconstruction completely home, just as their deconstructive strategy helps to reveal the profundity of this motif.

A remarkable characteristic of the Hongzhou deconstruction is its self-cancellation or self-effacement. The Hongzhou self-deconstruction is as compelling as its deconstruction of the position of others. One famous case is Mazu Daoyi's (709-988) self-effacement of his notion of "the mind is Buddha." When the notion is first taught by Mazu, it involves an attempt to oppose the misunderstanding of the Buddha nature as something outside or separable from the ordinary mind. It is a kind of deconstructive operation upon the reifying view of the Buddha nature. However, after he teaches this notion for a certain period, it is inevitably sedimented or abstracted from the original context. His students show the tendency to attach themselves to this notion. Then Mazu starts to teach a different notion that apparently runs counter to his original teaching, a notion now emphasizing that there is neither mind nor Buddha.[34] In this way Mazu keeps himself moving with different situations, avoids misleading students and helps them to eschew sedimentation, fixation, and reification. This self-effacement indicates that for Mazu, there is no need to establish any logocentric hierarchy. He does not privilege any notion at all. He is able to use any kataphatic terms in his soteriological teaching, whenever the situation requires; but any time he is also able to deconstruct the terms he has used.

Another famous example is Linji. Much attention has been drawn to his notion of "an authentic person without rank." But little heed has been paid to his self-erasing of this "authentic person without rank." The saying that there is an authentic person without rank, just like many other sayings, is a kind of soteriological expedient pointing to the existential transformation of personhood. The words themselves designate no reality of any metaphysical Self or absolutized subjectivity. Linji knows well that someone, among his audience, may understand the notion in a reifying way. Therefore, soon after his proposal of this notion, he suddenly declares: "What kind of shitty ass-wiper this authentic person without rank is!" (*CJ*, vol. 11, 7349; *Rinzai_roku*, 52. Cf. *ZTML*, 13). It lets people feel that Linji himself is not so serious about this notion. In fact, this non-serious attitude is simply a strategy of self-erasing. The aim of this strategy is similar to Mazu's. However, Linji may be the one, among other Chan masters, who uses the clearest language to deconstruct all kataphatic terms that Chan Buddhists have been using, including those used by himself. Let us take a quick look at some of his sayings:

> [M]y insight is different: I make no choice between the secular and the sacred without, nor do I stay in the root and foundation within. (*CJ*, vol. 11, 7352; *Rinzai roku*, 94; Cf. *RSML*, 11.)

> [Y]ou must understand right now that the person here listening to the *Dharma* has no [fixed] form, no characteristics, no root, no foundation, no [particular] place he abides, yet he is vibrantly alive. (*CJ*, vol. 11, 7353; *Rinzai roku*, 105; Cf. *ZTML*, 36.)

> There is no Buddha, no [*Dharma*], no training, and no realization. . . . Do not be deceived.[35]

Linji also points out: "The true *dao* is without substance" (*CJ*, 7359; *Rinzai roku*, 159; Cf. *ZTML*, 62). As we can see, all those terms, such as *ti* (substance), *ben* (foundation), *fo* (Buddha), *fa* (*dharma*), *zheng* (realization), used either by others or by himself, have no legitimacy of reification. In this aspect, Linji is unmistakably clear and quite radical. He is most resolute and exemplary in taking a stance of free flowing with all things and circumstances. His de-reifying maneuver, as it stands in the text, should not be ignored by any scholar who intends to treat him with a fair and critical attitude. The entire *Linji lu* is full of the spirit and energy of deconstruction and self-deconstruction. One characteristic of his discourse, shared by the discourse of other Hongzhou masters, is the use of both kataphatic and apophatic language. The Hongzhou masters both reconstruct and deconstruct Buddhist themes, notions, and concepts. On the one hand, they ceaselessly deconstruct all terms including their own; on the other, they never stop using positive terms. Deconstruction, for Hongzhou, is not the end of all kataphatic discourses. It is the companion to kataphatic discourse. The principle is to meet the requirements of all moving situations. The movement and development of a situation call forth both the continuous use of positive language for soteriological purposes and the continuous use of deconstructive language for the same purposes. The Hongzhou masters are always aware of this call of practice. They echo it and do both at all times without hesitation. This may be a good lesson for our contemporary thinkers in dealing with the situation of "after deconstruction."

Notes

1. Robert Magliola, *Derrida on the Mend* (West Lafayette, IN: Purdue University Press, 1986), 96.

2. Bernard Faure, Chan Insights and Oversights: An Epistemological Critique of the Chan Tradition (Princeton, NJ: Princeton University Press, 1993), 225.

3. Faure, Chan Insights and Oversights: An Epistemological Critique of the Chan Tradition, 225.

4. Deconstruction here is regarded as a contextual strategy or a situational operation of overturning oppositional hierarchies with the characteristic of self-subverting. Its main target is reification or substantialization. This is my definition of deconstruction from which I will start to examine Chan Buddhist deconstruction. Obviously, this broad meaning of deconstruction is not limited to Derridean deconstruction.

5. "Originally there is no tree of enlightenment,/Nor is there a stand with a clear mirror./From the beginning not a thing exists;/Where, then, is a grain of dust to cling?" Heinrich Dumoulin, *Zen Buddhism: A History*, trans. James W. Heisig and Paul Knitter (New York: Macmillan Publishing Company, 1988), vol. 1, 133. I have made a minor change.

6. *Dacheng wusheng fangbian men*. See *T.* 85, 2834.1273c. For the original words of the *Dacheng qixin lun*, see *T.* 32, 1666.576b; trans. by Yoshito S. Hakeda, *The Awakening of Faith* (New York: Columbia University Press, 1967), 37. Note that I translate the Chinese word *xinti* as "the whole of the mind" and avoid translating it simply as the substance or essence of the mind. To my knowledge, the Chinese word *ti* originally involves the meaning of body and the organic whole. It may even be distinguished from the English word "subjectivity" which involves the meaning of substance in modern Western philosophy. However, the *ti* in Chinese philosophy nonetheless reflects the relatively static dimension of the whole and is distinguished from the dynamic dimension of the *yong*, the functioning, even though the two are often considered non-dualistic. This makes a privileging of the static *ti* possible and the deconstruction of it necessary. In the *Dacheng qixin lun*, although the use of the *ti* and *yong* is mixed with another term *xiang* and does not indicate a mature Chinese usage, it has been broadly admitted that the text is influenced by Chinese thought. My rendering of the *xinti* as the whole of the mind is thus to take into consideration the historical-cultural background of the text and of the ensuing Chan adoption. It avoids any ignorance of the difference between the Western metaphysical appropriation and the one we are now examining. For Shenxiu's quotation and the relation of his treatise with the *Dacheng qixin lun*, see John R. McRae, *The Northern School and the Formation of Early Ch'an Buddhism* (Honolulu: University of Hawaii Press, 1986), 175, 221-223. Hereafter *NS*. Also see Bernard Faure, *The Will to Orthodoxy: A Critical Genealogy of Northern Chan Buddhism* (Stanford, CA: Stanford University Press, 1997), 41-45. Hereafter *WO*.

7. In this regard, we agree with Gadjin Nagao's position. In his "What remains in *śūnyatā*," Nagao points out, the *Dacheng qixin lun* "seems to put more emphasis on 'the mind of suchness'…." See Gadjin M. Nagao, *Mādhyamika and Yogācāra*, trans. Leslie S. Kawamura (Albany: State University of New York Press, 1991), 60.

8. Yinshun, *Zhongguo chanzong shi* (Taibei: Zhengwen Chubanshe, 1971), 141. For the English translation, see *NS*, 195.

9. Yanagida Seizan has called this a sort of "Chan sickness," a word taken from the early Chan writings. See Yanagida Seizan, *Shoki no zenshi 2: Rekidai hōbōki*, (Tokyo: Chikuma shobō, 1976), 12. Hereafter *Shoki*.

10. I take this sentence basically from Wing-tsit Chan's translation. See *The Platform Scripture*, trans. Wing-tsit Chan (New York: St. John's University Press, 1963), 51. Hereafter, *PS*.

11. *The Platform Sutra of the Sixth Patriarch*, trans. Philip B. Yampolsky (New York: Columbia University Press, 1967), 138 (with minor modifications). Hereafter *PSSP*.

12. "If in successive thoughts you practice it, this is called true existence" (*PSSP*, 148).

13. Tang Junyi, *Zhongguo zhexue yuanlun: yuanxing pian* (Taibei: Xuesheng Shuju, 1984), 3-11.

14. Junyi, Zhongguo zhexue yuanlun: yuanxing pian, 29.

15. Roger T. Ames, "The Mencian Conception of *Ren xing*: Does it Mean 'Human Nature'?" in Henry Rosemont, ed., *Chinese Texts and Philosophical Contexts* (La Salle: Open Court, 1991), 145.

16. Rosemont, Chinese Texts and Philosophical Contexts, 145.

17. Rosemont, ed., Chinese Texts and Philosophical Contexts, 149-150.

18. See, for instance, Mou Zongsan, *Foxing yu boruo*, vol. 2 (Taibei: Xuesheng Shuju, 1977), 1041-1069; He Guoquan, *Zhongguo chanxue sixiang yanjiu* (Taibei: Wenjin Chubanshe, 1987), 244.

19. Here I follow Peter Gregory tentatively in translating *zhi* as "awareness." See his *Tsung-mi and the Sinification of Buddhism* (Princeton, NJ: Princeton University Press, 1991), 215. But note that Shenhui's notion of awareness or intuitive knowledge nonetheless involves the element of cognition, even though it is intuitive and different from ordinary knowledge. Cf. Jan Yun-hua, "Tsung-mi: His Analysis of Ch'an Buddhism," *T'oung Pao* 58 (1972): 1-53, 40, note 1. Hereafter "Tsung-mi."

20. See Shenhui, *Tanyu*, in Yang Zengwen, ed., *Shenhui heshang chanhua lu* (Beijing: Zhonghua Shuju, 1996), 10. This edition of the *Recorded Sayings of Shenhui*, which I use for this essay, is not only a synthesis, based on careful comparison and examination, of the previous editions by Hu Shi and D. T. Suzuki, but also includes the most recent discoveries of the different versions of Shenhui's sayings. Hereafter *SHCL*.

21. Nanyang heshang wenda zazhengyi, in *SHCL*, 67.

22. Zongmi, *Chanyuan zhuquan jiduxu*, *T.* 48, 2015.403a; Kamata Shigeo, ed., *Zengen shosenshū tojo* (Tokyo: Chikuma shobo, 1971), 95. Hereafter *Tojo.* Cf. Jan Yunhua's translation in his "Tsung-mi," 40.

23. Nanyang heshang wenda zazhengyi, in *SHCL*, 119.

24. Zong Mi, *Yuanjue jing dashu chao*, *Xuzang jing* (I will follow its conventional spelling, *Hsu tsang ching*, hereafter *HTC*), vol. 14, 279d. Cf. Jan Yun-hua, "Tsung-mi," 49.

25. Huangbo Xiyun, *Chuanxin fayao*, *Chanzong jicheng* (Taibei: Yiwen Yinshu Guan, 1968) vol. 13, 8975. Hereafter *CJ.* Cf. *Denshin hōyō*, *Ui Hakujū yakuchū zenseki shūsei maki* No. 2, 4-16. Hereafter *DH.* Also see. John Blofeld, trans. *The Zen Teaching of Huang Po* (New York: Grove Weidenfeld, 1958), 36-37.

26. Zongmi, Zhonghua chuanxindi chanmen shizi chengxitu. *HTC*, 110.437d; Tojo, 336.

27. *HTC*, 110.435b; *Tojo*, 307. For the English translation see Gregory, *Tsung-mi and the Sinification of Buddhism* 237. I have made some changes.

28. *HTC*, 110, 436d; *Tojo*, 326. For the English translation see "Tsung-mi," 52.

29. Zongmi, *Yuanjue jing dashu chao*, *HTC*, 14.279b. For the English translation, see "Tsung-mi," 47.

30. The Sayings of Mazu Daoyi. *Jingde chuandeng lu*, fascicle 6, *T*, 51, 2076.246a.

31. Huangbo Xiyun, *Wanling lu, CJ*, vol. 13, 8987; *DH*, 78-79. Cf. *The Zen Teaching of Huang Po*, 90.

32. *Linji lu*, in *Guzunsu yulu*, fascicle 4, *CJ*, vol. 11, 7351. Yanagida Seizan, ed., *Rinzai roku* (Tokyo: Daizō shuppan kabushiki kaisha, 1972), 79; cf. Burton Watson, *The Zen Teachings of Master Lin-chi: A Translation of the Lin-chi Lu*, (Boston: Shambhala, 1993), 26. Hereafter *ZTML*; Ruth Fuller Sasaki, trans.*The Recorded Sayings of Ch'an Master Lin-chi Hui-chao of Chen Prefecture* (Tokyo: The Institute for Zen Studies, 1975), 9-10. Hereafter *RSML.*

33. *Linji Lu*, p. 7357; *Rinzai roku*, 145. Cf. *ZTML*, 55; *RSML*, 27. It is alleged that this hymn was written by the Twenty-Second Indian Patriarch, Manorhita. Probably, however, it was fabricated by Chinese Buddhists. In any event, the hymn quoted by Linji reflects Linji's own thought.

34. See *Guzunsu yulu*, fascicle 1, *CJ*, vol. 11, 7310. Cf. Cheng Chien Bhikshu, trans. *Sun-Face Buddha: The Teachings of Ma-tzu and the Hong-chou School of Ch'an* (Berkeley, CA: Asian Humanities Press, 1992), 78.

35. *CJ*, vol. 11, 7357; *Rinzai roku*, 140-141;. Irmgard Schloegl, trans. *The Zen Teaching of Rinzai* (Berkeley, CA: Shambhlala, 1976), 44-45; Cf. *ZTML*, 53.

Eight

Sudao:[1] Repeating the Question in Chan Discourse

Frank W. Stevenson

The duality of unthought/thought (silence/language) has always pervaded metaphysical and onto-theological discourse. That this traditional duality is logocentric is assumed by Robert Magliola's differentialism, grounded to a degree in both the Derridean *différance* of signifier-signified and the negative dialectic of Nāgārjuna's tetralemma, particularly the fourth lemma ("neither x nor y") with its pure "negative reference." Differentialism plays off/between and indeed "re-inscribes" the traditional unthought/thought or inexpressible/expression rift in Hindu-Buddhist thought, just as Derrida's deconstructive discourse, ever parasitical upon its host, *plays* off/between similar rifts in Platonic and Hegelian discourse.

Here I want to explore the connection of unthought/thought with another basic duality or pattern of betweenness in Chan Buddhism, that of question/answer. This immediately presents itself in the most naïve but also pragmatic reading of the *gong'ans* (J. *kōans*), those *wenda* (J. *mondō*) or question-answer texts (dialogues).[2] I am going to suggest a way of reading the *huatous* and *gong'ans*—our primary "case" will be *Wumenguan* Case 43—which sees the answer not as "disappearing into," presumably a more traditional view, but as "repeating" the question. Or: the question repeats itself, is (always) already a self-repetition. I then will come back to Magliola's differential treatment of the same *gong'ans* and *huatous* and try to show that his own (off-) Derridean readings in effect take the answer as a repetition of the question. My own reading here is grounded in a certain priority: I look first at the dynamic-dialectical (off-Hegelian but also off-Heideggerian) side of the paradoxes, where the experienced *temporality* of question-answer is paramount, and then move to that purely logical-dialectical side which Magliola (given his Nāgārjunan/Derridean proclivities) tends (or first appears) to foreground. The real issue is then perhaps the identity-and-difference of these two "modes."

Between the Word-Head

Xuyun said:

> Our sect advocates the Chan training. This training centers on "realization of mind (and) perception of self-nature," that is, an exhaustive investigation into one's fundamental face . . . There were many *gong'ans* (devised by the ancients but) later only *huatou*'s [word-heads] were taught such as: "Who is dragging this corpse here?" and "What was my fundamental face before I was born?" In the present day, the masters use the *huatou*: "Who is the repeater of Buddha's name?" . . . [T]he reply to "Who?" will invariably be the same: "It is Mind." Word arises from Mind and Mind is head of (i.e. ante-) Word. Thought arises from Mind and Mind is head of Thought . . . *Huatou* = . . . the mind before it is stirred by a thought. It is the mind in its undisturbed condition . . . [it] is the moment before a thought arises. As soon as a thought arises it becomes a *hua wei* (lit. word-tail). The moment before a thought arises is called "the un-born." That void which is neither disturbed nor dull, and neither still nor (onesided) is called "the unending."[3]

According to this meditative technique the student wants to "look into the mind" (the *huatou*, word-head or thought-head, pre-word, pre-thought) *just before* "it is stirred by a thought": "The *moment before* a thought arises is called 'the unborn' [my emphasis]. That void which is neither disturbed nor dull [blank, empty[4]], and neither still nor (onesided) [directional, in motion] is called 'the unending.'" We note first that the traditional (post-Nāgārjunan but pre- Magliolan) Chan view clearly foregrounds the "betweenness"-state of the *śūnyatā*-void (it is "neither x nor y"). Secondly, there is the temporal factor: we are dealing with an "imminent moment," the moment just before the word-head (pre-thought, pre-word/language) becomes the word-tail (thought, word/language, "expression"). But this betweenness of the imminent moment (or moment of imminent arrival at a thought) is of course closely tied to the betweenness-state of the "void" (or "devoid"): "neither disturbed nor quiet, neither still nor in motion" is a kind of physical description of the state-of-mind just at that (passing) *moment* of "arising thought."

But what would it mean for the student to meditate on a question of this sort? Perhaps the question is "held in suspension" at the moment before it emerges into thought as an "answer;" that is, the student wants to remain "in the question," the question is prolonged. We might say the question is "opened out"—even to the point that it swallows up not just its "answer" but (what may be the same thing) the questioner, who "falls into" it. "When a student looks into a *huatou* with the same steadiness with which a broken tile when thrown into a deep pond plunges straight down 10,000 *changs* to the bottom, if he fails to become awakened in seven days, anyone can chop off my head and take it away" (*CZT*, 24).[5] Here we might think of Heidegger: *Dasein* is the being that asks the *Seinsfrage*, question of being, thus opening himself into being and/or opening (the) being in(to) himself. But for Heidegger the *Seinsfrage* is fundamentally temporal, is temporality itself.

The Chan "question" is also a process of holding-in-doubt, is itself a (continuous) "state of doubt" (doubtful or skeptical state of mind), suggesting again the prolongation just before the "arising thought," the indefinite delay of that thought/answer:

> When one looks into a *huatou*, the most important thing is to give rise to a doubt. Doubt is the crutch of *huatou*. . . . This doubt should not be coarse; the finer it is, the better. At all times and in all places, this doubt alone should be looked into unremittingly, like an ever-flowing stream, without giving rise to a second thought . . . one should take no notice of either stillness or disturbance. (*CZT*, 38)

Now let us consider one of the most basic word-heads: "What was (or is) my fundamental face (original nature) before I was born?" (The traditional answer is/was, of course, "Buddha's face," "Buddha-nature."[6]) Again, temporality: it seems the student may be trying to "think back" to his earlier, earliest, "original" face/nature, in which case it is an indefinite or infinite (infinitely delayed) task, since he could never get to that point/origin/answer. (Here we think of answer as "origin of the question.") One way to look at a continuously prolonged question is as an indefinitely repeated question, formulated not as a repetition of discrete question-sentences ("What was my original face?" "What was my original face?") as in "chanting Buddha's name"—which we assume would establish it as a word-tail, a thought, one which would indeed "disturb the void of the mind"—but simply as a (pre-thought, threshold-of-thought) "continuously prolonged question." This again is thought (or mind) before it is "formulated" in words/language, so the easiest way to see it is perhaps precisely as that "state of doubt" mentioned above. But the point is again: here we would be (in a moment) *between* a continuous state of doubt/holding in suspension—which might be seen as a pre-conceptual (pre-discrete) repetition—and a conceptual state of (discrete) repetition.

While a more traditional (and/or more Heideggerian) interpretation of the continuously-prolonged (pre-thought) question—of that state of doubt, questioning state of mind—as "opening out" so that the questioner (his self, being) "falls into it" might account for the pressure of this moment-of-betweenness (e.g., as a kind of Heideggerian *angst* grounded in being/nothing interplay), we need to see that the moment of betweenness is itself a form of mutual reflection—pre-thought reflects thought, thought reflects pre-thought—and thus of repetition. While the image of the falling stone does suggest that the *huatou* meditator falls downward toward the "unthought," perhaps to be swallowed up by it, an "answer" is in some sense always (already) expected, that is, an answer other than that of the question-abyss which itself becomes the (its own) answer. A conceptualized or "voiced" answer is also expected/demanded, even if we remain suspended as long as possible just at the threshold of that voiced answer. But this expected answer, rather than (like the question-abyss) swallowing/answering itself, that is, rather than merging with or becoming the (its own) question, can only "repeat" the question.

We do also get the between-state marked out in terms of (logocentric, phonocentric) audible/inaudible sound (inner/outer, divine/human, or human/divine "voice") imagery, which is perhaps one way in which the description or conception of it gets away from temporality (and thus closer to Plato and Husserl if not Derrida[7]). For this praxis of "looking into the *huatou*" is indeed also a kind of inward seeing-hearing:

> . . . you should unremittingly and one-pointedly turn the light inwards on "that which is not born and does not die" . . . you should . . . turn inwards your (faculty of) hearing to hear the self-nature. "To turn inwards" is "to turn back." . . . When "hearing" and "looking" are no longer in pursuit of sound and appearance, they become fundamentally pure and enlightening and do not differ from each other . . . . If there is singleness of thought abiding in that "which is not born and does not die," without pursuing sound and form, this is "going against the stream;" this is called "looking into the *huatou*" or "turning inwards the hearing to hear the self-nature." (*CZT*, 41)

But here again we are at a point/moment "between two voices"—between the "original (unthought) voice" (voice of original or Buddha-nature) and the "voice" of the thought just about to be expressed in language. One of the best-known Zen *kōans*, "What is the sound of one hand clapping?" indeed plays with(in) the betweenness of unsound/sound or unthought/thought (though not explicitly between original voice/"present" voice) in a more self-reflexive way. Yet one is struck here by "'To turn inwards' is 'to turn back'." Does it imply "back in time," the temporal reversal already suggested by the quest for "original face (voice)"? Do then all *huatous* have, does even "Who is dragging this corpse here?" ("Who are you? Who is the mind/original self inside your body?") have this dynamic? Of course it does, if we think of it as a question about "original nature." But do all *huatous* have this reverse-time dynamic because they are asking about absolute "origins" or because in all of them the prolonged question (state of doubt) is itself a structure-of-repetition which has the sense of "going back" (in time) merely in the sense of "repeating it again" (going "back" to it again and again)? "Turning inwards is turning back": prolonged questioning is repeating, suspended doubt is repetition.

My case is of course made too easy by the *huatou* which Lu K'uan Yu tells us is most commonly used "in the present day": "Who is the repeater of Buddha's name?" The answer is "my (non-)self." Lu explains that while this word-head can apply also to those Buddhist schools/chants in which Buddha's name was repeated out loud,[8] it especially applies to the silent meditative praxis of Chan. Then we have a variation on the above problem. Is the meditator silently repeating (discrete, voiced) "Buddha-names" (implying that he is already into the zone of thought, word-tails), or silently repeating pre-conceptualized (voiceless) Buddha-names (what would this mean?), or (as we assume) at the moment between these two "states"? While Lu suggests the meaning of the word-head ("Who is repeating?") is really (again) "Who are you? What is your original mind/nature?" its actual terms give us something arguably more complex and self-referential: the "who?" in question (self as itself a "question") is the "who" that is already questioning/pre-thinking/*repeating* (the question/pre-thought). This is again a clue that questioning itself can be seen as a form of (self-) repeating, with the accent on the (self-reflexivity of the) "self." It could suggest a form of self-inscription within a pervasive text/textuality.[9]

Here is Lu's comment:

> ...when one is asked, "Who is repeating Buddha's name?" everybody knows that he himself repeats it, but is it repeated by the mouth or by the mind? If the mouth repeats it, why does not it do so when one sleeps? If the mind repeats it, what does the mind look like? As mind is intangible, one is not clear about it. Consequently some slight feeling of doubt arises about "who." (*CZT*, 38)

Predictably (logocentrically) the "inner voice" of the mind is given priority over the "outer voice" of the mouth: the former repeats (the name) even in (dreamless) sleep, the latter only while we are awake.[10] The "deep sleep" image reinforces the notion of the pre-thought (pre-word) as dwelling in the deep mind/unconscious: yet even here we get the repetition. Also, the repetition-potential of outer voice/thought/language gets qualified here. Yet this whole "narrative" of mouth/mind is set within the context of "doubting," used as an example of the doubting-procedure: when asked, "Who is repeating the name?" we will question/doubt that it is x, then question/doubt that it is y, where the latter doubting (that "mind" is repeating it) leads to a more "positive conclusion" (*CZT*, 38), so that in a sense the repetition-potential of the mouth/outer voice, in being "doubted," is simultaneously (intra-textually) being reaffirmed.

"Goat Horns" and "Original Face"

Though *kōans* or *gong'ans* ("public cases," the *an* is also "problem," "*event*") may be based on the *huatou* form of simple ("What?" "Who?" "Why?") question, in them the master can ask the student to solve a dilemma or paradox stated formally as such: "What is X and not-X?" We get the formal dilemma in *Wumenguan* Case 43:

> Shoushan holds up his bamboo stick, and says: "You monks: If you call this a bamboo stick, there's an impingement [*chu*, a 'coming into-onto,' as a goat's

> horns can]. But if you don't call this a bamboo stick, there's a parting [*bei*, a 'turning one's back']. Tell me, all of you, what do you call it?"[11]

"Not calling X an X" is clearly problematic (a "wrong answer") if it means that we "call X a Y," but what if it means "not calling it anything," remaining silent? Is silence also a "wrong answer" or merely a "turning one's back" or "refusal (to speak)"? "Calling X an X" seems (at least on the face of things) to have a univocal sense, and it is less obviously wrong or problematical: the most obvious problem here would be that then we have only the "name" (a "stick") and not the "actual thing." But again I want to first emphasize the temporality of the scene here: the monks are under the pressure of time, they must quickly answer with either an "affirmation" or "denial"—where denial can have at least the two senses mentioned. Or perhaps they have another option, one that only the most enlightened would hit upon. If, with a *huatou* like "What was your original face?" we want to "look at the question," hold it in mind just at the moment of pre-thought/thought betweenness, perhaps a similar strategy exists here: a student might hold the dilemma or doubt itself in his mind—"Is this X or not-X?"—just at the "imminent moment," remain suspended just on the "verge" of answering. But this "non-answer" is effectively a (silent/spoken) prolongation, thus (as suggested above) repetition, of the question: it is the *dao*-"way" of a *dao*-"answer" as imminent suspension.

Wumen's comment here is "Not get it with words, not get it without words, *sudao* (quickly reply)!" Or: "Without words, without silence,[12] answer now!" This does strongly suggest that we take the "Don't call it an X" as a silent "response," but either way we "can't get it" ("get the answer"), whether with a voiced assertion ("It is an X") or a silent non-assertion. (On the doubt-model of the *huatou* the latter would be the "denial" of a "not-thinking this is an X," the pure negative reference of the Nāgārjunan fourth lemma perhaps, which we would still need to distinguish from the "not-thinking it is anything"; this last comes closer to a complete "not-thinking" or total "silence.") The paradox of this dynamic (temporal) dialectic then becomes: "You must answer now, but you can't get the (right) answer either with words or without words." We are thrown back into a temporal-logical pattern in which the question (statement of the either-or dilemma) is effectively repeated. To "get" the answer (in other words to "get" the question) I would have to "answer now" by hanging in the moment between question (pre-thought, state of doubt of the dilemma itself) and (voiced) reply, where either (any) reply ("It is/is not X") would be "wrong." But this imminent or "arising" ("Answer fast"!) in-between state can be read as a "between of the between" since effectively we are between the imminent unvoiced/voiced state of the *huatou*'s "prolonged doubt"—which corresponds to the ambiguous (pre-thought/thought, unvoiced/voiced) option of "not-calling X an X" or "not-getting it without words"—and the voiced/thoughtful/logocentric answer, "X is X," "not-getting it with words." Of course, then there "is no answer"—but that is precisely what the "question" was telling us in the first place.

The answer could only be a repetition or "reformulation" of the question, of the temporal-dialectical *demand* (to be answered) of the dilemma; that is, it could only be a repetition (yielding a still more "imminent," more narrowly "in-between" state) of the question-answer (temporal-logical) betweenness.

Magliola's reading, which takes this *gong'an* mainly as a logical-dialectical (synchronic) "thought-exercise," gains momentum by interpreting the two Chinese terms. Magliola distinguishes his off-centric or differential reading from the logocentric Chan reading. In the logocentric reading, *chu* and *bei* mean simply (univocally) "assert" and "deny," and the dilemma is essentially that of medieval nominalism-realism:

> If one becomes too attached to the name, the word-sign "bamboo stick," one "falls for" the correspondence theory, and slights the real bamboo stick, which is, after all, other than its name. . . if one refuses the ability of the name, the word-sign "bamboo stick," to correspond to its referent, one cannot seize the real bamboo stick at all. ("Differentialism," 90)

Now Magliola's differential reading, which needs to bifurcate one of these two terms (*chu* and *bei*) so that we can get an X/Y versus a Y, that is, get an "and/or which is between the and/or of X and Y," relies on a highly suggestive and playful reading of the character *chu*. Its primary sense is "impinging on" (like a goat's horns) in the sense of "becoming attached to" or "involved with": thus "to assert," where the name has impinged upon its referent. But its secondary sense, Magliola claims, is to "impinge" in the sense of "bang into," "give offense to," thus correlating it with the meaning of its supposed "opposite" *bei* which clearly means "turn one's back on," "give offense to." "Perhaps it is with this recurrence in mind that Inoue recognizes *chu* and *bei* can have the 'same' meaning" ("Differentialism," 90).[13] We thus have a pattern of *chu*-entanglement/offense versus *pei*-offense, a further (more literal) refinement of *chu*-affirm/deny versus *bei*-deny, and—picking up Blyth's comment on another Chan *gong'an* that "You must do one thing, and at the same time do-it-and-not-do-it"—Magliola correlates the *chu*-entanglement with "not doing one thing" and the *chu*- and *bei*-offense with "doing one thing." "In short, the meaning of *bei*, which 'does one thing,' is reinscribed in *chu*, but in a veiled way, so that *chu* both 'does one thing and doesn't do it.'" That is, the logocentric meaning/discourse is reinscribed within the differential (and for Derrida "parasitic") meaning-discourse:

> If we . . . elevate the above to a sort of paradigm, it can become an analogy for the workings of the Buddhist "two truths" (*saṃsāra*/*nirvāṇa*). Buddhist bliss becomes the "free slide" to and fro, and performed at will, between "doing it/not doing it" [because there is a subversion of coherent meaning(s), this is differential] and "doing it" [because there is a retention of coherent meaning(s), this is logocentric]. In short, Buddhist bliss is the free slide between the differential mode and the logocentric mode. And each mode, while bearing its own

> integrity, is "shot through" with the "sameness" of the other mode, the "sameness" of reinscription . . . . ("Differentialism," 91)

Magliola further describes this reinscription, in the context of the logic of paradox, as a strategy of "taking the paradox literally." Thus while for logocentric thought either "X = 'all and only Y' and 'all and only not-Y'"—which is "a logical impossibility, so that the two logically preempt each other, and the mind is exploded into non-reason"—or "X is 'part Y' and 'part not-Y" (a "synthetic or mediating approach"):

> Differentialism, when tracking the logic of paradox, finds itself led to neither of the two customary solutions, but to reinscription . . . . Derrida is well-known for his assaults on traditional paradox, and on mediation in general. He regards them as mere "dialectical" variants of what has already been deconstructed . . . . Blyth . . . represents for us that movement in Ch'an which stresses literality—the logical literalness which refuses mediation. "The most important thing" about paradox, he reminds us, "is that it should not be explained away." Otherwise, he says, the sage is a "mere punster" and his *mondo* [*wenda*, question-answer] just "pseudo-Zen riddles." But how does reinscription work in terms of paradox?...[W]e are granting...that somehow *Wumen*'s paradox is "delivering" the solution. . . We are taking the Buddhist "at his word" . . . What remains is to take the paradox literally, i.e., at its word as expressed in rational terms. If "X is Y and not-Y" . . . then Y and not-Y are the "same." . . . Thus the recourse of off/reason, the hard dreadfulness of reinscription. The differentialist solution to *Wumen*'s paradox is "'with words' and 'with words,'" or, reversing direction, "'without words' and 'without words.'" This is a special kind of redundancy whereby the first term hides itself in the second term and usurps it. [Thus] the differentialist solution to *Wumen*'s paradox is "'with words,' and (veiled) 'with words,'" or . . . "'without words' and (veiled) 'without words.'" A Buddhist "sameness which is not identity." ("Differentialism" 92-93)

Now one might wonder here why, since "Y" and "not-Y" are (literally) "the same," we wouldn't also have the option of saying (in addition to "Y and Y" and "not-Y and not-Y"), "Y and not-Y," "with words and without words." In this case we would be reading the "Y and not-Y" literally, non-paradoxically, not-thinking (it as a paradox)—the praxis of not-thinking, which is what we are after. Although (Magliola's point) it is in not-thinking-it as a paradox that we think it as "Y and Y," "not-Y and not-Y," why not also "literally" (non-paradoxically) not-think it as "Y and not-Y"? Might this not also be a form of reinscription?

In any case the term "reinscription" suggests—and this view is reinforced by the fact that "with this recurrence in mind . . . Inoue recognizes *chu* [assert or assert/deny] and *bei* [deny] can have the 'same' meaning"—that we are now fully "caught" within a logical recursiveness which entails/is entailed by an intra-textual (intra-language) recursiveness, an on-going repetition which offers no possibility of "escape" from language/thought/logos, caught within the field of "free play," "free circulation of signifiers" in which, perhaps, any combination might come around. Derrida sees the "essential structure" of language/meaning as being one of iterability and citationality (within the pervasive language-machine),[14] a view which bears a certain relationship to the early Wittgenstein's notion of logical tautology ("Y is Y") as the redundancy of "pure logical form." Do we then read Magliola's "With words and (veiled) with words," where the "without words" has been usurped/appropriated/reinscribed as "with words," as merely this potential for any (randomly-chosen) signifier—though perhaps *a fortiori* one which signifies the "logical form" of the whole machine—to substitute for another? After all, they are all mere iterations or citations, "quoted usages" within the larger text, the larger "style" which, like the "veiled woman" of Nietzsche's *operation feminine*, as described in Derrida's *Eperons*, finally "puts all the truth in quotation marks."

Magliola holds of course that a full escape from thought/language becomes logocentric (the non-rational absolute being just as "essentialized" as the rational one), yet he wants the "Way of the Between," wants to "frequent the 'unheard-of thought' and also, 'with one and the same stroke,' allow the reinstatement of the logocentric too . . . ," since "for Nagarjuna the 'beyond knowing' allows for logocentric, i.e., language-bound knowing (in a way which frees him from Derrida's quandary concerning entrapment in language)." But how, again, does this apparently pervasive intra-textual model of "reinscription" allow us to get to or on this "Way of the Between," how does it give us a glimpse of the "unheard-of thought"? We assume the "silence" Magliola is after here lies precisely in the "betweenness"—that it is the silence/unthought between the (logo-phonocentric) "sound" of assertion and of non-assertion. But as long as we remain within the synchronic, logical-dialectical-linguistic model suggested above, it seems the silence of betweenness only comes in patterns of *repetition* within the larger system—becoming thus an off-silence and perhaps what Magliola would indeed want.

But let us return to the basic question-and-answer structure of our *gong'an*. The sage asks you to answer him by asserting/denying, using words/not using them: the "silence" of your answer (and/or of your understanding/enlightenment) can only be in some sense a repetition of (the silent or off-silent, unthought or off-thought kernel of) the question. This is already clear in Magliola's dialectical working out of the "solution": if the sage asks, "How can you (not-) think 'Y and not-Y'?" you must "answer" by (not-) thinking "Y and Y" or "not-Y and not-Y" (repetition with variation of the question) or (possibly also) by (not-) thinking "Y and not-Y" ("full repetition"). We get a variation on this, which points us toward a more empirical-temporal reading of the same *gong'an*, if we take the "silence of the between" here, and/or of the intra-textual (narrative, dialogic, question-answer) repetition, as lying in the very asymmetry of the Way of the Between itself (and/or of the *gong'an* itself, the "text") as an "off-track." In *Life-Worlds* Magliola speaks of the "law of aberrant reinscription" in Derrida's later texts, where "dissemination" becomes:

> the dissipating of decidability (the *dis*- here = in several directions), so that—like the case of a teletype machine out of whack—the aberrancy introduced within the limits of the machine brings about a random but inevitable return of several possibles, and these possibles are asymmetric to each other.[15]

Magliola's "unthought"—or rather interface of thought/unthought, or of (un)thought and thought/unthought—then could be seen to lie within the asymmetric nexus of (un)decidability, where any of several (logical) possibles may "return." This is in fact the whole strategy of "off-tracking" traces/*prajñapti* within the larger "body of textuality" that we get in Magliola's most recent book—taking textual "cuts" (*tranches*, as in "cutting" a deck of cards, the Mallarmean-Derridean dice-throw of *Dissemination*), looking for "unexpected" or "asymmetrical" linguistic-semantic connections and overlaps which seem "predetermined" (within the organic language-body, language-machine) yet "contingent" and so reveal the "continuity of rifts." But here I want to come back to my problem of Chan "question(ing)." To think (of) the unthought-unthinkable, inexpressible or "silent" side of the logos/off-logos difference here as lying in the open-ended nexus of pure contingencies, pure possibilities might just be to think (of) it as the radically open-ended and contingent nexus of the "question" itself—the question which could have any number of answers "returning" to it, and/or could be unanswerable. But the question/answer (unthought/thought) duality remains indeterminate: the asymmetric self-returning possibilities, those signifiers/citations within the self-repeating language-machine in one model, might be seen as possibilities of the (still unthought) question itself, and/or as its (thought/unthought, silent/voiced) answers.

But then Magliola's view of reinscription, as I have tried to suggest by slightly "expanding" it here, while it may seem logical-synchronic, has been all along assuming, perhaps even grounding itself in the temporal-dynamic side of the dialectic. Thus we have the repetition-and-reversal pattern of "manifestation and return"—contingent meaning-possibilities spun-out and (always already, though perhaps asymmetrically) returned/returning. Similarly, the problem of an unstable-dynamic "origin" lies (unspoken but assumed) at the heart of the Magliolan off-Derridean reading of the quintessential *huatou*: "What is/was your original face?"

> "Before your parents gave birth to you, what was your prior face?" introduces a hierarchy, a signified (factor) and signifier (mirroring activity). The question it poses necessarily drives the disciple back away from the signifier (his present human "face") to the signified alone, the "prior face" or Buddha-nature. As such, the question forces the dyad of Buddha-nature and particularized human face to rupture. In our terms, the "word" is the signifier and the "ante-word" the signified, and the intent of the *huatou* technique . . . is to shear off the word, and to raise the question—with Chan's "*great doubt*"—of "who?" Eventually this "free signified" should dissolve too, crumbling during meditation before the . . . off/rational . . . which reaches up and deconstructs it. The result is supposed to be *śūnyatā*, "devoidness" . . .[16]

This may be a variation on our "classical" *huatou* model in which one strives for a point between the logocentric unthought ("original face" as transcendental signified) and the voiced word/thought ("my face"). Here again we are suspended in a between-state: (logocentric-voiced) word is "sheered off" and we are reaching (our earlier reading foregrounds the temporal-dynamic sense) toward the pure (logocentric-unvoiced) signified, which "should dissolve too, crumbling...before the off/rational which . . . deconstructs it." That is (we assume) this "free signified" (unthinkable original face) dissolves within the signifier-signified rupture, *aporia*, unbridgeable difference of devoidness. But the question or thought-problem of (thinking) one's "original self-identity" has again already "posited" this same (or a similar) difference: the gap where we end up is the gap of the "question" which has been, in a sense, repeated. Or recirculated: any question or notion of "origin" is for Nietzsche/Derrida/Magliola (always already) a "copy," "rehearsal," "transcendental signifier." The "original face" must have been "already recirculated" as copy/rehearsal/signifier. Thus if the question posed by the *huatou*—the question of "who?"—"necessarily drives the disciple back . . . to the signified [transcendent origin] alone" then the question was by definition unanswerable, that is, "answerable" only by a breaking-down (of it) into (*śūnyatā*/devoidness as) the ongoing "return" of (asymmetric, contingent, off-silent) answer-possibilities.

And as we have seen, the problem of origin as repetition is explicitly stated as *huatou* "question" in the case of "Who is repeating Buddha's name?" If we reach toward the "mind" (transcendental signified) as "original repeater" and away from the speaking/repeating "mouth" (signifier)[17]—here the mouth-signifier (Saussure's "sound-image") becomes curiously self-reflexive, making it perhaps harder to ever "escape" from the gravitational field of its "echo chamber" and move toward the "already" self-reflexive, autonomous, *causa sui* signified—we remain "lost" (or perhaps for Magliola "found") within an indefinitely recursive (self-reflexive) pattern of "answer as repetition of the question." Indeed we might say that not only the (self-) "repeater" but also the whole dialectical pragmatics of question-answer is here placed within some sort of encompassing, indefinitely recursive, self-repeating "text."

"Open Mouth See Guts"

In the *Biyan lu* Case 3 we have a slightly unusual reversal of the typical *gong'an*'s question-answer dynamics (or "directionality"). Here the master answers an "ordinary question" (put by a student) with a paradoxical answer:

> Grand Master Ma was unwell. The temple superintendent asked him, "Teacher, how has your venerable health been in recent days?" The Great Master said, "Sun Face Buddha, Moon Face Buddha." ("FDD," 13)

What first strikes one here is that the paradox is given as answer to a question so open-ended as to be meaningless. "How are you?" is a question of ("mindless") ordinary conversation, a merely ritualized, formulaic question: this is clear when we contrast it (as polite "student's question") to the "philosophical" student's question ("What is Buddha?") or the *huatou*, or *kōan*, or paradox-questions posed by Chan masters.[18] The "openness" of this question, which could have any number of answers, contrasts with the openness of *huatou* questions like "What is your original face?" ("What is your Sun-Face-Buddha?") For in a quite different way "How are you?" is meaningless in its very openness (all-inclusiveness, as in "X = Y") and thus is answered/echoed by a paradox that transcends sense. The answer then could again be read as a certain form of repetition of the question, with variation. But in the "form" of the *kōan*, we also see a role-reversal: we might have expected the student to inquire about one of his "homework" *kōan*-paradoxes, "What is Sun-Face-Buddha/Moon-Face-Buddha?" and the master to answer with the absurdly incongruous, "How are you?" This context also makes clearer, now that we are forced to take it seriously, the radical open-endedness, thus meaninglessness, of such an "ordinary conversation" question and so of ordinary conversation. Thus this "expected" sequence is an inversion of the actual sequence here. They are both variations on "answering nonsense with nonsense," arguably what takes place in—is the "form" of—all *gong'an*'s.

In Chan tradition this "Sun Face Buddha" suggests eternity and "Moon Face Buddha" transience, fleeting time. Thus in reply to "How are you?" the master may be saying "I am alive/dead (alive and already dead)." The commentary goes: "Sun Face Buddha, Moon Face Buddha. When he opens his mouth you see (his) guts (*kaikou jiandan*[19]). Like two facing mirrors: inbetween there's no reflection." Magliola ("FDD," 13) comments on this "open mouth see guts": ". . . if the two Buddhas are one and the same (though not, of course, the logocentric 'self-same'), indeed you can see the viscera when the mouth opens—there's nothing inbetween! (Notice how this Buddhist text is 'somatic,' 'inscribed as human body'[20] . . .)." That is, if X is Y (mouth/mind is body or mouth is mind/body, the space between them collapses or disappears) I don't care, there is no "I," "I" am non-attached to all dualities such as sun and moon, mouth (active speech, life, perhaps being-awake as we saw in the *huatou* of the mouth/mind) and guts (transience, death, decay).

Both terms then could be *aporias*: *dan*-guts/gall could suggest both (logo- or off-centric) body and (logocentric) inner nature,[21] while *kou*-mouth could be both a merely physical (logo- or off-centric) "outer voice" like the one that talks/repeats Buddha's name only while we are awake (unlike the mind), and a (logocentric) "inner voice" (Derrida's Platonic sun-logos). Here we come back to the unthought/thought or silence/language betweenness, already suggested by the equivocal or *aporia* term "mouth" ("voice"). It is the same sort of betweenness we saw in our brief analysis of *huatou*'s: the moment just before pre-thought/pre-voice passes into thought/voice. "Open the mouth" could thus mean "open the mouth to speak" and/or "open/fall into the abysmal question," it catches both senses simultaneously in the "moment of opening." But then is the question we fall or open into to be the "guts"—"open mouth see guts"—as inner/deep body and/or as deep mind/nature ("moon" as unconscious)? We open the mouth—paradoxically (simultaneously) speaking and silencing the mouth—and fall into the silence of the deep mind/body? Or perhaps the fall/opening also goes the other way, from guts to mouth, into the opened question of the open mouth? Perhaps the fall from speech to silence is simultaneously one from silence to speech?

The last part of *Wumen*'s comment reads: "Like two facing mirrors: in-between there's no reflection." Magliola focuses on this line:

> A reflection is a signifier, just as mirrors are the receptive apparatus (and, in Buddhist allegorical terms, the mirrors are the "pure consciousness" which normally registers, without "attachment," all signifiers passing across it). The Commentary is making the point, however, that here there is no signifier at all . . . a signifier would be occlusive, not revelatory. . . In Derrida, absence-of-signifier would mean the "remainder" of the "pure signified" . . . —a "more" sur/passing even the sumptuous "free-play" of a Roland Barthes. ("FDD," 13-14)

Chan's "absence-of-signifier"—between two mirrors where "inbetween" there can be "no reflection" (no signifying of factors/signifieds)—becomes then Derrida's "opaque signifier": here "a signifier would be occlusive, not revelatory," it would (in the old Chan metaphor) simply "cloud the mirror" (cover it with dust). Thus (paradoxically) we seem to come closest to "having" a (transcendental) signified in this (pure) condition of the absence of any signifier/signifying (*signifiant*), a between-state of two purely-reflecting surfaces which are then reflecting . . . what? One another's pure "power of reflection" (of "signifying")? I should think that if there are no "occluding signifiers" here (signifiers which would have needed something to signify, something other than their own blank "source" in the mirror-surface), then the pure (blank) signified with which we are "left" could not escape the dynamic-differential fate of being an indefinite/infinite self-reflection and recursiveness—the on-going (postmodernist *mise-en-abime*, hall-of-mirrors) mirroring of mirrors (within mirrors). If this signified (sun = moon, mouth = guts, life = death) was the question-as-origin, it now gets repeated indefinitely (and "within itself," the problematics of an ever-narrowing betweenness both spatial and temporal) as its own "answer."

Thus we come back to our "question-answer" reading of the two mirrors in terms of a mutual "falling" or "opening-into" which reveals finally only the blankness of the question. It's a self-reversing movement, the "falls" (mouth to guts/guts to mouth) echo/repeat one another, the "question" (endlessly) repeats itself. It becomes the "non-sense" of its own betweenness. But if these two mirrors are "the same" they are still (as "signifiers") also "different"—sun and moon, mouth, and guts. Each is itself an *aporia*-term, a betweenness. There is also a certain asymmetry in their relationship: each can encompass the other, depending on how we "read" it. Sun/mouth can encompass moon/guts as the "open space" of logos-speech, in the heart or depths of which we find silence; moon/guts can encompass sun/mouth as the unlimited *khora* or body of "writing" of which "speech" is but one manifestation. Which come(s) of course to the same thing: the two sides of the sign, of language. This can also be seen as the *order* of sun-logos-male and the *chaos* of moon-body-female, where again either might be seen as encompassing the other.[22] But is there to be a mutual (non-) reflection between two "mirrors" when one encompasses the other, or is it precisely the image of the *mise-en-abime*, "abyss" of a hall of mirrors? Two "under-determined" mirrors, two "overdetermined" mirrors, one under- and one over-determined?[23] In any case they would "cancel each other out."

The Question of the Question

In *Derrida on the Mend* Magliola cites Streng, who distinguishes Nāgārjuna's "dialectical" from "correspondence" and "intuitive" truth-structures in Indian thought.[24] But beyond this picture of the Nāgārjunan tetralemma as a negative dialectic which, rather than "expressing an absolute by not-expressing it" (apophatic theology), simply (or not so simply) "denies the illusion that it exists,"[25] beyond the conception of a non-empty ("devoid") *śūnyatā*, of *nirvāṇa* as *saṃsāra* which points toward Magliola's differentialism as an off/rationality in which rationality is "reinscribed," most striking here is Streng's/Magliola's characterization of Nāgārjuna's "dialectic" itself. While it is not reified, "is never an independent force or first cause, but is operative only in relation to phenomenal or ideal entities [both of which it deconstructs]," this dialectic is nonetheless "the spiritual *answer* to the problem of grasping after self-existent entities. It is the means of quelling the pain found in existential 'becoming' which results from longing after an eternal undisturbed entity" (*DOM*, 93-94, my emphasis).

This is, when we see Nāgārjuna's tetralemma as a schema of (non-) assertion which reveals or points toward (*prajñapti* as "conductal clue") the devoidness of *śūnyatā*, the trace of thought/unthought or logos/off-logos difference, we are also seeing it as a praxis, a "way" (*dao*) of discourse/understanding /existence. If we "off-track" within this dialectical truth-structure then the dialectic is also itself a dynamic "off-track(ing)"—the "Middle Way" is an "Off-Way."[26] We have to keep in mind this dynamism of the whole dialectic, the directionality of the trace and dynamic force of the "one stroke" of dialectical betweenness—

> Nāgārjuna's Middle Path, the Way of the Between, tracks the Derridean trace, and goes "beyond Derrida" in that it frequents the "unheard-of thought," and also, "with one and the same stroke," allows the reinstatement of the logocentric too . . . (*DOM*, 87)[27]

—if differential Buddhism will be able after all to solve/dissolve the problem, open or close the *aporia* (*wumen*, "gateless gate") of post-structuralism, "go beyond Derrida" in this way (though here we are by no means being sent back to the Hegelian solution).[28] Magliola ties this sense/force of the Nāgārjunan dialectic as dynamic "Way" (process of change, of "transmutation") directly to the problematics of thought (language)/unthought (inexpressible) by quoting Sprung:

> It follows that the middle way is not a means to some final truth; it is not a path leading to knowledge. Whatever it is, it is the end of theory, and of [logocentric] knowing. It is the practice of wisdom, not a means to it. Is he [Nāgārjuna] telling us that the end of philosophical thought is not the answer to a question with which it began nor even the end of a quest, but the transmutation of "thought" into what is more than thought: into a "way"? Does the middle way not supervene at precisely the point where thought is driven beyond itself, having failed to achieve its aim—that of making sense out of all matters brought before it? Is the end of philosophy to discover that philosophical questions all along, were not in the service of philosophical answers? (*DOM*, 94)

Strung seems to suggest that when thought is changed into a "way" then the issue is no longer one of "answering the question" with which one "started." This raises the (no doubt unanswerable) question: does this sort of Nāgārjunan (and Chan) praxis then leave us "within" the question, within our questioning? Does the "way" supervene at the point where thought is driven beyond itself (into a way), having failed to "answer its question(s)," precisely because this way is the "way of the question"? Again we come back to the *aporia* of silence/language or unthought/thought. But if "answering" (as a positing or positive "determination") is logocentric whether occurring within thought/language or within an absolute state of silence/non-thought, we are left wondering about the more ambiguous (logo- or off-centric) status of (thought or unthought) "questioning"—of the Way of/as questioning. I am suggesting here that the way of questioning takes us "beyond thought" because it is what comes just before thought, that it is fundamentally neither thought nor unthought but pre-thought, always (already) emerging in the imminent zone or moment between silence and saying.

Loy feels that Derrida cannot go so far as Nāgārjuna in the direction of an "absolute silence" or "cessation of language":

> [For Nāgārjuna] the serenity (or "beatitude": *śiva*) we seek is the coming-to-rest of all ways of taking things, the repose of named things (*sarvopalambhopaśamaprapancopaśamah*). His commentator Candrakīrti (seventh century A.D.) glosses the verse as follows: "The very coming to rest, the non-functioning, of perceptions as signs of all named things, is itself *nirvāṇa*... When verbal assertions cease, named things are in repose; and the ceasing to function of discursive thought is ultimate serenity." Contrast this to Derrida's problematization of the difference between signifier and signified . . . For Der-

> rida, what is problematic is the relationship between name and concept; so it is not surprising that he concludes with an endless recirculation of concepts. But notice what is signifier and what is signified, for Candrakīrti: The nonfunctioning of perceptions as signs for named things is *nirvāṇa*. . . The important thing in Buddhism is that the coming-to-rest of our using names to take perceptions as self-existing objects actually deconstructs the "objective" everyday world.[29]

For Loy then Derrida remains trapped within language (as Magliola has also suggested) because while he questions or even "breaks down" all signifier-signified connections he limits (the possible domain of) his "assertions" to this zone of linguistic signs, so that he "concludes with an endless recirculation of concepts" (one might have said "signifiers" here); Buddhism wants us to "stop speaking" in a more radically empirical sense (tied directly to perception/understanding of objects in the world) and thus, in a more fundamental and final way, to "become silent." Coward, on the other hand, speaks of a school (Bhartṛhari's) of Hindu thought in which we do remain within language, within that "pregnant silence" which lies ready to explode/disseminate into speech/meaning at the very heart of language:

> The Absolute word-consciousness has within itself a trace, an impulse, toward differentiation into thought and spoken speech . . . there is a pent up pregnancy within *Śabdabrahman* that predisposes the silence of *paśyantī* to burst forth in thought and speech. The ultimate silence, after all negation and purification has occurred, remains within the unity of language. And that unity contains within itself the seeds of difference which create the possibility for the multiplicity of language to burst forth.[30]

And—here Coward takes us back to pre-"*Dénégations*" writings like "Violence and Difference" (on Levinas) and "Edmond Jabés and the Question of the Book"—this seems to be quite close to a certain theme in Derrida:

> Silence is seen [also] by Derrida to be dynamic in nature. Rather than being the cessation of language, as suggested by Sankara and Mādhyamika, Derrida's silence is the origin, the source of all speaking, and yet a source that locates itself in the quiet between the letters of his writing. Language, both ours and God's, originates not in God's speaking but in God's keeping still—it "starts with the stifling of his voice and the dissimulation of his face. This difference, this negativity in God is our freedom, the transcendence and the verb which can relocate the purity of their negative origin only in the possibility of the Question."[31]

Here of course we shift the terms of our discussion somewhat by bringing into play (the possibility or "question" of) a Judaeo-Christian, monotheistic discourse; but then no doubt we are already entering into "cross-cultural" terrain when we do (off-) Derridean readings of Hindu-Buddhist texts.[32] And arguably the same sort of "silence" is at stake—that is, the same human longing to dwell in a silence at the heart of language and existence, a silence which paradoxically itself longs to burst (as with the force of an exploding question) into sound and sense.

Notes

1. "Quickly say (answer)!" The comment on Shou-shan's question, "What do you call it?" in *Wumenguan* Case 43 is: "Not with words, not without words, quickly say!" (See the later discussion.) "*Dao*," speaking or going "through," can of course mean "way" as well as "say," as in the first line of the *Daodejing*—"*Daokedao, feichang-dao*"—often translated something like "The way that can be spoken of is not the constant Way." Needam claims in *Science and Civilization in China* (*History of Scientific Thought* II [Cambridge, UK: Cambridge University Press, 1954], 228) that the character for *dao* has a "head on the right and foot on the left" in its oracle bone form, suggesting a simultaneously contemplative/pragmatic way.

2. And here it may seem we are dealing with a quite non-Platonic form of dialogue.

3. Lu K'uan Yu, *Chan and Zen Teaching: First Series* (London: Century, 1960), 22-23, 37. Hereafter *CZT*.

4. Magliola quotes Streng: "Nagarjuna 'is not saying that the true eternal state of reality is a blank; the calmness of nirvana does not refer to an ontological stratum beneath or behind the flux of experienced existence.'" *Derrida on the Mend* (Indiana: Perdue University Press, 1984), 94. Hereafter *DOM*. See note 23 on "dark" versus "blank noise" (Serres, chaos theory).

5. These are the words of "Ancestor Kao Feng." A "*chang*" is "a measure of ten Chinese feet" (Lu's note). But wouldn't the true seeker of the "original face" have wanted his *own* head to be cut off?

6. Magliola (see later discussion) reads this "original face" in terms of the signifier (my own face)/signified (Buddha's face) split.

7. For Plato the divine/inner voice is of course the truer *logos*; against this "logocentric" voice Derrida sets the deferral or difference of "writing" based on the pure repetitions of "external memory" (*hypomnesis*). (See "Plato's Pharmacy" in *Dissemination*.)

8. Or in "language/thought"—paradoxically, since this way seems more robotic and thus "mindless"—perhaps it is Mindless because performed "in thought."

9. See the later discussion.

10. The Mind is "always speaking" (Buddha's name), even when we sleep—it is perhaps a kind of "constant *Dao*" where we take *Dao* as "speaking." The mouth/outer voice, though, only speaks while we are awake. This gives us an interesting variation on Descartes' final certainty (after much hesitation) that he is "not now dreaming." Descartes assumes that if he had merely dreamed the assertion "*Cogito ergo sum*" it wouldn't have been a "real thought," a "clear and distinct idea," thus wouldn't have "counted." The *huatou*, interestingly enough, virtually reverses the priority, since here the fact that the "voice" continues even in sleep is what validates it. (A key issue for Freud, and by extension Lacan—and Descartes?—is dream-sleep versus dreamless sleep; here the *huatou* presumably gives priority to the latter.)

11. Robert Magliola, "Differentialism in Chinese *Ch'an* and French Deconstruction: Some Test-Cases from the *Wu-Men-Kuan*," *Journal of Chinese Philosophy* 17 (1990): 87-97, 89. Hereafter "Differentialism." *Chu* has the *chueh*-animal horn radical on the left, but the lower part of the right-hand component is a graph often used for invertebrates. Thus its "positive" meaning as "come into/onto" or "attach" is really a physical "touching"—in one combination it means the "sense of touch" and, in another, an insect's antenna(e). It clearly also has (as Magliola says) the "negative" meanings of "ram," "offend." *Pei*, which has "north" over "moon," though "moon" here may mean "meat"—see the later discussion of *tan*-"guts"—means "back (side)," "reverse (side)," "behind," "turn one's back on" but also (sometimes) "to remember," "learn by rote." The senses of "re-

versal" and "rote memory"—Derrida's *hypomnesis*, contrasted with the Platonic doctrine of *anamnesis* or "living memory" in "Plato's Pharmacy"—are suggestive in light of the later discussion.

12. Magliola's suggestion. "Differentialism," 91.

13. "See Blyth, 281": Magliola's note. That they have the same and also opposite meanings is of course the key point. Both characters can clearly mean "offend" or "repel," thus "reverse"— are they the same because they reverse each other as in two facing mirrors (see the discussion of "Open Mouth See Guts")?—while the *chu* also (in its positive sense) means "touch." (See note 11.) But if the name actually "touches" its referent/signified/object might it not merge/disappear into it? Then we *would* after all have just the signified (word/signifier having disappeared)— apparently the contrary of *pei*-"refusing to assert" but also (more clearly than if we only have the "name" or "signifier" as in the interpretation Magliola suggests here) the "same" as it?

14. At least since "Signature Event Context" (1971); English translation, *Margins of Philosophy* (1982), trans. Alan Bass (Chicago: University of Chicago Press, 1982): 307-330.

15. Robert Magliola, *On Deconstructing Life-Worlds: Buddhism, Christianity, Culture* (Atlanta: Scholars Press, 1997), 159-160. Hereafter *DLW*.

16. Robert Magliola, "French Deconstruction with a (Buddhist) Difference: More Cases from the Gateless Gate and Blue Cliff Record," *Studies in Language and Literature of National Taiwan University* 3 (1988): 1-25, 10. Hereafter "FDD."

17. That mouth which "cannot speak/repeat while we are sleeping," as the mind can.

18. Though in fact we might say a novice's question of the form "What is Buddha?"—which could be met by the master's blow or, as here, his paradox—is just as formalistic or formulaic as "How are you?"

19. Here the character for open mouth (*kuo*) reflects/echoes the sun, while guts (*dan*) has the moon (meaning also "meat") as its radical on the left—and something very like that bold, offensive "goat-horn" on top of its right-hand component. This *dan* ("guts") in its first meaning is "gall;" then "courage;" "internal parts, e.g. of a vessel;" "tube of a tire, etc." "Gall" as in "gall bladder" and "liver bile (fluid)," thus a certain kind of "inner nature" (as in "courage," "guts"). Could *dan* then (also) have meant "inner nature" or "inner voice" in this sense, as contrasted with the "outer voice" of the open mouth? *Dan*'s possible sense as "inner tube" could lead to various more-or-less "convoluted" readings on the theme of (inwardly-coiled) repetition and recursiveness.

20. See discussion of *dan*-"guts"—especially as "inner tube"—in previous note.

21. Note 19 again: "guts" as "intestines" and/or as "courage," "inner spirit."

22. We may assume that Kristeva's semiotic *khora* encompasses, as a kind of infinite space or womb, as chaos or even nonsense, the "rational limit" of (male) symbolic-representational language, just as Derrida's body of writing as recursive possibilities of *citation* (more clearly figured as "mother's womb" by Kristeva, Cixous, and Irigary) encompasses logocentric speech, and just as the Nāgārjunan/Magliolan *śūnyatā* as devoid/difference (and *chaos*?) "encompasses." The problem then becomes the "symmetry" of a two-way ("equal") reflection of/as "betweenness" versus the "asymmetry" of a devoid/difference that encompasses. Hesiod's *Theogony*, the writing/written body of Nietzsche, Derrida and French feminism and Serres' "background noise" (see following note) suggest that "chaos" (whose Indo-European root *gheu* means "yawn," "gape" and "gums") encompasses "order."

23. I suspect there may be (as yet unexplored) connections between the Nāgārjunan/Derridean/Magliolan dialectic—*śūnyatā* as the devoid(ing), off/rational, voice/unvoiced difference—and Serres' interpretation of chaos theory in physics in terms of "dark noise" (babble, nonsense, indetermination of primordial disorder) which first self-orders into (meaningful) "sound" (tuned in out of static on the radio) and then, as the hyper-logical order of logical tautology, becomes the overdetermined redundancy of

"blank noise" and "decays" back into "dark noise." (See e.g., *Genesis*, trans. G. James and J. Neilson [Ann Arbor: University of Michigan Press, 1995].)

24. While in the correspondence structure "language and reality, here the 'ultimate reality,' can match and the 'logic of mutual exclusion' holds," in the intuitive structure the "'whole point of inner control is to realize one Reality pervading each particular manifestation of the Reality' . . . and the 'logic of convergence' holds." But the "'dialectical structure' . . . escapes the principle of identity and does not impute identity of any kind to *śūnyatā*" (*DOM* 93).

25. Thus simply "not-expressing" it, or "not-expressing by not-expressing" it. The latter formula suggests the imploding series of metalanguages which are Magliola's Nāgārjunan *prajñapti*.

26. Nāgārjuna himself calls of course his Way the "Middle Way" (hence *Mādhyamika*).

27. Magliola continues here: ". . . for Nāgārjuna the 'beyond knowing' allows for logocentric, i.e., language-bound knowing (in a way which frees him from Derrida's quandary concerning entrapment in language); and still Nagarjuna's 'beyond knowing' is not itself logocentric" (*DOM*, 88-89).

28. Well, arguably it remains an open question—opened in "another" way by the synchronic move beyond Hegel of French (post)structuralism.

29. Harold Coward and Toby Foshay, *Derrida and Negative Theology* (Albany: State University of New York Press, 1992), 249-250.

30. Coward and Foshay, *Derrida and Negative Theology*, 211.

31. Coward and Foshay, *Derrida and Negative Theology*, 221. Coward is quoting Derrida in "Edmond Jabes," *Writing and Difference*, trans. Alan Bass (Chicago: University of Chicago Press, 1978), 67.

32. Cross-cultural "comparison" is of course the central thrust of Magliola's whole project.

Part Five

Deconstructing Life-Worlds

Introduction

Deconstructive operation does not and cannot limit itself to a deconstruction of a text. A reflection on the meaning of deconstruction tells us why that should be the case. Deconstruction functions by marking a gap in a text. The gap is not an exceptional occasion that happens only in a certain text but the reality of a text. That is because a text is written in language which is not a solid essence but works on a differential identity. A text always carries a gap in itself as well because it is a record of our thinking and we do thinking in language. What this consideration on the constituents of a text implies to us is that a text is never a closed entity, but an overflow of both written and unwritten meanings. An attempt to confine the unbounded-ness of a text can be made only by an intentional act of exclusion.

This also tells us how the relationship between theory and practice changes in deconstruction. The Western philosophical tradition has maintained the position that philosophy does not have to include practice. The illusion that philosophy is not involved with the realm of practice has blinded us to believe that in philosophy we speak a purely objective language in our search for the universal Truth. Some have contended that because philosophy deals with the objective Truth, it speaks a language, which is gender neutral, which is not ethnographic nor a reflection of a specific social class. However, philosophy is performed by and through language that is always already differential; philosophy is written in a text whose meaning is subject to context; and philosophy is done by a philosopher who is a concrete reality with a gender, ethnicity, and specific social class. Deceiving us into thinking that it is not involved with the particularities in life-worlds, philosophy has justified a transformation of a small "t" (truth) into the capital "T" (Truth). Such a practice in philosophy has also been reflected in the structure of our life-worlds, in which the dominance of a particular (small "t") truths acting as the (capital "T") Truth in the exclusion of other small truths has become a regular practice. Deconstruction of the philosophical appropriation of a written text, then, cannot but be extended into a deconstruction of another text which we call *life*. A life-text is like any texts in the world: fully charged, context-bound, and inscribed within past, present and future.

Robert Magliola's experiment (if we may call it that) with his own life-text in his book-text, *On Deconstructing Life-Worlds: Buddhism, Christianity, Culture*, gives us some ideas about the scene of the encounter between philosophical differentialism and life-worlds. As Youru Wang states, "Reality itself is deconstructive." The violent function of trace and *différance* (or karma and dependent co-arising) is always already there, fully functioning regardless of our awareness or non-awareness of their operation.

Jane Augustine reads the "text" of Magliola's book, in which "the inscription of a Christian personal history lies crosswise under his Derridean Buddhist deconstruction," from the perspective of her own life-text as a Buddhist practitioner. Violation of the rules/laws of genre is inevitable here. Not only the boundary between philosophy and religion, but those between philosophical theory and practice, between Christianity and Buddhism, and between fiction and truth(s) become blurred as these genres become intertwined in Magliola's text: life inscribes them all. This, however, must be distinguished from "anything goes" logic, with which both postmodernism and Asian thought (especially Chan Buddhism) have frequently been confused in the West.

Locating Robert Magliola's work in the "differential" space between Buddhism and Christianity, Eastern practice and Western intellect, and philosophy (theory) and experience (life-worlds), Augustine describes Magliola's deconstructive literary style as arising from his meditations on Buddhist *śūnyatā*. Augustine sees that Magliola's familiarity with *śūnyatā* deconstructs his Christian training, which is noticeable in his interpretation of the temple "veil rent in twain" at Jesus's death. The "veil rent in twain" to Magliola is a revelation of the "God rent 'between'." The veil rent in twain also represents Magliola's life itself as he describes it as being caught in the double-cross, the chiasm between *saṃvṛti-satya* and *paramārthasatya*, *saṃsāra* and *nirvāṇa*. Exploring the deconstructive movements in Magliola's life, Augustine is convinced that when theology is deconstructed through Buddhist *śūnyatā,* that is, "[w]hen the conceptual veil is torn, it is not nothing that is revealed." Instead, "A primal vow, an ethical choice," Augustine writes, "came with the liberation of intelligence, *prajña,* through the emptying-out of fixed ideas, that is, through suffering."

Unlike Augustine, who confirms the possibility of ethical commitment in Magliola's Buddhist deconstruction, Gad Horowitz criticizes Magliola's deconstruction in particular and Buddhism in general for their failure to provide a source of ethical obligation for an individual. According to Horowitz, Magliola's Buddhist/deconstructive interpretation of life's "double bind" is based on his profound acceptance of the various contradictions of life. Magliola, however, allows one exception: one's obligation to loving-kindness, one's binding to other human beings. Horowitz notes that by this statement, Magliola exempts the ethical obligation from the double-binding context of life. "What is the secret of the happening of this divine exception?" Horowitz asks. To Horowitz, "Magliola's Buddhism—like Buddhism in general—does not seek to account for the *ethically obligatory* quality of the Buddhist vow." Horowitz finds the ground for this vow in Emmanuel Levinas, in whom "this 'must' precedes the ego 'I', as its inescapable orientation to the other which is not an alter ego...but the inaccessible, inconceivable, non-phenomenal, always already past and always to come . . . vulnerable yet Authoritative Other . . . ." Hence, to Horowitz, the ethical question Śākyamuni faced "after" his enlightenment regarding whether he should or should not share his enlightenment with others should come "before" his enlightenment. The priority of the ethical is not logocentric or theocentric, Horowitz argues, for it "has always already come 'before' any 'first'." Horowitz concludes with the claim that this Levinasian ethic as a first philosophy is also central to deconstruction as he finds it in the recent works of Derrida, which strongly suggest that there is a logic of ethical testimony at work in deconstruction. (JYP)

Nine

The Veil Rent in Twain: A Buddhist Reading of Robert Magliola's Deconstructive Chiasm

Jane Augustine

Philosophy is the enemy of experience: that rubric heads this essay, this attempt. It is not a proper philosophical essay, formally argued, but a congeries of fragments, "off-center," "differential," "off/rational" in Robert Magliola's terms, arranged as associated rather than connected ideas. Nevertheless, it tries to shape an argument: Magliola's brilliant, *sui generis* deconstructive literary style arises from his personal experience of *śūnyatā,* "emptiness" or "devoidness," within meditation as distinct from his intellectual encounter with its logic in the Mahāyāna Buddhist texts.

These meditations on the meaning and implications of "emptiness"—the essencelessness of all phenomena—emphatically deconstruct his Christian theology with its positing of a "real" God as Being, the ultimate essence. Caught in conflict, Magliola therefore interprets the Biblical account of the Temple "veil rent in twain" at Jesus' death to reveal a "God rent 'between'." Symbolic associations to the "rent veil," the cross or chiasm, the slippery "between," and Derridean "difference" open up his preoccupations: to stay "between" Buddhism and Christianity, eastern practice and western intellection; to compare Nāgārjuna and Derrida; to apply "devoidness" in the reform of Christian doctrine; and to stretch language to show how things 'go on.' His intricate, multi-tonal "differential" discourse, *sous rature*, makes a radical new contribution to post-modernist thought.

"Between"

Śūnyatā, which cannot be invented, only discovered, which is not a "holy" or mystical experience,[1] neither conceptual nor ineffable,[2] makes possible a literary form that deconstructs logocentric "reality," the phenomenal world made of concrete sense-data and abstract ideation. Magliola's language asserts, then denies. It crosses itself out in palimpsestic chiasm, leaving a trace of the erased under-text. It is *śūnyatā* thought-language, emptied of concept, non-existent.

***

The argument appears short-circuited. How to talk about something non-existent? Words tend to essentialize. They make a "thing" appear even if it's not "really" there. Pursuit of the argument means abandoning it in favor of narrative, metaphor, poetic symbolization, "off-center" language usages that inherently manifest *sous rature*, under erasure.[3] Poetry makes no truth claims *per se*. This shift in emphasis emulates Magliola's own move from organized philosophical exegesis in *Derrida on the Mend* to autobiographical, generically innovative disquisition in *On Deconstructing Life-Worlds: Buddhism, Christianity, Culture.*

***

"Christianity," a loaded term, intrudes awkwardly an experiential fact in the "text" of Magliola's life. Not fully erased, the prior inscription of a Christian personal history lies crosswise under his Derridean Buddhist deconstructions. It is what is deconstructed by *śūnyatā* and makes necessary that deconstruction. It offers an excuse for this essay's lopsided procedure through the explication of one favorite Magliolian word, "between," its cognates and associations in the account of the "veil rent in twain."[4]

***

In *Derrida on the Mend* (134), Magliola cites the New Testament account, in Matthew 27:50-1, of the rending of the veil of the Temple[5] when Christ died on the cross, that great, sad moment of final disillusionment for his friends:

> Jesus, when he had cried again with a loud voice, yielded up the ghost. And, behold, the veil of the Temple was rent in twain from the top to the bottom; and the earth did quake, and the rocks rent; . . . . (*KJV*)

Or, in the tamer, modern New Revised Standard Version:

> Then Jesus cried again with a loud voice and breathed his last.

> At that moment the curtain of the temple was torn in two, from top to bottom. The earth shook, and the rocks were split....

Magliola interprets this passage to mean that "the One God of the Jewish religion, of which the Temple is the allegorical type, was revealed to be a God rent down the middle (rent 'between')" (*DOM*, 134).

***

"Between" as a key term in Magliola's writing represents his effort to escape the net of logocentrism, that is, conceptualization. "Between" is not a noun; it doesn't quite name anything. It makes virtually no sense except through its linguistic cognates, "twain, twin, two," and its Germanic prefix "be-" with its implications of process going on, a conductal, slippery situation, the opposite of "be" as in "to be," *esse*, to be some clear-cut defined "thing" or essence.

Luckily, Magliola fell "between." Or not luckily but inevitably. "For nothing can be sole or whole/that has not been rent," said Crazy Jane to the Bishop, as overheard by the poet William Butler Yeats.[6]

***

Magliola is a logician. The Roman Catholic Church, specifically the Jesuits, prepared him intellectually to do what he does extremely well—philosophizing, following phenomenology's tracks to Derrida's logic, which he then embraces, annotates and expands. Jesuit intellectual training "took" in Magliola, just as an inoculation "takes" in one's body, by soaking into every tissue and staying there. He loves logic and reasoning; they drive him in his search for meaning. He is also in love with the abstract goals of that search—truth, goodness, ultimate reality—and wants to maintain them undivorced from the practical goal, justice in this world, now. He *will* make it "four-square," the city of God, the ideal society envisioned in the Book of Revelation (21:16).

Philosophy is the enemy of experience: therefore logic breaks down. Magliola is a passionate logician; therefore he practices contemplation as a Carmelite tertiary among Theravādin monks in Thailand. He writes passages of learned and meticulously-reasoned argument; therefore he criss-crosses his arguments with puns, coinages, *kōans*, metaphors, metonyms, definitions, derivations, prayers, exclamations, incantations, mantra, onomatopoeia, scriptural citations, anecdotes, cultural commentary, a mix of English with foreign tongues—Latin, Greek, French, German, Italian, Spanish, Japanese, Chinese, Sanskrit, Hebrew, plus nonverbal punctuation signs deranging and fragmenting these: slashes, hyphens, parentheses, brackets, capitals, italics, dashes, caesurae, irregular line spaces, excess letter spaces, stanzaic breaks, hexagrams, and ideograms from the *I Ching*—and when prefabricated print-forms run out, hand-drawn icons, a cross, a skull. And footnotes: genial loquacious *midrash* that revivify a nearly lost subgenre.

All this in place of deadly correctness, the solidified syntax that generates logocentricity. Rupture, disruption, rending, "cross-hatch," crux, cross, double-cross. The meanings of the words fall somewhere "between."

***

SWOOSH SWOOSH of the double-edged ("two-mouthed") sword of *prajña*—intellect—that cuts both ways, cutting the roots of both self and other.[7] The big X that Xs out belief in entities of any kind. The crucifixion of belief.

Life-worlds

In *On Deconstructing Life-Worlds*, narrative comes onto Magliola's *mille fleurs* linguistic playing-field, bringing experience to bear on philosophy in a reprise and amplification of the logic developed in *Derrida on the Mend.* More precisely: we see the actual beginnings of Magliola's discovery of *śūnyatā*, emptiness, or "devoidness," as he prefers to translate the Sanskrit, that is the "Middle Way" between nihilism and eternalism (*ODE*, 27). As a practical path between these extremes, *śūnyatā* itself manifests "between-ness" in the constant shifty interplay between its two aspects, known as the "two truths": the relative truth of the phenomenal or mundane world, *saṃvṛti-satya*, *saṃsāra*, and the ultimate or absolute truth, *paramārtha-satya*, *nirvāṇa*, "awareness of the essencelessness of things" (Misra in *DOM*, 95).

***

Corollary to the argument: Magliola's Christian practice and his Buddhist practice require each other, and both of them require emptiness.

***

On the Mend. We say people are "on the mend" when they are recovering from illness. Recovery takes place because of illness. The "mend"—that which is mended and the act of mending—takes place because of the rending. "The veil rent in twain" reveals *śūnyatā*, but there must be a veil to tear. Two aspects of reality, two truths.

***

When Jesus died on the cross, the "veil rent in twain" created a gap, an opening for a new idea of God to enter. But what is revealed is not so easy to say. One way it was said is that God "was made flesh and dwelt among us" (John 1:14). But Jesus was not merely flesh; he was the one on whom John the Baptist saw "the Spirit descending from heaven like a dove" (Matt. 3:16). The perennial insoluble philosophical question surfaced historically yet again: what explains the connection, if any, between form and non-form, or matter and spirit? Mahāyāna Buddhists attempt to answer this question by expounding the view of the *Trikāya*, or "Three Bodies"[8] under the non-theistic rubric of emptiness. Jesus' death launched the early Christian Church's ongoing theistic struggle to describe the concept of a Triune God. Magliola enters this ever-open field, observing that:

> Christ's revelation of the Blessed Trinity, when taken in its several scriptural formations, sends incongruent (better, 'decongruent') messages proclaiming a Trinity which is sacred différance. (*DOM*, 134)

His learned and exhaustive argument for a "differential" Trinity, that is, differing from the entitative historical formulations, is directed at both theologians and "off/thinking" mystics, both Christian and Buddhist, and is summarized in an analogy and word-play quoted from the 15th-century Christian Hebraist Johannes Reuchlin:

> as the four-lettered and hence "stable" name of God, (the Tetragrammaton, הוהי, or Yahweh) is "destabilized" by a fifth letter to make the Messianic name (the name of "Jesus," i.e., Joshua, השוהי adds the letter *shin* to the Tetragrammaton and means "Yahweh saves,"), so too does Christ's Trinitarian teaching subvert an entitative notion of God and announce a God of perpetual alterity. (*DOM*, 149)

The word-play, the key element here, is "off/rational," deployed in response to Derrida's "great contribution" and anguished recognition that:

> the logical disproof of logocentrisms such as self-identity reduce finally to a disproof of the very syntax of language, the very syntax of logic, the very syntax of thought; furthermore, that such disproof invalidates the disproof itself; and furthermore, that one nonetheless *cannot* (literally *cannot*) reject the disproof *nor* reject logic. One rides in-between, as it were. . . . (*DOM*, 151)

That is, "emptiness" also is empty. The thinker also exists in a constant state of change, alterity, moving between ideas, perceptions, reactions, "frequenting"—another favored Magliolian term—both *saṃvṛti-satya*, the relative truth of the appearances of everyday logocentric life, and *paramārtha-satya*, the ultimate truth that nothing exists behind those appearances. In undercutting the purported solidities of experience by philosophical reflection, we rend "the veil" that hides our intelligence and insight.

Multiple interpretations accrue to the "veil rent in twain" (*IB* VII, 609-610; *NIDNTT*, 794; *NIB*, 493; *JBC*, 64-65). Generally, it symbolizes the end of Judaism's view of God and of atonement, with its attendant rituals. The Letter to the Hebrews elaborates the symbolism: Jesus is the new High Priest who has entered the Temple's inner sanctuary, the "Holy of Holies," the presence of God, by the transformed blood sacrifice of himself to secure "an eternal redemption from sin" (Heb. 9:6-14). The rending of the veil—in Greek *katapetasma*, a temple curtain (*NRSV*, 96)—is here interpreted as symbolic of Jesus' tortured body on the cross:

> Therefore, brethren, since we have confidence to enter the sanctuary by the blood of Jesus, by the new and living way which he opened for us through the curtain, that is, through his flesh, and since we have a great priest over the house of God, let us draw near with a true heart.... (Heb. 10:19-22, *RSV*)

***

Magliola's "true heart" kept him going when he was turned out of the house of God, when both the church and its absolutized theology failed him:

> I identified with the starving Christ spindled on the Cross, torso arched out and sagging.... Without this precise Christ-figure, archetype for me of sacrificial love—the 'milk and honey' drunk in with my mother's milk, with my *italianità*—I could never muster the strength to *perdure,* to keep serving others. (*DLW*, 26)

If no theology offered meaning or reward, what made him want to keep serving others? A primal vow,[9] an ethical choice, came with the liberation of intelligence, *prajñā*, through the emptying-out of fixed ideas, that is, through suffering. When the conceptual veil is torn, it is not nothingness that is revealed (*ODE*, 2-3).

***

The 'veil' might also be seen as symbolizing the conceptual dividing line between life and death. When torn apart, it reveals a vision of a greater life, an inconceivably vast, beautiful, profound eternity that incorporates and obviates being born and dying, which are human beings' most binding preconceptions. The revelation comes through the opening or gap, an opening that is empty, lacking self-identity, *anātman*.

***

The Buddha saw that the "veil" of philosophy, or preconception, blocks intelligence. It has to be torn apart in order that light—enlightenment—may be shed on experience, that is, for human suffering to be relieved. The "veil rent in twain" reveals a greater vision—the God "between." "The tear is not ineffable, yet/you cannot name it" (*DOM*, ix).

Magliola—Veil Rent in Twain

But most clearly, the "veil rent in twain" represents Magliola himself, as is painfully shown in *On Deconstructing Life-Worlds*. Philosophy is the enemy of experience—that is, abstraction is the enemy of particulars, generalization the enemy of specifics. Philosophy, the high abstract medieval Christian theology of the Roman Catholic Church became the enemy of Magliola's development as a human being when, as a young man, he tried to take up a religious vocation—an experience that drove him close to madness.

X, the double cross. Pulled two ways at once, the rational mind searching upward, the "lowly" body starving, spindled on internal crux (*DLW,* 13, 26). Magliola's mind is somatic. When he is depressed, ill, unloved, he gets thin. When he sits in meditation, he gets "fat and sudsy" (*DLW*, 44). Food is love. You don't have to be Italian to know that—it's not a particularly theological truth.

"If a man learns theology before he learns to be human, he will never learn to be human," said Ludvig Holberg, the 18th-century Danish poet and metaphysician.[10] Theology imprisoned the young Robert and blocked, for a time, his learning how to be human. The highest good and truth that he knew created the obstacles that prevented him from realizing them in actuality. "Rent in twain," he fell "between" philosophy and experience into the human mess—that is, into the confusion of individual, partial, distorted consciousness hedged around by the world's confusions and aggressions, *saṃsāra.*

It was a liberating fall. His life became "unveiled." It opened up, became experientially rich, interesting, successful, sexual, riddled with mistakes and unhappiness, intractable, rendering up a new set of obstacles that drove him into his virtually unique four-track intellectual path with credentials in comparative literature, philosophy, Buddhology, and Christian theology.

But this very multiplicity of accomplishments testifies to felt impediment. No one language or discipline will suffice to express truth. In the preface to *Derrida on the Mend*, he outlines his quest, his motives, and the path that led him to write the book:

> For a considerable number of years I have been plying the fabric (*tantra*: 'warp-threads') of phenomenology, hermeneutics, and 'theory of text'. For a long time already I have been researching Buddhism. And...using Buddhist meditative forms—adapting them to my prayer life as a Carmelite tertiary. (It is fair to say, indeed, that my practice has been more rigorous than casual.) One be/wildering day several strands crossed: I found that Derridean deconstruction and Nagarjunist Buddhism, the former to dismantle the principle of identity, the latter to dismantle an entitative theory of *dharmas* resorted to the 'same' logical techniques. But in the Nagarjunist 'text'—as rational and off/rational discourse and as meditative experience—there is an 'excess', a 'surplus', which continues *dissémination* and still 'preserves' organic theories . . . while introducing a 'differentialism' which liberates and bears bliss. (*DOM*, ix)

"Differentialism" is the shortcut term that summarizes Magliola's revolutionary contribution to postmodernism. The "Nagarjunist 'text'," set in quotation marks, does not refer to a piece of writing, but to an experience of *śūnyatā*, the primal "devoidness" that is not at all a blank but is expressive, the unconditional condition that permits manifestation of the apparent phenomenal world (*ODE*, 3).

The metaphor of the "veil rent in twain" comports with Magliola's metaphors of "fabric," "strands," "threads." The Sanskrit word "tantra," literally "thread," in Buddhist context means "continuity," referring to that which continues throughout the cycles of birth and death as well as to a set of advanced Indian and Buddhist practices. The "thread" also metaphorizes *pratītya-samutpāda*, "dependent co-arising" of phenomena which have no independent existence, the world of appearances ("CHW," 30). Magliola quotes Nāgārjuna, linking his insight with Derrida's:

> We declare that whatever is relational origination [dependent co-arising] is *śūnyatā*. It [*śūnyatā*] is a provisional name [i.e., thought-construction] for the mutuality (of being) [dependent co-arising] and, indeed is the middle path. (MK XXIV: 18; quoted in *DOM*, 116).

Magliola adds:

> Notice that even the name and concept of *śūnyatā* are "provisional," i.e., "crossed out." *Śūnyatā*, like Derridean *différance*, should not be hypostasized and cannot be framed by ratiocination. Remark as well that *śūnyatā* is the "middle path." Clearly, Nagarjuna means *middle* in the sense of *between*, tracking its 'and/or' [absolute constitution and absolute negation] *between* the conventional 'and/or' proposed by entitative theory. *Śūnyatā* is not voidness but devoidness.

If Derrida and Nāgārjuna are two strands in the weave of Magliola's deconstructive thought, "Carmelite tertiary" too cursorily summarizes the third strand, his Christian religious practice which would seem necessarily imbricated in the essentializing *nominans-nomen*, "God." It is a crux, the crux, cross-roads, *carrefour*, intersection. What becomes of his Christian practice after *śūnyatā* unpacks the Christian theology that so deeply formed him? It is a life question, not a theoretical one.

The relative truth of the emptiness of the phenomenal world actually begins to be experienced by everyone at birth, in bewilderment. Nothing makes sense; every assertion is contradicted. Education comes later, the necessary effort to make sense, that is, to impose concepts and make the world workable.

Magliola discovered absolute truth—the devoidness of concepts—through intellectual investigation of the Prāsaṅgika-Mādhyamika, particularly the Mādhyamikan dialectic of the tetralemma, the logical "four-square." With the Prāsaṅgika-Mādhyamika, he refuses to posit any construction that might arise after deconstruction. He rejects the Yogācāran "mind-only" position and assertions of "buddha nature" that sometimes appear in Zen texts (e.g., *DOM*, 96). He calls these views "centric" Buddhism, too conceptual and in that respect no different from "centric" Christianity. Although he asserts as the profound basis of his logic the fourth lemma of the Mādhyamika dialectic—"phenomena are neither existent nor non-existent"—he recognizes that the "emptiness of emptiness" permits logocentrisms to be seen as valid in context, though always subject to the unending process of deconstruction.

There must be a veil to tear. The manure of experience nourishes the root of the lotus of enlightenment.

Magliola had to put up with a lot of shit in his everyday life. Intellectual success could not touch or change his pain. Philosophy is the enemy of experience. In *Derrida on the Mend* he tells us that he researched Buddhism—that's philosophy. *On Deconstructing Life-Worlds* tells us that at a particular point, living with his family in Indiana, he began Zen sitting practice—that's experience. He doesn't tell us why he began Zen sitting, but I think he did it because he was miserable. A "loveless marriage" succeeded the loveless monastic life he had left earlier. Power-driven machinations of academics succeeded those of ecclesiastics. Philosophy was no consolation. It failed utterly to connect with, let alone remedy, the extreme suffering that brought him near to breakdown.

Suffering, the first "noble truth" declared by the Buddha, is not an idea but a direct observation of the way people are. You don't have to be Buddha to make this observation. You know it already. You're anxious, uncertain, manipulated by external circumstances, clinging to ideas supposed to bring a good outcome, trying to sort things out by conventional rational means. No amount of thinking changes the situation, since thinking—conceptualization—is the problem. The only help is to let go, as in Zen sitting. There is basically only one way of doing nothing.

Zen sitting practice, however, at least in the Japanese style, does 'nothing' in a style of almost military rigor—"like boot-camp," said a Buddhist woman friend of mine, who did not further pursue the Zen path. This rigor, however, appealed to Magliola's internalized monastically-formed standards. Awareness of the lack of absolute truth in the Christian theological concepts let him see more deeply the power of the sacred that manifests non-conceptually through its symbolic representation in the ritual, ceremony, and aesthetics of Roman Catholic church life.

In the practice of sitting, thoughts come and thoughts go, tangled, not one more valuable than another, emptying themselves out. "Between" marks this place, an intersection in which one path is indistinguishable from the other, and neither is a path. This intersection, *carrefour*, crossing, cross is a crux.

Crux is also double-bind—that is, the effort undertaken toward a specific goal is so driven by preconception that it thwarts arrival at the goal in actual fact—as Magliola came to see:

> Derrida's deconstructive work exposed for me one of the most sinister of historical binds: the philosophical Tradition's *hot desire* to know how 'matters really go on' (sic) had again and again generated the argumentative sleights-of-hand which had thwarted chances for a closer approximation of how matters 'go on.' Derrida also shows me how the 'intention to mean' necessarily commits itself to 'repetitive' structures (grammar, lexic, etc.) which thwart, displace, intention (*DLW*, 104).

The crossings-out in his writing show Magliola's intention to avoid these repetitive structures. He "frequents" them, that is, visits them momentarily and then finds them gone, which is the nature of thought, the interior "text" discovered in meditation. When the time comes to write out that text, he commands himself not to be repetitive. His writing is *exercitia*, wrestling with the angels of theology and the demons of natural life who interchange their masks continually.

The original approximative "off-center" thesis of this essay aimed to show that Magliola encounters emptiness primarily in experience, not philosophy. That experience is of words, of language, languages, and languaging. Words drive logic. Magliola's world is a word-world to which he would not have access if he did not retreat from it in wordless meditation. His literary style falls "between" words in its effort to split the hard rock of concept. It is not a surface manipulation of ideas, not a set of signifiers pointing dualistically to signifieds, not a rhetoric in the pejorative sense but the actual substance, *sous rature*, of his philosophy. His message is the medium.

I have not done justice to the richness and complexity of Magliola's thought. He does not need to reconcile theism and non-theism, *ātman* ("soul") and *anātman* ("no-soul"), those irreconcilable extremes, because there is nothing to which they refer. Yet they form a chiasmic text or diagram (*DLW*, 115) in his mind, a *prajñapti*, an arrangement of "thought-constructs" that lead in differing directions logocentrically but that, contemplated together in meditation as both empty, set the meditator free.

Magliola denies any holistic expression that might arise out of the "emptiness of emptiness," but his practice has restored to him *consolatio*, the comforting sense of divine presence that he had lost more than thirty years before. Perhaps it is simple well-being. According to the Tibetan Buddhist *shentong* tradition (*ODE*, 3), the nonconceptual experience ensuing from the meditative realization of emptiness reveals "the clear light nature of mind" which is unnameable but cognizable and registers "the union of bliss and emptiness."

St. Thomas Aquinas, writing in 1271 in a commentary on the *Nicomachean Ethics* of Aristotle, "adopts with approval the statement that among human operations the most pleasurable is the contemplation of truth . . . . [T]he purity and enduring nature of this contemplation arise from its objects, which are free from matter and from change." In the light of Christian revelation, according to Aquinas, the contemplative should always keep his mind on immortality. He should

> strive to live an intellectual life, with his sensitive powers subject to reason, for intellect is the best of his powers, being immortal and god-like. In fact, the happy contemplative who lives an intellectual life and makes the good of his intellect his chief care is most beloved by God.[11]

***

Magliola is that "happy contemplative" whose reply to Aquinas is to carry on the medieval European tradition by contemplating and questioning the objects of matter, change, and mortality in an Asian monastery. Still, the contemplation is pure, spacious; it is the basic goodness of the "clear light nature of mind" out of which *prajñā*, intellect, arises. The light on his path produces both the deconstructive method and recognition of the primal condition of *śūnyatā*.

But emptiness could not have come to him had he not persisted in being a Christian with the Church's structure to drive and block him.

Saṃsāra and *nirvāṇa* are opposites. They are the same, inseparable. Philosophy and experience are enemies. Love thy enemy. Magliola's goal is ethical—to seek truth in order to "help to heal the world" (*DLW*, xi)—that is, to end suffering and bring happiness. His writing is the means to this end through its union of *prajñā*, *upāya*, and *karuṇā*—intellect, skillful means, and compassion.

In the beginning of *Derrida on the Mend* he promised to introduce "a 'differentialism' that liberates and bears bliss." Differentialism's constant wordplay manifests the Logos of the word made flesh—not blasphemous—in creating what Edith Wyschogrod in her preface to *On Deconstructing Life-Worlds* praises as a "groundbreaking work of Catholic theology" (*DLW*, ix).

It is self-breaking, too, neither Catholic nor theological. The fruition of the work is beyond the work, it is the life itself, the ongoing life of the mind that crosses itself chiasmically in literary and literal reinscription. "The 'criss-cross' sayings of the old monks . . . ." (*DLW*, xiii). Magliola wrote in a letter: "For text is Writing is Life. Rising/Falling constantly. Garbling all the while."

Notes

1. Geshe Rabten, "The Commentary to the Heart of Wisdom," in *Echoes of Voidness* trans. and ed. Stephen Bachelor (Boston: Wisdom Publications, 1983), 30. Hereafter "CHW."

2. This essay's discussion of *śūnyatā* and its logical explanation in the Mādhyamaka dialectic comes out of the oral teachings of Buddha Śakyamuni transmitted primarily through the Kagyü and Nyingma lineages of Tibet. Particular sources are pages 108-198 in the Vajradhatu Seminary transcripts of lectures on the Mahāyāna given in 1975 by the Vidyādhara Chögyam Trungpa Rinpoche (1939-1987) and *The Open Door to Emptiness* [hereafter *ODE*] by the Venerable Khenchen Thrangu Rinpoche (1933-), Chief Abbot of the Nalanda Institute for Higher Buddhist Studies at Rumtek Monastery, Sikkim and abbot of Thrangu Tashi Chöling, Boudhanath, Nepal. Thrangu expounds Nāgārjuna's teachings based on Chandrakīrti's commentary. Tenzin Gyatso, the 14th Dalai Lama (1935-), also expounds them in *Buddhism of Tibet and the Key to the Middle Way*, from the Gelugpa lineage's slightly different perspective on teaching method. There is no fundamental disagreement in the views expressed.

3. "Erasure" is an important metaphor for Robert Magliola. Fundamentally, he analyzes what survives "under erasure"—that is, under the crossing-out of the deconstructive method—as Derridean *différance* (e.g., *Derrida on the Mend* [West LaFayette, Indiana: Purdue University Press, 1984], 20, hereafter *DOM*), the concept at the root of Magliola's theory of "differentialism." Literarily, the metaphor emphasizes RM's method of undoing his statements in constant evasion of the essentializing tendency of language.

4. Although the *Revised Standard Version* of the Bible is standard, the *King James Version* of the Bible (Authorized Version) translation takes precedence in this essay for accuracy, vigor, and consistency. The Greek gospel uses the same word for tearing of fabric and the splitting of the rocks (*The New Revised Standard Version-New Interlinear Version Parallel New Testament Greek and English*, 96). "To rend" also suggests more force than "to tear."

The following abbreviations will be used for different versions of the Bible:

IB: *The Interpreter's Bible* in Twelve Volumes (Nashville: Abingdon Press, 1951), 31st printing, 1980. Exegesis by Sherman E. Johnson. Commentary by George A. Buttrick, vol. VII, "Matthew," 609-610;

KJV: *King James Version* of the Bible (Authorized Version, 1611);

NIB: The *New Interpreter's Bible*;

NIDNTT: *The New International Dictionary of New Testament Theology*, ed. Colin Brown (Exeter: Paternoster Press, 1978);

NRSV: *The New Revised Standard Version*—New Interlinear Version Parallel New Testament Greek and English with interlinear translation by Alfred Marshall (Grand Rapids, MI: Zondervan, 1990);

RSV: *Revised Standard Version of the Bible*, 1952;

UBD: *Unger's Bible Dictionary*.

JBC: John L. McKenzie, S. J. "The Gospel According to Matthew," in *The Jerome Biblical Commentary*, vol. 2. *New Testament*. Eds. Raymond E. Brown, S. S., Joseph A. Fitzmyer, S.J., Roland E. Murphy, O. Carm. (Englewood Cliff, N.J.: Prentice Hall, 1968).

5. In the Temple of Herod, as in the Mosaic temple, there were two curtains. One hung between the outer court and the outer sanctuary, the *Holy Place*, "which contained one golden candlestick, a single table of showbread, and one altar of incense." The "veil" said to be "rent" hung between the outer and the inner sanctuary, the *Holy of Holies*, "which was empty," entered only on the Day of Atonement by the High Priest (*UBD*, 1082; *IB*, 610).

6. William Butler Yeats, "Crazy Jane Talks with the Bishop," in *The Collected Poems of W. B. Yeats* (New York: Macmillan, 1959), 254-255.

7. Robert Magliola, *On Deconstructing Life-Worlds: Buddhism, Christianity, Culture* (Atlanta: Scholars Press, 1997), 3, 15. Hereafter *DLW*.

8. In "The Trikāya," Shunryu Suzuki Roshi describes the "Three Bodies" in discussing the *Lotus sutra*: "Form and color of Dharma, and nature of Dharma, and Dharma itself: Nirmāṇakāya Buddha, Saṃbhogakāya Buddha, and Dharmakāya Buddha." In the Mahāyāna, the Saṃbhogakāya Buddha is thought to have form, a 'subtle body', but Suzuki also describes it as "Truth itself" as well as "the source of Śākyamuni Buddha," the incarnated or Nirmāṇakāya Buddha-form, which comes about as the result of the Saṃbhogakāya vow to help all beings (*Windbell*, San Francisco: San Francisco Zen Center, n.d. [c. 1970], 16. Hereafter *W*).

9. Gad Horowitz, at the IAPL 1999 panel at which these essays were discussed, pointed out that Magliola's vow to serve oth*ers precedes his philosophical encounter with śūnyatā* and does not depend upon a religious idea. It is more deeply ingrained in the human condition than concept. This observation is linked with the Mahāyāna Buddhist view that the Nirmanakāya Buddha came into the world by vow, out of the Saṃbhogakāya intentionality, rather than by *karma*, the usual cause and effect that propels the *saṃsāric* world (*W*, 9). The primacy of Magliola's vow and his suffering from witnessing injustice also comport with Derrida's "infinite 'idea of justice', infinitely irreducible," which motivates action in the world. See Mark Lilla, "The Politics of Jacques Derrida," *The New York Review of Books*, XLV: 11 (June 25, 1998): 36-41, 39.

10. Baron Ludvig Holberg (1684-1754), *Selected Essays of Ludvig Holberg*, trans., intro, and notes by P. M. Mitchell (Lawrence, KS: University of Kansas Press, 1955), 51.

11. Encyclopedia Britannica, 1957 ed. Vol. 8,767.

Ten

emmanuel, robert

Gad Horowitz

Robert Magliola's *On Deconstructing Life Worlds* is motivated by the Bodhisattvic desire to help others cope with evil and suffering through Buddhist/deconstructive meditative frequenting of the double binding happenings of human existence—essentially a teaching of profound *acceptance* of all goings on. However, this work is punctuated by periodic assertions of an absolute obligation binding on all human beings to work for a better world and justice. Magliola's Buddhism—like Buddhism in general—does not seek to account for the *ethically obligatory* quality of the Bodhisattva vow. I suggest that such an account can be found in the teaching of Emmanuel Levinas. I suggest that ethical obligation is the 'prior' 'condition' even of Śākyamuni's experience of enlightenment and his decision to share it with humanity. The Bodhi tree would also be Jacob's ladder.

1

In *On Deconstructing Life-Worlds*, Robert Magliola lets us know: "the main reason for this book: if you sense your life is a bind/double bind I will give you a way to cope."[1] The desire in this book is Boddhisattvic desire: to give. In this book Robert describes and gives ways of healing which he found through much travail at the (non)intersections of Buddhism, deconstruction, and Christianity. Through derridean and nagarjunist analytic deconstruction, and especially through deep meditation on the devoidness of all happenings, one can learn how to cope with evil and suffering, "letting the spectacle of the world go on without me (i.e. without ME) letting go, letting be," observing and affirming "the rising and cessation of all 'things'" (*DLW*, 78). This is a practice of *frequenting* the binds/double binds which describe how the devoid happenings of this world devolve. "As in Derrida, the world of 'cause and effect' proceeds: it is not destroyed but deconstructed, not evaded but obviated."[2] Robert indicates that such healing, for those who are like him in this respect, follows or goes along with surrender of the "Awake-Dream" of an omnipotent Creator whom we can expect to provide "justice" and "fairness" within our life experience (*DLW*, 99) even though He makes happen or allows the happening of not only good but also evil, the triumphs of the wicked and the tortures of the innocent.

Many of us will have found it necessary, like Robert, to pray to God to deliver us from belief in that God (*DLW*, 79). The God of healing, like the worlding of the world of "cause and effect," "seems to work as a Bind" (*DLW*, 104). "God is a Bind/Double Bind" like Derrida's *différance originaire* (*DLW*, 158-159, 163). Derrida "strongly compares *différance originaire* (the 'prior' difference enabling no and not—no talk in language) and 'God' as pure difference (the 'prior' difference making possible the 'naming' of beings and their negations)" (*DLW*, 159). "Irreducible binds/double binds . . . are clues, somehow, to the very constitution of God" (*DLW*, 127), "God is the name of this bottomless collapse of language,"[3] bind and double bind after bind and double bind, infinite retreat of binds/double binds. Only such a view of God could "make sense for me," says Robert, "out of the unspeakable injustices of human history." He goes so far as to suggest that Nazism was an "inevitable moment," one of those "foredoomed...waves of recurrence" of Evil which must forever mark the unrolling of "history" (*DLW*, 115-116). Surrender the expectation of justice, practise the meditative frequenting of the double binds of your existence and "eventually the double binds become salubrious" (*DLW*, 117). "Christ's wounds—our wounds—are turned all glorious" (*DLW*, 127). "The enlightened person is detached from every circumstance and thus can celebrate every circumstance . . . in a 'playful Samadhi'...one can even enjoy hell."[4]

But wait. Robert cautions: "there attaches, however, a certain moral apostil: because the deconstructionist is teaching . . . everyone is obliged to kindness."[5] Caveat meditator. And the question arises: *why* is the deconstructionist teaching? Why and whence this *obligation* to kindness? A search of *On Deconstructing Life-Worlds* reveals numerous similar caveats: Robert rejects, at least for himself, the "kind of Buddhism which would simply affirm good and evil in the world as the inevitable play of Samsara" (*DLW*, 69 note 32). His religious practice is not "escapism" because he believes in "direct action," even "leftist," "socialist" action to "make the world better," to "stop aggression/oppression" (*DLW*, 70). Marx's prescription of communism: "from each according to her/his ability, to each according to her/his need" is for Robert a "holy maxim" (*DLW*, 70, note 34). Why is it holy? He declares his commitment "to ethics, and to working out the project of goodness-at-all-costs" (*DLW*, 75). Why at all costs? Like a good deconstructionist Buddhist Robert refuses to "lay claims to absolute or universalized truth" (*DLW*, 79-80); however, in a footnote, this refusal is interrupted: "Except for one conviction, which I insist is binding on all: the obligation to loving-kindness" (*DLW*, 80 note 60). And he writes of his decision to "try (his) utmost to do good, and *for the rest* (my emphasis) affirm (and observe...). The rising and cessation of all 'things'" (*DLW*, 78). How does it happen that there is this exception, this absolute truth, this obligation binding on all human beings, which takes precedence over the practice of meditative frequenting of the binds and double binds of the devoid happenings of God and the world? What is the secret of the happening of this divine exception, and what kind of devoidness is its devoidness? Whence is the peremptory, compulsive, compelling passion in Robert's work for doing good and for justice, which somehow assumes a kind of priority—behind his back—in relation to the teaching of analytic derridean and nagarjunist deconstruction and of non-clinging meditative practice? Is this passion a response to the commandment of God—not the Omnipotent One from whom Robert prayed to be delivered—but God the name of the Other Who interrupts cause-and-effect, being-and-non-being, invoking and evoking the self as infinite obligation to the other person?

One will have recognized in these words the teaching of Emmanuel Levinas. Though Robert Magliola disavows any calling to contribute to the "theoretics of justice and expectation," referring his readers instead to Deleuze, Guattari, Baudrillard, "and so on" (*DLW*, 99 note 94), is it not the case that his confessions of commitment and obligation resonate not those pagans but the Jew? Though (perhaps) he doesn't hear it loud and clear, is there a calling after (or before) all, and a certain implicit or muffled theoretics? The disavowal somewhat double bound, crosshatched, by a "prior" avowal or vow?

Magliola's text, very much like the Mahāyāna Buddhist tradition to/of which it is a contribution, does not go behind the Bodhisattva's Vow, the promise, to account for the VOW-nature of the vow, to explain the obligatory quality, the *must*-ness of the "I must 'do good'." The Bodhisattva vow gives no account of itself other than the familiar formulation of Compassion as the manifestation in the world of cause and effect of insight into emptiness. But...the question: "why the must? Why the *VOW*?"

2.

Emmanuel Levinas' phenomenological or post-phenomenological research indicates that this "must" precedes the ego "I," occupies, pre-occupies, animates, breathes the "I" as its inescapable orientation to the other, which is not an alter ego, i.e. not "another Same" and not the other *of* the same, but the inaccessible, inconceivable, non-phenomenal, always already past and always to come, utterly powerless, vulnerable yet Authoritative Other, who shines in the faces of all actually existing others as the Face.

The vow is not freely assumed by a preexisting "I." There is no preexisting I. The I *is* the vow. The erring sinful creature (and God knows there is no creature, not even the most righteous Tzaddik, who is free of sin/error) disavows the vow to greater or lesser extents without affecting its primordial inescapability. The Bodhisattva, the Bodhisattva in Robert or Whoever, Someone/No one, "Personne," is the human fully living the ethical responsibility, or more precisely the struggle with ethical responsibility, Israel, which characterizes, defines, the human.

Buddhist insight into devoidness/emptiness whether we think of it as prior to or co-arising with compassion is at bottom discovery of the "pour-l'autre" of the human self—its (non)essential dispossession or home-leaving. It's not a matter of I taking refuge/leaving home. Rather, leaving home *is* the I correctly understood. In Levinas' words, "its very closing" or selfhood "is a turning inside-out. . . ..An inside-out without an inside."[6]

The Boddhisattvic self—our true nature, or Buddha nature, if it is all right to say so—shows itself in this perspective as a "putting into question of the self" which poses "itself directly as de-posed, as for the other . . . . The departure from oneself" can only be "the approach of the neighbour."[7] That is why the Bodhisattva *must* help not only by teaching the devoidness of self and of things and of all happenings but by helping in every way, by insisting on justice in this world. God simply is this powerless yet obsessively authoritative insistence on justice, or, as Levinas puts it, "God" is the "signification" that comes to mind when the *conatus essendi* or right to life is shaken by the question: do I deserve to live? "If I am for myself, what am I?" asks the Bodhisattva Rabbi Hillel.

The world of cause and effect *can* be deconstructed, obviated, phenomenologically speaking, and it *must* be deconstructed, obviated, ethically speaking, because the call of the Other, the approach of the Other who has always already escaped my comprehension, has created me as desire, as response to and for the Other. What is beyond the ego, says Levinas, is its very own constitutive "non-indifference" to the Other, its "disinterestedness . . . as the just judgment, and not a nothingness," i.e., not a simple spacious devoidness of ego (*GCM*, 11). Not its devoidness/suchness, then, but this devoidness/suchness *as* the incumbent pre-occupying proximity of the other, dis-possession by the other, infinite obligation to the other, impossible to discharge, finish, or fulfill. The teaching and the experience of non-importance, of devoidness, which may indeed if we are fortunate dis/empower us to be insightful/blissful/compassionate even in hell, gains its significance and importance from the Commandment: be ye just. So the self is Bodhisattva, Buddha, Christ, Saint, Messiah, and Tzaddik: "At the very bottom of my 'position' within myself [there is] my substitution for the Other" (*GCM*, 10). But all of the above are not God. "God" is the signification of human signification which "cuts across all phenomenality." Cuts across, cross-hatches (The translator elaborates: "trancher: contrasts with it, interrupts it, puts it to an end temporarily at least." One might add-from inside/outside) (*GCM*, xi)...the signification that "comes to mind" when I hear the call. Another Levinasian term which belongs here is "illeity": impersonal intersubjectivity, indicating not an I-Thou dialogue relation but an asymmetrical relation, between I and a commanding utterly vulnerable He—the *alterity* of the other person.

Immediately following Śākyamuni's experience of enlightenment under the Bodhi tree, the Buddhist legend tells us, he *had to decide* whether or not he would share, give, teach, in spite of the likelihood that others would be unreceptive or uncomprehending. According to the legend he was persuaded by the god (God?) Indra. Would Levinas say that this story should be turned inside-out? The struggle with obligation/decision would come first, though not in any chronological synchronic sense. The Bodhi tree would also be Jacob's ladder. The inescapable call of the Other would be the "prior" "condition" of the search for enlightenment, and of the experience of enlightenment, the decision to teach, and the teaching. As in the case of the Israelites whose response (not without struggle) to the giving of the Torah was: "Naáseh Vénishma—we will do it and (then) we shall hear the word," it would be the commitment, even before there is any apparently or conventionally autonomous ego to assume it, which would precede, condition and evoke the ego and its insights and sharings and refusals/inabilities to share. The obligation, in the darkness of the Other (Moses sees only God's back) is the no-space in which the light of insight-compassion can appear. The ethical question faced by Śakyamuni "after" his enlightenment is "before" his enlightenment, the *first* question (ethics is first philosophy, says Levinas) the question posed to the first human born to Adam and Eve: Am I my brother's guardian? All religion, according to Levinas, answers Yes, Yes, that is what I am. I alone am my sister's guardian ("shomer"—watchperson, guardian, caretaker, preserver). The tree is the tree of the "knowledge" that we must first choose between good and evil. Eve is God's angel: first eat the apple, then we'll talk. The orthodox Lubavitch writer Zalman Posner puts it this way: "Yes, Yes, He is omni-this and omni-that, but what do we need him for? For defining good and evil."[8] Just obey the commandments, do God's will, do good, *then* we can talk about talking about language and the "bottomless collapse of language." For Posner this is "thinking Jewish." He's not far from Levinas and, strange as it may seem, not far from the Bodhi tree.

According to the legend, the Buddha proclaims, immediately following his liberation, "I Alone am the World-Honored One." Levinas would make it more clear than has ever been done how far this is from any boastful or even not boastful assumption of Superiority or Power, worldly, churchly, or "spiritual": My obligation places upon me the burden of the entire suffering creation, weighs on me as the very *meaning* of me, on myself *alone* (on every myself but not as deduction from any general rule of reason, thus never on "*you*"); and this, Levinas tells us, is the "infinition of the infinite," or "the glory," the "glory of God."

Again, this is not the God from whom Robert prayed to be relieved, but the God who is nothing other than the approach of the Other: "It is as if the face of the other man, who from the first 'asks for me' and orders me were the crux of...the surpassing by God of the idea of God and of every idea in which he would still be intended, visible, and known, and in which the idea of the infinite were denied by thematization or in presence or representation" (*GCM*, xiv). In *Fragments of Redemption*, Susan Handelman cites Isaiah 43:10: "You are my witnesses, says the Lord"—and the appended midrash: "If you are my witnesses, I am God, but if not, not."[9] Or as Moshe Idel puts it, transmitting a Kabbalistic tradition, the Torah "looks not so much for salvation by the intervention of God as for God's redemption by human intervention."[10]

In Flannery O'Connor's story "A Temple of the Holy Ghost" recounted by Robert in *On Deconstructing Life-Worlds* (127-130), when the hermaphrodite "freak" on display in the country sideshow admonishes his audience—"God made me this way . . . if you laugh he may strike you the same way," it is the Face of the Other which speaks, commanding, imploring, don't kill me, don't make me a "freak." Robert is close to this when he suggests that this figure "is the very emblem of God's Divine out-and-indwelling." But he is far from this, I think, when he says: "How can a good God 'will' such a birth-in-the-world. O'Connor's hermaphrodite affirms and does not dispute" (*DLW*, 130). I don't think Levinas could abide any idea of a *God* who "makes" "freaks" anymore than a God who could "will" the devoid happening of Auschwitz, or, for that matter, the bombing of Baghdad.

Is there some trepidation in relation to my language of priority, ultimacy, firstness? I think that Levinas knows as well as Magliola and Derrida that "*différance originaire*" or "God" or "any 'ultimate' would be asymmetrically but doubly bound into its 'traces' in the 'other-than-ultimate'" (*DLW*, 168) "....always entrammeled, entangled (1) in *ad hoc* situational difference, whichever one happens to be happening at the time and even (2) in the empty traces which 'it' (there is no self-identical 'it' of course) is singularly 'then and there' constituting" (*DLW*, 169). There is no logocentric "prior." Levinas says: "even if it cuts across all phenomenality" the signification "God" always signifies in a "phenomenological concreteness" (*GCM*, xi).

But he shows as well that the ultimate is nevertheless, in a certain most *significant* sense, ultimate. A kind of cross-hatching much like Magliola's discourse of bind and double bind, but with a systematic, explicit, Judaic, ethical difference, which Robert needs if he is to account for his "musts." The priority of the ethical is not logocentric and not theocentric, has always already come "before" any "first." If we go for help in relation to this issue to Levinas' crucial distinction between the ethical call, the *Saying* and the commonsensical, philosophical, phenomenological, theological, or gnoseological *Said*, all saids betray traces of a Saying, and are uttered by a Saying that nevertheless "does not enter as a contextual or intertextual element [i.e., 'presence'-gh] into any said." That Saying "in its contentless and nondiscursive repetition...is always new..." and has always already passed when its message is heard.[11] Thus it is always coming from an "immemorial" past that has never been present, a pre-original past, from a future that will never arrive, and therefore cannot be thought of as an origin, ground, arché. The "primordial" ethical saying is an-archic, inaudible in itself, cutting across the devoid saids of what Robert calls "the ever erratic going on" (*DLW*, 169).

3.

"Logocentric," says Robert, is "any concept or even 'experience' taken as 'closed' so that its parts adequate . . . to it and/or to each other.... (thus, even 'no frame' is a frame)." But "what really happens is measured...by what/how much is *missed* . . . . In the 'less' or 'more' which is *left out* (emphasis in original) happenings really go on." It is "this lack" that "generates what 'goes on'" (*DLW*, 172).

That which is left out: alterity: for Levinas is "ultimately," in terms of human significance, the alterity of the other person, the Other; the approach, appeal, incumbency of this ever escaping Other generates the selfing that goes on. A Buddhist might say: "that which cuts across *saṃvṛti-satya* (conventional logocentric truth) is *paramārtha-satya* (absolute truth of devoidness)" but for Levinas the imperative of gratuitous love, the ethical Saying, cuts across truth, all truths of happenings-and-their-devoidness. The saying of the saids "is" what "cuts across" them. There is much cross-hatching going on, but for Levinas the arms of the cross, though equal in some sense, are ultimately not equal. And it may be that Derrida would agree, for it is not at all difficult to find a similar sense of the priority of the ethical in some of his more recent writings.

For example, in an interview with Derrida, the question is posed: "is there a logic of ethical testimony at work in deconstruction?" Derrida answers: "Yes, it is absolutely central to it. Testimony, which implies faith or promise governs the entire social space. I would say that theoretical knowledge (truths of happenings and their devoidness-gh) is circumscribed within this testimonial space (the space of the ethical Saying). It is only by reference to the possibility of testimony that deconstruction can begin to ask questions about knowledge and meaning." And referring directly to Levinas' perspective, Derrida says: "It is because... [of] the infinity of the other...the infinite alterity of the other ...that I must describe my relation to him/her ethically and not in a purely phenomenological fashion.... In order to describe things in themselves...in order to be a phenomenologist to the end I have to interrupt phenomenology. That is what is meant by self-interruption, which is another name for *différance*."[12] The ethical saying which cuts across, cross-hatches, interrupts all truths, all saids, all happenings, is self-interruption, *différance originaire*, the bottomless collapse of language, all of which, as we have already heard, are among the names of God.

Notes

1. Robert Magliola, *On Deconstructing Life-Worlds: Buddhism, Christianity, Culture* (Atlanta: Scholars Press, 1997), 109. Henceforth *DLW*.

2. Robert Magliola, "French Deconstruction with a (Buddhist) Difference: More Cases from the *Gateless Gate* [*Wu-men-kuan*] *and Blue Cliff Record* [*Pi-yen-lu*]," *Studies in Language and Literature* 3, no. 1:1-25, 20.

3. Jacques Derrida, *On the Name*, ed. Thomas Dutoit (Standford: Stanford University Press, 1995), 51.

4. Magliola, "French Deconstruction with a (Buddhist) Difference: More Cases from the *Gateless Gate* [*Wu-men-kuan*] *and Blue Cliff Record* [*Pi-yen-lu*], 19.

5. Magliola, "French Deconstruction with a (Buddhist) Difference: More Cases from the *Gateless Gate* [*Wu-men-kuan*] *and Blue Cliff Record* [*Pi-yen-lu*], 19.

6. Joseph Libertson, *Proximity* (The Hague: Martinus Nijhoff, 1982), 225. (Autrement Qúetre 1974, 63. Joseph Libertson's translation in *Proximity*, 1982, 225.)

7. Emmanuel Levinas, *Of God Who Comes to Mind* (Standford, CA: Stanford University Press, 1998), 13. Henceforth *GCM*.

8. Zalman Posner, "Think Jewish," *Wellspring* (Boston: Spring 1997), 22.

9. Susan Handelman, *Fragments of Redemption* (Bloomington: Indiana University Press, 1991), 286.

10. Moshe Idel, *Kabbalah: New Perspectives* (New Haven: Yale University Press, 1988), 179.

11. Adrian Peperzak, "From Intentionality to Responsibility," *The Question of the Other*, eds. A.B. Dallery and Charles Scott (Albany: SUNY Press, 1989), 16-17.

12. Richard Kerney and Mark Dooley, eds. "Hospitality, Justice and Responsibility: A Dialogue with Jacques Derrida," in *Questioning Ethics* (New York: Routledge, 1999), 81-82.

Part Six

Questioning the Self, Questioning the Dialogue

Introduction

Previous chapters in this volume have discussed major currents of Buddhist thought in the context of deconstructive operation. As we read through them, we might have asked ourselves what has facilitated such a sudden "close-up" look at Eastern-and-Western thoughts that have long been considered irreconcilable (See my General Introduction for more on this issue).

The coming together of Buddhism (Eastern thought) and deconstruction (Continental philosophy), however, was not a rupture without a prelude. Derrida himself has identified the five precursors for his *différance* (Nietzsche, de Saussure, Freud, Heidegger, and Levinas); deconstruction is a point reached through the long process of Western metaphysics' self-de-essentializing practice. Two essays in Part Six demonstrate the wide range of this procedure by discussing Buddhist thought alongside pre-Derridean philosophies, especially in connection with existentialism and phenomenology.

One noticeable difference between the Continental metaphysical tradition and Buddhist thought has been that the subject-object dualism maintained in the former contradicts the latter's nondual stance. Simon Glynn explores how Jean P. Sartre's existentialism (and partly Husserlian phenomenology as well) reveals the problem of subject-object dualism and the limits of reflective subjectivity (and Cartesian Ego-Cogito), and thus facilitates a close encounter between Continental thought and the Buddhist non-self theory.

Buddhism claims that there is no permanent independent self, for the self from the Buddhist perspective is nothing more than a combination of five aggregates of form, sensation, its perceptions, mental formation and consciousness. In its criticism of Descartes's reification of the reflective Cogito that exists independently of what is reflected upon, Sartre's understanding of the self comes close, Glynn argues, to that of Buddhism. Building upon Hegel and Husserl, Sartre brings our attention to the phenomenal fact that our reflection is always a reflection of something, and our experience of consciousness has never been that of an independent objective thing in itself. Hence, our consciousness is a nothing, for it is no thing or object. As Sartre states, "Existence precedes essence," which

Glynn links to his claim that our volitional acts (the Fourth Aggregate in the Buddhist theory of the Five Aggregates) do not necessarily contradict the theory of self as desire. This also explains, Glynn contends, the responsibility of an individual, as an agent to attain *nirvāṇa* to liberate her/himself. If the Buddhist individual is insubstantial and subject to change, like Sartre's individual who is free to make the choice of commitment, that individual is free to choose to change herself and to free herself from the bondage of *saṃsāra* and transmigration.

Steven Laycock further elaborates on the non-substantial nature of reflexivity and consciousness, major concepts in the construction of modern subjectivity. Consciousness, Laycock declares, "*is* a blind spot." The privileged position consciousness occupied in the construction of modern subjectivity becomes ambiguous at best if consciousness is that which it is not, as demonstrated by Glynn in the case of Sartre. One of the many examples Laycock provides us in his variations on the theme of non-substantiality of consciousness is his interpretation of Narcissus. According to Laycock, the meaning of Narcissus' story lies neither in the possibility that he was "absorbed in his own reflection" nor that he failed to possess him-self: Narcissus demonstrates the impossibility of maintaining subject-object dualism except when one is standing aloof from reality.

Concluding the volume, E. H. Jarow brings our attention to the problematic nature of comparative study itself. Jarow asks: What do we mean by "Buddhism" in its singular form, as if it has maintained one unified form despite its two thousand five hundred year history in which it has been spread around the world? And why Buddh*ism*? The same can be asked in the case of Judaism or Hinduism, whereas the "unconscious usage of 'Christianity' as a unique emblem suggests its assumed preeminence over all mere 'isms'." Is it even legitimate to study Buddhism from "theological or philosophical perspectives" without considering its life-world? Jarow even attempts to deconstruct deconstruction itself, as he states: "practitioners of 'secular deconstruction' dismiss 'any and all notions of religiosity as logocentric' and thus practice exclusivism."

According to Jarow, Buddhism has grown out of a "parasitic" relationship to its host cultures, be it in Brahmanic India, China, Tibet, or elsewhere. The "heterodoxies" of different Buddhisms born out of the combination with different cultures defy such a reified project as a "comparative study." By the same token, the project risks the danger of turning Derridean deconstruction into an emblem, "an icon in the play of culture." As an alternative to a potential reification of the encounter between Buddhisms and deconstructions, Jarow suggests that the encounter need to "move further into imagination." By this, Jarow is referring to, among other things, our ability to "live" deconstruction: "how to live, not just how to think, after walking through the mine field of disproved assertions, tombstones of truth claims." At this point, it seems that we are going back to the issues Cai and Loy raised earlier in the volume: how do we define the relationship between philosophy and religion, theory and practice, deconstruction, Buddhism, and the life-world?

Are they really so distant from one another? Is philosophy the enemy of experience, as Jane Augustine repeatedly tells us? Is deconstruction possible without living it as well? Does Derrida still remain within a realm of text that cannot include life-text? And is it not the case that Buddhism requires a certain form of foundationalism, as Roger Jackson suggests, and if so, how deconstructive can it be? Is deconstruction possible without some totalizing gesture in order to distinguish itself from other -isms, systems, and trends? Where do we draw the boundary?

Questions remain to be resolved. As Jean-Francois Lyotard tells us, the postmodern spirit is a stranger to the declarative mode. Instead, postmodernity asks: is it happening? It is the spirit of Merleau-Ponty's interrogation in which the questioner opens her/himself for the encounter with the questioned. And this is the play of Chan *gong'an* meditation, in which practitioners constantly dismantle the closed system of the human mind and linguistic boundaries. (JYP)

Eleven

Sartre, Phenomenology, and the Buddhist No-Self Theory

Simon Glynn

The ego is traditionally held to be synonymous with individual identity and autonomy, while the mind, which is closely associated therewith, is widely held to be a necessary basis of cognition and volition, and the responsibility following therefrom. However, Buddhist epistemology, Existential Phenomenology and Poststructuralism all hold the notion of an independently subsisting self-identical subject to be an illusion. This not only raises problems for our understanding of cognition (for if such a self is an illusion who does the perceiving and who is deluded), and volition (who initiates acts), but also therefore for the notion of responsibility (for in the absence of an independently subsisting subject there appears to be no autonomous agent), while for Buddhism it also raises an additional problem for the doctrine of reincarnation (for in the absence of such a self it is unclear who is supposed to be responsible for failing to overcome desires and attachments, and concomitantly gets reincarnated). Arguing for such "no-self" theories the paper attempts to demonstrate how such difficulties can nevertheless be resolved.

The Buddhist No-self Theory

As is well known, Buddhists account for the development of a sense of self in terms of five *skandhas* or aggregates. These are: 1) Form, or the Body; 2) Sensations and Feelings; 3) Perceptions; 4) Mental Formations, or the habits and traits etc. that guide our volitions; and 5) Six Consciousnesses; one of each of the sensations coming from our five senses, and a consciousness of non-sensory or "mental" experiences.

While our immediate experience provides incontrovertible evidence of the existence of these *skandhas*, Buddhists draw our attention to the fact that, on account of their changing nature, they cannot, either individually or collectively, constitute a *persisting* self. Further they point out that there is absolutely no evidence, empirical or otherwise, to support the common inference that they are changing *appearances* of a *persisting* self, of an *independently subsisting* receiver and/or container of cognitive experiences, and/or source or origin of volitional dispositions, etc. Consequently while not denying the existence of a "self" understood as a collection of dependent and constantly changing *skandhas*, the self understood as an independently subsisting, unchanging or persistent, center of identity, is, for Buddhists, illusory. And it is this view that, following convention, we shall refer to throughout as the "no-self" theory.

Western Philosophy: the Self as the Mind

Accepting, along with the Buddhists, that for most of us our sense of identity involves *some* reference to our bodies (the first *skandha*), nevertheless Western Philosophy has tended to assume that it is largely with our "minds," broadly conceived as equivalent to our egos, that our sense of identity ultimately rests, a view attested to by a simple thought experiment. Asked whether, if after undergoing a "mind transplant" with another person, X, they would wake up in possession of X's body, or X's mind, individuals will almost invariably claim that it is X's body which they would then posses; their sense of identity thus being associated with their "minds."

In light of this it therefore becomes evident that a precise understanding of the nature of our minds is indispensable to our understanding of our existence and identity.

The Cartesian Reification (the Reflective Cogito) and the Sartrean Critique

Now notwithstanding whatever we may conclude concerning the *relationship* between the brain and the mind, clearly the mind as such has no height, width, depth, color, or shape, etc., which is to say no material existence. As Husserl affirms, "... psychic being (or Mind as we would call it) in and for itself has no spatial extension and (consequently) no location."[1]

Nor is Descartes' claim that, in contradistinction to the *res extensa* of the material world, the mind is *res cogitans*, a presumably unextended or immaterial thinking (and, we might add, experiencing) substance, convincing. For quite apart from the seemingly *ad hoc* nature of the notion of an immaterial "substance," even if one allows that what Descartes meant to indicate was simply the immateriality of the mind, careful attention to the phenomena will reveal that we no more have any non-sensory experiences of the mind—as we do of unicorns, centaurs, mermaids, and other immaterial objects—than any sensory experience of it.

Nor should this surprise us unduly, for notwithstanding Descartes' reification[2] of the mind (albeit as an immaterial, as opposed to a material, thing), a moment's thought will confirm that, whatever it may or may not be, the mind is no sort of thing or object, either immaterial or material, but precisely a subject. Indeed, Sartre, building upon Hegel's analysis of the three stages of consciousness,[3] explains the Cartesian mistake, of conceiving the subject as though it where an object, in terms of what he calls "impure" reflection.[4]

According to Hegel, then consciousness progresses from a primordial *awareness* or "sense certainty" of what he supposes to be relatively undifferentiated sensations, via a kind of cognitive reflection, to a second stage, namely that of *perception*, in which such sensations are organized to the point where we experience a number of discreet objects, differentiated from one another, and, (most germanely), from the subject; a subject which is, moreover, itself reflectively differentiated from other such subjects. From here, however, consciousness proceeds, by way of a more profound, philosophical, reflection, to a third stage; an *understanding* that, though epistemologically *distinguishable* or differentiable, individual identities are reciprocally co-constituting, and thus, like the two poles of a magnet, ontologically *inseparable* from one another. (See *POM*, 217 ff, *LH*, 191.)

Taking these insights of Hegel's as his initial point of departure, Sartre exposits the progression from what he refers to as "*impure*" reflection, characteristic of the second stage, to the "*pure*" or philosophical reflection of the third stage. Thus *impure* reflection is, for Sartre, an act of "*perception*" by which the subject, paradoxically affecting to "stand outside" or adopt "a point of view" upon itself, "sees," or *represents* itself (presumably iconically) to itself, as a quasi-object, or what we might refer to as a mind, understood as a reified "thing." While *pure* reflection is, by way of contrast, a philosophical act of *understanding* by which "consciousness" as we might refer to unreified awareness, realizing that in self-reflection it is (awareness or consciousness) itself—understood as a *reflective* subject (or consciousness) rather than as a reflectively reified or *reflected* quasi-object (or "mind")—upon which it reflects, *presents* or *presences* itself, to itself, as (just such) a *reflective* subject or conscious awareness; a subject (or consciousness) which, again in line with the Hegelian analysis, is intrinsically related to (which is to say conscious of) the world,[5] and to other subjects.[6]

Beginning then with the impure self reflection which he rejects, Sartre tells us that: "it must be remembered that all the writers who have described the *Cogito* have dealt with it as a reflective operation, . . . performed by a consciousness *directed upon consciousness*, a consciousness which takes consciousness as an object . . . we are in the presence of . . . two consciousnesses, one of which is consciousness *of* the other (*TE*, 44)." In such impure reflection then the "reflecting consciousness (mistakenly) posits the consciousness reflected-on, as its object" (*B&N*, liii). Invoking the self evident fact that self "reflection . . . demands that the reflective be that which is reflected on,"(*B&N*, 151), that "the reflective is the reflected on" (*B&N*, 155), and that in consequence, "[a]ctually the consciousness reflected on is not present . . . as something outside reflection . . . on which one can take a point of view" (*B&N*, 155). Sartre concludes that "Consciousness of self is not dual" (*B&N*, lii).

Thus Sartre abandons Cartesian reifying self-reflection, by which *reflective* or *reflecting* consciousness would make the *reflected* consciousness an *object* of reflection, in favor of a model in which the *reflection* that consciousness has of itself is as *reflecting subjectivity*; a *reflection reflecting* (*reflet-refletant*), which is to say a *reflection* which reflects the very act of *reflecting* in which, in self-reflection, it is engaged. As he writes of: "the reflection-reflecting. The reflecting exists only in order to reflect the reflection, and the reflection is a reflection only in so far as it refers to the reflecting. Thus the two terms . . . point to each other" (*B&N*, 173).

This, as Hazel Barnes (the translator of *Being and Nothingness*, and a leading Sartre scholar), points out, "easily suggests to Sartre the idea of a game with mirrors" (*B&N*, 151, Footnote 8). A game which should, I believe, be conceived of as two mirrors, placed opposite and parallel to each other (thus "pointing to each other"), such that each, appears in the reflection of the other as reflecting the other, just as the other's reflection appears in it as reflecting it. In each case the reflection therefore appears as reflecting (see *B&N*, 152). And it is this pure "inner" (see *B&N*, 151 & *TE*, 41) form of self reflection, in which the reflection of the mirroring subject is mirrored to itself as mirroring or reflecting itself, in which the "reflection is *also* the reflecting" (*B&N*, 173), which captures the mirroring or reflecting subjectivity of consciousness.[7]

Consciousness as Nothingness

No thing or object, either material or immaterial, consciousness is then, quite literally, nothing (see *TE*). While in so far as we have argued that it is consciousness that defines human identity, it therefore follows, that "Human reality is ... itself a nothingness" (*B&N*, 440).

But while not a thing or object, human mental activity or consciousness, which we essentially are, nevertheless remains, as reflecting subjectivity, conscious of objects, events, dispositions, etc. Indeed to be more precise we are conscious or aware of sensations and feelings (second *skandha*), perceptions (third *skandha*), mental formations, or the habits and traits etc. that guide our volitions (fourth *skandha*), and we are, in addition, not only aware or conscious of all of this, but, as we have seen in Sartre's exposition of pure self-reflection, conscious that we are conscious of it (fifth *skandha*).

In sum, Sartre begins by drawing our attention to the phenomenologically evident fact that we have no experience of consciousness as an independently subsisting and unchanging (material or immaterial) object or thing "in-itself" (*en-soi*), no experience or awareness of an undergoer of cognitive experiences or originator of volitional dispositions, etc. From here he proceeds, in exact accord with what he acknowledges to be the "the essential principle of phenomenology" (*TE*, 44)—that, "All consciousness, as Husserl has shown, is consciousness of something" (*B&N*, li, see also *TE*, 41, 44), or "*intentional*" (*I*, 222-6, 214) as Husserl would express it—to point out that we are, nevertheless conscious of, or present to, ourselves, in pure self-reflection, as an ever changing aggregate of these conscious experiences and volitional dispositions themselves. And in so doing Sartre does nothing less than provide phenomenological confirmation of the Buddhist no-self theory.

The Phenomenological and Buddhist Notions of Consciousness

As fellow Existential phenomenologist Martin Heidegger affirms, "A person is not a Thing, not a substance, not an object."[8] Indeed if, as we have argued, persons are essentially identified with our consciousness, and if, as Husserl asserts, "It is intentionality which characterizes *consciousness*" (*I*, 222), then as Heidegger affirms, "Essentially the person exists only in the performance of intentional acts" (*B&T*, 73). While if as Husserl also asserts, "We understand under Intentionality the unique peculiarity of experiences to be the consciousness of something" (*I*, 223), then the person exists, only as consciousness of something; a point well recognized by Buddhists. As Dōgen puts it: "I came to realize clearly that Mind is no other than mountains and rivers and the great wide earth, the sun and the moon and the stars."[9]

That is to say that, consciousness may be understood, as so too may human existence, as what Husserl has referred to as a subjective "Pole" of *experience*[10] or *experiencer*, known only in relation to the *experienced*, which is to say its world.[11]

That this is no idle metaphysical speculation, but accords exactly with our empirical[12] experience, is evident from the fact that, so far from encountering ourselves as reified egos, who experience, or come to experience, the world, etc., we experience ourselves always already experiencing the world, as *experiencers*, inextricably united with the *experienced*, in *experience*; the epistemological distinction between self and world being, as both developmental and cognitive psychology have demonstrated, a product of subsequent reflection. As Husserl puts it: "it is only through reflexion . . . that such a thing as consciousness or conscious content can become known" (*I*, 210).

Indeed, as a consequence of such reflection: "we continue to distinguish—despite the necessary interrelationship—the experience itself from . . . the content of experience . . . in experience we must distinguish between a subjectively and an objectively oriented aspects" (*I*, 214-15).

From Intentional Pole to Deconstructed Difference

Moreover Husserl continues: " . . . to this two-sidedness there corresponds, to a considerable extent at any rate, a division (though not any real separation) between . . . pure subjectivity (and) . . . objectivity . . . " (*I*, 215, second addition in parentheses mine). Concomitantly, as Vasubandhu concurs: "Where there is an object there is a subject, but not where there is no object. The absence of an object results in the absence also of a subject . . . . It is thus that there arises the cognition which is homogeneous . . . . The tendencies to treat object and subject as distinct and real entities are forsaken . . . ."[13] For as indicated previously, like the two poles of a magnet, the subjective and objective poles of experience, experiencer and experienced, self and other, though epistemologically distinguishable, are existentially inseparable; their identities as subject and object each being dependent, as in Hegel's Master/Slave dialectic (*POM*, 229-40), upon their *relation* to, or *difference* from, the other. As Derrida puts it: "Subjectivity—like objectivity—is an effect of *différance*, an effect inscribed in a system of *différance*."[14]

From Intentional "Pole" of Cognitions to Author of Volitions?

However, as Heidegger has pointed out: ". . . by maintaining the thesis that every subject is what it is only for an Object and *vice versa* . . . the terms thus correlated—like the correlation itself—remains ontologically indefinite. At the bottom however the whole correlation necessarily gets thought of as "somehow" being and must therefore be thought of with regard to some definite idea of Being" (*B&T*, 252).

In other words, the *epistemological* relatedness of experiencer to the experienced in experience is a concomitant of the fact that we are already *existentially* related to the world, already *ontologically* embodied (as Being-in-the-world or *Dasein* as Heidegger calls it) within it; a view in accordance with Buddhism as indicated by the first *skandha*. Indeed, commenting on Descartes' famous "*Cogito Ergo Sum,*" Heidegger observes that "The '*sum*' (my existence or the fact that "I am") is not the consequence of thinking, but vice versa; it is the ground of thinking..."[15]

Now while it is clear that such embodiment requires a body (first *skandha*), the body, as an ever changing collection of cells, that are themselves constituted by ongoing food and energy transactions with the environment, is anything but independent and unchanging, and therefore completely consistent with the Buddhist denial of an independently subsisting and unchanging self; and this notwithstanding the fact that, (as already indicated by the thought experiment involving a "mind transplant"), human identity is not, in any event, primarily derived from the body.

Ontologically embodied (the first *skandha*) within the world as it is, if our consciousness or awareness is to survive, it must, first and foremost, be *practical*. And indeed *Dasein's* first explicit conception of itself as Being-in-the-world is as being always already surrounded by a world of "ready-to-hand" or practical instrumentalities (see for instance *B&T*, 95-104); a world to which we relate volitionally, as indicated by the fourth *skandha*. Sartre concurs, claiming that it is "[the] intention," which, as is clear from the context, is, unlike cognitive intentionality, practical or volitional, which "is the fundamental structure of human reality" (*B&N*, 477, see also 476), a view reiterated by Merleau-Ponty, who writes that "Consciousness is in the first place not a matter of 'I think that' but of 'I can'."[16] And, as indicated in the fourth *skandha*, such *volitions* are directed by *habits* and *dispositions*, the latter of which, at least, presumably reflect our *desires* and *attachments*.

However, unlike the cognitive aspect of the subject which, as we have seen, is constituted exclusively in relation to objects of cognition, and thus as a "pole" of cognition, the volitional aspect indicated by the fourth *skandha* implies an author or/and director, who, initiating and guiding actions in conformity to habits and dispositions, would apparently have to exist prior to these volitional "effects"[17]; a seemingly independently subsistent, persistent aspect of the subject, which would, as such, be at odds with both contemporary and traditional "no-self" theories alike.

Existence and Essence

Recognizing this apparent dilemma, Sartre sets about circumventing it by distinguishing *existence* from *essence*. Having done so, he claims that in contrast to objects, the essences or persistent identities of which (or *what* they are) are always already given, along with their substantial existence (*that* they are), thus condemning them from the beginning to be *what* they are, for human subjectivity or consciousness, "existence precedes essence" (*B&N*, 568). This then leaves such subjective consciousness free to define itself by the choice of end or "fundamental project" (see *B&N*, 480, 564), which, he claims, constitutes a human's *essence* or identity. "[H]uman reality," he tells us, "is . . . a being which is originally a project . . . which is defined by its end"(*B&N*, 453, see also 443).

Thus while the *existence* of consciousness, which is to say aware subjectivity, provides the authorial agency for our choice of fundamental project, and, with the aid of the body, the concomitant volitional acts, it is these projects and acts which define, not to say *constitute*, individual *essences* or identities along with their associated habits and dispositions rather than vice versa. In which case the existence of conscious awareness is, prior to the projects and associated volitional acts which define individual identities, impersonal or prepersonal. As Sartre confirms, "I am nothing save this concrete project . . . this project . . . is nothing other than the choice of myself . . . " (*B&N*, 564). Nor should it be inferred that the individual or personal identity or "essence" constituted by such a choice is thereafter necessarily permanent, or even persistent, for consciousness is always free to abandon one fundamental project for another (see *B&N*, 436-439) to "effect a rupture with its own past" (*B&N*, 436), and in so doing, to change its identity.

In sum then, so far from accounting for the volitional acts which articulate the volitional tendencies (or fundamental projects) mentioned in the fourth *skandha*, in terms of a *persistently* self identical individual subject *subsisting* prior to, and therefore *independently* of, these acts, thereby undermining any no-self theory, Sartre has, by distinguishing existence or being from essence or identity, been able to argue that it is these very acts, and the choices embodied therein, that constitute the identity of individual subjects, and therefore their existence *qua* individual subjects. On this view, and in exact concurrence with Buddhism, individual or personal identity is an *insubstantial* and *impermanent product* of the desires and/or attachments which, presumably, occasion the acts and concomitant choice (of fundamental project) which define or constitute it. And therefore, by choosing differently, any "subject" is always capable of reinventing him/herself as *essentially* different, to the extent that, in the limiting case of the complete absence of desires or attachments, and thus of the projects to which they give rise, individual identity would dissolve altogether, resulting in escape from *saṃsāra*, escape from reincarnation.

No-self and Reincarnation

This being so, then to conceive of any particular individual self making this escape and reaching a state of *nirvāṇa*, is, as is well recognized, a misconception. For, if individual identity is the product of the desires and attachments which give rise to the "fundamental project" which constitutes it, and the absence of such desires and attachments, and the concomitant dissolution of individual identity, is a precondition of escape from *saṃsāra*, then clearly "nobody ever enters *nirvāṇa*." But if individual identity is an illusion, then equally it appears that even when *nirvāṇa* or cessation of desires and/or attachments is not achieved, there is in reality no self to be reincarnated; a conclusion seemingly at odds with the Buddhist doctrine.

However, this apparent paradox is easily dispelled once we come to understand that it is not individual identity *per se* which Buddhists take to be illusory, but rather its supposed persistence and subsistent independence; its subsistence and persistence independently of the desires and attachments which give rise to the actions and choices which, as we have just argued, constitute it. Indeed, in giving rise to the choices and actions which emanate from the aggregates or *skandhas* in which they arise, such desires and attachments not only thereby constitute the identities of these aggregates or *skandhas*, but also, as we shall see, give rise to the very *existence* of further *skandhas*, and influence their desires and attachments, and thus the choices and actions, which constitute their *identities* in turn; and it is in this sense, as we shall argue, that such desires and attachments, and the identities to which they give rise, can be said to be reincarnated.

Thus to begin, the very existence of the first *skandha*, the very fact *that there are*/"we have" physical bodies is, rather obviously the result of our forbearers' sexual desires, and the procreative acts to which they gave rise, as so too therefore is the existence of the other *skandhas* (two through five), which is to say the fact *that* there are/"we have" experiences, mental states, and dispositions. For quite clearly, without bodies, their sense organs and brains, there could be no such states or dispositions. Furthermore, in determining who exactly had sexual relationships with whom, and when, our forbearers' desires and attachments determine the genetic, and therefore the physical, characteristics of such bodies, or *what*, in the *genetic* or *physical* sense, they/"we" are.

Further our desires and attachments which, in giving rise to our actions and choices, constitute our identities—which is to say who or *what*, *psychologically* speaking, we are—arise, if not directly from the genetic structure we derive from our forbearers, then from the interaction between these *genetically* structured bodies, including brains, and the world or *environment*; a world that includes not merely natural elements, but artifacts as well as social, economic and cultural relations and institutions, initially formed by our predecessors. As Foucault explains, while: ". . . the subject constitutes himself in an active fashion, by the practices of the self, these practices are nevertheless not something that the individual invents by himself. They are patterns that he finds in his culture and which are proposed, suggested and imposed on him by his culture, his society and his social group."[18] And these social and cultural, not to mention economic, relations and institutionalized practices, which we inherit from our predecessors, reflect, as Deleuze and Guattari have explicated in detail,[19] the desires and attachments of those, (our predecessors), who constituted them.

This being so then as we can hopefully now see, not only do our *predecessors'* desires and attachments give rise both to our physical existence or embodiment and to our particular *genetic nature*, but in also shaping the artifactual, economic, social, and cultural *environments* which *nurture us*, *their* desires and attachments influence *our* desires and attachments,[20] and thus the choices and actions which constitute our identities. While our desires and attachments are, in turn, not only responsible for the procreation of our *successors* and for determining their particular *genetic nature*, but also for shaping the artifactual, economic, social and cultural environment that will *nurture them*, and thereby influence *their* desires and attachments, and thus the choices and actions which will constitute their identities, and so on and on.

Thus, our desires and attachments give rise to actions and choices which, in addition to constituting our identities, are responsible for both the genetic physiology, and the economic, social and cultural etc. practices and institutions which, together, structure or form the identities—which is to say the desires and attachments, along with the actions and choices which constitute the identities—of our successors; while our desires and attachments, etc., were in their turn structured or formed by the practices and institutions of our predecessors.

From the above then it is now clear that what is reincarnated is not an independently subsisting persistent self that would undermine the Buddhist "no-self" doctrine, but desires and attachments, and the impermanent and dependent identities constituted by choices and actions deriving therefrom. Our desires and attachments, derived from the genetic legacy, practices, and institutions reflective of the desires and attachments of our predecessors, are in turn reflected in the genetic legacy, practices and institutions which form our successors; and in this way these desires and attachments, together with the identities to which they give rise, are passed on, or reincarnated. In this sense then, as Huang Po has observed:

> . . . mind, beside which nothing exists, . . . is without beginning, is unborn and indestructible. It . . . has neither form nor appearance. It does not belong to the categories of things which exist or do not exist . . . . It is that which you see before you . . . .[21]

Identity, Autonomy, and Freedom

We have seen above then how desires and attachments, and the impermanent identities constituted by the actions and choices to which they give rise, may be passed on, and that when understood in this way the doctrine of reincarnation is indeed compatible with the "no-self" theory. However, the question that now arises is whether, in the absence of an independently subsisting, persistent, self, we have the necessary autonomy to be responsible, as Buddhists claim, for failure to escape *saṃsāra* for *nirvāṇa*. For if we are indeed nothing but the *skandhas*, and if these, so far from being independent and persistent, are, as we have argued, constituted and shaped by genetic inheritance and/or a continually changing artifactual, economic, social, and cultural environment, then so too, or so it would seem, will be our choices and actions, in which case we cannot be held responsible for them.[22] In sum then, if the view that one is an independently subsisting self is indeed an illusion, then there is no one to be held responsible for failing to escape *saṃsāra*, and no independent person capable of initiating escape therefrom.

However while the feelings, mental formations, habits and dispositions, etc. which constitute the *skandhas* are certainly, *in the first instance* at least, the products of (our) genetic inheritance and environment, and thus, from a Buddhist perspective, of the *karma* responsible for their constitution, the ability to reflect upon, and thus become conscious of, all this (the fifth *skandha*), makes it possible, as here, to understand ("our") desires and attachments, their role in sustaining the illusion of an independently subsisting, persistent self, and the suffering associated therewith. Moreover such reflection also makes it possible to become conscious of, and understand, abstract concepts, and, most significantly, the formal relations between concepts, or reason. And once *The Age of Reason*[23] has been attained it is possible to employ and develop the rational capacity for analysis, abstraction, extrapolation, interpolation, and synthesis etc. This enables critical evaluation of, and articulation of alternatives to, (our) hitherto environmentally or/and genetically determined ways of perceiving, conceiving and understanding, ourselves, others and the world, (our perspectives), along with the values, attitudes and beliefs related thereto. This in turn facilitates the re-evaluation of our choices—including that of the "fundamental project" which defines identity—and the judgments and actions etc. associated therewith, thereby guaranteeing our freedom.

Surprisingly enough then, and exactly contrary to preliminary intuitions, an initially dependent, insubstantial, consciousness or subject, being able to change its identity, and the choices, judgments and actions which define and emanate from it, may be free, while an independently subsisting subject which, like an object, must apparently be and remain persistently self-identical unless and until caused to change by some "externally" determining (environmental)[24] factor, may not be. Thus it seems that only if and insofar as human consciousness, like Heraclitus' river, or a candle flame, is an insubstantial process, a constant surpassing of itself as it was, towards what it is not yet, and as such impermanent or non-self identical (see *B&N*, 478, see also 479 & 549) can it, of its own volition, escape being what it initially discovers itself to be already constituted as, and therefore be truly free. Sartre concurs, informing us that "The distinguishing characteristic of consciousness . . . is that it is . . . impossible to define . . . as coincidence with itself" (*B&N*, 74) and concomitantly that it ". . . is defined . . . as being what it is not, and not being what it is" (*B&N*, lxv; see also 492, 566).

On this view then the Buddhist notion of the self as insubstantial and non-persistent consciousness is not only compatible with, but is a necessary precondition of, freedom, and therefore of responsibility for escaping or failing to escape *saṃsāra* for *nirvāṇa*. For only such an insubstantial and non self-identical consciousness, thus able to free itself of those genetic and environmental factors which seem to be determinative of the characteristics or essential identity of a substantial being, may make choices which eventually result in such radical transformations that s/he might literally, rather than figuratively, become an essentially different person, or, in the limiting case, choose to reject or transcend altogether those desires and attachments that are, as we have seen, the precondition of any sense of identity whatsoever.

Finally then, as Dōgen concludes:

> To study the self is to forget the self. To forget the self is to be actualized by myriad things. When actualized by myriad things, your body and mind, as well as the bodies and minds of others drop away.[25]

Notes

1. Edmund Husserl, *The Crisis of European Sciences, and Transcendental Phenomenology*, trans. David Carr (Evanston, IL: Northwestern University Press., 1970), 216, my additions in parentheses. Subsequent references to Husserl's writings will be noted in the text as follows:

I: *Ideas*., trans. W. R. Boyce-Gibson (NY: Collier, 1962).

Incidentally, the fact that consciousness has no material existence, and cannot therefore be said to occupy space, may seem to pose *a priori* difficulties for the notion of a "mind" or consciousness transplant, referred to previously. However following Sartre's analysis of the convergence of perspectives, it may nevertheless have spatial co-ordinates. See Jean-Paul Sartre, *Being and Nothingness*, trans. Hazel Barnes, (New York: New York Philosophical Library, 1956), 316-318. Subsequent references to Sartre's writings will be noted in the text as follows:

B&N: Being and Nothingness

TE : *The Transcendence of the Ego*, trans. F. Williams & R. Kirkpatrick (New York: Farrar, Strauss & Giroux, undated).

2. In this context I use the term reify to indicate the view of the mind as a thing or object, when, as we shall argue, as supposedly a subject, it is no sort of object, either material or immaterial, at all.

3. See particularly Hegel's analysis of the movement from the "perception" of the self as a reified object (the second stage) to the "understanding" of self as a subject (the third stage), in G. W. F. Hegel, *The Phenomenology of Mind*, trans. J.Baillie (New York: Harper, 1967), esp. Ch.IV, 217 ff. Subsequent references to Hegel's writings will be noted in the text as follows:

POM: Phenomenology of Mind.

LH: *The Logic of Hegel* (or "Lesser Logic," abstracted from *The Encyclopedia of Philosophy of Science*), trans. William Wallace (Oxford: Clarendon Press, 1975).

4. This theme and distinction between pure and impure reflection run throughout Sartre's work. However for a basic understanding see particularly (*TE*, 44-45 & *B&N*, lii-liii, 151-153, 155, 160-161 and 173).

5. Thus Sartre tells us that "All consciousness, as Husserl has shown, is consciousness of something" (*B&N*, liii) which is to say it is essentially or "intentionally" related to the world of objects.

6. Thus following Hegel's recognition that self-consciousness arises from its relation to other self-consciousnesses who make me "self-conscious" (*POM*, 229), Sartre tells us that "I see *myself* because somebody sees *me*..." (*B&N*, 260, see 259-261), that individuals' identities are self-conscious because reciprocally co-constituted.

7. For a fuller and more complete exposition of this distinction between pure and impure reflection, and of many of the other points that follow from it, see Simon Glynn, "The Eye / I of the Paradox: Sartre's View of Consciousness" in *Sartre: An Investigation of Some Major Themes*, ed. Simon Glynn (Aldershot and VT: Gower, 1987).

8. Martin Heidegger, *Being and Time* (1927), trans. J. Macquarrie & E. Robinson (New York: Harper & Row, 1962), 72. References will be given in the text hereafter as *B&T*.

9. Dōgen, *Shōbōgenzō*, in *Zenrui*, No.10, as quoted by Philip Kapleau in *The Three Pillars of Zen* (New York: Doubleday/Anchor, 1989), 215.

10. See, for example, Edmund Husserl, *Cartesian Meditations*, trans. D. Cairns (The Hague: Nijhoff, 1970), 66.

11. This notwithstanding the fact that, in addition to such "empirical consciousness," Husserl himself actually also subscribed to a Transcendental ego, for as Sartre demonstrates in *The Transcendence of the Ego*, such a conception of consciousness is as empirically unverifiable as it is functionally unnecessary.

12. I am using the term "empirical" here, as I do throughout, in the phenomenological sense, which is to say as depending upon experience regardless of whether such experience is sensory experience of material object and events, etc., or non-sensory experience of immaterial objects (such as centaurs and unicorns), events (such as dreams and memories), and states (such as emotions) etc. Thus while phenomenology certainly distinguishes sensory experiences and their objects from non-sensory experiences and their "objects" as being different in kind, unlike the so called "naïve" empiricism of the type advocated by Locke and Co., it does not start with the metaphysical presumption that only the former can provide the basis of genuine knowledge, nor dismiss the latter as altogether insignificant.

13. Vasubandhu, *Triṃśikā-vijñapti-kārikā*, in *Buddhist Texts Throughout the Ages*, trans. E. Conze (New York: Harper, 1964).

14. Jacques Derrida, *Positions*, trans. Alan Bass (Chicago: University of Chicago Press, 1981), 28.

15. M. Heidegger, "What Is a Thing," in *Martin Heidegger: Basic Writings*, ed. D. Krell (New York: Harper & Row, 1976), 279. My addition in parentheses.

16. Maurice Merleau-Ponty, *The Phenomenology of Perception*, trans. Colin Smith (London: Routledge & Kegan Paul, 1962), 137.

17. Cause must, of course, precede the effect to which it gives rise.

18. Michel Foucault "The Ethics of Care for the Self as a Practice of Freedom" in *Philosophy & Social Criticism* 12 (1987), 122, quoted in John McGowan, *Postmodernism and its Critics* (Ithaca, NY: Cornell University Press, 1991), 140-141.

19. See G. Deleuze & F. Guattari, *Anti-Oedipus: Capitalism and Schizophrenia* (London: Athlone, 1977).

20. Rom Harré and others have shown how our emotions or feelings are socially constructed. See for example, Rom Harré, ed. *The Social Construction of Emotions* (New York: Blackwell, 1986).

21. *The Zen Teachings of Huang-po*, trans. & ed. John Blofeld (London: Buddhist Society, 1958), 29, as quoted by David Loy in "Indra's Postmodern Net" in *Philosophy East and West*, vol. 43, no. 3 (July 1993): 481-510, 505.

22. Indeed even if, contra Buddhism, one were gratuitously to invoke the aid of a metaphysical soul as a potential basis of autonomy, any choices and/or actions emanating from it would be determined by its nature and therefore far from free.

23. This is, of course, the title of the first book of Sartre's "Roads to Freedom" trilogy.

24. Of course if genetics indeed plays some part in the constitution of our values, attitudes and beliefs, etc., upon which our choices are based, then if it became possible to influence the values etc. of an already existing subject by genetic intervention, genetics would also become an independent determining and therefore in this sense "external," factor.

25. Dōgen in *Moon in a Dewdrop: Writings of Zen Master Dōgen,* ed. Kazuaki Tanahashi (San Francisco: North Point Press, 1985), 50, quoted by Davide Loy in "Avoiding the Void: The Lack of Self in Psychotherapy and Buddhism," in *The Journal of Transpersonal Psychology*, vol. 24, no. 2 (1992), 173.

Twelve

Self and Self Image

Steven W. Laycock

There are things like reflecting pools, and images, an infinite reference from one to the other, but no longer a source, a spring. There is no longer a simple origin. For what is reflected is split *in itself* and not only as an addition to itself of its image. The reflection, the image, the double, splits what it doubles. (Jacques Derrida)[1]

> My uttered "I" *need not reflect* the intending factor which "places" the "I" . . . since reflexivity has dissolved, the moment wherein the human mind is "together" and, thus, capable of knowing (naming) *other things* no longer exists. (Robert Magliola)[2]

No matter how faithful, no matter how accurately descriptive it might be, reflective [*re*]presentation, could disclose *the self only* if it were possible to speak of consciousness it[*self*], consciousness *as such*; *only,* that is, if it presented the "self" of [*self-*]consciousness; *only*, once again, if consciousness maintained an ontic/ontological and transtemporal integrity; *only* if it refrained from its perplexing habit of flinging itself centrifugally beyond itself, deferring its very being beyond "itself," of lodging itself in that which it *is not.* Consciousness is not only "beside itself," ek-static, it *is* its own ecstasy. Findlay puzzles: "How can mind be thus `ecstatic', thus self-transcendent, we are inclined to ask, and it does not seem a sufficient answer at a sufficiently deep level of reflection to say that such ecstasy, such self-transcendence, is the very mark of the mental."[3] But the question that we are "inclined to ask" belies the suspicion that consciousness might be otherwise, that it might simply rest in itself without throwing itself away. If self-transcendence becomes a question, we must assume that self-immanence is original or normative. And we seek to resolve (not solve) Findlay's quandary by showing that the very "self" of self-consciousness is its self-alienation, its self-dispersal. Transparency, self-transcendence, ecstasy is not the "mark" of consciousness, its essential structure, but its very being. Cautiously echoing Sartre, it is not simply that consciousness is "what" it is not, but far more radically, that its very *being* resides "elsewhere." It is *that* which it is not.

It is to Robert Magliola's enduring credit that he bears clear, effective, and eloquent witness to the centrifugal, disintegral, unstable, and phenomenologically elusive comportment of the self. That he can do so in a single phrase—"reflexivity has dissolved"—is extraordinary. Only a self that displays itself in presence, that imbibes the character of ideality—"the possibility of a return ad infinitum" (*SP*, 9-10)—could bear reflexive relations of being conscious *of itself*, appearing *to itself*, being *itself*—to itself. But consciousness is not ideal. And crediting the Buddhist insight, the emptiness and impermanence of all things ensures that ideality is a conceptual mirage. Magliola, with Derrida, is determined to "think-out" the "un-thought-out" logic of presence, "its 'principle of principles', that is to say, its intuitionism, the absolute privilege of the living present . ..." ("TT," 39). Consciousness is "apocalyptic," explosive, deferring both being and appearing beyond "itself," or rather, deferring self to other. And for Derrida, the apocalyptic is "a transcendental condition of all discourse, of all experience itself, of every mark or every trace (*MP*, 87).

Merleau-Ponty declares that "consciousness has a '*punctum caecum*' . . .,"[4] a blind spot. In the Buddhist analysis offered here, consciousness does not "have," but rather *is*, a "blind spot" in the sense that, lacking reflexivity, it cannot appear to "itself." Magliola quotes Derrida with evident approbation: "nonpresence and nonevidence are admitted into the blink of the instant. There is a duration to the blink, and it closes the eye" (*DOM*, xi). While the eye is, in the perennial trope, an ineluctable condition of visibility, it cannot see itself. Indeed, "[e]ven the sharpest sword cannot cut itself; the finger-tips cannot be touched by the same finger-tips. *Citta* [mind] does not know itself."[5] Again: "reflexivity has dissolved." Mind is not—as the thematic amalgam of [*con*]sciousness wherein, presumptively, the consciousness is present *to itself*—"together." Or in Magliola's words, in this presumptive moment of togetherness, the moment at which consciousness would be seamlessly one in its self-presence, it "no longer exists." It cannot, in principle, get its act together. And this, of course, engenders a cascade of implications with regard to the nature of subjectivity and its purported alliance with "objects." In the immediacy of experience, no contrast is possible between subject and object. Thus "*other things*" (objects)—cannot exist (*as* objects), the subject cannot exist (*as* subject), and the self cannot exist as an objectification of subjectivity. As Henry says, "[t]he subject is not the opposite of the object, it is the opposite of being" (*DOM*, 159). "As a Vietnamese monk of the eleventh century said, '*The free man sees all, but nothing is seen by him.*'"[6]

The humorous (if also repellant) story of a friend who underwent an eye operation sharpens the point. Under local anesthesia, both of her eyes were extracted from their sockets by suction and placed in a tray immediately below. She tells me that in this remarkable situation, one of her eyes could actually see the other. Of course, we commonly see our "own" eyes in the mirror. Or rather, we see the reflection of our eyes. My friend's experience involved the unmediated perception of one eye by the other. But the point still stands. *This very eye cannot see itself.* At best, the extraordinary perception of one eye by the other models the event of reflection in which the mind objectifies its own activities. The reflecting consciousness is not, and cannot be its own object, for "reflexivity has dissolved."

As Dōgen observes, "[s]ince there is no mind in me, when I hear the sound of raindrops from the eaves, the raindrop is myself."[7] This does not entail the absurd project of identifying "two" ostensible non-identicals. Wittgenstein sagely discerned that "to say of two things that they are identical is nonsense, and to say of one thing that it is identical with itself is to say nothing at all."[8] Thus, Hegel is surely correct in affirming that "no mind thinks or forms conceptions or speaks, in accordance with the law of identity, A is A, and ... no existence of any kind whatever conforms to it"[9] (*TLP*, 136-137). Concomitantly, Dōgen is not expressing the unmistakably dualistic claim that the raindrop (one thing) is identical with the self (another), but is rather abnegating dualism in its most pervasive and subtle guise. For the eye, there is no eye. For the mind, there is no mind. And for the subject, there is *no subject*, and thus, no counterposed *object*. For enlightened perception, the raindrop is not an ontically independent object *identical* with the self. It is rather *non-different*. For in immediate experience, there is, and in principle can be, nothing, no thematic posit, no discernible feature, in terms of which subjectivity can be distinguished from objectivity.

Nor is Dōgen postulating the Self as a Great Object, a great *One* that absorbs or sublates the multiplicity of narrowly circumscribed selves and swallows up manifold objectivity. Counting is duplicity. To count—even to one—assumes a dyad of counter and counted. And monism is accordingly self-contradictory. Reality has no "outside," and cannot be enumerated. "One" applies only to that which can display its exterior. But this display would be a "view from nowhere." For reality embraces all possible vantage points. And the division of "inside" from "outside" already entails a "second" beyond the "one" counted. Dōgen's radical non-dualism is incompatible with the postulation of reality as unitary or single, as a [*uni*]verse, a bounded *whole* delivered to our intuition in a single (*uni-*) turn (*versus*), and is incompatible, *a fortiori*, with the perception of this purported unity as identical with the self. In Berg's almost comically paradoxical expression, "I'm not here so I see everything ...."[10] But this "everything" is not "an" everything, a [*uni*]verse or *a* (single) universal Self. As Being is not *a* being, so, also, the All is not *an* all—and as *a* being is not at all. The eighth-century Chan teacher, Zhi of Yunzhu, affirmed: "There is seeing, but nothing is seen." A monk queried: "If there is nothing seen, how can we say there is any seeing at all?" Said Zhi: "In fact there is no trace of seeing." The monk inquired: "In such a seeing, whose seeing is it?" In Zhi's retort: "There is no seer, either."[11] Egolessness (Pāli: *anattā*; Sanskrit: *anātman*) motivates the question, "Where is this "I"? What does it look like?"[12] And an expectable Buddhist reply is that it has no "look." It "looks like" nothing at all. Or to echo Magliola's words, "reflexivity has dissolved." Consciousness is not related *to itself* for it has no self, no "it[self]," to serve as terminus of reflexive self-relation. Consciousness is not *a* consciousness. Nor can there be a plurality of consciousnesses. One counts only what can be subsumed under a category. And consciousness, as the ground and possibility of any category whatsoever, is not—"itself"—subject to subsumption. Being transcategorial, it is also transordinal and indenumerable. To front the word "consciousness" with the indefinite article is to betray a failure of insight.

Though perhaps an object of thought, a plaything of theory, the "I," apprehended—not *a la* Sartre, as a transcendent *Gestalt* of states, actions, and qualities, the objectified exterior of consciousness—but as the agent of perception, the "seer," the agency whereby ontic plurality is disclosed, is in no way present in our immediate experience. Rejoining Shenxiu's poetic postulation of the mirror-likeness of mind (*xin ji mingjingtai*), Huineng (638-713 C.E.), the sixth ancestral teacher of the Chan tradition, responded that there never was a mind-mirror (*xinjing yi feitai*). The reciprocal repulsion of these diptych claims is, however, merely apparent. On deeper investigation, we find not only compatibility, but also co-implication. For if mind-heart (*xin*) is, indeed, like a mirror (*jing*), or like a mirror-stand (*jingtai*), then, like a mirror, it cannot reflect itself. And if consciousness is, indeed, like the eye, then nothing reflected, nothing perceived, is "itself." For the mirror, there is no mirror.[13] Or rather, any mirror standing before the mirror is not the "original" mirror itself. Or again, whatever stands before the mirror as an object of reflection is not "itself" a mirror at all. Indeed, "[t]o see one's double is to see oneself dead" (*WNOW*, 22). For the mirror, in its reflective functioning, is precisely that which withholds itself from objective representation. Or again, in the interplay, in the *mise-en-abime*, one mirror reflected within another without end, there is, as Derrida suggests, "no longer a source, a spring." The construal of the reflected image as an "addition" assumes the originary status of the object. If "there is no longer a simple origin," then the object is no longer unitary and independent, a unit of being, but a moment of an internal doubling, a co-conspirator in ontological duplicity. This is echoed in Trinh thi Minh-ha's observation that "When i say 'I see myself seeing myself,' I/i am not alluding to the illusory relation of subject to subject (or object) but to the play of mirrors that defers to infinity the real subject and subverts the notion of an original 'I'" (*WNOW*, 22).

In exactly this way, "the concept of a nonunified or decentered (the usual terms are *egoless* or *selfless*) cognitive being is the cornerstone of the entire Buddhist tradition."[14] Consciousness is "decentered," not merely in its being perpetually displaced beyond direct figural objectification, but more radically, in its being entirely incapable of objectification in any way. And the unenlightened, experientially insensitive, response to this deprivation of center, this self-effacement, is narcissistic. As Dillon observes, "we find the familiar figure of philosophical Narcissus still absorbed in his own reflection. . . . Narcissus has always sought his reflection outside himself. He has always sought what he lacks to be himself in the Other that is beyond himself: Narcissus has always been decentered."[15] Merleau-Ponty concurs: "I am a self-presence that is an absence from self" (*VE-E*, 250). Thus, "[v]ision . . . is the means given me for being absent from myself, for being present at the fission of Being from the inside . . . ."[16] Yet both claims retain a subtle vestige of externalism. We could be in a position to describe Narcissus as "absorbed in his own reflection" only from a certain elevation, a position external both to Narcissus and his reflection, from which original and its purported supplement could be displayed and compared.

Despite the deep-lying insight of these claims, we must insist that Narcissus is not "narcissistic" at all. In Bulfinch's classic interpretation, Narcissus "fell in love with himself."[17] Edinger proposes an antipodal interpretation. For him, "Narcissus represents the alienated ego that cannot love ... because it is not yet related to itself. To fall in love with the reflected image of oneself can only mean that one does not yet possess oneself"[18] (*BM*, 161). But if "reflexivity has dissolved," then self-relation is an illusion. And Narcissus could love only at the cost of being deluded. In neglecting Narcissus' own standpoint, both interpretations fall short of the demands imposed by a rigorous phenomenology. *For Narcissus* (not *for us*), the object of passionate admiration is not himself but the elusive youth that he spies in the silver water. It is only by standing outside of Narcissus' situation, by taking up an external vantage point, that we can call attention to the purported duality of "original" and reflection and posit a cognitive "mistake." And likewise, it is only from the altitude of reflection, the *pensee de survol*, that the subject/object schema has any application to the description and analysis of our experience. From its "own" standpoint, consciousness reveals neither consciousness "itself" nor a reflection or representation of consciousness. In its engagement, it provides no materials from which the conception of self could be constructed.

Moreover, were Narcissus to desire himself, he would, as engaged consciousness, cease to be. The desire for oneself—one's self—is a confession of default, the admission of a failure of self-possession. And as Borch-Jacobsen observes, "if I *desire* to be (an) I, if I *desire* myself, it must, following elementary logic, be because I am not it. Thus, this singular desire, by and large, is the desire of no subject."[19] Narcissus neither loves nor desires "himself." He could be himself, and could desire to be himself, only by failing to be.

The mirror, understood not as a manifest presence, an object in the room made visible by its frame (or perhaps its stand), the glare of light refracted from its surface, the discoloration of its glass, the irregularities of its taint, but as the pure functioning of mirror[*ing*], is constituted precisely by its having no presence, no opacity, no "self." It "itself" cannot be seen. It "is" its very *not being* for us. Its "presence" is precisely its absence. And for it, from its "own" point of view, there is neither ownness nor position-taking. As Levin remarks, "to be 'possessed by' the visible is to be a *cogito* dispossessed: an ego not in total possession of itself; an ego not totally present to (for) itself."[20] But consciousness is not simply lacking a few degrees in "total possession of itself," thus referring to an ideal and ideally realizable fullness of self-presence. It is totally lacking in self-possession. Yet this momentous absence is constitutive. For the mirror, *to be* is exactly *not* to possess a self. In Dews' explanation, "[t]his is because, however many times it is reduplicated, the image of the observer seeing him- or herself, which appears in the mirror, must always remain the object of an uncaptured *pre-existing gaze*."[21] It is not that the mirror is "devoid" of self, that a void remains where the self *could*, perhaps *should*, be. It is not that the mirror has been dispossessed of that which belongs to it by right, that which is most intimately its "own," that *de facto* selfhood is simply exchanged for *de jure* selfhood. Rather, the mind-mirror is essentially, necessarily, originally selfless. Self is not an unspeakable residue that remains after all objectivity has been excluded. "A Cartesian," writes Merleau-Ponty, "does not see *himself* in the mirror; he sees a dummy, an 'outside' ...."[22] But this is not to say that the mirror "itself" is the self posed against this "outside." *For* the mirror, there *is* no mirror "itself." Heidegger claims that "man everywhere and always encounters only himself."[23] But we could see our own reflection in the mirror of Being only if we knew what we look like. But we have never seen "ourselves" directly and are not in a position to construe the world as our image.

Imagine a perfect mirror, a mirror completely free from flaws, discoloration, glare, any phenomenal trait that would call attention to "itself," announce itself, stand as a locus of opacity. The perfect mirror is utterly self-effacing. Or rather, it has no "self," no opacity, to efface. Or rather, still, its "self" is exactly its absence of self. Seeing a reflection in a perfect mirror is indistinguishable from perceiving the purported "original." Phenomenologically, the "two" are the same experience. The one cannot be discriminated from the other simply on the basis of its visual properties. From a purely phenomenological point of view, we cannot tell whether the qualities of the object are "in" the mirror or "out" there in the world. And likewise, we cannot be in a position to affirm that the gossamer presence, the ectoplasmic sheen, that consciousness offers to itself in self-presence is "within" consciousness. And neither can we affirm, warranted only by the experience of self-presence, that consciousness is pure revelation, opening upon a mist of opacity entirely external to it. Experientially, there is neither "inside" nor "outside." The distinction is theoretical, metaphysical, but not phenomenological. Experientially, it is *exactly as if* the presence of self-presence were in consciousness. And it is also, with perfect fidelity to experience, *exactly as if* consciousness opened upon a presence outside itself. The two seemings are undecidaole. But this has dramatic consequences for a theory of consciousness. For it turns out that the category of immanence is vacuous.

An object or objectivity is "immanent," in the Husserlian sense, if its being and its appearing are one, if, in Sartre's words, it conforms to "the absolute law of consciousness for which no distinction is possible between appearance and being."[24] It is not easy to find an appropriate illustration. A headache might be said to be "immanent" inasmuch as there is no more, and no less, to the headache than its being felt. Its being is its appearing. But if a single headache can diminish in intensity over time, it gives itself off in a series of aspects, and thus exceeds, in its being, any particular appearing. There is one headache, but many appearances. Thus, no appearance can straightforwardly coalesce with the headache. Far from immanent, the headache turns out to be transcendent. An object is transcendent if there is always more "to" it (more being) than can ever appear in any array of appearings. The acts and events of consciousness have typically been regarded as immanent. Yet any phenomenal opacity by which the act "itself" is revealed to consciousness is ambiguous. We cannot tell, simply by reflection, whether this presence is "inside" or "outside." It is *exactly as if* both were equally and undecidably true. And for this reason, an act or event "of" consciousness is transcendent. There is always more than one way to see the act: it can appear *as if* its presence were intrinsic and also *as if* this same presence were simply revealed through it. The being of the act does not simply coalesce with its appearing, since there are always at least two appearings. Or perhaps we should say that to the extent that being and appearing do coalesce, consciousness is then internally divided, doubled.

In the more general case, consciousness is thought to offer itself to itself reflexively. Yet this purported self-presence is infected by the same ambiguity. And in principle, consciousness cannot simply *be* its appearance to itself without internal diremption. The implication is inescapable: not only are its acts transcendent, but consciousness "itself" is transcendent, perpetually eluding any self-presentation. Any phenomenon that announces itself as the "self" consciousness is not, and cannot be, consciousness itself. Thus, as Paul Klee avers, "I cannot be caught in immanence."[25] Consciousness is not "in" itself.

There is in Sartre's early thinking a strain of insight remarkably similar to the Buddhist repudiation of concealed, interior, substantial being. Consciousness is "all lightness, all translucence" (*TE*, 42). Yet it offers to "impure and conniving" reflection—a modality of reflection "which effects … a passage to the infinite" (*TE*, 64) and thus "affirms *more* than it knows" (*TE*, 65)—an "outside," a certain indistinctness, a ghostly haze, "as if interiority closed upon itself and proffered us only its outside; as if one had to 'circle about' it in order to understand it . . .(*TE*, 84). The *Larousse* of Sartre's French, defines "translucidity" (distinct from "transparency") as "that which allows light to pass without at the same time permitting one to see objects clearly through its thickness: frosted glass is translucid."[26] The translucent is, to some degree, in some respect, opaque. It is "impure," muddied, imperfectly capable of transmitting illumination, as if an otherwise crystalline consciousness were pervaded by a darkening cloud of color or discernible quality that offered to reflecting consciousness "something," however subtle, to *see*. The transparentism of Sartre's clearer insight is spoiled by the assumption that indistinctness, this ectoplasmic pervasion, "is interiority seen from the outside; or, if one prefers, indistinctness is the degraded projection of interiority" (*TE*, 85). And it is thanks to this ghostly presence that consciousness is visible to reflection.

Sartre seems to have been only marginally aware of the incompatibility of these two models, and modulates unconsciously from a transparentist to an ectoplasmic (translucentist) conception of consciousness. Yet, *pace* Sartre, while consciousness may be "pure translucidity," it is, nonetheless, "pure"—and a merely translucid consciousness is "impure," clouded and diffused in some degree by a permeating positivity of phenomenal quality. Moreover, the admitted shift in his thinking—not quite a *Kehre*, but an imperceptible passage, a not-entirely-recognized incongruity—from an anonymous consciousness to a conception of [*con*]sciousness—a knowing (*scientia*) ineluctably accompanied by (with: *con-*) a non-positional awareness of the event of knowing "itself"—is clearly a movement *away from* a transparentism. In some moods, Sartre will insist that the least hint of content, a wisp of discoloration "in" consciousness, "would slide into every consciousness like an opaque blade." It would "tear consciousness from itself," and would be "the death of consciousness" (*TE*, 40). Yet if "[a]ll is clear and lucid in consciousness . . ." (*TE*, 40), there should be no ectoplasmic haze, no indeterminate qualitative pervasion, no "matter," no *hyle*, no matter how subtle.

Moreover, the translucid is transparent in one respect and opaque in another. If consciousness is translucid, it admits of "respects," thus becoming multiperspectival, and thus exceeding in its *being* any particular *appearing*. If transcendence is invariance (thus in/difference) across the varying and differing modes of appearance (respects), then consciousness would be transcendent. Yet if consciousness, voracious for presence, is like "[t]he spider which draws things into its web, coats them with its own drivel, and slowly swallows, reducing them to its own nature,"[27] it preys upon the different and can hardly be "indifferent" to differing manifestations of presence.

If consciousness is present to it[self], it is self-predatory, it devours its "self." Yet this macabre feast is necessarily partial. For if Uroboros, ingesting his own tail, were to complete his grisly repast, there would remain not only no tail, but no snake. We are not spared "that primitive illusion . . . according to which to know is to eat—that is, to ingest the known object, to fill oneself with it (*Erfullung*), and to digest it ('assimilation')."[28] Were consciousness "itself" transcendent, were it to possess an "itself," consciousness as reflectively known would remain "in the same place, indefinitely absorbed, devoured, and yet indefinitely intact, wholly digested and yet wholly outside, as indigestible as stone ... the 'digested indigestible' . . . ."[29] But a consciousness governed by "the absolute law of consciousness for which no distinction is possible between appearance and being" (*TE*, 63) cannot—in principle—display itself in a manifold (or even a duality) of "respects." Consciousness is the "identity of appearance and existence."[30] It is "pure 'appearance' in the sense that it exists only to the degree to which it appears."[31] To whatever extent, in whatever way, it appears, it appears exactly *as it is*. It cannot appear in alternative "ways." And the suggestion that transparency and opacity are second-order traits, and do not, then characterize the "itself" of consciousness, is metaphysical, not phenomenological.

In Corless' quip, "Descartes said, 'I think therefore I am,' but Buddhism replies, 'Think again'."[32] Sartre did, in fact, "think again," and recognizes that "the consciousness which says *I Think* is precisely not the consciousness which thinks" (*TE*, 45). This reflective "synthesis of two consciousnesses, one of which is consciousness *of* the other" (*TE*, 44) is "detotalized," decentered, ruptured. Or in Magliola's elegantly simple description, the human mind is not "together." Sartre, no less than Buddhism, would reject Valery's assumption that "[b]etween what I say and what I hear myself say, no exteriority, no alterity, not even that of a mirror seems to interpose itself ... The [interior] voice ... can accomplish the circular return of the origin to itself" (quoted in "AT," 127). For Valery, interior speech is "[l]ike a closed circuit" and is "similar to the snake biting its tail" (quoted in "AT," 287). But in a rumination more consonant with Sartre's view, "Who speaks, who listens? It is not exactly the same ... The existence of the speech from self to self is the sign of a *cut*" (quoted in "AT," 189). In reflection, consciousness is cut off from "itself," its unity fractured. It is severed, breached. And to this extent, the ventriloquism of Sartre's reflective synthesis is Derridean. "Do not forget," admonishes Derrida, "that you are the nucleus [*le noyau*] of a rupture"[33] (*WD*, 67)—*are*, not "have." For Derrida, "[t]here is no longer a simple origin," for "what is reflected is split *in itself* and not only as an addition to itself of its image. The reflection, the image, the double, splits what it doubles" (*OG*, 9). In Dews explication, "[t]here is no domain of `phenomenological silence,' of intuitive self-presence prior to the representational, and therefore divisive, function of language."[34]

The projected affirmation, "I Think," on the part of the reflecting consciousness which merely *says* "I Think," but does not think—or which, rather, is represented as saying so, since, unthinking, it is also mute—is an echo, the reflection (or re/flexion) of a primal institution of voice. Ventriloquism is the comportment of "a consciousness which imprisons itself in the world in order to flee from itself" (*TE*, 80), thus projecting upon the *I Think* "a degraded and bastard spontaneity, which magically preserves its creative power even while becoming passive" (*TE*, 81). The *cogito* is "an ontological puppet, whose inventor [i.e., Descartes] at the same time sketched a new figure of the philosopher as transcendental-talking ventriloquist. . . ."[35] Thus, [*c*]*ogito* means everything, except *I think*,"[36] for "reflexivity has dissolved" (*DOM*, 8). In Derrida's rather cryptic remark: "A more or less argot translation of the *cogito*: `I am therefore dead'" (*Glas*, 92). Or as Blanchot puts it, "[w]hen the Cartesian "I think, therefore I am" is written it is, in effect, rewritten as 'think, therefore I am not'."[37] The I recuperated in reflection has already elapsed. To be in a (reflective) position to say "I think" is, then, no longer to think. Sartre assumes, by contrast, that prereflective consciousness enjoys an authentic spontaneity, a legitimate originality of which the reflective representation is but a faded duplicate. But originality is lost in the reflective synthesis. The presumptive "original" may impress its outlines upon the reflective representation, but the representation, in turn, determines and informs its object, the "original." Or in Derrida's words, there is "an infinite reference from one to the other, but no longer a source, a spring" (*OG*, 9). Or rather, the source "is born of this very eluding, like a situated mirage, a site in a directionless field. It is nothing before being sought, only an effect produced by the structure of the movement. The source is therefore not the origin, it is neither at the departure or the arrival" ("AT," 287). Reflection can only recapture an elapsed event of thinking, a discarded husk, and not the live upsurge of present and engaged consciousness. And Derrida has shown us that "there is no longer a simple origin."

Though deceptively positing its object as present, reflection can never be strictly simultaneous with its posit. And as co-determinants, "reflection" and "original" mirror each other without primacy. As Trinh thi Minh-ha confirms, "[n]o primary core of irradiation can be caught hold of . . . ." Indeed, "[i]n this encounter of I with I, the power of identification is often such that reality and appearance merge while the tool itself becomes invisible" (*WNOW*, 22). Derrida writes:

> And when we ask the question: 'Who has been the subject of this experience' this question is perhaps already an answer, if, for the one who introduced it, it was affirmed through him in this interrogative form, substituting for the closed and unique 'I' the openness of a 'Who?' without answer. Not that this means that he simply had to ask himself: 'What is this me that I am?' but much more radically he had to seize hold of himself and not let go, no longer as an 'I?' but as a 'Who?,' the unknown and sliding being of an indefinite 'Who?.'[38]

In reflection, as in prereflective consciousness, the mind-mirror "becomes invisible." There is neither primary reality nor a merely apparent representation, but the endless free fall of reflection within reflection swallowed up in the "abyss" of the *mise-en-abime*. And if "reflexivity has dissolved" in interminable oscillation, Magliola's postulation of the ineluctable failure of "togetherness" on the part of mind is thereby validated.

Notes

1. Jacques Derrida, *Of Grammatology*, trans. G. C. Spivak (Baltimore: Johns Hopkins, 1976), 9. Hereafter *OG*. The following abbreviations will be used for Derrida's works:

"EW": "'Eating Well', or the Calculation of the Subject: An Interview with Jacques Derrida," in Eduardo Cadava, Peter Connor, Jean-Luc Nancy, eds., *Who Comes After the Subject?* (New York: Routledge, 1991).

Glas: trans. J. P. Leavey and R. A. Rand (Lincoln: University of Nebraska Press, 1986).

"AT": "Of an Apocalyptic Tone Recently Adopted in Philosophy," *Semeia*, 23 (1982).

MP: *Margins of Philosophy*, trans. Alan Bass (Chicago: Chicago University Press, 1982).

SP: *Speech and Phenomena and Other Essays on Husserl's Theory of Signs*, trans. David B. Allison (Evanston, IL: Northwestern University Press, 1973).

"TT": "The Time of a Thesis: Punctuations," in Alan Montefiore, ed., *Philosophy in France Today* (Cambridge: Cambridge University Press, 1983).

"WD": *Writing and Difference*, trans. Alan Bass (Chicago: University of Chicago Press, 1978).

2. Robert Magliola, *Derrida on the Mend* (West Lafayette, IN: Purdue University Press, 1986), 8. Hereafter *DOM*.

3. N. J. Findlay, *Ascent to the Absolute: Metaphysical Papers and Lectures* (New York: Humanities Press, 1970), 244.

4. Maurice Merleau-Ponty, *The Visible and the Invisible*, trans. Colin Smith (New York: Humanities Press, 1962), 247.

5. T.R.V. Murti, *The Central Philosophy of Buddhism: A Study of the Madhyamika System* (London: Allen & Unwin, 1987), 317-318.

6. Trinh Thi Minh-ha, *Woman, Native, Other: Writing Postcoloniality and Feminism* (Bloomington: Indiana University Press, 1989), 23. Hereafter *WNOW*.

7. Quoted in Kotoh Tetsuaki, "Language and Silence: Self-Inquiry in Heidegger and Zen," in *Heidegger and Asian Thought*, ed. Graham Parkes (Honolulu: University of Hawaii Press, 1987), 206.

8. Ludwig Wittgenstein, *Tractatus Logico-Philosophicus*, trans. D. F. Pears and B. F. McGuinness (Atlantic Highlands, NJ: Humanities Press, 1974), 5.5303, 52.

9. Wittgenstein, Tractatus Logico-Philosophicus, 136-137.

10. Stephen Berg, "To the Being We Are," in *Beneath a Single Moon: Buddhism in Contemporary American Poetry,* eds. Kent Johnson and Craig Paulenich (Boston, MA: Shambhala, 1991), 31.

11. Daisetz Teitaro Suzuki, *Zen Buddhism* (New York: Doubleday Anchor, 1956), 207.

12. Daisetz Teitaro Suzuki, *The Zen Doctrine of No-Mind: the Significance of the Sutra of Hui-Neng* (*Wei-Lang*), ed. Christmas Humphreys (New Beach: Samuel Wiser, 1981), 115.

13. For a fuller exposition of the narrative implications of the gathas of Shenxiu and Huineng, see Steven Laycock, *Mind as Mirror and the Mirroring of the Mind: Buddhist Reflections on Western Phenomenology* (Albany: State University of New York Press, 1994).

14. Francisco J. Varela, Evan Thompson, and Eleanor Rosch, *The Embodied Mind: Cognitive Science and Human Experience* (Cambridge, MA: The MIT Press, 1992), xviii.

15. M. C. Dillon, "Preface: Merleau-Ponty and Postmodernity," in *Merleau-Ponty Vivant* (Albany, NY: State University of New York Press, 1991), x.

16. Maurice Merleau-Ponty, The Primacy of Perception and Other Essays on Phenomenological Psychology, and the Philosophy of Art, History and Politics, ed. James M. Edie (Evanston, IL: Northwestern University Press, 1964), 186.

17. Thomas Bulfinch, *Bulfinch's Mythology* (New York: Gramercy Books, 1979), 102.

18. Bulfinch, *Bulfinch's Mythology*, 161.

19. Mikkel Borch-Jacobsen, "The Freudian Subject, from Politics to Ethics," in *Who Comes After the Subject*?, eds. Eduardo Cadava, Peter Connor, Jean-Luc Nancy (New York: Routledge, 1991), 66.

20. David Michael Levin, "Visions of Narcissism: Intersubjectivity and the Reversals of Reflection," in Dillon, "Preface: Merleau-Ponty and Postmodernity," 69.

21. Peter Dews, Logics of Disintegration: Post-Structuralist Thought and the Claims of Critical Theory (London: Verso, 1988), 87-88.

22. Merleau-Ponty, The Primacy of Perception and Other Essays, 170.

23. Martin Heidegger, *The Question Concerning Technology and Other Essays*, trans. W. Lovitt (New York: Harper and Row, 1977), 27.

24. Jean-Paul Sartre, *The Transcendence of the Ego: An Existentialist Theory of Consciousness*, trans. Forrest Williams & Robert Kirkpatrick (New York: The Noonday Press, 1972), 63. Hereafter *TE.*

25. Quoted in Merleau-Ponty, The Primacy of Perception and Other Essays, 188.

26. Translucidite: "qui laisse passer la lumiere, sans permettre toutefois de voir clairment, les objets a travers son epaisseur: les verres depolis sont translucides." Quoted in Phyllis Sutton Morris, "Sartre on the Self-Deceiver's Translucent Consciousness," *Journal of the British Society for Phenomenology*, vol. 23 (1992), 105.

27. Jean-Paul Sartre, quoted in "Introduction" to *The Philosophy of Jean-Paul Sartre,* ed. Robert Denoon Cumming (New York: Vintage, 1965), 19.

28. Jean-Paul Sartre, *Being and Nothingness: An Essay on Phenomenological Ontology,* trans. Hazel E. Barnes (New York: Washington Square Press, 1971), 258-259.

29. Sartre, Being and Nothingness, 739.

30. Sartre, Being and Nothingness, 17.

31. Sartre, Being and Nothingness, 17.

32. Roger J. Corless, *The Vision of Buddhism: The Space Under the Tree* (New York: Paragon House, 1989), 125.

33. Jacques Derrida, *Writing and Difference*, trans. Alan Bass (Chicago: University of Chicago Press, 1978), 67.

34. Dews, Logics of Disintegration, 19.

35. Gerard Granel, "Who Comes After the Subject?," in *Who Comes After the Subject?*, 148.

36. Michel Henry, "The Critique of the Subject," in *Who Comes After the Subject?*, 116.

37. Maurice Blanchot, *Thomas the Obscure*, trans. R. Lamberton (New York: David Lewis, 1973), 99.

38. Maurice Blanchot, *L'Amitie* (Paris: Gallimard, 1971), 110.

Thirteen

Zen Flesh, Bones, and Blood: Deconstructing Inter-Religious Dialogue

E. H. Jarow

> Even Buddha is lost in this land
> the immensity takes us all with it,
> pulverizes & takes us in
> Bodhidharma came from the West
> Coyote met him (Diane de Prima)

1

The synchronic and the diachronic, intertwined like a helix: can they ever be truly fleshed-out, taken out of their flesh and observed systematically? Or may the act itself be so injurious, that the eating of its fruit plunges you into an infinite regress of intimation, with any notion of origin shrouded in the murky narrative of myth? The Buddha, where is his beginning? In a *Śākya* tribe by the foothills of Nepal? In the overarching *dharmakāya*, buddhafields containing the "four immeasurables,"[1] or in the countless *sambhogakāya* array of jewel-quality emanations (*anantaguṇaratnavyūha*)?

Bodhidharma, it is said in the *Blue Cliff Record*, came to China from the west and was greeted by Emperor Wu of Liang, who wanted to know the highest meaning of the holy truths. "Vast emptiness, nothing is holy," replied Bodhidharma. "Who, then, is facing me?" asked the emperor. Bodhidharma's reply: "I don't know."[2]

Bodhidharma came from the west, but west of what?—of vast emptiness, with one shoe in his hand,[3] a *mudrā* of unknowing, but a *mudrā* just the same, a gesture containing, acknowledging its own erasure. Was this the first *gong'an* (but that would be another beginning)? The overtone of the *gong'an* is enigma, but the undertone is the tribunal; *gong'an* (Japanese *kōan*) is literally a "public case," and such a tribunal implies a confrontation with the other, a narrative discrepancy. Myths of origin are for the docile ear, confrontation thrives on difference; on "you," "me," and all the judgments and presuppositions that are brought to the table. It only admits to provisionary resolution. Confrontation becomes narrative/s, discourse as war (and despite its image of non-violence, Buddhist traditions have had their share of war); but war has often been (and continues to be) a form of commerce, as in discourse, and the exchange of words, like flesh, like goods, is constantly shifting. Fortunate is the one who can navigate their vehicle in the bazaar.

The Chan Buddhists, therefore, adopted a practice of confrontational dialogue rising from the precincts of indirection, not meant to inform—but to incite, to push one beyond the comfort-zone level of *écriture*. And perhaps there is only *gong'an*, every act a hermeneutic one, a translator's conundrum, with beginnings and endings being more or less impossible within the context of narrative, as Derrida tells us (*il n'y a pas de hors texte*[4]). And this, from another perspective, may very well be the condition of *saṃsāra* itself, the irredeemable movement of language and thought through a history which proceeds from other movements of language and thought, even while imagining, hoping, and waiting for its own conclusion. Of course, the Buddha was said to be beyond all this—just as Jesus was said to have overthrown the money changers in the temple. But that too is narrative, which gets exchanged with other narratives, publishing companies, compendiums, etc. And narratives, be they *Theravāda*, *Mahāyāna*, *Vajrayāna*, and on down, tend to contend with one another.

When the philosopher Spinoza declared that he was no longer looking for "truth" in scripture but was looking for "meaning," a door cracked open onto the helix-like phenomenon of undecidable multiplicity, a humbling awareness of otherness that only appears as "contemporary" from a reductive station. And the Buddha, supposedly, knew this well; he refused to speculate upon origins, anointed no successor, and created no "ism." Still, "isms" abounded and abound. This seemingly contemporary (post-modern) explosion, this multi-juxtaposition —not only of religions and ideologies, but perhaps more importantly of restaurants: Chinese, Japanese, Italian, Mexican, Vietnamese, Senegalese, Indian, Egyptian on the main streets of cosmopolitan cities—cannot be isolated from the matrix of an underlying historical process. This process includes the enlightenment overthrow of absolutism (that allows more than one kind of food in a community), humanism (that allows common citizens to dine in restaurants), the scientific method, technological amplification, globalized "free-trade" (that allow for the transport and processing of both food and credit), and the space-to-earth vision of the "whole planet" (that turns the meeting with the other into something more than a one-time fantasy adventure). All these ideas underlie the current conglomeration of contingencies, multi-cultural formations, and mass-media leveling, a mass-confrontation, a truly delicious catastrophe. And whether pasta came from China or Italy, it is now in your own kitchen, and the unavoidable deep-interfacing on mass, multi-levels; economic, electronic, or otherwise, spawns a collective need for the revisioning of both unity and difference, a need for interpretive communities—religious, secular, and in-between—to recognize each other in some newly functional way, beyond traditional modes of inclusiveness or exclusivity: at least enough to allow currency to flow. It is in recognition of this turbulent and thickly interlaced atmosphere that one may begin to somewhat consciously approach the phenomenon of inter-religious dialogue in its mytho-historicity.

To see this situation as merely "contemporary" or "post-modern" is to see from a certain perspective. One can always find precedents, previous narratives. In the thirteenth century, long after the well-worn silk route had brought members of many different cultures irrevocably together, Mongke Khan, ruler of the Mongolian court, assembled representatives of the religions of the earth. In May of 1254 he held a conference of "world religions."

> Here you are, Christians, Saracens, and *tuins*, and each one of you claims that his religion is superior . . . The Khan would like you all to assemble together and hold a conference . . . to enable him to learn the truth.[5]

The erstwhile Franciscan missionary, William of Rubruck, argued the Christian case against Buddhists, Moslems, and others, and assumed that he would surely win the day. He was quite chagrined, therefore, when he was summoned to an audience with Mongke Khan to hear the verdict: "We Mongols believe," the Khan declared, before expelling William from the Mongol court, "that just as God has given the hand several fingers so he has given mankind several paths."[6]

An early interfaith affirmation, fingers on a hand (an excellent metaphor for the construct of the "five great religions of the world" that is often taught in Introduction to World Religion courses at American colleges), hands that can hold tea cups, sit around tables, and nod in agreement on neutral territory: certainly a development beyond previous efforts to proceed against the enemies of God and cleanse the face of the earth, "so that there will be only one shepherd and one fold," no matter what fold it might happen to be.[7] But perhaps, such affirmations and their respective assemblies, in any space and time, have not gone as far as some might like to believe. For there are often implicit revisionary agendas embedded in inter-religious dialogue, academic and otherwise, conscious or not, and they need to be brought to the foreground. In this paper I would like to focus on contemporary inter-religious dialogue, and on the peculiar role that "Buddhism" often plays in it, particularly in the light of deconstruction.

Robert Magliola's work, *On Deconstructing Life-Worlds*, subtitled *Buddhism, Christianity, Culture*, will be our jumping-off point. This volume courageously interweaves life-events, personal and cultural history, Prāsaṅgika-Mādhyamika dialectics, and Trinitarian theology. A series of comparative juxtapositions between Derridean deconstructive practice and Mādhyamika philosophy is applied to a third (Christian) tradition, and is presented as a potentially creative and even healing force. Can the discourse of deconstruction reveal variant threads of the "Holy Trinity" in a new light, much as Nāgārjuna lays bare, in his fourfold de/constructs, absolutist assumptions, thus revisioning *śūnyatā*? There is much energy here and fertile ground for "re-imaging" staid concepts. Not only in Magliola's text, but in recent works that are bringing deconstruction, through philosophy and poetics, into a more conscious and above-board meeting with religious discourse.[8] For Plato et. al. may indeed by the fountainhead of the Western philosophical tradition, but the tradition has moved and breathed to the beat of Christendom, not only through ideas and practices, but through rhythm and image as well. And those who traffic in deconstruction must dialogue with it (or better yet, jam with it) just as the secular state has had to.

In my more cynical moments, I have wondered if Magliola's bringing of the "Trinity" into his conversation between Nāgārjuna and Derrida is representative of an effort to spare Christian discourse from the ravaging aspects of deconstruction, the "long-live the death of God" aspect of it, which he sees as stemming from defensive misreadings. But this may be what we all are doing, from Derrida on down, in one form or another. After all, the "splitting" awareness of *différance* alters the *Gestalt*, reconfigures the paradigm, offers another *darśana* (the Sanskrit word that encompasses "vision," "seeing" and "being seen," "meeting," and revelation). My primary concern here, however, is about the sense of "culture" that follows "Buddhism" and "Christianity" in Magliola's title, which is why I am employing "beat" and "image" as opposed to "idea" or "belief." For movement, the rhythmic-diachronic way in which one moves, the ritualized calendar-beat to which one moves, and imaging—the shadows to which one moves—as in the constant correctives of airplane trajectories, may be among the pivotal aspects of culture. And I cannot help but wonder about the tendency to push the culture of movement and image into the back seat when totalizing concerns become paramount. This is not an argument against comparative philosophy or theology, but a questioning of the separation of idea from image, from process, of synchronic from diachronic.

If one sees the Trinity as an unalterable theological emblem, does it have the same fluidity as an unnameable absolute, or a non-absolutist absolute in the case of Buddhist thinking? After all, why stop at three major significators: Father, Son, and Holy Spirit? Why not a mother? Can we have a son without one? The historiography of Christendom certainly attests to an exalted "Mother" just as the emergence of the "Pure Land" and the coexistence of deity yoga and pantheons of savior-*bodhisattvas* alongside anti-theologies of emptiness attest to a personal-devotional impulse in Buddhist-based cultures. Perhaps a daughter must also be born to perpetuate the chain of signification which repeats the fourfold tetralemma, the quaternity, whose center incarnates into mirror images of its own evolutive journey, the jeweled net of Indra. What I am wondering about here is the carte-blanche, too synchronic, extrapolation of religious doctrine from the variegated difference of culture that surrounds it. For this kaleidoscope of culture is, after all, the incarnation. The cross and the crescent, the domed vault, the stupa, and the six-pointed star—they all move with the tides and configure in time like pebbles on a beach. Can our snapshots or wrought-iron frames ever do them justice?

While moving through figurative mine-fields of religious texts, doctrines, and histories, then, it may be helpful to simultaneously backtrack and ask some elemental questions. First of all, what do "Buddhist" and "Christian" refer to? I am not just being semantic here. "Buddhism" is a label that Western European scholars affixed to a series of pan-Asian religious practices about three hundred years ago, and the continued unconscious usage of "Christianity" as a unique emblem suggests its assumed preeminence over all mere "isms" (Judaism, Buddhism, Hinduism, etc).[9] When we speak of "religions" in terms of institutions, or in terms of sets of texts and ideas, do we risk forfeiting the fabric of the living culture? Magliola himself is quite strong in this regard:

> For I maintain that all philosophies, even the most "rationalist," "impersonal," and "objective," write from and are written by their life-events, the theater of their lives, no matter from how deeply below the surface such psychic stage-machinery may happen to pull its strings, work its levers.... [10]

What applies for the person applies for the disciplines as well. Do theological or philosophical perspectives, separate from anthropological and sociological ones, do justice to the phenomenon known as "religion?" When Buddhism is bracketed under "religion," is its central argument being "defanged?" And do any of the fore-mentioned perspective-methodologies reflect religious experience itself in any way shape or form? One can argue that we are speaking of apples and oranges here, but one of the stronger charges against deconstruction has been that it offers no praxis, no living water (a similar criticism has often been leveled, from outside of the tradition, against the Buddhist concept of *śūnyatā*). And it is life itself, the theater of living, embodied experience in all its dimensions, that invariably holds us, that keeps pulling us back, that demands our energy and attention.

Doctrinal "containers" tend toward the pure synchronic, they see through the flesh of history, through the undulating movements of traditions in time, through the figure/ground relationships of a community's lived experience and its corresponding doctrines. When ideas themselves are stripped of the "thick yellow loam" of their respective cultural environments and histories, their skeletons do reveal a very particular outline.[11] As does an x-ray, if you will, which may pinpoint inconsistencies in a body (and thus be a crucial diagnostic tool), but may also poison a body (x-ray radiation is toxic), or even make one forget that we are dealing with a body at all. To forget the body is to forget the ground upon which we stand, the *topos* that characterizes our living environment. And such "forgetting" has often been perpetuated by uncritical practices of observation; reliance upon an "informant" who would never reveal women's religious practices and initiatory ceremonies to a male outsider, for example, or satisfaction with being shown a Buddhist temple and a series of practices that registers with previous knowledge about the "high tradition" while remaining totally ignorant of a temple a couple of miles away, frequented by thousands every full-moon evening, in which shamanic rites are performed, never to be observed or written about in the texts of observers.

The "Hindu" temple (and let us not forget that Buddhist traditions emerged out of and thrived alongside of *varṇāśrama* Indian culture) is built in the macrocosmic form of an allegorical body, the temples to the Buddha entering into *parnirvāṇa* in Sri Lanka are fully embodied, flanked by planetary gods and local shamanic deities of war who rise on flying peacocks. Buddhist temples in Tibet, like Christian churches in Europe are flanked with a plethora of figures, *bodhisattvas*, protector deities, helpers, and the like. The vast anti-figure of *śūnyatā* is itself embodied in the implacable form of the Buddha (a sculptural icon that grew out of Greek—at least partially influence), in the *kālacakra* mandala teeming with peaceful and wrathful deities in various *loka-s* (realms), in the institution of the *saṅgha* and the communities that support the *saṅgha*, in *dharma*; not only as "element" or "teaching" but also as the cohesive energetic (√*dhr* "to hold") that allows one to live, to walk on a path that may be envisioned as the very body of the Buddha (*dharmakāya*).

2.

Embodiment implies multiplicity, for no known body exists outside of its generative and relational context. And as Buddhist texts powerfully delineate through the teaching of interdependent co-arising (*pratītya-samutpāda*), there is no discernible origin, no ultimate resting place, no metaphysical scaffolding from which to separately observe the human condition. To work under the assumption of a transcendental reality may provide solace, but it may also devalue the theater of the world. To work under the assumption of a particular localized origin invokes the tribal/familial myth that can reconstruct a coherent or quasi-comfortable past and preserve a secure, structured, and purposeful vision of the future, until the boats of an admiral Perry, or a Columbus, arrive on the shore. Neither strategy opens to the challenge of alterity, to the inevitable tribunal in the arena of common discourse when faced with the other.

In inter-religious encounter, this plays out through the machinations of exclusivism, inclusivism, and pluralism, and such play has given rise to entities such as "comparative religion," "interfaith dialogue," "*Derrida on the Mend*," and "pluralism projects" such as Diana Eck's CD on Religious Pluralism in America—produced and marketed with a certain amount of fanfare, and receiving accolades from the White House and other appropriate places.[12] Exclusivism, the absolute privileging of one's own tradition, fortifies evaluative difference and must defend itself against the dangers of multiplicity. In this regard, practitioners of "secular deconstruction" have often engaged in their own form of exclusivism, all too easily dismissing any and all notions of religiosity as *logocentric*. It is no wonder, then, that the Buddhist voice has been a latecomer to this conversation. For Buddhist voices (as opposed to a "Buddhist religion") revel in the undermining of assumed metaphysical certainties. It took Magliola, in *Derrida on the Mend*, to bring Nāgārjuna and other Buddhist voices into the arena of the discourse on deconstruction, and the efforts of the academy to marginalize his work have been considerable.[13] Inclusivism, the more subtle privileging of one's tradition, in which one accepts other modes of religious discourse as subordinate to (or leading up to) one's own, embraces the other on its own terms. Interestingly enough, Buddhist traditions (like others) have often employed this strategy as a means to further their expansion. Padmasaṃbhava "subdued" the deities of the Bon Po and put them to work for the Buddha, and the tutelary spirits of Japan, the *kami*, are said to have "welcomed" the Buddha into their territory. What I want to primarily address here, however, is the "pluralist response" which professes to honor the other in a new world of tolerable differences.

Pluralist discourse seems to part from the missionary calling to cleanse the face of the earth. It even appears to break ground, opening up a new space of acceptance and respect in a global reality of deep diversity. Upon closer examination, however, pluralistic thinking and its corollary discipline of "Comparative Religion" often remain very much in the exclusivist category by distinguishing themselves from "relativism," or from their understanding of relativism. Diana Eck, for example, asserts that pluralism must entail a "commitment" (that relativism does not), "commitment" here referring to pre-existing forms of religiosity, names, texts, and institutions (*DLW*, 193-195). The construct of religion is privileged over the antichristic secular deconstruction of religion. Thus, in this particular world of religious pluralism, members of various denominations, holding the proper credentials, can sit down and commiserate at the same table of "World Religions." We may no longer have a world of partisans for Christ, but we will at least maintain a world of partisans for "the Divine." Having Buddhists at this table, however, could place the word "God" under erasure: "vast emptiness, nothing is holy." But "Buddha" ("awakening")—as an "ism"—can be safely taken into the fold. The radical challenge of the "*dharma*," which refers to neither God, nor metaphysical underpinning, nor institutional power, is no longer an issue. Instead, we have "Buddhists" and we can take solace in a "World Religions" that promotes values of tolerance, well-mannered interchange, peaceful coexistence, and diversity. In this construct, Buddhism becomes a part of the "totalizing process" of the pluralist project, as the discourse of suffering, its origin, and its cessation, is safely framed by the cadre of accepted tradition.

"Co-existence" like "comparison," however, resists cross-hatching, as it resists cross-dressing. Those invited can sit down at the table with their different costumes, but no one ever gets naked. This is quite a step back from the deconstructive position in which getting naked may be understood to be a philosophical impossibility, but is at least entertained. Perhaps we are back with Spinoza, not looking for truth, but looking for meaning. But meaning, as deconstruction demonstrates, calcifies all too easily. For meaning (Gk. *meinen*) is a complaint, a defense, and an intention that may be embarrassed when the repressed returns with a vengeance, as it tends to do. Coincidentally, the word for "meaning" in Sanskrit (*artha*) is synonymous with "power" and is frequently employed in the discourse of statecraft (i.e., *Ārthaśāstra*). Among earlier exercises in the statecraft of "religious pluralism" was the first "religious census" initiated by the British government in India in 1871, to determine the communal breakdown of their colony's population. Prior to this, the word "Hindu" was primarily used by invaders (and the word "Buddhist" was just beginning to move into printed discourse).

What the "religious pluralism in America" model leaves out of its package are huge pieces of the last hundred and fifty years of history: the rise of the secular community, the proliferation of countless sub-cultures, splinter-religions, sects, life-style communities, holistic healing centers, zen lunatics, and ever increasing numbers of "trans-denominationalists" who could not care less what label you give to them. And this is a particularly acute oversight in terms of Buddhist traditions in the West which have often moved in through the open gate of secularism. Angarika Dharmapala, for example, challenged the delegates at the parliament of World Religions in 1893 declaring that only Buddhism, without the encumbrances of an overdetermined foundation (not to speak of a God), could dialogue with Western science.

Moreover, the possibility that secular culture, meaning contemporary culture, may contain within itself the seeds for the reemergence of living-sacral experience—a culture of awakening that may no longer need the trappings of any religious institution—is too much for many pluralists to bear. The democratic and agnostic imperatives of the scientific, secular world are potent forces, however; no "world-religion" has been founded in a democracy.

In New York City, one of the most highly participated-in annual rites—Halloween (arguably a sacral event)—has erupted from the streets. The leering ghouls have returned through the cracks in the pavement to demand their due. This is quite reminiscent of Tibet, where dancers, wearing brightly painted masks of the wrathful deities, perform annual ceremonies to insure a good harvest by warding off those spirits who would oppose it. These are examples of "religious culture," and they are rarely brought into the conversation.

If we begin to add ritualized "deep-play" sporting and entertainment events into the pluralistic mix (to employ the terminology of Clifford Geertz)—the stuff of which lives are made—then even a visit from the Pope pales before a night at the Oscars or a day at the Superbowl. The "deconstruction grill" now manifests itself as totems staring out from the grills of automobiles and the sides of football helmets in great religious rituals of mock-war. But the predilection to drive while looking through the rear-view mirror is as deeply ingrained a habit as is one's mother-tongue. After all, "religions," like our own imaginary ego-narratives, desperately need to maintain themselves.

A recent *Utne Reader* featured a "Designer God" cover article in which the author queried a number of selected "religious leaders" about the American tendency to "create your own religion"—to mix and match: a Zen bell from here, a Tibetan bowl from there, a cross and a star, whatever feels right.[14] A good number of those surveyed strongly disapproved of such temerity, criticizing the "cafeteria approach" in which the "taking an idea from here and there is like stealing bricks from ancient temples to build a rickety shrine of one's own."[15] Such judgments, however, all too easily corresponded to the strongly vested institutional interests of those surveyed. How would they have reacted to Padmasaṃbhava forcibly bringing the *dharma* to Tibet, mixing and matching with the Bon tradition when necessary? And how might the guardians of religious institutions react to the following statement of Jacques Derrida?

> For me there is no such thing as religion. Within what one calls religions—Judaism, Christianity, Islam, or other religions—there are again tensions, heterogeneity, disruptive volcanoes, sometimes texts, especially those of the prophets, which cannot be reduced to an institution, a corpus, to a system.[16]

The invocation of a reified "pluralism," like "comparative religion" then, may often be a back door attempt to save what cannot be saved. It is easy to forget that the now-established "religious classics" are deeply hybridized texts themselves. The Hebrew Scriptures, New Testament, the *Bhagavadgītā*, and the Lotus-Sutra are all highly-interwoven works drawing from a wide-variety of source threads. If a hallmark of modernity/post-modernity has been people's ability to choose, or better yet to create, their own religion (or not to), this must entail *bricolage*. And what we call "Buddhism" has been woven from variant strands since its inception. The 7th century "Cold-Mountain" poet Han Shan mused that:

> Most T'ien-t'ai men don't know Han Shan
> Don't know his real thought and call it silly talk[17]

The "T'ien-t'ai men," were the socially approved synthesizers of their day, working to organize the truth-claims of a mass of Buddhist texts that they had inherited by arranging them into complex hierarchical constructs. This, I have heard, also goes on in mental institutions that are unfortunate enough to have more than one inmate who believes himself to be Jesus Christ. The various avatars often form their own hierarchical order that may revise but not completely obliterate original truth-claims. And religion worth its salt is founded on some sort of truth-claim. By even entertaining "the other," you are already admitting, on some level, the insufficiency of your own exclusive position. Just by entering into debate, William of Rubruck had already lost. For, in Lacanian terms, the entrance into language is a self-compromise.

For years, scholars of religion wrote about the great "three traditions" of pre-industrial China: "Confucianism," "Taoism," and "Buddhism"—although no one but a professional priest would ever identify himself in such a manner. It was just not conceivable from the lens on the scholar's bookshelf that people could "do" Buddha at a funeral, Confucius at a graduation, and Lao-Tzu at a village festival, or embroider their own combinations to suit the time and circumstances. But this has been the case, and it has been the reluctance of the writers of descriptive and philosophical discourse to experience and acknowledge the living field of religion, the *différance* of religion, which often resembles a carnival more than a sanctuary or study, that keeps re-creating distinctions between high and low, academic and popular, mind and body, self and objective world.

Buddhist traditions grew up in the shadows of Brahmanical orthodoxies and in a mass of "heterodoxies": Jains, Ājivikas, and others, and as Buddhist teachings have migrated, they have often acted as "parasites" onto host cultures, be they found in China, Tibet, Japan, or Vietnam. The parasite/host relationship is one form of exchange, of dialogue if you will, for each takes on the trappings of the other. If one tries to extrapolate some "pure doctrine" of emptiness out of this, one easily loses sight of the other side of the *rūpam śūnyataiva śūnyataiva rūpam* coin: that emptiness is none other than form. And if there is no pure, original form, no original indigenous clear lake of self, then "parasite" ceases to be a dirty word (glossed in my thesaurus as "bloodsucker, freeloader, mooch, and leach") and one moves into the realm of acknowledged interdependency. Indeed, it might very well be because of this understanding that Buddhist traditions have been able to adapt and mutate into creative forms that are in no one's playbook. When asked if the *bodhisattva* could appear as a machine, the Dalai Lama did not reject the possibility.[18]

Just as Caputo finds "Jewishness" in Derrida's thinking, the Buddhist notion of how things are appears through a variety of unexpected situations. I am speaking here of culture, of mixing and matching; from D. T. Suzuki's skillful means of serving thick green tea to Jack Kerouac and his spontaneous prose friends, to John Cage sitting silent in front of a piano, to physicists and biologists discussing causality and evolution with the Dalai Lama, to the deeply Americanized versions of Zen and the art of whatever you are doing. Therefore, I would suggest that if we move the lens onto culture; onto arts and letters, athletics, media, architecture, and business, we will find emerging forms of the *dharma* co-existing in a play of differences, and that these forms equally partake of the "lotus land of purity."

3.

Much discourse under the label of "deconstruction" is both playful and pernicious; a *saṃsāra* of the mind. It leaps back on itself, squirms around like a cat, seems to be enjoying its idol-breaking movement, and yet is filled with its own gods and their legions, who slip through its pages, Pan, Dionysus, Hermes—all still alive and well in new garbs. Perhaps, Derrida himself has become a sort of god, not the person nor the corpus, but the icon in the play of culture, "Derrida" like "Joe Montana" has a resoundingly heroic ring to it, albeit in its own sphere. The name becomes an icon that often attracts a certain configuration of images: "destructive, atheist, nihilist, threatening," etc. It becomes reified. It becomes a "religion," "Deconstruction," like "Buddhism," becomes an emblem that precludes engagement: a lot of labels being read, not a lot of tasting. But the helix, like the yin yang Moebius Strip, like the double-bind, always comes back upon itself: the latter Derrida writes on such subjects as "forgiveness," "death," and the "messianic." Perhaps then, the meeting of deconstruction and Buddhist traditions needs to move further into the imagination, toward the imagistic and rhythmic realms of poets and shopkeepers (Nietzsche would be aghast) as well as the causal realm of the philosophers, toward a simultaneous consideration of multiplicity rather than the extrapolation of one form or of a number of forms. How would entertaining the ideas of the *sākara-vādins*, for example, who offer the possibility of ultimate images that do not have a completely constructed nature (*parikalpitasvābhāva*) and are thus present even upon enlightenment, affect the discourse of emptiness?[19]

William Blake's remark on the evolution of the religious dimension describes the revisionary pluralism project well. In the *Marriage of Heaven and Hell*, Blake contends that

> The ancient Poets animated all sensible objects with Gods or Geniuses, calling them by the names and adorning them with the properties of woods, rivers, mountains, lakes, cities, nations, and whatever their enlarged & numerous senses could perceive. And particularly they studied the genius of each city and country, placing it under its mental deity.
>
> Till a system was formed, which took advantage of, & enslaved the vulgar by attempting to realize or abstract the mental deities from their objects: thus began Priesthood; Choosing forms of worship from poetic tales. And at length they pronounc'd that the Gods had order'd such things. Thus men forgot that All deities reside in the human breast. (Plate 11)

Perhaps it is time to take Blake's propositions a bit more seriously. Animism need not be relegated to the temporal primitive, especially when one acknowledges its reappearance in the mass media. "Real living is meeting," said Martin Buber, and meeting requires animation, *darśana*. What if, instead of maintaining the reified construct of "a religious tradition," we invited its participants into the realm of free play—of course free play is bound by its own internal logic, but Magliola reminds us that "deconstructing is not destructing," and religion, as ultimate performance art, as metaphorical vessel, as a generative grammar of mythos, manifests itself as the free-play of writing, revised and rewritten through anyone's examined life.

The post-Derridean project that Magliola ascribes to, "how to achieve liberation while practicing deconstruction" (*DLW*, 167), is an authentic challenge because it incorporates the body: how to live, not just how to think, after walking through the mine field of disproved assertions, tombstones of truth claims, what practice can rise out of these ashes? Deconstruction may not be destruction, but do its traces leave any semblance of a path? After all, it is the *mārga* that the historical Buddha is said to have offered along with the fundamental insights into incompleteness, unfulfillment, insubstantiality, and interdependency. But perhaps the *mārga* itself has just been another self-preservation strategy of the reified institution: the *saṅgha*. After all, the way that can be named is not the way, and the Buddha-figure in modern dress, J. Krishnamurti, went around insisting that "truth is a pathless land." Perhaps getting lost is necessary, is even the initiatory prerequisite to any form of authentic liberation, whatever that may be.

The meeting of East and West has happened and will happen again. Deconstruction has also happened, and will happen again. What happens to a Buddhism that has already been deconstructed, not dismissed but encountered? Something may indeed shift, especially if the encounter is held in the flesh as well as in the word, and is sustained long enough to bypass the conditioned reactions and counter-reactions of heresy. And perhaps, through the grid of idea, tradition, and institution, a field can be opened for another kind of dialogue: a culture of awakening that need not perpetuate the discourse of the observer and its corollary infinite regressions through the *bhāvacakra*, because it is willing to abandon the separate certainty of its own position, it is willing to listen without the customary forms of protection, it is willing to relate, it is willing to change, it is willing to enter the stream.

Notes

1. In Sanskrit, *catvāryapramāṇāni* (*Vimalakīrti Nirdeśa Sūtra*, I) cited in Robert Thurman, *The Holy Teachings of Vimalakīrti* (Pennsylvania and London: Penn State University Press, 1981), Chap. I, Note 48 and p. 149.

2. *Blue Cliff Record*, trans. Thomas and J. C. Cleary (Boulder: Shambhala Publications Inc., 1977), 1. I have taken the poetic liberty of rendering "Empty without holiness" as "Vast emptiness, nothing is holy." For this is how it was delivered to me *via* oral tradition, and in the spirit of *Chan* I am offering this rendering as it was heard, likewise with Bodhidharma coming from the West.

3. It is said that Bodhidharma appeared to Sung Yun of Wei "carrying one shoe in his hand," *Blue Cliff Record*, 5.

4. Jacques Derrida, *De la grammatologie* (Paris: Editions de Minuit, 1967), 227-228. English translation, *Of Grammatology*, trans. Gayatri Spivak (Baltimore: Johns Hopkins University Press, 1974), 158.

5. Peter Jackson with David Morgan, *The Mission of Friar William of Rubruck* (London: Hakluyt Society, 1990).

6. This meeting is cited and discussed by Stephen Batchelor in *The Awakening of the West: The Encounter of Buddhism with Western Culture* (Berkeley, CA: Parallax Press, 1994), 79-100.

7. Igor de Rachewiltz, *Papal Envoys to the Great Khan* (London: Faber and Faber, 1971). Cited in Batchelor, *The Awakening of the West*, 84.

8. See, for example, John Caputo's *The Prayers and Tears of Jacques Derrida: Religion without Religion* (Indiana University Press, Bloomington, 1997).

9. See James Hillman, *Interviews* (Dallas: Spring Publications, 1983), 79.

10. Robert Magliola, *On Deconstructing Life-Worlds: Buddhism, Christianity, Culture* (Atlanta: Scholars Press, 1997), xv. Hereafter *DLW*.

11. "Thick yellow loam" is quoted from Hillman's *Revisioning Psychology* (New York: Harper & Row, 1976), 67.

12. Diana L. Eck, *Encountering God: A Spiritual Journey from Bozeman to Banaras* (Boston: Beacon Press, 1998), 46. Eck employs the theological terms of "exclusivism," "inclusivism," and "pluralism," and I am following her terminology here.

13. See *DLW* for a brief account of this marginalizing process

14. *Utne Reader*, July-August, 1998.

15. *Utne Reader*, 27.

16. Derrida, cited in *Deconstruction in a Nutshell: A Conversation with Jacques Derrida*, ed. John D. Caputo (New York: Fordham University Press, 1997), 21.

17. *Cold Mountain: 100 Poems by the T'ang Poet Han-shan*, trans. Burton Watson (New York: Columbia University Press, 1962), # 57.

18. Personal Notes from *Conference on Buddhism and the Sciences* held at the Union Theological Seminary, New York City, 1993.

19. Sara McClintock, "Sākara and Nirākara Yogācārins," *Buddhist Academic Discussion Forum*, March 24, 1999.

Afterword

Robert Magliola

This Afterword was invited by Jin Y. Park, so I could comment 'in the manner' of my after-words during the 'Close Encounter' session in Buddhism/Deconstruction/Magliola (at the International Association for Philosophy and Literature annual meeting, 1999), but comment at length and—to use one of Derrida's favorite puns—*au pied de la lettre*. Deconstruction always comes 'afterwards', and, I am convinced, precisely because it is *making* our very 'going forward', it is always—despite rumors to the contrary—somewhere around (and around). Given the pressure of time and space, I have opted to comment only on the contributions which most pique me, keeping in mind Vajra Yoginī and her *khatvānga* (sharp trident-staff).[1] Tibetan dakinis, you will recall, are spiky and pique us, but teach needed wisdom. As for those contributors whose papers I do not address, they should be doubly complimented, because any deconstructionist knows that what is missing is so often the key to the most crucial. In Jin Y. Park's case this is preeminently true, because her work has been/is/shall be most crucial for the success of this volume, this collection.

***

Roger Jackson's paper claims that my work "both overstates and underestimates" Nāgārjuna's affinity with Derrida. Insofar as Jackson thinks I deny 'foundationalism' of any sort to Nāgārjunist Buddhism, I presume he means that I 'overstate' Nāgārjuna's affinity to Derridean anti-foundationalism. Insofar as Jackson declares Nāgārjuna's Mādhyamika "does not—*contra* Magliola—'reinstate the logocentric'," I presume he means that I here underestimate Nāgārjuna's affinity to anti-logocentrism. That Jackson drastically mis-takes my argument is due to his drastic mis-taking of Derridean deconstruction, and that he mis-takes Derridean deconstruction turns out to be no surprise, given that his declared sources are Jonathan Culler and Richard Rorty, two American academics who have managed quite nicely to flatten Derrida's philosophical elegance, in Culler's case by (intentionally?) reducing deconstruction to the needs of the domestic literary establishment and in Rorty's case by (intentionally?) sterilizing deconstruction so it can better serve 'philosophical pragmatism'. Jackson seems to think Derridean 'logocentrism' means no more than philosophical 'essentialism' and/or 'substantialism': in short, he affiliates the term to the 'essentialist' thinking critiqued—in their own ways—by the Analysts, and by Wittgenstein, and by (the Anglicized versions of) Heidegger. He cites Culler's explanation of "theories grounded on presence," but shows no sign that he understands the more radical nature of Derrida's project, namely, that 'logocentrism' refers to any holistic structure whatsoever, including the self-identical appearance of any element (even an element such as a number or a word), or the relatedness of any elements to each other ('codes' and 'logics' included). In Derridean terms, then, it almost goes without saying that Nāgārjuna *does* reinstate the logocentric, in that he (in Jackson's words) "affirms the conventional world" as long as it is understood to be—according to *paramārtha-satya*—truly empty of self-nature (*svabhāva*). That the conventional world—even though only because of *saṃvṛti-satya*, i.e., ignorant or concealing truth—*appears* to act according to codes, would be enough, already, to qualify it as 'logocentric' for Derrida.

Jackson seems to argue that in fact Nāgārjuna understands *pratītya-samutpāda* to be on the side of the conventional (where it operates as the Buddhist version of causality, the "positive counterpart to the concept of emptiness"); and *śūnyatā*, 'emptiness', to be on the side of ultimate truth. To the extent that Jackson's Nāgārjuna seems to retain an 'early Buddhist' definition of *pratītya-samutpāda*,[2] and I conclude this because Jackson seems to make it the law of 'what obtains' (though of course he grants that 'what obtains' is *established* in turn by *śūnyatā*), even *pratītya-samutpāda* becomes logocentric in Derridean terms (in fact, even a confluence of instantaneous 'causes' would be 'logocentric'). I disagree with Jackson's interpretation of Nāgārjunist *pratītya-samutpāda*, but I do of course agree that Nāgārjuna in several ways successfully affirms the conventional, and that he does so in a philosophically subtle and convincing way. I argue that Nāgārjuna's affirmation of tne conventional is necessarily a reinstatement of logocentrism because the world—conventionally taken—appears *concretely*, and behaves according to *laws* (laws are coherent, thereby 'holistic', formulations). And I argue that Nāgārjuna's several means for reinstating the logocentric can be of great help to Derridean thought, in that they—concomitant with an unmitigated deconstruction—allow for a 'validation' of logocentrism.

Because Nāgārjuna's *Mūlamadhyamakakārikās* [henceforth, *MMK*] 24:18 delivers the climactic conclusion that "*pratītya-samutpāda*[3] is *śūnyatā*" ("dependent-arising is emptiness"), I follow the Prāsaṅgikan reading, Candrakīrti's in particular, and the subsequent mainstream Tibetan Prāsaṅgikan tradition, which declare that "all phenomena are dependent-arisings":

> The term 'dependent-arising' not only refers to a process of production and of coming into existence but also to those things which are produced and come into existence. Phenomena themselves are dependent-arisings; a pot is a de-

pendent-arising; a consciousness is a dependent-arising; an emptiness is a dependent-arising, and so forth. (*ME*, 164)

If everything is a dependent-arising, it hardly makes sense to identify it with one pole of a positive/negative polarity, the "positive counterpart to the concept of nothingness," as Jackson does. Rather, dependent-arising is nothingness. Of course Nāgārjuna in the same *MMK* 24:18 reminds us that *śūnyatā*, 'nothingness', is itself only a provisional name, a "dependent designation," and the Gelukba Prāsaṅgikans explain that in fact each phenomenon is constituted by its unique emptiness or 'unfindability':

> The emptiness of one thing, though no different in color, shape, and so forth from another emptiness, is not the emptiness of another thing.[4] . . . If the emptiness of one thing were the emptiness of another, one would be forced to accept that the lack of inherent existence of a pot is the lack of inherent existence of a person and that the apprehension of the inherent existence of a pot is the apprehension of the inherent existence of a person, but this is clearly not the case. (*ME*, 408)

For the Gelukba, the basis for Nāgārjuna's distinction between the 'two truths' is more epistemological than ontological, since the division is not in reality but only between "objects of knowledge" (*ME*, 412). Since truths are defined as "those things that exist the way they appear," only "ultimate truths (*paramārtha-satya*, [Tb] *don dam bden pa*) or emptinesses, qualify as truths" in the strict sense (*ME*, 405). "The other various and sundry objects do not exist the way they appear, except to Buddhas." These objects are *saṃvṛti-satya*, 'truths-for-a-concealer',[5] i.e., they exist the way they appear only for an ignorant consciousness. "Truths-for-a-concealer are falsities, appearing one way and existing another" (*ME*, 405).

Reality, then, is a stream of 'dependent-arisings', of 'unfindables'.[6] The Prāsaṅgikan tradition calls them, literally, the 'unfindables', because a core-identity, *svabhāva*, is—in each case of an apparent holism—truly 'unfindable'. When Nāgārjuna says "all things obtain for him for whom emptiness obtains" (*Vigrahavyāvartanī*, 70), he means that 'unfindables', dependent-arisings, establish or 'constitute' the world (*ME*, 168). And this is why I dissent not only from Jackson's positioning of *pratītya-samutpāda* as 'positive' and over-and-against the *śūnyatā* to which he makes it the positive pole; but also why I dissent from his employ of a foundationalism-deconstruction polarity—which he adapts from Rorty—as the organizing principle of his paper throughout. Foundationalism and deconstruction, as Jackson presents them, are too much like the extremes of 'substantializing' and 'nihilating' which Buddhism 'cuts off'. In Gelukba terms—if one were to adapt what Jackson calls the 'Anglo-Saxon' terms of 'foundationalism'. and 'deconstruction'—one would say that, for a beginning practitioner, reality seems a stream of 'emptieds-out' of 'foundations'. Or, in what are comparative but of course not identical terms, a Derridean could say that life is a stream (or better, a tangle) of logocentrisms-as-deconstructed.[7] In

Gelukba terms, for an advanced practitioner, reality is a flux of unfindables which establish what appear to be foundations.[8]

The foregoing Prāsaṅgikan version of the 'two truths', then, makes it clear that the 'world-taken-conventionally' is *saṃvṛti-satya*, or 'truths-for-a-concealer', and not—as Jackson implies—the 'world-taken-as-dependent-arisings'. Dependent-arisings are, rather, the emptinesses-of-things, (a provisional name for) *śūnyatā*, the Middle Way. (The Middle Way is neither substantialism nor nihilism; the Middle Way is the stream of unfindables.) But nonetheless I have been claiming that a prime contribution of the Prāsaṅgika Mādhyamika is its capacity to teach western deconstructionists how to reinstate the validity of holisms (Derridean 'logocentrisms') while retaining deconstruction. And Candrakīrti himself emphasizes that "Mādhyamikas are skilled in presenting what conventionally exists" (*ME*, 411). For a Prāsaṅgikan, how can 'truths-for-a-concealer' still be 'valid', so logocentrism is reinstated?

Nāgārjuna of course says in *MMK* 24:10, "Without relying on conventions/ The ultimate cannot be taught./Without realizing the ultimate/Nirvāna is not attained" (*ME*, 401). The Prāsaṅgikans explain that an adept rejects not only the extreme which is substantialism, but also the extreme which is nihilism, since s/he "has not damaged (or refuted) worldly conventionalities that are like reflections," and thus "has not damaged actions and their fruits" (*ME*, 402). Conventionalities are *saṃvṛti-satya* or 'truths-for-concealers' because they do not exist the way they appear (they 'appear' holistic[9]), but this does *not* mean that one should therefore *throw away* appearances (to do so would be nihilism). In short, appearances can still be *provisionally* manipulated in terms of expresser, expressed, and holistic referent. In order to retain the distinction—within *saṃvṛti-satya*—between mundane truth and falsity (the distinction between a so-called 'real' face, say, and a picture of a face), the Prāsaṅgikans discriminate according to whether or not the 'appearance' can perform the functions consistent with its appearance (see *ME*, 421). "The difference between a picture of a cow and a cow is that the former cannot perform the functions of a cow but the latter can" (*ME*, 542).

***

The history of the Sanlun schools, China's appropriation *en titre* of Mādhyamika, is the subject of an increasingly impressive body of scholarship. The Sanlun schools, on Chinese terrain and in Chinese terms, continue the Mādhyamikan competition with Yogācāra and other Buddhist traditions. Generalized Mādhyamikan influence spreads much wider, undergoing mutation and even syncretization with Yogācāric and other systems. In this regard, Chan supplies what has been for me a very interesting configuration, because—as Youru Wang's essay in this anthology shows—it sometimes pits Mādhyamikan deconstructive moves against Yogācāric and other more holistic formations, such as those of Tiantai and Huayan. When dealing with intersections of Derridean and Chanist deconstruction, I have sometimes characterized citations from various Buddhist monks as more deconstructive or conversely more centric, but I am unaware of any place in my work where I have either characterized a monk's work in general as 'centric' or limited Chanist deconstruction to Southern Chan: and I must declare the usually careful Bernard Faure's allegations to the contrary—as referenced in Youru Wang's paper—quite gratuitous indeed.

My own argument has been that the Chinese Mādhyamika, like its counterparts elsewhere, constitutes a better venue, coming and going (coming/going), for a Derridean to meet Buddhism than do other Buddhist venues. This is not to deny that the Chinese Mādhyamikans 'shape-up' their philosophical representations more than the Indian and Tibetan Mādhyamikans do (i.e., Chinese predilect plastic thought-models), but still the Chinese Mādhyamika can be very serviceable, indeed, to deconstructionists. And within Chinese Mādhyamika I have adhered to those lineages which most resist what becomes a growing trend, viz., treatment of Nāgārjuna's tetralemma[10] as a 'climbing-ladder', a ladder of negation leading to a transcendent. In a Zennist such as D. T. Suzuki one finds a modern-day culmination of this trend, as in Suzuki's declaration that "Nāgārjuna's famous doctrine of the Middle Path of Eight No's breathes the same (Upanishadic) spirit (Absolute Reality is to be described by No, No!)" [the parenthetical remarks are also Suzuki's],[11] so in *DLW* I agree with Hsueh-Li Cheng's critique[12]:

> Cheng is pointing out that Suzuki's version of Nāgārjuna's 'Eight Negations' makes them behave like a classic negative theology. That is, Suzuki's version assumes an Absolute Reality transcending the human attributions which the Eight Negations negate. Cheng would instead take the Eight Negations as a canceling-out of four dialectical (and therefore logocentric) opposites, such as, for example, 'annihilation' and 'permanence'. For him the Middle Path does not involve the negated pairs, but neither is there an Absolute which transcends them. (*DLW*, 107)

In Chinese Buddhism, the Mādhyamikan notion that myriad *reality* is *not* a holistic formation *in any way at all* is well represented, indeed perhaps best represented, by Ji Zang's famous deployments of the tetralemma, so I heartily concur with Ellen Y. Zhang's choice of topic, and the considerable attention Zongqi Cai likewise gives it. Ji Zang, with arguments analogous to those of the Tibetan Prāsaṅgikans, rejects an ontological reading of the 'two truths' and calls them instead "the two truths qua standpoints" which function epistemologically.[13] Two of Ji Zang's famous deployments of the tetralemma are "the three levels of two truths," and "the four levels of two truths." Ming-Wood Liu diagrams the first deployment as follows:

THE THREE LEVELS OF TWO TRUTHS

MUNDANE TRUTH	SUPREME TRUTH
(1) Existence	Emptiness
(2) Duality of 'existence' and 'emptiness'	Non-duality of 'existence' and 'emptiness' (neither 'existence' nor 'emptiness')
(3) **Duality** of 'duality' and 'non-duality'	Neither 'duality' nor 'non-duality'

[I supply bold print here, to distinguish, in my discussion below, third level duality from second level duality.]

Ji Zang explains the third level this way:

Although the deluded ones [, on hearing the second form of two truths,] abandon the two extreme [ideas of "existence" and "emptiness"], they in turn get bogged down in [the idea of] "middle-way." Hence, [the Buddhas address them] the third time [, and] explain that not to become attached to the "middle-way" after-leaving far behind the two extremes [of "existence" and "emptiness"] is the supreme truth, and that the two extremes and the middle-way are all mundane truths.[14]

The second level's affirmation of both existence (C. *you*) and emptiness ('non-existence', negation of *you*) is the "duality" represented in Liu's diagram above, in the third-level mundane truth; and the second level's denial of both existence and emptiness is the "non-duality" also represented in the third-level mundane truth: in short, the third-level mundane truth is *both* affirmation *and* denial of both existence and emptiness, and thus the third-level mundane truth is itself a **duality**. Ji Zang says that the affirmation of both existence and emptiness is an extreme of one-sidedness (that is, an extreme of choosing extremes), and must be cut-off. And he says that the denial of both existence and emptiness is an extreme of 'middle-ness' (of 'centrality' in this sense,[15] of choosing non-extremes) and must be cut-off too. Cutting-offness must be cut-off because ironically this too can deceive.[16]

Insofar as the three levels of the two truths—even the supreme truth of the third level—are representational (and 'logocentric' in Derrida's sense), they are not 'awakening' (Sk. *bodhi*), but rather, function heuristically, as "instruction"[17] (at their best, acting as *prajñapti*, in the sense of 'privileged clues' to 'awakening'), and must be eventually "discarded," says Ji Zang.[18] But, citing a famous line from Seng Zhao, he continues, "'They resemble a man produced by magic: this man is not non-existent, yet, being a product of magic, is not a real man'. . . . This is true of all things. Therefore they are not to be discarded."[19] The three levels are to be discarded and not-discarded. There are two points I wish to make here. Firstly, as *not-discarded*, "what is dual is not dual, and what is not dual is dual" (Ji Zang in *HCP*, 298). In this our anthology, many of the treatments of Buddhism emphasize that 'what is dual is not dual', but very few also affirm that '*what is not dual is dual*', and thus—in my opinion—many of the essays lapse ultimately into a very deep-structured but no less grounded *holism*. Some, perhaps, even slide into a '*oneness*'. My second point is that the three levels are not discarded because they are *not* best-conceived as a *climbing-ladder*. They are *prajñapti*, yes, but not a ladder, and here I think I disagree with both Zong-qi Cai and Ellen Zhang. A ladder suggests that one climbs the rungs, and then leaps from the top to a transcendent, discarding the ladder.[20]

The supreme truth of the third level, "neither duality nor non-duality," is 'neither affirmation nor denial of both existence and emptiness (non-existence)'.

When the three levels of double truth are *not-discarded*, "nor denial of both existence and emptiness (non-existence)" means the non-duality of the third-level supreme truth is *dual.*[21] Not non-existence as well as not non-emptiness.[22] I would maintain that this negatively overlapped formula (typically Chinese in its grammar), '*what is not non-existent*', insofar as it is still somehow *there* (in poetic terms we can perhaps say, there as *shadow*), generates its own fascinating evocations of Derridean *trace*. But the main point I wish to make here is that there is an intentional equivocation in Ji Zang's remarks about the *status* of the third level, in relation to the preceding two levels. As formulaic representations of standpoints, Ji Zang *does* treat the three levels incrementally, so he says in both *On the Lotus* (*T* 34.396c1-7),[23] and *On the Two Truths* (*T* 45.91a16-b4),[24] that "the three forms of two truths have as their respective objects of instruction the common people, the two vehicles [Hīnayānists and immature Mahāyānists], and the inferior bodhisattvas."[25] *However*, when the three levels are deployed experientially, as *prajñapti* intended to initiate *bodhi*, 'awakening',[26] they are not incremental at all. In fact, Ji Zang says their function then is to push the meditator's experience into non-abidingness, which—along with non-acquisitiveness (non-grasping)—constitutes 'awakening'.[27] That non-abidingness is *the* key to the Mādhyamikan version of awakening, so that the 'middle way' is defined specifically as non-attachment,[28] permits me parenthetically to note here how this further justifies my claim in *DLW* that 'movement-under-erasure' is Mādhyamika's privileged clue.[29]

Ji Zang goes on to say "that practitioners of sharp faculties require only the instruction of the first form [level] of two truths, whereas practitioners of dull faculties have to go through the instruction of all three forms [levels] of two truths before they can achieve awakening."[30] Surely, this indicates that experientially the three levels are not a ladder, nor are they meant to lead to a mystical experience apart from the ladder. Indeed, regarded from the experiential perspective, the supreme truth of the third level, neither non-existence nor non-emptiness, seems to off/circle back to the first level, 'existence' [mundane truth] and 'emptiness' [supreme truth]. The practitioner stays with the 'ladder', but it is no ladder-to-be-climbed in any teleological sense. Non-abidingness, 'awakeness', is to scramble up and down the ladder at will. Brian Bocking, in his *Nāgārjuna in China,*[31] emphasizes that, for the Mādhyamika, 'awakening'—while of course an advanced *jnānic* event—is not an irrational or non-cognitive event:

> The precise nature of the relationship between the Mādhyamika dialectic on the one hand, and the practical path to liberation on the other, which Chi-Tsang [Ji Zang] tried to explain systematically through the idea that 'refutation is at once an awakening to the true dharma', remains one of the elusive aspects of Mādhyamika in the Middle treatise which contribute to its appeal. (8)

Bocking argues that refutation's role as *practical meditative* path derives from Nāgārjuna himself:

> Much of the force of Nāgārjuna's assault on received notions derives from the very repetitive, even meditative, systematic application of the same

> Mādhyamika critique to a number of different topics (this is the reason for entitling each chapter in the present translation 'Contemplation of ...' rather than 'Examination of ...'). (8)

The Mādhyamikan 'wakefulness', then, rides up and down the ladder at will, and—an important corollary for us—as *jnānic* happening it is beyond merely conceptual thought but not 'beyond thought'. If such wakefulness answers to any messages in Derrida's post office, it is to Derrida's queries of the 'unheard-of thought', the 'impossible' writing.[32]

Non-abidingness is also the specific lesson of Ji Zang's second deployment of the two truths, "the four levels of two truths." Here Ji Zang adds a fourth level to the three levels already treated, and the function of the fourth level is purely pedagogic: the fourth-level mundane truth represents the three prior levels in their entirety, and the fourth-level supreme truth represents 'non-difference of the three levels of two truths': "We speak about these three categories [levels] (of two truths) in order to make (people) realize (the) non-(difference of the) three (categories of two truths). Only non-dependence [non-abidingness] and non-acquisition [non-grasping] are called the (true) principles."[33] The 'non-difference' which is the supreme truth is of course not a monistic formation nor even transcendental in the sense of departure from the other three levels.[34] Rather, the 'non-difference' represents the back-and-fro fluidity of non-abidingness. Otherwise, abidingness and non-grasping would cease to be the true (as opposed to merely provisional) norms of 'awakening'. In the aptly chosen words of Ellen Zhang's paper, the "tetralemmatic space . . . indicates a complex interplay between the conventional and the ultimate in the infinite process of happenings." The 'non-difference' is a process more analogous to Derrida's 'sameness which is not the self-same' than it is to any holistic formation whatsoever.

Given all the above, it should be clear that Ji Zang's fourth-level supreme truth—though inscribed in the Chinese tradition and argued in a Chinese register—enables the 'reinstatement' of logocentrism according to a Mādhyamikan justification considerably like the one we saw in the Prāsaṅgika-Mādhyamika.[35] Simply put, if *all* three levels of two truths, mundane and supreme, can be navigated (like a *navette* shuttles to-and-fro, Derrida could say), and this very navigation of the fourth-level mundane truth (= the first three levels) is the fourth-level supreme truth, *then* the first-level mundane truth (logocentric existence[36]) is enabled *too*. This navigation, as non-abidingness, is empty, so Thomé Fang can gloss Ji Zang by saying "Apart from the *śūnyatā*, there is no materiality, and apart from the materiality, there is no *śūnyatā*."[37]

***

David Loy's paper aims to show how Buddhism, and more specifically the Huayan school and the doctrine of Indra's Net, can deliver postmodernists and deconstructionists[38] from the "bad infinity" of dissemination and the "endless recirculation of concepts" (*sic*). Loy chooses as his emblem for 'good infinity' the famous Indra's Net of the *Avataṃsaka Sūtra*, no doubt so this perfectly coherent net (in which everything perfectly interpenetrates and identifies) can outshine the endless (and often tortuous) disseminations of Derrida. The Huayan school appropriates from both the Mādhyamikan tradition (Sanlun school) and Yogācāric/Vijñānavādic tradition (Weishi, Consciousness-Only school). Loy's philosophical arguments are a combination of Mādhyamikan 'emptiness' interpreted in a Yogācāric (and specifically Vijñaptimātratātic way, i.e., the emptiness is coordinated in terms of the trisvabhāva-theory[39]), and Huayan formulations such as absolute Pure Mind (Huayan's version of Pure Mind differs somewhat from Tiantai's, but both are developments[40] of the *ālaya*-tradition). I have no objections, and have never had objections, to the deployment of what can be considered the more holistic theories often associated with Far Eastern Buddhism,[41] since my attitude has always been that doctrinal formulations in Buddhism function as *prajñapti*, and *prajñapti* should suit occasion and personality-type. What I have maintained and do maintain is that more holistic theories are not an expedient venue for meeting deconstructionists and a postmodern age.[42] Most Derrideans are 'Continentalists'[43] ignorant of Buddhism and for whom Buddhism is bizarre (ironically, most fail to apply what should be the *ad hoc* deconstructive maneuver, viz., unconcealment of *why* they are thus marginalizing Buddhism). Even before the dice are thrown, holism in a Buddhist context, or even what *sounds* like the *rhetoric* of holism, is enough to drive Derrideans away. Perhaps this should not be the case, but it is.

In my treatment of Loy's paper, I shall try to vindicate Derridean deconstruction in the face of what are—in my opinion—prevalent but quite gross misunderstandings of what Derrida is up to/about. Then I shall explain what in Loy's presentation of Buddhism is so 'holistic', and thus counterproductive in terms of 'skillful means'. Then I shall explicate how, at several crucial points and upon several crucial issues, Mādhyamika differs from Loy's representations. The most egregious misreading of Derrida, and the most harmful in that it closes-off any understanding of him from the start, is that 'he just deconstructs language'. Indeed, in his paper "The Deconstruction of Buddhism," in Coward's and Foshay's collection *Derrida and Negative Theology*,[44] Loy says outrightly that ". . . Derrida's approach is still logocentric, for what needs to be deconstructed is not just language but the world we live in and the way we live in it, trapped within a cage of our own making. . . ." This misrepresentation, that Derrida deconstructs just language, appears in several of this anthology's papers, and Loy's version of the misrepresentation (from the Coward/Foshay collection) is even quoted as a reference in this regard. Loy's paper in this our current anthology engages in the same false charges, to wit: "But the textual dissemination liberated by Derrida's deconstruction will not be satisfactory unless the dualistic sense of self—not just its discourse—has been deconstructed"; though there are some hints of backtracking, as when it says, "Today Jacques Derrida argues that the meaning of such a multi-dimensional space can never be completely fulfilled, for the continual circulation of signifiers denies meaning any fixed foundation or conclusion. Hence texts never attain self-presence, and that includes *the text that constitutes me*" [emphasis mine]. *Today* Derrida argues suchwise? The fact is that as early as *Derrida on the Mend* (1984), I had already demonstrated the contrary of what Loy and so many other detractors charge, and had already shown much evidence,[45] of which I here just include the following quotation from *De la grammatologie* (published 1967, very early indeed).[46] In *De la grammatologie*, and here I cite from the English translation (1976, still very early),[47] when discussing *différance*, Derrida reports:

> that it is in the specific zone of this imprint and this trace, in the temporalization of a *lived experience* which is neither *in* the world nor in another 'world', which is not more sonorous than luminous, not more *in* time than *in* space, that differences appear among the elements or rather produce them, make them emerge as such and constitute the *texts*, the chains, and the systems of traces.[48]

Of course this is already the point, that *différance*, here the garble (or 'chiasm' or 'double-bind') of time and space (time/space) deconstructs the dichotomy of inside and outside, so a dichotomy of language and reality is always already false. Geoffrey Bennington, in his intriguing collaboration with Derrida called *Jacques Derrida*, cites *Margins of Philosophy* and *Psyché: Inventions de l'autre* to make the 'same' point:

> Whether we try to secure it on the side of the subject or on that of the object, the passage to language presupposes not a prior meaning that signs would then only have to express, but a certain continuity that we are here calling "the same" (and which is none other than *différance* [see *Margins* 17]). . . . This "continuity" (which is made up only of difference and caesuras) forbids us from accrediting the idea of an abyss between language and world or experience, but also, for example, between readable space and visible space (*Psyché* 106).[49]

In *Buddhisms and Deconstructions*, this current anthology, it seems to me Ian W. Mabbett points up the problematic very well, viz., that not only language, but all the goings-on-of-the-world, are textual: "When we speak of deconstruction, then, there is no unique given reality with which we can identify it apart from *the phenomenal world itself, which is a text*, a structure of seeming structure whose real nature can be recognized to be incapable of consistent characterization once it is seen for what it is" [emphasis mine].

When Derrida says that there is no 'outside-the-text' (*hors-texte*),[50] he means that *différance* 'sets everything at work', and 'sets everything at work' in a textual way. That is, life behaves in a textual way. But texts, for Derrida, behave according to garbled deferments in time/space (the "systems of traces"), disseminations which both give rise to the apparent 'logocentric' levels and disestablish them with a single stroke (*un seul coup*), an off/analogy to the Buddhist 'two truths'.[51] Along with its comparisons[52] of Derridean and Nāgārjunist deconstruction of the principles of 'identity' and 'personal identity', I would think one of the main contributions of *DOM* was the comparison of Derridean dissemination and Nāgārjunist dependent-arising. And my definition of dependent-arising was (and is) Mādhyamikan and often specifically Prāsaṅgikan, again because such a definition intersects Derridean thought better than does the Yogācāric definition of dependent-arising which Loy (and several other of this anthology's authors) make sure to invoke. In Derrida, 'writing' is 'written large' ("All is writing"), i.e., it refers to the iterability of the 'mark'[53] and the binds of diagram/program.[54] Because this Derridean 'writing' is how life goes on (so in my own work I use the *majuscule* and call it 'Writing'), and since it functions according to a decapitated contingency (dependency without a depended-upon), it vitiates self-presence. This process has more than a passing similarity to Nāgārjunist dependent arising, and—a fact often grossly misunderstood—does not require physical writing, graphs on a page, etc. (what I call 'writing' in my own work, using the *minuscule*). Derrida finds that writing 'written small' (the graphs on the page) is an effective *clue* to how all life goes on,[55] that is, all life functions according to time-and-space deferment/iterability.[56] In short, writing is a clue to Writing. Derrida does *not* mean that speaking/hearing work *less* according to deferment/iterability, but only that speaking/hearing are more *deceptive*. Because speakers/hearers usually sense themselves—at least existentially—in closer proximity to each other than do writers/readers, they tend to ignore the deferment/iterability which 'operate(s)' even speech-acts and spoken discourse.[57] In fact, however, "all speaking [and hearing] and writing and thinking and doing are all Writing."[58]

In *DOM* I gave much attention to the "quandary" the implications of which Derrida was working out and continues to work out: namely, that he acknowledges humans are in linguisticity (the double-binds of phonic and graphic marks, of tongue/hand and ear/eye, etc.), but he still acts as if he can check against 'experience' to judge whether a given linguistic construction is more or less indicative of how life's text goes on (see *DOM*, especially 44, 45). Back then and now too, I have suggested—and it is here that David Loy and I most agree—that the meditative *jnāna*[59] are the condition for such validation ('validation' as in Latin *validus*, [making] 'healthy'). Indeed, the *-on the mend* of my book-title was intended to entrap the double-bind of Derrida 'on the mend' in the senses of (1) mounting and deconstructing the logocentric mend (while *upon* it, undoing it), and (2) regaining health (the idiom, 'on the mend') by means of a Buddhist connection. Mark Taylor, in his review of *DOM* back then, missed (by *too* wide a mark) the point of the title (and my book).

Derrida continues, as he has for going on forty years, "to reinscribe the 'necessary but impossible moments' he always has—albeit always with the necessary but impossible *décalages*," and in *DLW* I have tried to note how "Left-handedly, perforce, . . . Derrida has most clearly changed."[60] In terms of writing/Writing, Derrida has much developed his discussion of double-bind, of the mark, of the 'floating graphic trait', of 'counting', of *sériature*, of liaison/striction.[61] Because David Loy and Frank Stevenson both seem to ignore that Derridean *différance* undoes the silence/language opposition as much as it does the subject/object opposition, so that silence is Writing too, I here insert a few remarks on silence. Because life (and space) temporalizes[62] (which requires *repetition*), *mark* in this context becomes the repetition-trait which necessarily always already *precedes* the act of signifying, and any meaning whatsoever. Time is forever passing, so silence no less than non-silence is marked, and thus is Writing. In *DLW* I intersect with Nāgārjuna in this regard:

> And in this Derridean sense, Nāgārjuna's *śūnyatā* is also marked, traced, because—as explained above—if it is to be true to Buddhist *anitya* and 'relatedness' both, it must be a going-on of pure negative reference, of pure *différance*. For Derrida, 'literal' silence belongs to textuality as much as speaking does, and writing does. Regarding the privileged Buddhist silence of the enlightenment experience and of *paramārtha*, the fact it is privileged would make it no less marked: on the contrary, enlightenment would be to 'frequent' Writing. Wise to pure *différance*, the silently Wise adept would be pure *différance* and its trace, a 'marked silence', a silence 'marking (serene) time' (*DLW*, 144).

As the Prāsaṅgikan Mādhyamikans convincingly argue—you will recall—dependent-arising (the flux of 'unfindables', the marks, traces) is/are *paramārtha-satya* (not *saṃvṛti-satya*) is/are *śūnyatā*.

The Huayan [Flower-Wreathe] School is identified with totalism[63] by so many scholars (and so calls itself) because in it "the all is one" and "the one is the all" (*HCP*, 347). Its claim is to recapitulate earlier schools of Buddhism and cap-them off with its holistic version of the one true Dharmadhātu ('dharma-realm'). Wing-tsit Chan summarizes as follows: "The whole Huayan philosophy centers around its fundamental concept, the Universal Causation of the Realm of Dharmas (elements of existence). The Realm of Dharmas (Dharmadhātu) connotes the whole universe, which in the belief of the school, is fourfold. It involves the Realm of Facts, the Realm of Principle (*Li*), the Realm of Principle and Facts harmonized, and the Realm of All Facts interwoven and mutually identified."[64] Whereas for the Consciousness-Only School (Weishi), perfect reality, as consciousness-only, is in perpetual transformation, for the Huayan School, Perfect Reality does not *change*.[65] As indicated previously, my resort to Mādhyamika is primarily driven by a motive analogous to *upāya*, 'skillful means'. I know well that the Huayan lineages are rich and diverse, and—as is the case with all great philosophies—interpretations of exactly how the Huayan system works have varied and vary, sometimes very much. Like all great philosophical systems, Huayan has generated many controversies internal to itself, not to mention polemics with other schools. I am not aiming here to stereotype Huayan or build it into a straw man (or straw wreathe) so it can more easily be burnt down. My point, rather, is that—*a priori*—the key ideas of the Huayan School, and even more so, the rhetoric associated with the school, alienate the deconstructionist: s/he turns a cold shoulder. Whereas the Mādhyamika philosophy, especially in its Prāsaṅgikan variants, takes *paramārtha* as a stream of unfindables, an open-ended flux which resists recuperation into a 'unity' of *any* kind, Huayan's Dharmadhātu supplies the idea of the mutual identification of one and many,[66] and the image of perfect harmony. No doubt, Huayan—like all Buddhist schools—intends its chosen ideas and images to serve only as *prajñapti*, but this is in fact my point: precisely on this score, vis-à-vis deconstruction, Huayan's unitariness doesn't pass muster.

The holism of Huayan exposes itself well in "Indra's Postmodern Net," Loy's paper reprinted in this collection. In sharp contradistinction to Ji Zang's Mādhyamika (which regarded non-duality as yet another one-sidedness to be cut-off), Loy's Huayan affirms Non-Duality. Loy explains the Net's 'paradoxicality'[67] (what he calls later in his paper its "polyvalence"): "If each jewel in Indra's Net mutually conditions and is conditioned by all the others, then to become completely groundless is to become completely grounded, not in some particular, but in the whole web of interdependent relations. The supreme irony of my struggle to ground myself is that it cannot succeed because I am already grounded—in the totality." When Loy addresses "the post-structural realization that the meaning of a text cannot be totalized," his rhetoric shows his hand. "From a Buddhist perspective," he says, the post-structural realization "—that language/thought never attains a self-presence which escapes differences—is an important step towards the realization that there is no abiding-place for the mind anywhere within Indra's Net." *Within* Indra's Net.[68] The rhetoric of inside/outside, and non-abidingness is unbashedly *inside* the holism. Ji Zang's adept, you will recall, experienced non-abidingness as the privileged Buddhist 'awakening', but Ji Zang, Chinese though he be, in general shied away from (or refused to indulge) a rhetoric of boundaries.

In order to avoid boundaries, Derrida in his early work writes of Writing as the "same which is not identical" (*Writing and Difference*[69]), and Bennington glosses by calling it, after Derrida, "the non-enveloping figure of invagination" (*JD*, 304); and Derrida in his later work develops more and more the figures of the double-bind[70] and 'contamination'[71] because they thwart closure, unmarked space, and other hallmarks of holism. My own work has intersected the Derridean "sameness which is not self-same"[72] and various Mādhyamikan and Chanist versions of dependent-arising (the 'going-on' of life) precisely to avoid holism.

In my opinion, one-sided commitment to 'non-duality' has another bad consequence, too. Loy's several disavowals of *fixation* on truth, and even his quotation of the Buddha's "It is not proper for a wise man . . . to come to the conclusion: 'This alone is Truth, and everything else is false'," are swallowed up in a (well-nigh triumphalist?) recuperation in Note 5: "Awareness of mutual identity and interpenetration [the two Huayan doctrines accounting for Dharmadhātu] is rapidly developing into the only doctrine that makes sense anymore, perhaps the only one that can save us from ourselves." This reads/sounds like a lapse back into the Onto-Theology that Loy elsewhere disavows. I have signaled already in *DLW* in several places that my work in Catholic theology aims to show how even Christ's "that all may be one" (John 17:21) is not reducible to a logocentric oneness,[73] and my current project is to argue that God's 'oneness' is 'more than logocentric oneness while not spilling over into twoness'. In the case of the Buddhist-Christian Dia/logue in which I have been and continue to be active, I am working out a non-holistic way of thinking based on the fact that Buddhism on its 'side' and Catholicism on its 'side' both grant that members of the other party-in-dialogue can—without leaving their own religion—be 'liberated/saved'.[74] Indeed, both religions—while maintaining the 'ultimacy' of their own religion, and even their vocation of witness to the other party (so relativism is precluded)—even have their (different) ways of accounting for why the other religion functions, and functions benignly. My main attention in this problematic is upon the 'ultimates' involved, be they Buddhism's nirvānic/Bodhisattvic modes or Catholic Christianity's 'God and beatific union in/with God'. In short, what can it mean for us that these two sets of truths (and other sets too, Jewish, Moslem, Hindu, etc.), each utterly different from the others (so pluralism, common ground, and so on, are preempted),[75] go-on, devolve, in the world? Chiasm:—'ultimates', be they the nirvānic/Bodhisattvic modes or God (and union in/with God[76]), DOUBLE-BIND each other in *regressio infinitiva*: and this chiasm can be *prajñapti*/clue to what Buddhists call nirvānic/Bodhisattvic modes and Catholic Christians call God. (The double/binds double-bind with the other religions,—I here treat Buddhism and Catholicism because these are the venues of my work.) In holistic terms, the riddle does not (logocentrically-) 'compute'. It translates only as 'There is [*il y a*] more than one one-and-only-truth (but each is still truly a one-and-only-truth)'.

David Loy's comments on specific stanzas of the *Mūlamadhyamakakārikās* enable me to clarify some outstanding differences between the Mind-Only approach (at least, Mind-Only in its Chinese/Japanese extension) which he favors, and the Mādhyamika, especially the Prāsaṅgika-Mādhyamika.[77] Loy cites the famous *MMK* XXV: 9 in Sprung's translation, which is accurate enough here[78]: "That which, taken as causal or dependent, is the process of being born and passing on, is taken non-causally and beyond all dependence, declared to be nirvāna." Loy operates within those traditions which identify *pratītya-samutpāda* with the 'confluence of (positive) causes' which—because they are *anitya* (impermanent) and insubstantial—are *saṃsāric*: that is, everything is 'causal' and 'dependent' and thus belongs to the 'process of being born and passing on' (*saṃsāra*). *Nirvāṇa*, then, is treated as a mode which escapes away from this causality or dependency. But Mādhyamika interprets passages such as *MMK* XXV: 9 in a different way, a way not to be confused with what Loy calls Mādhyamika but which is really a Yogācāric subsumption of Nāgārjuna into a Mind-Only frame. Mādhyamika retains Nāgārjuna's crucial deconstructive move, namely, the deconstruction of *pratītya-samutpāda* taken to mean 'confluence of causes'.

'Confluence of causes' maintains a residual entitativeness, Nāgārjuna argues, because the model it proposes is of particular causes (little momentary holisms) converging to burst apart notions such as 'thing' and 'gross causes' (all of which are macro-holistic formations). But even micro-holisms are residually substantial, says Nāgārjuna. In fact, says Nāgārjuna, 'confluence of causes' is just a more sophisticated form of holistic 'cause and effect' (by extension, he would have necessarily argued—had he been still alive—that Huayan's 'everything causes everything else, which is equivalent to saying everything is caused by nothing',[79] is the biggest macro-holism of all). Nāgārjuna proves that holistic formations of *any* kind, including even the law of cause(s)-and-effect(s), are not empty, and violate Buddha's true and ultimate teaching on emptiness. So what Nāgārjuna does is define *pratītya-samutpāda* as *śūnyatā*, that is, as the emptiness of what falsely appears as holistic.[80] If the notion of causality is to be used at all, then, it must be used to mean that *emptiness* is causality. "Because emptiness works, therefore everything works" (*MMK* XXIV: 14). When Candrakīrti says "The term 'dependent-arising' not only refers to a process of production and of coming into existence but also to those things which are produced and come into existence," he means that emptiness is the process, and that emptinesses are the (true) phenomena themselves (see full quotation supplied earlier in this paper). What really is caused by emptiness falsely appears (to unknowing persons, to 'ignorant' persons) as a holism. That is why, for the Mādhyamika, Nāgārjuna's assertion that "the limit of *saṃsāra* is the limit of *nirvāṇa*" (*MMK* XXV: 20) makes sense only because '*saṃsāra* is empty' and therefore is *nirvāṇa* for s/he who can fully cognize this emptiness (or, as the Prāsaṅgikans point out, 'these streams of unfindables, these emptinesses').[81]

Thus, Madhyamakins interpret Loy's cited passage, *MMK* XXV: 9, in a different way from his. Consistent with Nāgārjuna's argument (throughout the *MMK*) against 'confluence of causes' and 'dependent-arising' so taken, Mādhyamikans understand *upādāya*[82] (lit. 'having acquired', Sprung's 'taken as causal') and *pratītya* (lit. 'dependent', as in Sprung) to refer here to the holistic causality and dependence that Nāgārjuna proves to be in fact empty. (In Derridean terms, we would say that Nāgārjuna deconstructs 'logocentric', i.e., holistic causality.) "That which, taken as causal or dependent," that is, *holistically* (logocentrically), is "the process of being born and passing on," i.e., *saṃsāra*, 'truth-for-a-concealer', an illusion. That the Sanskrit in *MMK* XXV: 9 uses *ājavamjavībhāva* ('revolving of birth-death state', Sprung's 'process of being born and passing on') is taken to comport saṃsāric ignorance. But that which, taken holistically, is an illusion, "is, taken non-causally and beyond all dependence [the Sanskrit just has the negation, 'non-dependently'] declared to be *nirvāṇa*." That is, in Nāgārjuna's words, "everything works" because its true working is *śūnyatā*, and the jñānic cognition of the 'unfindables' of saṃsāric life is nirvāṇic.[83]

Several of Loy's references in the *Mūlamadhyamakakārikās*, especially *MMK* XXV: 24, belong to a family of stanzas in which Nāgārjuna discusses 'serenity', 'quiescence', 'cessation'. *MMK* XXV: 24 reads, in the translation from Sprung that Loy quotes, "Ultimate serenity is the coming to rest of all ways of taking things, the repose of named things: no Truth has been taught by a Buddha for anyone, anywhere." Actually the Sanskrit has *prapancopaśamah*, 'cessation of concept-processing' (McCagney has simply "cessation of all thought"), so ultimate serenity is the "coming to rest" of 'concept-processing', that is, of holistic or logocentric thought. Just as when the stanza says that "no Truth has been taught by a Buddha" (or "no doctrine has been taught [*dharmo* ... *deśitah*]) by Buddha"), what is meant is that the teaching of the Buddha, necessarily in logocentric terms, is not *paramārtha-satya*, i.e., direct cognition of emptiness. Rather, the Buddha is deploying logocentric language as 'skillful means'. The stanza does not mean that 'cessation' is a better *prajñapti* than movement, since Nāgārjuna has cut off *both* logocentric arising and cessation: "Where the range of thought is renounced, that which can be stated has ceased to be valid. Indeed, the nature of events is like liberation, non-arising and non-ceasing" (*MMK* 18: 7).[84] Since the Prāsaṅgika-Mādhyamika, for reasons already explained, takes 'dependent arising' as the flux of 'emptinesses' and Nāgārjuna tells us 'dependent-arising' is the 'middle way', no wonder that it can be argued, and argued very efficaciously, that 'on-the-moveness' is a most effective *prajñapti.* Rather than calling 'cessation' the Buddha's "slogan," it is—after all—'dependent-arising' which the Dalai Lama chooses to call *the* "slogan" of the Buddha (*ME*, 17). And I prefer 'on-the-moveness' as *prajñapti* because it intersects so well with Derrida's 'movement *sous-rature*'. Even to the extent that Hopkins can report that for the Gelukba, "Every emptiness is, in turn, qualified by an emptiness, necessitating an infinite regress, but this does not entail a fallacy. . . ."[85] And even to the extent that for the Gelukba the Buddha's Enjoyment Body "disintegrates moment by moment" but "its continuum remains of the same type, unlike an ordinary body which becomes sick, old, and so forth; thus it is immortal but still impermanent" (*ME*, 345; see also 121-122). Forever changing and 'on-the-move'.

***

In his close critique of my reading of two *gong'an,* Frank Stevenson reinterprets them in terms of his own theory of repetition. His essay not only informs and delights, but also gives me the opportunity to further explain—at least insofar as I can write/read my own writing[86]—the cuts (*tranches*) my two pertaining essays[87] are/were intended to make in those marvelous decks of cards which constitute the *Wumenguan* and *Biyanlu*. When dealing with the *Wumenguan* case XLIII ("Shoushan's Staff," the 'Goat Horns' *gong'an*), Stevenson asks why—since I am seeking the praxis of literality—I do not generate as an alternative 'answer' the "full repetition" of the question, so an answer to Wumen's challenge, 'without words/with words, quickly say!' becomes 'without words/with words', that is, a full repetition of the question. I do not generate such an answer because my project differs from Stevenson's. The article in question was commissioned by Taiwanese Buddhists who wanted me to demonstrate how various Derridean maneuvers can serve a hermeneutics of *gong'an*. In case XLIII I am aiming to show the veiled reinscription of a term in its opposite, be it—as in the *gong'an* itself—the veiled reappearance of *bei* in *chu* (its *manifest* opposite); or—as in Wumen's commentary—the *veiled* appearance of 'without words' in 'with words' (its *manifest* opposite), or the inverse, the veiled appearance of 'with words' in 'without words'. My answer to Wumen indeed examines literality, but in order to show how reinscription can *mask* itself. Stevenson's proposed alternative, while of course literal, is also *flat*. It can hardly function as a *prajñapti* pointing towards a Mādhyamikan version of the Buddhist 'two truths', the two truths whereby—for everyone except Buddhas—'samenesses' (*paramārtha-satya*) are masked by holistic appearances (*saṃv□ti-satya*).

When dealing with *Biyanlu* case III ("Sun Face Buddha, Moon Face Buddha"), Stevenson suggests that my reading—to the extent it takes "no reflection" (on the surfaces of the Buddha-mirrors) to mean 'absence-of-signifier'—comes "closest to 'having' a (transcendental) signified." Again, he is working a different *tranche* from mine—my aim here was/is to show a Derridean maneuver, the severing of signifiers from signifieds; and I go on to contrast what would be—

on the one hand—the more expected Derridean option in this context, namely, covering by way of occlusion (so, the 'signifiers' turn out to be opaque, blockages instead of revelation), and another Derridean option, 'absence-of-signifier' (leaving the 'remainder' of the pure signified, one of the alternatives in Derrida's famous deconstruction of Saussurean-style linguistics).[88] Taking the two facing Buddha-mirrors as 'pure signifieds' in this sense, I interpret them in the Chanist terms at hand here, the terms of the 'pure consciousness' tradition, but in this situation the 'pure consciousness' is hardly a transcendental signified: Stevenson is right when he says the two facing mirrors become necessarily a "postmodernist mise-en-abyme, hall-of-mirrors": this blissful recursiveness[89] can function, indeed, as a Buddhist *prajñapti*.

***

When I sort the deck of cards, the essays of Jarow, Augustine, and Horowitz cross each other repeatedly in the same suit, and in particular under the sign of so-called 'interreligious dia/logue',[90] that wildest of cards which—I would argue—serves best when it does not aim to trump. Insofar as this anthology is *centered* on Buddhism/deconstruction, I have relegated the last part of this Afterword to afterwards, i.e., I forego detail and comment in abbreviation. But comment I do, because a text centered on Buddhism/deconstruction must of course give 'that which is marginalized' a chance to trespass on/in the center.[91] Religions utterly differ but can still instruct each other, most productively when they call the 'other' religion to that 'other' religion's own repressed (but still utterly distinct) reserves. At the I.A.P.L.'s Buddhism/Deconstruction session in 1999, the Venerable Mettanando, a Theravada monk and scholar from Thailand, and my university-colleague there, supplied us a case in point, when he said the Christian doctrine of the Word emerging from the Silence of the Father can challenge a Buddhist to probe into the "reason for the cosmic manifestation of the lineage of Buddhas." Conversely, in my own work I perceive Buddhism to summon Christianity to better develop a theology of God's impersonality.

It should be clear that I cannot resort with E. H. Jarow's notions of "multiplicity" and "free-play," though I grant his life-world may find them very workable indeed. By 'multiplicity', Jarow seems to mean the array of life-worlds taken as an array of bodied singularities (singularities each with a history, of course, the "thick yellow loam"): here he should look to Gilles Deleuze, perhaps (and at the I.A.P.L. session in 1999 Chung-min Maria Tu's fine paper served Deleuze well), but I find this concrete 'multiplicity' too much the dialectical opposite of 'abstract unity'. As already indicated, my work deploys a Derridean 'negative reference' which results in 'sameness which is not identity', a more (doctrinally) Buddhist formulation than Jarow would allow. As for Jarow's "free-play" (American 'trans-denominationalism', and religion by individual *bricolage*, and so on), it dances to the beat of Jean Baudrillard and Mark Taylor, perhaps, but my take on postmodernism is more Derridean.[92] Derrida deals in hybridization and contamination, indeed, but his emblem here is botanical/biological *grafting*, i.e., the imported body functions with the host, but remains utterly different (by 'pure negative reference', that which constitutes the 'sameness which is not self-same'). When Derrida—in a passage Jarow cites—says that within what one calls 'religions' there are tensions, heterogeneity, and "sometimes texts, especially those of the prophets, which cannot be reduced to an institution, a corpus, to a system," he is arguing precisely against *reductionism*: what one calls a religion is not exclusively adequated to its logocentric formations, and—indeed—the life of a religion is often most alive in its "disruptive volcanos." He is not discarding the role of the logocentric, nor of bodily formation. The prophets do not mix nondescriptly—they speak first to their own people (though what they say can be reinscribed into other peoples).

For example—why did Derrida begin, more than thirty years ago, to lecture on Plato, and why did I find him still, at Irvine in 1996, lecturing on Plato, persistently critiquing him, deconstructing him, over and over again, in ever new ways? It is because Derrida discerns himself as belonging with the Platonic body somehow.[93] Derridean deconstruction positions itself within the body, taking on its assumptions so as to uncover where/how that body dissimulates an appearance of holism. And, you will note, Derrida typically stays with the body he deconstructs: he persists in the deconstruction, often doing so by means of other bodies, but my point is—Derridean deconstruction typically *stays with the body*. Plato-as-deconstructed, for example, continues to supply ever new and fertile scripts for Derrida. Deconstruction does not make it a practice to 'quick-search' one body after another, to 'process' one body after another, in some *capitalist* frenzy. (This is not to deny—in the case of a macroscopic formation like a culture, tradition, and so on—that one has the right in conscience to leave one body for another, or even to hybridize bodies,[94] but such a decision is hardly a trivial matter.) Mark Taylor is no congener of mine precisely because I think his hodge-podges trivialize difference. When J. Hillis Miller lectured at National Taiwan University some years ago, he began by saying he was American and Protestant, and that American Protestantism—in its 'protest' against 'Roman' Catholicism—exemplifies the deconstructive act. I countered by saying that Protestant Christianity had abandoned the body of 'Roman' Catholicism and as such—whether Protestantism be right or wrong to have done so—in my opinion it certainly was not *deconstructive* of Catholicism in doing so. The opposite of Catholicism, maybe, and thus instructive for Catholicism sometimes (Protestant 'Higher Criticism' of the Bible, for example, stimulated Rome to develop its own differing Higher Criticism of the Bible[95]), but not deconstructive of Catholicism. Still, I give Taylor and Miller their due: people like Taylor and Miller exist so that people like me can exist, and people like me exist so that people like Taylor and Miller can exist. The world is disposed *thus*, but it takes philosophers in particular a long time to come to terms with such inevitable discordance. It took me a long time.

When Rick Jarow implies, then, that my doctrinal treatment of the Trinity is a preemptive defense against the more "ravaging aspects of deconstruction,"[96] he confuses defensiveness with what is really otherness. I *choose* to stay with the body which is Catholic Christianity, and thereby, my Faith constitutes me in this regard as Jarow's 'other'. I humbly suggest that his operative subtext is that *he wants me to be like him*. He should—in my opinion—come to understand that for me (and there have been many others like me), Trinitarian theology is not a merely 'abstract' exercise, but is cross-inscribed into my concrete meditative-life, my prayer-life, and all my bodied experience. And I hasten to add that for a good number of the many Buddhist monks I know (I teach seminars in Mahāyāna Buddhism to Theravāda monks at a Graduate Institute of Philosophy in Thailand), the doctrines of *anicca/anitya* and *śūnyatā*, far from being merely abstract, are inscribed as praxis. When Jane Augustine in her essay says that "Philosophy is the enemy of experience" and "the high abstract medieval Christian theology of the Roman Catholic Church became the enemy of Magliola's development," I detect the same refusal to come to terms with me in my otherness. What I negatively critique in *DLW* is *not* philosophy and medieval theology, but rather (1) the Jansenist-style exclusion of the sōmatic, an exclusion which characterized practical training in American, not Italian, Jesuit seminaries during the 1950s (a Jansenism which at that time was perhaps Irish-American in provenance, and all the more ironic, given the historical antagonism of Jansenism and the Jesuits)[97]; and (2) the American Church's legalist attitude towards both morality and spirituality (whereas Italian Catholicism, more indulgent, knew to soften rigor according to situation and in-the-application). Let American Buddhists, perhaps tempted to exoticise and idealize the Asian monastic *sangha*, not forget that Buddhist monasteries had/have their psychic troubles too, as witness this account of early 20th-century Chan monks in China:

> One hears of monks who found it impossible to make any mental breakthrough either because they were "stupid" or because they could not stop thinking about their parents, wife, children, and the other things they had left behind. At first they would be unable to keep their minds on anything. Then they would begin to have hallucinations and "talk nonsense." At this point they were usually locked in a room and a Chinese doctor called to examine them. Some recovered, some died. According to one informant, fatalities were most common during meditation weeks and the bodies were not buried immediately.
>
> It was felt that their deaths must be retribution for sins committed in former lives, so they were wrapped in quilts and left to be disposed of when the meditation weeks were over.[98]

As for Jane Augustine's claim that *DOM*'s 'between' represents "Magliola's effort to escape the net of logocentrism, that is conceptualism," I must again demur. Better to say my effort is to escape from the net of logocentrism to the condition of 'torn net', or 'logocentrism-as-deconstructed'. Such a condition commits neither what Jarow calls the fallacy of 'totalization' nor what he calls the fallacy of the 'synchronic'. In terms of inter-religious dia/logue, and the formatting thereof, it means that I bypass the models of "exclusivism, inclusivism, and pluralism," and opt for the 'negative reference' I have already explained: dia/logue opens onto (the *prajñapti* of-) negative overlaps in temporal/spatial *regressio infinitiva*, 'infinite retreat'. In short, (1) in dia/logue with Buddhists, I try to respect and understand the doctrine, history, and, insofar as possible, the praxis of Buddhism (and Buddhist scholars in Thailand have endorsed me to teach Buddhism academically, in the classroom), while recognizing Buddhism as utterly distinct from Christianity (see my related Note, in section on Loy); and (2) when writing Christian theology (an utterly different project from the above), I often am inspired by Buddhism, so that I can find an utterly distinct counter-point in Christianity's own reserves,[99] and also can join those who are trying to work out what would have happened[100] if the Christian revelation had traveled primarily Eastwards into a Buddhist mind-set, and developed a theology there.[101]

I appreciate Jane Augustine's essay for its realization that *DOM* writes a different stage in my life from *DLW*. Several of this collection's essayists have—in my opinion—treated my work synchronically, whereas these my two books in philosophy/religion, plus my pertaining anthology-papers and articles, punctuate very different moments in time/space. I also appreciate Jane Augustine's essay for its references to *DLW*'s rhetorical 'style' (where much of the book's philosophy actually takes place), a style which she says "crosses itself out in palimpsestic chiasm, leaving a trace of the erased under-text." The style (as well as the semantic, of course) is an attempt to enact the density of phenomenological life, and specifically in its character of frustration, i.e., how—on the experiential level—life seems to 'cross itself out', giving with one hand and taking with another. Double-binds can function, according to Buddhism, as a clue to the nature of *saṃsāra*, since saṃsāric life is frustrating until it is truly recognized/frequented as devoid. According to Catholic Christianity, double-binds are caused by the Fall, but can function in our lives as the personal crucifixion whereby—in/with/through Christ—ourselves and the world can be transformed into Easter-glory. In *DLW*, on the stylistic level the residue or 'trace' of the 'erased under-text' mimes those subtle recurrences in life which can sometimes serve to signal, no matter how obscurely, life's subtextual purposefulness. These recurrences 'fall short of perceptible meaning but are too much for mere chance'. For a Buddhist, they can represent the 'unfathomable' turns of personal *karma* (only advanced adepts can recognize precisely how their *karma* influences their life-events[102]), and for a Christian, they can represent the hidden designs of God's providence. Following Derrida's lead, in *DLW* I sometimes deploy 'floating graphic traits' as a device, and I do so in order to stylistically 'act-out' subtle recurrence.[103] In the case of double-binds, I sometimes cryptically inscribe them into *DLW*'s 'textual body' in the French postmodern literary manner, as when—for example—the Index acts-out my treatment of Glitch in the theology of the Trinity (glitch-in-holism as fertile, as 'clue' to how God works, *DLW*, 175-190) by an apparent 'glitch' or typographical error in the Index entries for "Generating" and "Glitch"[104] (196). Most readers have missed one of the most cryptic inscriptions—the Biblical reference to my quotation (*DLW*, 4) of "Where the Body (Gk. *sōma*) is . . ." is wrong (the correct reference is Luke 17:37), but perhaps readers should consider what the substituted reference can mean.

A truly liberating Buddhism, no matter whether it be a 'nirvāṇic' or a 'Bodhisattvic' Buddhism,[105] teaches that double-binds are a choice opportunity to recognize *all saṃsāric* life (including a so-called prosperous/long-lived/'fulfilled' saṃsāric life) is *duḥkha* ('unsatisfying', frustrating) in-the-long-run because of attachment. Catholic Christianity teaches that double-binds are a blessing (though they may not seem so at the time) because they are a choice opportunity to (1) shatter egoism, and (2) participate in Christ's redemptive suffering. In Christian terms, *DLW* affiliates crucifixion with Christ's call, "If anyone wishes to come after me, let him deny himself and daily take up his cross [chiasm, double-bind, crux], and follow me" (*Lk* 9: 23; *Mk* 8: 34), though any reader is free to draw responsible yet different conclusions from/about *DLW*'s text: the opaque density of the text is like phenomenological life's opacity, yielding to disseminating interpretations. The teaching that Christians can participate in Christ's redemptive act, i.e., that they can have the honor of joining their (technically superfluous) suffering with His (perfectly efficacious and infinitely sufficient) suffering, in order to save others, has been historically the heart of Roman Catholic spirituality,[106] and has distinguished it in particular from the Reformation churches (which believe the teaching impugns Christ's efficacity). The Catholic interpretation draws largely from Colossians 1:24, "Now I rejoice in my sufferings for your sake, and in my flesh I fill-up what is lacking in Christ's afflictions for the sake of his body, that is, the church." The teaching is of special interest here because it seems to intersect so incisively the Mahāyāna teaching of Bodhisattvic compassion (most Mahāyānists affirm all human beings are on the road to becoming Bodhisattvas).

Jane Augustine addresses *DOM*'s reference (134) to the Temple-veil torn down the middle from top to bottom (*Mt* 27:51). *DOM*'s author intended citation of this Biblical passage anagogically, so it becomes God's imagistic revelation that *holism* does not do justice to the Divine nature/working. Jane Augustine also calls attention to Hebrews 10: 19-22, which of course presents the Rending of the Veil as a figure for Christ's slashed flesh, through which we can truly enter the Holy of Holies. *DLW*'s author intended to assimilate his own grief and even his occasional despair to this dark passing through the slashed curtain which is Christ, Christ dying and rising, and Christ saving him. Sometimes Jane Augustine's essay sounds so vindictive that I think she fails to detect the tenderness which Catholics feel for Christ, and for (what they affirm as) His Church which—despite all the bitter failings of its human members—they still consider His 'mystical body'. That the author is working on a theology which argues Logos-as-concept doesn't alone do justice to Christ or His mystical body, but needs (ever unending) supplement from Logos-as-deconstructed, does not diminish his fidelity.

At the end of his feisty essay, Gad Horowitz rightly converges Emmanuel Levinas and the late-phase Derrida on the question of ethics,[107] and then adds a recapitulative 'said' about Levinasian 'ethical saying': "The ethical saying which cuts across, cross-hatches, interrupts all truths, all saids, . . . is *différance originaire*, the bottomless collapse of language, all of which, as we have already heard, are among the names of God." I co-passionate Horowitz's fierce Judaic drive to justice, and have always considered myself bound to it as its bond-servant. By virtue of this same bond, he surely must indulge me and let me re-address *DLW* for him, since—to put the matter as Roland Barthes would—

Horowitz 'writes' an *DLW* very different from the *DLW* Magliola wrote. That he does so would be a very acceptable state-of-affairs as long as he were attentive to my grammar, semantic, and (at least my) proximate intertexts. Deconstruction subverts texts, even shockingly, but does so precisely by a minute respect for the 'letter of the text'. (When Derrida writes of the 'postal network', the point is *not* that we should aim to falsely address, but that a message to a greater or lesser extent thwarts/is-thwarted *despite* our intention: meaning inevitably 'drifts', but in philosophy we should not encourage or cultivate the drift.) My replies to Gad Horowitz's essay are four, and each re-addresses a passage from Horowitz falsely addressing (or sometimes even misquoting) a passage from me.

(1) "In a 'playful *samādhi*', one can even enjoy Hell." This refers to Katsuki Sekida's gloss on the *Wumenguan*, Case Two. In my article "French Deconstruction with a (Buddhist) Difference," I report it (p. 19) without affiliating myself to it. Horowitz attributes it to me, and conflates it with his montage of citations from *DLW* quoted out of context. Even so, he has the gist of the Chan/Zen commentators wrong. They are explaining that when one is undergoing ordeal *and there is no physical recourse*, an awakened mind can *detach from* the ordeal, even to the extent that it can celebrate whatever in the circumstance is not evil (the evils, the three poisons of hatred, greed, ignorance, cannot be celebrated because they only vitiate experience and are harmful to self and others). *Mutatis mutandis*, it should not be difficult to envision how someone under torture might be able to relieve himself somewhat by mentally detaching from the pain and concentrating on the abstract color of the fire, say, or the innate beauty of shapes.

(2) I do not pray to God to be delivered from an omnipotent God who "makes happen or allows the happening of not only good but evil," as Horowitz says. The point made in *DLW* (79) is that I prayed for "letting-go/letting-be." I was beginning to realize that I had been imposing my design on God rather than the other way around. I was beginning to learn, instead, the trust in God that the *akedah* narrative (the 'Binding of Isaac') teaches us Abraham displayed. Horowitz implies that a theology of Divine double-bind (*DLW*, 188-189, etc.) implies a deceptive God. The motif of 'dissimulation' comes from Derrida, who derives it from midrashic commentary on Sacred Scripture, but—as I say in my Prolusion (*DLW*, xvi)—my script deviates very conspicuously from his in many respects. Divine 'dissimulation' is necessarily loving (189), as when Christ in the Eucharist dissimulates His Divinity by hiding under the false appearances of wine and unleavened bread (128).

(3) I do not believe that Nazism was an "'inevitable moment', one of those 'foredoomed. . . waves of recurrence of Evil'." Horowitz quotes passages that represent Derrida's treatment of evil and evil's 'aberrant reinscription' (*DLW*, 115-116, 163), though it is important to realize that Derrida nowhere affirms evil nor does he refuse to fight it.[108] His point, rather, seems to be that evil is always with us in history: the problematic of its recurrence is what he is trying to delineate. I cite the Derridean problematic in my treatment of meditation, so the beginning meditator knows not to allow spontaneous visualizations free-rein (116). When one enters or exits deep meditation, the human psyche is more vul-

nerable than usual to demonic manipulation. The meditator must commit to "the daily practice of loving-kindness, and to the rejection of malice," especially "when entering/exiting the sacred darkness." In the pertaining section of my book, I am proposing a kind of meditation intended for believers of any religion or none, so I do not propose my specific Christian belief about evil. I believe there is a personal/impersonal Evil which is very real, persistent, and heinous, whereas I can find no evidence Derrida so believes. Buddhism, for its part, tends to define evil as evil behavior (the three or five poisons) arising ultimately out of ignorance. I inscribe my personal belief about evil throughout *DLW*'s 'oto-autobiographical' Part One. Two examples: (i) Near the beginning of the long sequence which is "part elysian, part sheōl, and part grand-guignol" (37-52), evil appears—from out of Genesis 4:7—as the chiasmic Satanic 'croucher'[109] (40) who/which then continues to disseminate in the text, often as the 'crouching at your door' image; (ii) Late in my life I confront and repudiate a stubborn streak of evil in myself, my refusal to forgive—"So, noting the etymology, I decided on 'No more Harlequin!': no doubt I *did* store up too much rancor, the Devil's own very 'bad blood' . . . His/her/its bad blood-juice; Yes, I had to learn to *forgive* instead, to forgive even gargoyles" (107). The crypted subtext reinforces my message, since the curious reader will consult a dictionary and find the following etymology: "Harlequin, from MF *Halquin*, . . . goblin-leader of a troop of malevolent spirits."

(4) "Surrender the expectation of justice, practice the meditative frequenting of the double-binds of your existence and 'eventually the double-binds become salubrious'." This montage from Horowitz practices hodge-podge postmodernism, perhaps, but in my opinion falls short as responsible philosophy, Derridean or otherwise. In the context of *DLW*'s 117-119, the purpose of the meditation is to help come to terms—on a deep psychic level—with *what cannot be changed* and has the character of frustration. Examples would be irremediable birth defects or the death of loved-ones, especially if they adversely bind-us up, sending us into suicidal depression, etc. One is reminded of St. Teresa of Avila's dictum, "Lord, give me the grace to change what I should change and to accept what I cannot, and the wisdom to know the difference." In the Catholic Christian tradition, it is by personally passing through one's own version of Christ's crucifixion, one's own agony, that one attains His Easter-glory "all glorious." "I have been crucified [*sunestaurōmai*, co-crucified] with Christ; it is no longer I who live, but Christ who lives in me" (*Gal* 2:20).[110] On an intersecting track, the various Buddhist traditions require a death to ego which can be abetted in particular by adversity, and in Chan/Zen one finds that the 'Great Death' and subsequent 'gates' are often 'won' only by passing through agony.

"Surrender the expectation of justice," the first phrase in Horowitz's montage-sentence, does not appear anywhere in my work. What I say is the following: "The Awake-Dream I woke from was the expectation that within my life experience, my *Lebenswelt*, the world could be perceived, could be *detected*, as a just world" (*DLW*, 99). The pertaining footnote in *DLW* even establishes that the above attitude "was—existentially—my psychological state-of-affairs" during the (past) interval in my life about which the oto-autobiography is attempting a narration. Nonetheless, I in fact stand by the assertion even now. The point being made is that I came to terms with my *incapacity* to *detect*—in the experiential *appearances* around me or in history—that the world is just. I came to terms with the fact that 'life seems grossly unfair', and especially unfair to the poor and weak (whom I, for religious and humanistic reasons, most honor, *DLW* 130). Nowhere and at no time do I let such incapacity deter me from working actively for justice in the world, as Horowitz himself readily admits.

Faith in Christ and His teaching enables me to continue as an avenger for justice in the face of an apparently cruel world. Avowal of the inescapable vow, response to the prior ethical obligation to the concrete Other—and here I happily invoke the Levinasian terms—enables the Jew as an avenger for justice no matter how the world phenomenologically appears (and especially *if* it appears cruel, one might add). Faith in the Eightfold-path's accuracy enables a Buddhist to help others and not to give-up in the face of an apparently unfair world.[111] When s/he is sufficiently 'awakened', s/he can cognize the karmic justice of the world, and faith that helping others is fruitful (for others and oneself) becomes unnecessary. The sufficiently awakened Buddhist continues to help others all the more, but can cognize karmic pattern and thus more effectively steer individuals towards greater liberation. In Mahāyāna Buddhism there is the Bodhisattvic vow, to which even beginners can pledge themselves, viz., not to cease working to liberate others (even by transfer of 'personal' merit), until all sentient beings are liberated.

Gad Horowitz tells me that I need "a systematic, explicit, Judaic ethical difference" if I am to account for the binding nature of my 'infinite obligation' to/for justice. I reply that the Christian tradition affirms the prior Ethical Saying to be God the Father and the concrete perfect Response to be (the Jew whom it calls) Christ in his Divine/human nature. His crucifixion/resurrection is understood to be the perfect 'turning inside out' for others, so that all others can do likewise in/through Him. Bearing the 'burden of the entire suffering creation' is His Glory, our glory. That I am working on a theology which deconstructs what is an exclusively holistic *prise* of these teachings in no way means I don't accept the teachings (in fact, it means I *do* accept the teachings, *DLW*, 105-107).[112] Not that he need agree at all, but surely Gad Horowitz knows that Christians believe the Vow is *always already* (*ex eternitate*, and "before the foundation of the world"[113]) Jesus/Joshua the Christ, and references to this theology appear repeatedly in *DLW*. Two examples: "'Jesus thrown everything off balance' [quoted from Flannery O'Connor's "A Temple of the Holy Ghost"]. . . . I must always choose in the best interest of the world's suffering Displaced, —no matter how or where they suffer" (130); and "to give myself, body and psyche, to be consumed by all the sentient beings around me, . . . until 'nothing' is left: consider the case of Jesus consumed in Communion" (129).

The problematic of justice in Buddhism utterly differs from that in the Judeo-Christian tradition. All three 'turns of the wheel' of Buddhism, contemporary Theravāda, Mahāyāna, and Vajrayāna, are in their classical formulations purely 'self-help' traditions. One's destiny is determined by one's own volitional acts. Even the so-called 'other-help' schools normally supply 'other-help' only in order to better position the recipients to liberate themselves (Pure Lands often supplying ideal meditation conditions, for example). Karma, the law of perfect justice, is always in effect: each 'self' (understood as a cluster of impulse-formations, not a soul), over a series of many lives, gets what it deserves. Moreover, *śūnyatā*, the nothingness(es) of things, is accessed only by 'non-discrimination', including non-discrimination between good and evil. Masao Abe, representing the main Chinese and Japanese traditions here, puts it this way:

> In Buddhism, on the other hand, religious transcendence is not God as the supreme good but *śūnyatā*, which is neither good nor evil; and the relation between ethics and religion is realized to be fully discontinuous, not only in the move from ethics to religion, but also in the move from religion to ethics. This implies that in Buddhism, ethics is to be established in the religious dimension not directly—as God's commandment in the case of Christianity—but dialectically through the realization of *śūnyatā*. . . .[114]

Thus, for most Buddhists, justice is important but belongs to saṃsāric life. In Mahāyāna and Vajrayāna, anyone with Bodhisattvic intent can actively help people, serve others, in the world, and the religious narratives are replete with stories of utter self-sacrifice for others. Bodhisattvic activity is normally understood to be effective in proportion to its practitioner's degree of awakening, and it is in this sense that ethics is established (to use Abe's term) "dialectically": the more 'awakened', the more one can have an ethical effect in saṃsāric life. Jane Augustine's essay alludes to the more developed Mahāyānist version of the Cosmic Buddhas whom Ven. Mettanando, a Theravādin, referenced in his session-paper. The Sambhogakāya vow sends Buddhas into the world, but it is important to realize that even their help is indirect, i.e., they help others help themselves.[115]

Westerners have long blamed Buddhism for much of the East's 'undeveloped social conscience', and part of this indictment derives from a misunderstanding of the above 'indirection' (while, of course, part derives from real disagreement, i.e., the parties understand but disagree). It is true, I think, that among the essays in this anthology, and among the papers from the I.A.P.L. session which initiated it, there is much to abet the western stereotype of Buddhist 'non-involvement', at least in terms of what is *omitted* from discussion. Perhaps Hsiao-yu Sun's fascinating "From the Lying Truth to the Truth about Lying: Jacques Lacan and Buddhist Thought," a session-paper which unfortunately could not be anthologized here, best exemplifies the problem for us when it says in its Buddhist section:

> All the phenomena, when viewed in the light of this wisdom, is lying insofar as it conceals the ultimate truth. So we have to develop both awareness and equanimity at both the conscious and unconscious levels and to be mindful of everything but not to react to it.

An informed Buddhist knows that such awareness/equanimity enables the practitioner to cognize the world better and thus intervene at will when help is needed, but in the history of Buddhism 'non-reaction' has often been understood by the masses as a call to social 'non-involvement'. Nonetheless, I have my doubts about the overall validity of the western indictment. If Buddhism has often failed to implement the ethical reserves in its teaching, so has Christianity. Over the long haul, Buddhism has been both more pacifist and ecologically sensitive than Christianity, and it is the Christian nations which brutally colonized the East, not the other way around. As the various Christian institutions have been undergoing salutary deconstruction (of themselves), so too have the various Buddhist institutions (e.g., the Theravādic Ven. Buddhadasa deconstructed Theravāda). Crosswise, the religions have been 'instructing' each other. Sulak Sivaraksha in Thailand and the various networks of [politically/socially] Engaged Buddhists, Dharma Master Cheng-yen in Taiwan and the Tzu Chi Foundation, were perhaps inspired in part by western models, but they have revived (long-untapped) political/social reserves in their own Buddhism, and now exercise global influence. The Benign Action-Sword of Amoghasiddhi is swinging a wide swathe.

Some words at the last, about Ven. Mettanando's Buddhist deconstruction of Christianity's "Beatific Vision," as he presented it at the I.A.P.L. session. His deconstruction pertained to dia/logue, insofar as it deployed Buddhist 'Wisdom' to deconstruct Christian 'Love'. The Ven. Mettanando's paper ended with the following teaching-story:

> (At the end of their trips through the *Bardo* [a Tibetan Vajrayānist term, meaning 'intermediate stage(s)' between death and rebirth], a Catholic priest and a Tibetan Gelukba monk and a Theravāda monk suddenly find themselves facing a huge globe of serene blinding light—) The Catholic priest says, "This is what I have been expecting from you, Lord! Oh, how much I do love You, my Lord!" The Tibetan monk says, "I know this is not real! It is just a projection of my thought!" The Theravāda monk says, "I know even this is not permanent!"

The intention of Ven. Mettanando was to deconstruct the doctrine, normative for most Christian denominations, that the Faithful in Heaven experience the Beatific Vision of God, and that this is the Ultimate Beatitude possible. For most Buddhists, the notion (and experience) of 'Beatific Vision' is mired in the epistemological split of subject and object (and therefore of desire), with God as the 'object'. From his Theravadic perspective, Ven. Mettanando distinguished between Christianity's emphasis on 'Love', which requires exchange between two identities; and Buddhism's emphasis on 'Wisdom', which dissolves identities. In Thailand, the Ven. Mettanando and myself have never been able to come to terms on the relative roles of Love and Wisdom, but I continue to remind him that Christian *agapē* does not involve an 'object [or subject] of pleasure', and also that there is in both the *sophia*-tradition of Greek Christianity and the Thomist tradition of Roman Christianity a 'wisdom' which is distinguished from 'charity' but understood to be equally involved in heavenly beatitude. St. Thomas Aquinas, for example, much emphasizes that in beatific vision the human intellect is raised to the intellectual vision of God as supreme truth. The 'vision' is called such only by way of metaphor[116]; the union is not that of subject and object (or subject and subject), since in the union the created intellect "participates in some divine likeness" not belonging to a "created intellect" (the Blessed are "partakers of the Divine Nature," the New Testament says in 2 Peter 1:4). I propose Derridean chiasm and 'sameness constituted by pure difference' as helpful ways of 'talking about' such a union. Ven. Mettanando should not have the Catholic priest exclaim, when looking at the serene blinding light, "This is what I have been expecting," since the chiasmic reinscription of God and the 'Blessed in heaven' would necessarily bring about a union the actual experience of which is beyond finite human expectation.

Ven. Mettanando has the Theravāda monk see the "huge globe of serene blinding light" too, and exclaim, "I know even this is not permanent!" I presume the monk means that the "globe" appears as an object, and thus too must be impermanent. Knowing that in *nibbāna* there is no intact form, the monk concludes that he has not arrived yet. As for the Tibetan Buddhist monk, he exclaims, "I know this is not real! It is just a projection of my thought!" Here perhaps the allusion is to the famous Tibetan 'terma' text of the Nyingma tradition, the *Great Liberation Through Hearing in the Bardo*,[117] attributed to Padmasambhava. According to this Sacred Text, in the second day of the *Bardo* there appears the "mirror-like wisdom, dazzling white, luminous and clear," shining forth from the heart of the Tathāgata Vajrasattva and his consort and piercing your eyes so "you cannot bear to look at it" (*TBD*, 43). The Text says that to attain liberation, a traveler through the *Bardo* must choose this light, though it is terrifying, and not the "soft smoky light of the hell-beings," which is non-blinding and seductive, but an illusion. A Tibetan monk would know that to recognize a Tathāgata in the *Bardo* is "not dependent on his [the monk's] perception" (*TBD*, 13), and thus is *not* an illusion; to see the soft smoky light is dependent on his perception, and thus *is* an illusion. Since Venerable Mettanando's Tibetan monk is *not* supposed to consider Tathāgata Vajrasattva's blinding light a "projection," maybe our Ven. Mettanando is being a very naughty and deconstructive Theravāda monk here, putting a Theravādin's words in the Tibetan monk's mouth. Normative Theravāda rejects the very notion of *Bardo*, and the Vajrayānist [and Mahāyānist] doctrine of Tathāgathas is judged a flagrant violation of the Buddha's 'four seals'.[118] And dear reader, all of this constitutes in its own way a welcome rhetorical turn for me the 'author' of this Afterword, because it lets me stop abruptly, at a deconstructive end.

Notes

1. Those interested can check on the *khatvānga* in Tsultrim Allione, *Women of Wisdom* (London: Routledge and Kegan Paul, 1984), 34; and compare Magliola, "Sexual Rogations, Mystical Abrogations: Some Données of Buddhist Tantra and the Catholic Renaissance," in Clayton Koelb and Susan Noakes, eds., *The Comparative Perspective on Literature: Approaches to Theory and Practice* (Ithaca, NY: Cornell University Press, 1988), 208-211; and Magliola, "Differential Theology and Womankind: on Isaiah 66:13,"

in Philippa Berry and Andrew Warnick, eds., *Shadow of Spirit: Postmodernism and Religion* (London and N.Y.C.: Routledge, 1992), 219-220.

2. That is, to cite Jackson, "if x, then y; if no x, then no y" (see Jackson's essay earlier on, in his section treating the Pali Canon).

3. For the etymology of *pratītya-samutpāda*, see Jeffrey Hopkins, *Meditation on Emptiness* (Boston: Wisdom Publications, 1996), 161-173. Henceforth cited by the abbreviation *ME*.

4. Nonetheless, it is worth noting that—as in the case of a Buddha—"when emptiness is directly cognized—that is to say, without the medium of concepts and images—all emptinesses throughout all world systems are simultaneously known" (*ME*, 407). The emptinesses are "like fresh water poured into fresh water" (*ME*, 407). That the "emptiness of one thing . . . is not the emptiness of another" implies not only the Mādhyamikan stream of dependent-arisings but also the ongoing of Derridean *traces*, which are the configured but moving marks of 'absence', 'lack', not-thereness. On Derridean traces, see 'traces/marks' entry in the index of my *On Deconstructing Life-Worlds: Buddhism, Christianity, Culture* (Atlanta: Scholars Press, American Academy of Religion, 1997; Oxford: Oxford UP, 2000) [henceforth *DLW*]. Of course Derrida does not address the vast and 'simultaneous' cognizing which the Prāsaṅgikas attribute to Buddhas.

5. Or "truths-only-for-a-concealer-of-suchness," the Gelukba say, because the 'unfindability' of each thing is its *suchness* (*ME*, 405 and 218-219).

6. From the side of the practitioner just beginning to access 'unfindables', one can call a dependent-arising an entity's 'emptied-outness': dependent-arisings seem to be a flux of *emptied-outs*. The awakening consciousness 'empties-out' holisms appearing in the 'ignorant consciousness', because holisms are false, i.e., only 'truths-for-a-concealer'. But the Prāsaṅgikan tradition points out that actually unfindables are not emptieds-out, because such a formulation implies that each phenomenon establishes its own unfindability, whereas the opposite is the case, each unfindability establishes a phenomenon. Moreover, unfindables are necessarily concatenated because they are *dependent*-arisings, and cannot 'found' themselves.

7. Derrida is not a Buddhist, of course, nor is he all that familiar with Buddhism as a philosophy. The most I am claiming are some philosophical intersections of Derridean thought and Buddhist thought, and this in order to open-up Derrideans to a Buddhism I think can help them in many ways: "Intersections are lines-crossing-each-other. Lines have no 'width', so when crossing each other they cannot have ground 'in common'" (*DLW*, 191).

8. For the Prāsaṅgika Mādhyamika, *pratītya-samutpāda* is a sign of the *non*-true existence of things; on the other hand, for the Vaibhāsikas, Sautrāntikas, and Cittamātrins, *pratītya-samutpāda* is "a sign of things' *true* existence" (*ME*, 167), which is one of the reasons I have always affirmed Mādhyamika, and especially Prāsaṅgika Mādhyamika, instead: what I call the 'centered' (in Derridean sense) Buddhist schools do not address a Derridean's needs.

9. To all but Buddhas.

10. 'Tetralemma' renders what is *catuṣkoṭikā* in Sanskrit, meaning 'four ends' [four extremes]; and *siju* in Chinese, meaning 'four phrases' [four lines].

11. See D. T. Suzuki, *Outlines of Mahāyāna Buddhism* (New York: Schocken, 1963), 102-3.

12. In Hsueh-Li Cheng, "Emptiness: Exoteric and Esoteric Buddhism," *World Sūtric and Tantric Buddhist Conference Report* (Kaohsiung, Taiwan: Fo Kuang P, 1988), 121.

13. See Ji Zang, *On the Mahāyāna* [*Dacheng xuanlun, Profound Treatise on the Mahāyāna*] in *Taishō shinshū daizōkyō* [hereafter *T*], 45.1567-10, as cited and translated in Ming-Wood Liu, *Mādhyamaka Thought in China* (E. J. Brill: Leiden, 1994) 142.

14. Ji Zang, *On the Lotus*, *T* 34.396b.19-29, as cited and translated in Liu, *Madhyamaka Thought in China*, 149.

15. Yu-lan Fung's preferred translation, in his *History of Chinese Philosophy,* Vol. II, trans. Derk Bodde (Princeton: Princeton University Press, 1953) [henceforth *HCP*], 296. See also Wing-Tsit Chan's translation, in his compilation, *A Source Book in Chinese Philosophy* (Princeton: Princeton University Press, 1963), 360.

16. Thomé H. Fang in his *Chinese Philosophy: Its Spirit and Development* (Taipei: Linking Pub. Co., 1988), puts it this way, following Ji Zang: "Hard dualism and non-duality should not be called the authentic: The wondrous authenticity in Prajnā must surpass the coupling of sheer dualism [the extreme of choosing extremes] with the non-duality [the extreme of choosing non-extremes]," 202.

17. Liu, *Mādhyamaka Thought in China* , 150-151, citing Ji Zang.

18. See *On the Two Truths* [*Erdi yi*], *T* 45.91-92, cited and translated in *HCP*, 297-298.

19. *On the Two Truths*, *T* 45.92, in *HCP*, 298.

20. It is Chan in its Yogācāric variants that most popularizes 'throwing away the ladder' upon 'awakening'.

21. The duality of the supreme truth is also non-dual, of course, since 'neither are both existence and emptiness affirmed', but my point is that most of our contributing essays—at least according to Ji Zang and many other Mādhyamikans—fall into the opposite error; and to this extent, these essays fail to deploy Buddhism in expedient terms: fail, in short, to deliver deconstructionists their summons/summoning.

22. When the three levels of two truths are *not* to be discarded, Ji Zang treats the third-level supreme truth according to what logicians call the *undistributed* mode. Supplying many passages from Ji Zang's pertaining texts, Fung makes it clear that only the undistributed mode can apply (see *HCP*, 296-298). For explanations of the distributed and undistributed modes, see *DLW*, 118, 165, and also its index-entry 'neither x nor non-x (4th lemma)'. Ellen Zhang's often so informative paper does not treat the third-level supreme truth in the undistributed mode (and in her diagram the formulation in symbolic logic is in distributed mode).

23. Cited in Liu, *Madhyamaka Thought in China,* 152.

24. As cited in Liu, *Madhyamaka Thought in China*, 152.

25. Liu, *Madhyamaka Thought in China,* 152.

26. From Sk. *bodhati*, 'awakes, understands', extended form of Indo-European root *bheudh-*, 'to be aware, to make aware'. The word 'enlightenment' misrepresents the Sanskrit, insofar as 'light' imagery descends from the Indo-European *leuk-*, 'light', which becomes, on the Sanskrit side *rocate*, 'shines', and on the Old English side, *leoht*, 'light'. Translating *bodhi* as 'enlightenment' has the disadvantage—when dealing with Derrideans—of carrying the word 'light'. On 'light' imagery, see Derrida's "White Mythology," collected in his *Margins of Philosophy,* trans. Alan Bass (Chicago: University of Chicago Press, 1982). Also, see entry 'braille disseminating series' in index of *DLW*, for Christianity and a 'saving darkness'.

27. See Liu, *Madhyamaka Thought in China*, 141, 149.

28. "Chi-Tsang [Ji Zang] applies to the middle way the same descriptions he gives of non-attachment," Liu, *Madhyamaka Thought in China*, 153. See also Liu's references to the *Large Treatise*, etc., in order to show that the Mādhyamika in general interprets the middle way to mean non-abidingness.

29. See *DLW*, 152-153. Of course I in turn am invoking 'movement-under-erasure' as an expedient emblem for better summoning deconstruction, since Derrida's off/tracking does not accord well with 'quiescence' or, *afortiori*, 'absolute quiescence' as emblems.

30. Liu, *Madhyamaka Thought in China*, 151, paraphrasing Ji Zang,Commentary on the Middle Treatise, T 42.28b11-13.

31. *Nāgārjuna in China,* Studies in Asian Thought and Religion series, vol. 18 (Lewiston, NY: Edwin Mellen Press, 1995).

32. In Derrida's usage, the thought that can be 'heard' is naively logocentric: the thought that can be read would be 'writing', that is, 'differential' marks. But I think an 'impossible' writing such as Mādhyamikan *prajnā* he has not met yet.

33. Ji Zang in *On the Mahāyāna*, *T* 45.15c5-11, translated in Liu, *Mādhyamaka Thought in China* , 150-151 (supplied parenthetical words are Liu's).

34. It thus clashes not at all with Derridean *différance/différence*.

35. It is just that even Ji Zang sometimes resorts to thought-models and a representational rhetoric more plastic, that is, more 'modeled' or 'shaped-up', than those the Gelukba usually employ, so I prefer—for my purposes—the Tibetan Mādhyamika.

36. Not that the first-level supreme truth, and some variants of the other levels, are not *logocentric* too, for Derrida, but the first-level mundane truth is the simplest representation of 'existence', and my aim at this juncture is to show how Mādhyamika can validate (and thus, for Derrida, 'reinstate') even a *grosso modo* logocentrism in a convincing way, and all in the midst of a continuing deconstruction.

37. Fang, *Chinese Philosophy*, 205.

38. Not that postmodernism and deconstruction are 'one-and-the-same'. See my discussion of E. H. Jarow's paper, ahead.

39. See Loy's section on "Causality" and his footnote 8. As for Huayan's assimilation of the *trisvabhāva*-theory, see Fang, *Chinese Philosophy*, 313-314; and *HCP*, 346-348.

40. See *HCP*, 383-384, for comparisons of Weishi, Huayan, and Tiantai.

41. Chan/Zen being sometimes the paramount exception among Far Eastern Buddhist schools. Its non-holistic, deconstructive bent sometimes drives it to deconstruct the holisms of other schools, and even the holisms of its own Yogācāric current.

42. This is not to deny that deconstruction and differentialism also suit *my* personality-type, and have constituted an important, indeed crucial, lesson in my own life-history. See *DLW*, 71-79, 98-104.

43. That is, Europeanists who belong to either the English-speaking world or the Latin American world, or to Continental Europe itself.

44. H. Coward and T. Foshay, eds., *Derrida and Negative Theology* (Albany: SUNY Press, 1992), 227.

45. See *Derrida on the Mend* (Lafayette: Purdue University Press, 1984; rpt., Purdue University Press, 2000) [henceforth, *DOM*], especially 42-43. Includes pertaining citations of Derrida, and references to him.

46. Jacques Derrida, *De la grammatologie* (Paris: Editions de Minuit, 1967).

47. *Of Grammatology*, trans. Gayatri Chakravorty Spivak (Baltimore: The Johns Hopkins University Press, 1976).

48. Derrida, *Of Grammatology*, 65.

49. Geoffrey Bennington and Jacques Derrida, *Jacques Derrida* (Chicago and London: University of Chicago Press, 1993; pbk. 1999) [henceforth, *JD*], 111; see also *JD*, 102-103, 113-114, for many other pertaining references to Derrida, and discussion.

50. See also Bennington (*JD*, 84), as he reverses Derrida's opponents (and with great success): "We have begun to cast doubt on everything that can apparently *limit* deconstruction to language (this is our only chance of understanding that there is nothing outside the text)" [emphasis mine].

51. I have long argued that the Buddhist 'two truths' are implied in Derrida's own work (though no doubt in too inchoate a form). Ian Mabbett in his paper finds likewise.

52. As heretofore explained, the comparisons are, at most, intersections: they are *not* grounds-in-common.

53. For Derrida's treatment of 'mark', see in particular his early essay, "Signature Event Context" (*Margins of Philosophy*); and his later "Ulysses Gramophone: Hear Say Yes in Joyce," trans. Tina Kendall and Shari Benstock, in Bernard Benstock, ed., *James Joyce: The Augmented Ninth* (Syracuse, N.Y.: Syracuse University Press, 1988), 27-75.

See also the references at the index-entry for "Mark" in Peggy Kamuf, ed., *A Derrida Reader: Between the Blinds* (N.Y.: Columbia University Press, 1991)

54. See references of index-entry for "program/diagram" in *DLW*, and for "Program" in Kamuf, *A Derrida Reader*.

55. That is, physical graphs only can function because they are spatially distinct from the writer and from each other, and temporally sequential. These factors—to put the matter logically/logocentrically—enable 'ourselves' too, and all life, since reality is spatial and temporal.

56. That is, even space and time are double-binded/bound (time/space): they necessarily undo, deconstruct each other: they *defer* (space precludes one-point-only-ness, time precludes one-moment-only-ness), and they *iterate* (non-one-pointedness and non-one-momentness pull at each other, deconstruct each other, deflect each other). Thus *différance* devolves, 'goes on'.

57. See Derrida, the essay "Tympan" in his *Margins of Philosophy*.

58. *DLW*, 180. See *DLW*, 179-181, for citations of Derrida and a discussion.

59. Though, following the Mādhyamika, I regard the jnānic states as more cognitive than Loy usually regards them. The jnānic states are supermundane but cognitive, and not a leap to the non-cognitive. And in them the debris of rationality can continue on as 'traces'. The reader may find it interesting to compare what I call Christianity's 'differential mysticism' (*DLW*, 190; also 110-119). No doubt there are other differential mysticisms too, including several Jewish kinds (which, for many psycho-biographical reasons, seem unavailable to/for Derrida).

60. *DLW*, 158. For the 'changes', see Part Two, section (ii), "Double-Binds and (Derrida's) 'Dénégations'."

61. For liaison/striction, see *JD*, 95, 309, and *passim*.

62. And, as I noted previously, time *spatializes* (thus, time/space double-bind).

63. For example, see Junjiro Takakusu, *The Essentials of Buddhist Philosophy* (Honolulu: University of Hawaii Press, lst ed., 1947; 3rd ed., Office Appliance Co., 1956), 108; and Wing-tsit Chan in *A Source Book in Chinese Philosophy*, 406.

64. Wing-tsit Chan, *A Source Book in Chinese Philosophy*, 407. Thomé Fang explains the Dharmadhātu of Huayan as follows: "Taken in its all-inclusive unity, this One True *Dharma-dhātu* verifies the omni-presence and omni-potence of the creative Mind constitutive of the noumenon of all the phenomenal worlds, diverging itself into (a) the differentiating Realm of Events, (b) the integrative Realm of Reason, (c) the interpenetrative Realm of Reason and Events [*li* and *shi*]; and (d) the interlacing Realm of all Events" (Fang, *Chinese Philosophy*, 320).

65. See 'Comment' on point three in Fa Zang's Treatise on the Golden Lion [Jin shizi zhang], in Chan, A Source Book in Chinese Philosophy, 409.

66. See, for example, "Hundred Gates to the Sea of Ideas of the Flowerly Splendor Scripture" ["Huayan jing yihai baimen"], Chan, *A Source Book in Chinese Philosophy*, 423.

67. Paradoxical formations, unless they are double-binds and not really 'paradoxical' at all, are 'logocentric' for Derrida. See *DLW*, 171-172; and Derrida on 'intercut', 'interlace', etc., in *Truth in Painting*, trans. G. Bennington and I. McLeod (Chicago: University of Chicago Press, 1987), 255-382.

68. Whereas Sākyamuni's net—at least as an emblem and *prajñapti*, can be quite entangled indeed, as even Dogen knew well. David Putney cites one of Loy's main sources, Dōgen, declaring, "My late master [Rujing], an ancient Buddha, said, 'A gourd is really the tangles of wisteria vines'," and Putney explains, "The gourd is a *fruition* of the entanglement of vines. . . . It is the seeing of things precisely as entanglements, the way they are or have become (*yathābhūtam*), that leads to the realization that entanglement is part of the path to wisdom. It is the continued actualization and continued expression of the entanglement of the kōan as enlightenment" (see Putney, "Dogen: Enlighten-

ment and Entanglement," in *Buddhist-Christian Studies*, Vol. 17 [1997], 35, 40). Derrida's net of course comes with holes and is all garbled-up. And as I have shown elsewhere, it can even be said the Christian net, the apostolic Net of the Fishermen, is best thought of as ever 'brimming over and in-the-process-of-tearing' (Luke 5:6—"and their net was being torn [*dierrēgnuto*]"). See Magliola, "Inside/Outside and the Difference: Attitudes towards the Church in Some Novels by Graham Greene and Shusaku Endo [*Nei/wai yu yanyi— geleian gelin yu yuanteng zhouzuo bufen xiaoshuo dui jiaohui de taidu*]," trans. Shu-chen Chiang, in A. Bramkamp, ed., *Proceedings of the First International Conference on Literature and Religion* [*Diyijie guoji wenxue yu zongjiao huiyi lunwenji*] (Taipei: China Times, Ltd., 1987), 118-119.

69. Trans. Alan Bass (Chicago: University of Chicago Press, 1978), 152.

70. It is the open-ended overlap of a double-bind which 'thwarts' closure and thus deconstructs. For discussions, see *DLW*, 100-102 et seq., 188-189, and index-entry 'binds/double-binds'. Note Derrida's teaser, cited by Kamuf (*A Derrida Reader*, 599) from Derrida's *Glas*: "All the examples are thus cut out and cut across each other. Look at the holes, if you can" (210).

71. *JD*, 306, 310, for discussion, and references to Derrida.

72. Or "sameness which is not-identity."

73. That is, neither ontological 'oneness' nor numerical 'one'.

74. Catholic Christians hold that the non-baptized can still be saved by Christ's Redemption (which, Catholicism says, *alone* can save human beings) if they obey the 'natural law' and God's Providence wills a design for them other than the grace of knowing and affirming Christianity. Most Buddhists believe that non-Buddhists can qualify for the Divine Vehicle, and can ascend as high as the First Dhyāna Heaven. See Ven. Yin-shun, trans. Wing H. Yeung, *The Way to Buddhahood* (Boston: Wisdom Press, 1998), pp. 8-10, 49, 97-99. My point is that the two religions teach that members of other religions can achieve a (degree of) beatitude. Catholic theologians, while *retaining* their religion's doctrines, should ask the question, "Why does God work, in many specific cases, through other religions which do much good and flourish? And do good and flourish according to doctrines utterly different from Catholic ones? What implication does this have for our understanding of God, i.e., what we call the 'theology of (the nature of) God'?" And Buddhist philosophers, while *retaining* their Buddhism, should ask, "Why is the 'God' of Catholic theology/mysticism more like what we Buddhists call Dharma (in its sense as 'law of the universe') than like what we Buddhists define as a Divinity (such as the 'refuge of Brahma' [see Yin-shun, *The Way to Buddhahood*, 10])? What implications can this have for the Buddhist classifications of non-Buddhist vehicles, and the nature of truth?" In Thailand, the famous Ven. Buddhadasa was beginning to ask such questions. Not that there is an 'answer' in the sense of a 'solution' or discovery of 'common-ground'. But neither does the inquiry become a 'blank sheet without traces'. There are debris. And the double-bind perpetuates.

75. In Thailand, where I teach in an (interfaith) Graduate Institute of Philosophy and Religions, the Buddhist philosophers and Catholic theologians cannot find common-ground. Though agreeing on the truth of many assertions ('Selfishness is a grave moral fault', 'The world is impermanent', etc.) and the good of many practices (monastic chant, silent meditation, etc.), we find that inevitably the truths/practices said to be 'held-in-common' are based on more elementary teachings which are uniquely Buddhist or Christian: indeed, the more 'ultimate' the process of reduction becomes, the more absolute the difference between Buddhist and Christian justifications of *why* such-and-such is true/good.

76. Which, by the way, is also a chiasm. That is, I would argue that chiasm is a better clue to understanding 'beatific union in/with God', at least in Catholicism's sense, than straightforward 'sameness' and 'difference' are.

77. Mind-Only "means that nothing exists apart from consciousness. 'The word *mere* [Skt *mātra-*, 'only'] is used to deny that there are any real things aside from consciousness' . . . . On the other hand, 'the dharmas, etc., as inseparable [*sic*] from consciousness, do exist'" (*HCP*, 319). Mind-Only theorists claim that they 'keep to the middle path' by neither adding something to consciousness-alone, nor reducing consciousness to nothingness. The *svabhāva* of 'sole imagination' (*parikalpita-laksana*) and 'dependency' (*paratantra-laksana)* are idealistic in formation, and the character of 'ultimate reality' (*parinispanna-laksana*) is Wisdom-only, the wisdom of absolute Mind. Loy himself approvingly quotes Yongming's assertion, "The One Mind can take in all minds and return them to the One Mind. . . ." Such a formulation, though it may serve as a *prajñapti* for some, is simply too 'foundational' to summon deconstructionists. Loy denies that "metaphysical idealism" is involved, since *paratantra-laksana* breaks-down the subject-object dichotomy, but he begs the question. 'One Mind' itself is an idealistic formulation. The further claim that Mind-Only describes meditative experience also begs the question. Meditative experience in Yogācāra accesses truth, indeed, *becomes* truth, and if—when representing to others—it chooses idealism as its *prajñapti*, my objection is not obviated. For the complicated history and controversies indigenous to Mind-Only theorists, see Fang, *Chinese Philosophy*, 257-292. For the Prāsaṅgikan Mādhyamikan refutation of Mind-Only, see *ME*, 367-381, 611-614.

78. Except for its renderings of the negations as 'beyond', which is perhaps too interpretive.

79. See Loy's paper,—"To say that an event . . . is caused by everything in the universe is finally equivalent to saying that the event is caused by nothing."

80. See my pertaining explanations and references earlier in this paper, where Jackson's exposition is analyzed.

81. See also the Tibetan Gelukba reading of the Heart Sūtra's "Emptiness is form and form is emptiness," in *ME*, 413.

82. The Sanskrit, romanized, reads "*ya ājavamjavībhāva upādāya pratītya vā_/ sa 'pratītyānupādāya nirvānam upadiśyate//.*" See the Poussin edition (with variations in brackets from de Jong's edition) of Nāgārjuna's *MMK*, romanized and accompanied by McCagney's translation, in the Appendix (137-218), Nancy McCagney, *Nāgārjuna and the Philosophy of Openness* (Lanham, Md.: Rowman and Littlefield, 1997), 207.

83. Debate over the subtleties of 'unfindables' and *saṃsāra* is one of the most exciting scenes of Tibetan *Prāsaṅgika* polemic. See *ME*, 405-439. For some pertaining distinctions between '*nirvāṇa*-with-remainder' and '*nirvāṇa*-without-remainder' in the Gelukba's *Prāsaṅgika* tradition, see Daniel Cozort, *Unique Tenets of the Middle Way Consequence School* (Ithaca, NY: Snow Lion Press, 1998), 253-258.

84. I use here McCagney's translation. The "range of thought" which is renounced is logocentrism, that is, concepts, logic, words, grammar, images, etc. All these are of course holistic. See *DLW*, 144, on how *nirvāṇa*, at least insofar as it can be emblematized via *prajñapti*, can still be 'marked' in a Derridean sense. The McCagney translation renders *anutpannāniruddhā* as non-arising and non-ceasing. In *DLW*, 151-154, I discuss the Sanskrit of *MMK* 18:7 more closely (and of *MMK* 18:9 too), but for the English translation I use Streng.

85. *ME*, 407. The Gelukba's use of 'infinite retreat' here intersects remarkably with Derrida's *mise-en-abyme* of 'traces'.

86. A necessary proviso, it seems to me, because with Derrida I agree that our textual webs outgrow us. The Thai and Burmese Buddhists whom I know all emphasize that Buddhism's 'first truth' means 'uncontrollability', that *saṃsāra* necessarily escapes our 'control'. Wisdom requires us to accept the factor of uncontrollability, all the while realizing as well that 'good acts' do sooner or later effect changes for good.

87. "French Deconstruction with a (Buddhist) Difference: More Cases from the *Gateless Gate* (*Wumenkuan*) and *Blue Cliff Record* (*Piyenlu*)," in *Studies in Language*

and Literature (National Taiwan University), vol. 3 (1988), 1-25; and "Differentialism in Chinese Chan and French Deconstruction: Some Test-Cases from the *Wumenguan*," in *Journal of Chinese Philosophy*, vol. 17 (1990), 87-97.

88. Of course 'absence-of-signifier' must come 'under erasure'. It is 'impossible', among other reasons because it would be contradicting the definition which hatches it. But it is a 'Derridean impossible'. That is, for Derrida, either 'pure signified' or 'pure signifier', from under the scratches of erasure, still functions as a better 'clue' to how life goes on than does the undeconstructed signified-signifier dyad. Most often, Derrida privileges the 'pure signifier' when he can. See my discussion in *DOM*, 10-28; and my comparison to Nāgārjuna, *DOM*, 107-109; *DLW*, 139-142.

89. Stevenson seems to ignore that Derrida argues 'recursiveness' too is writing, and a clue to Writing.

90. I use the diagonal sign to demarcate 'dia' from 'logue', and signal our experience in Thailand, where the Gk. root *dia* is best interpreted to mean 'separate' or 'through': the *legesthai* > *legein*, 'to speak', is pierced through and separated by the *dia*.

91. Would that most American conferences on 'postmodernism and religion' or 'deconstruction and religion' did likewise, by allowing Buddhism in.

92. In my own work I take Derridean deconstruction to belong to postmodernism in a loose sense, in that postmodernism broadly defined can comprise any movement which breaks down holisms. Derrida's ways of breaking down holisms deploy negative reference rather than indiscriminate mixing. Derrida himself disavows postmodernism in large part to avoid identification with the latter mode (and also, of course, because he eschews the right-wing and capitalist implications of some postmodernism). My description of various Derridean maneuvers in terms of postmodernism appears in Magliola, "The Off/Figural: Postmodernism in Italian Architecture and American Poetry" [*Tuokui de nixiang—yidali jianzhu yu meiguo shi de houqi xian-daizhuyi*], trans. Shu-chen Chiang, in Yao-fu Lin, ed., *Proceedings of the National Conference in Literary Criticism* [*Wen xue piping yantaohui lunwenji*] (Taipei: National Taiwan University Press, 1986), 122-141.

93. Not that he does not belong with other bodies too, including the Jewish one which is alternately his parasite and his host.

94. One thinks of Derrida's Joyce's 'Jewgreek/Greekjew'.

95. I disagree with those contemporary Catholic theologians who affirm one 'scientific' model of Biblical hermeneutics, so that all Christians can 'objectively' cooperate in this 'objective' enterprise. See Magliola, "Two Models of Trinity—French Post-Structuralist versus the Historical-Critical: Argued in the Form of a Dialogue," Oliva Blanchette, Tomonobu Imamich, and George F. McLean, eds., *Philosophical Challenges and Opportunities of Globalization,* Vol. II (Washington, DC: Council for Research in Values and Philosophy, 2001), 401-425.

96. In reference to which, Jarow raises the question of an excluded 'fourth' in the Trinity. I discuss Jung's famous critique of the Trinity in terms of a 'fourth' in "Transformation Theory and Postcolonial Discourse: Jung by Lacan by Derrida (Bar Sinister Descent)," in Robert Lumsden and Rajeev Patke, eds., *Institutions in Cultures: Theory and Practice* (Amsterdam: Rodopi, 1996), 239-260.

97. And which continues—it seems to me—in truncated form today, in most American seminaries. The Jansenist puritanism is gone, but still missing is a positive emphasis on corporality in the prayer-life (through iconic meditation, devotional *affectivity*, etc.)—all highly developed in Catholicism's medieval, Renaissance, and Baroque periods, and vital for a celibate's psychosomatic health. Without an affective and somatic prayer-life, erotic repression can easily occur, and the consequences can be devastating indeed.

98. Quoted in Yoel Hoffmann, *The Sound of the One Hand* (New York, N.Y.: Basic Books, 1975), 24-25.

99. To give a very practical example, the rules for detachment prescribed by Jean-Jacques Olier (French Berullean School, 17th cent.) follow a rationale very similar to those of Theravāda Buddhism, but utterly differ in that they are driven by/target utterly different motives/objectives.

100. Or can happen, a very different story.

101. It is worth noting that in terms of a Hindu mind-set, such a project is already well-advanced (Raimundo Panikkar, Bede Griffiths, and others).

102. For the preponderance of Buddhists, there can be only faith in the Eightfold-path, and its potential to eventually lead them to this 'recognition' and finally, liberation.

103. For Derrida's own use of 'floating graphic traits', see the section so-named in Magliola, "Derridean Gaming and Buddhist *Utpāda/Bhanga* (Rising/Falling): How a Philosophical Style Can Devoid Substantive Field," electronic (online) *The International Journal for Field Being*, Vol. I (summer 2001) http://www.iifb.org/ijfb/RMagliola-2.htm.

104. The second line of the "Generating" entry is intercalated into the "Glitch" entry, where it becomes the second line: thematically, the relation of the First and Second Persons in my treatment of the Trinity involves a kind of structural 'intercalation'. *DLW*'s index is contrived in many ways to theatricalize what Jane Augustine calls the "trace of the erased under-text."

105. Both 'nirvānic' (Theravādin) and 'Bodhisattvic' (Mahāyānist) Buddhism regard the 'karmic' paths as inferior. 'Karmic' Buddhism refers to a life-style aimed towards rebirth (earned through merit-making) in a more 'successful' life in worldly terms, i.e., a life of wealth, health, and filial progeny. Nirvānic and Bodhisattvic orientations seek to escape all karma, whereas a 'karmic' orientation seeks to make 'good karma'.

106. Christ is understood to give Christians, out of His generosity, the privilege to throw in their lot with Him, i.e., to participate in the redemptive act, though Christ's infinite merit alone suffices to save humankind. The co-participation of Christians is superfluous but enables them to be *alteri christi* ('other christs'), that is, to be transformed more thoroughly into Christ. According to Roman Catholicism, grace does not 'cover-over' the believer from the outside, but transforms her/his very nature. Christification is a union in/with Christ which I think can be better 'talked about' in terms of Derridean chiasm than it can in terms of ontic/ontological philosophy. Christification crosses Tibetan Vajrayānist 'identification with the deity' ('deity-yoga') in intriguing ways.

107. Though there remain significant differences between them. See *JD*, 302-310 on Derrida, Levinas, and the 'quasi-transcendental'. In "Dénégations" and elsewhere, Derrida relates the Torah's 'Injunction-Promise-Ethic' more and more to his earlier notion of the prior (yet temporally entrammeled) condition which enables humanity's 'no' and 'not-no' (*DLW*, 159). Derrida's treatment of the ethical 'no' and 'not-no' continues through the 1990s, and is proliferating now more than ever. See, for example, all of his *Spectres of Marx*, trans. Peggy Kamuf (London: Routledge, 1994; orig. Fr. ed., 1993); and "Foi et savoir" (1996) in the collection *La Religion* (Paris: Seuil, 1996).

108. See *Spectres of Marx*, trans. Peggy Kamuf (New York, London: Routledge, 1994), 174-175.

109. I derive this interpretation from the Christian, not the Jewish, interpretive tradition.

110. For a treatment of Mary as prime exemplar of co-crucifixion with Christ, see Magliola, "Appropriative and/or Imitative Use(s): Some Cruxes—Greek, Latin, English, French, Sanskrit," in Han-liang Chang, ed., *Concepts of Literary Theory East and West* (Taipei: Shu Lin Press, 1993), 184-191, where I treat at length Luke 2:34-35 ("and a sword shall pierce your soul too").

111. See Yin-shun, *The Way to Buddhahood* on "faith" (the index supplies many pertaining page references).

112. When I say "I do not lay claim to absolute or universalized truth" (79-80), I mean that I do not claim to understand the relation between my monotheism and the de-

fining truths/beauties of a religion such as Buddhism, of which two of the defining and pivotal doctrines are (a) rebirth and (b) the rejection of an eternal God who creates all the universe. From the Judeo-Christian side, God as Double-bind is a way of accessing the above problematic of relation.

113. John 17:24. For a differential treatment of Psalm 110, v. 3, "Before the daystar, like the dew," see pp. 34-38 of my "Postmodern Literariness and the Bible: On Psalm 110, Piquant Piqué," in *Studies in Language and Literature* (Taiwan), Vol. 4 (Oct. 1990), 31-41.

114. Masao Abe, "A Rejoinder," in John B. Cobb and Christopher Ives, eds., *The Emptying God: A Buddhist-Jewish-Christian Conversation* (New York: Orbis, 1990), 183.

115. The electronic *Journal of Buddhist Ethics*, so readily accessible via internet, is an excellent site for accessing scholarly papers on all these issues.

116. See Aquinas, *Summa contra gentiles*, LIII, trans. Joseph Rickaby (London: Burns and Oates, 1905).

117. See Guru Rinpoche according to Karma Lingpa, trans. and commentary, F. Fremantle and Chogyam Trungpa, *The Tibetan Book of the Dead: The Great Liberation through Hearing in the Bardo* (Boston and London: Shambhala, 1987) [*TBD*]. Also compare Robert Thurman's resourceful trans. of the same (New York: Bantam, 1994).

118. Normative Theravāda maintains that a Vajrayāna Tathāgatha violates the third seal, that all phenomena are selfless, and the fourth seal, that *nirvāṇa* is peace (so after *nirvāṇa*-without-remainder there cannot be Mahāyānist beings/states). Sambhogakāya body is said to violate the first seal, that all produced bodies are impermanent and the second, that all impure bodies are miserable. See *ME*, 345-346.

Selected Bibliography

William Edelglass

Buddhism and Deconstruction

Cai, Zong-qi. "Derrida and Seng Zhao: Linguistic and Philosophical Deconstructions." *Philosophy East and West* 43, no. 3 (1993): 389-404.

Corless, Roger. "On Deconstructing Life-Worlds: Buddhism, Christianity, Culture" (review). *Buddhist— Christian Studies* 19 (1999): 216-219.

Coward, Harold. *Derrida and Indian Philosophy.* Albany: State University of New York Press, 1990.

Coward, Harold G. and Toby Foshay. *Derrida and Negative Theology.* Albany: State University of New York Press, 1992.

Della Santina, Peter. "The Madhyamika and Modern Western Philosophy." *Philosophy East and West* 36 (1986): 41-54.

Elberfeld, Rolf. "'Lieu': Nishida, Nishitani, Derrida." *Revue Philosophique de Louvain* 92 (1994): 474-494.

Foshay, Toby Avard. "Denegation, Nonduality, and Language in Derrida and Dōgen." *Philosophy East and West* 44, no. 3 (July, 1994): 543-558.

Garner, Richard T. "The Deconstruction of the Mirror and Other Heresies: Ch'an and Taoism as Abnormal Discourse." *Journal of Chinese Philosophy* 12 (1985): 155-168.

Katz, Nathan. "'Prasanga' and Deconstruction: Tibetan Hermeneutics and the 'Yana' Controversy." *Philosophy East and West* 34, no. 2 (1984): 185-204.

Kim, Hyŏnghyo. "Tekst iron kwa Wŏnhyo ŭi sasang ŭi nollijŏk tokpŏp." ["Textuality and logical reading of Wŏnhyo's thought"]. In *Wŏnhyo ŭi sasang kwa kŭ hyŏndaejŏk ŭimi* [*Wŏnhyo's thought and its significance in modern times*], 1-122. Seoul, Korea: Han'guk chŏngsin munhwa yŏn'guwŏn, 1994.

Loy, David, R. "The Mahayana Deconstruction of Time." *Philosophy East and West* 36, no 1 (1986): 13-23.

———. "The Clôture of Deconstruction: A Madhyamika Critique of Derrida." *International Philosophical Quarterly* 27 (1987): 59-80.

———. "The Deconstruction of Buddhism." In *Derrida and Negative Theology*, edited by Harold Coward and D. Foshay. Albany: State University of New Yorik Press, 1992: 227-253.

———. "Language Against its Own Mystifications: Deconstruction in Nagarjuna and Dogen." *Philosophy East and West* 49, no. 3 (1999): 245-261.

———. ed. *Healing Deconstruction: Postmodern Thought in Buddhism and Christianity*. Atlanta: Scholars Press, 1996.

Magliola, Robert. *Derrida on the Mend*. West Lafayette, IN: Purdue University Press, 1984.

———. "Postmodernism on the Brim: A Differentialist Manifesto." *Krisis* 3 (1985): 91-111.

———. "Sexual Rogations, Mystical Abrogations: Some Données of Buddhist Tantra and the Catholic Renaissance." In *The Comparative Perspective on Literature: Approaches to Theory and Practice*, edited by Clayton Koelb and Susan Noakes, 195-212. Ithaca, NY: Cornell University Press, 1988.

———. "Differentialism in Chinese Ch'an and French Deconstruction: Some Test Cases from the Wu-Men-Kuan." *Journal of Chinese Philosophy* 17 (1990): 87-97.

———. *On Deconstructing Life-Worlds: Buddhism, Christianity, Culture*. Atlanta: Scholars Press, 1997; New York City and Oxford: Oxford University Press, 2000.

———. "French Deconstruction with a (Buddhist) Difference: More Cases from the Gateless Gate [*Wu-men-kuan*] and Blue Cliff Record [*Pi-yen-lu*]." *Studies in Language and Literature* 3, no. 1 (1988): 1-25.

———. "Derridean Gaming and Buddhist 'Utpāda/Bhanga' (Rising/Falling): How a Philosophical Style can Devoid Substantive Field," electronic on line journal *The International Journal for Field-Being* 1 (2001) <http://www.iifb.org/ijfb/RMagliola-2.htm> Jan 1, 2005.

Matilal, Bimal Krishna, "Is 'Prasanga' a Form of Deconstruction?" *Journal of Indian Philosophy* 20 (1992): 345-362.

McCort, Dennis. *Going beyond the Pairs: the Coincidence of Opposites in German Romanticism, Zen, and Deconstruction*. Albany: State University of New York Press, 2001.

Odin, Steven. "Derrida and the Decentered Universe of Ch'an Buddhism." *Journal of Chinese Philosophy* 17 (1990): 61-86.

Pickering, John. "Buddhism and Cognitivism: A Postmodern Appraisal." *Asian Philosophy* 5 (1995): 23-38.

Wang, Youxuan. *Buddhism and Deconstruction: towards a comparative semiotics*. Richmond: Curzon, 2001.

Buddhism and Western Thought

Abe, Masao. *Zen and Western Thought.* Edited by William LaFleur. Honolulu: University of Hawaii Press, 1985.

———. *Zen and Comparative Studies*. Edited by Steven Heine. Honolulu: University of Hawaii Press, 1997.

Abe, Masao and Steven Heine, eds. *Zen and the Modern World: A Third Sequel to Zen and Western Thought.* Honolulu: University of Hawaii Press, 2003.

Abelsen, Peter. "Schopenhauer and Buddhism." *Philosophy East and West* 43 (1993): 255-278.

Altizer, Thomas J. J. "The Buddhist Ground of the Whiteheadian God." *Process Studies* 5 (1975): 227-236.

Ames, Van Meter. "Zen and Pragmatism." *Philosophy East and West* 4, no. 1 (1954): 19-34.

———. "Zen and American Philosophy." *Philosophy East and West* 5, no. 4 (1955): 305-320.

Anderson, T. "Wittgenstein and Nagarjuna's Paradox." *Philosophy East and West* 35 (1985): 157-169.

Applebaum, David. "The Fact of Reason: Kant's 'Prajna'—Perception of Freedom." *Journal of Indian Philosophy* 15 (1987): 87-98.

Baran, Gary L. "A Buddhist and a Hindu Critique of Descartes." In *East-West Encounters in Philosophy and Religion*, edited by Ninian Smart. Long Beach: Long Beach Press, 1996.

Betty, L. Stafford. "The Buddhist-Humean Parallels: Postmortem." *Philosophy East and West* 21, no. 3 (1971): 237-254.

Bosart, William. "Sartre's Theory of Consciousness and the Zen Doctrine of No Mind." In *The Life of the Transcendental Ego*, edited by Edward S. Casey. Albany, NY: State University of New York Press, 1986: 126-150.

Bossert, Philip J. "Paradox and Enlightenment in Zen Dialogue and Phenomenological Description." *Journal of Chinese Philosophy* 3 (1976): 269-280.

Bouquet, A. C. "Stoics and Buddhists." *Philosophical Quarterly* (India) 33 (1960): 205-221.

Bugault, Guy. "Buddhist Anthropology vis-à-vis Modern Philosophy and Contemporary Neurophysiology." *Journal of Indian Council of Philosophical Research* (1990): 69-76.

Chatterjee, Dipankar. "Skepticism and Indian Philosophy." *Philosophy East and West* 27, no. 2 (1977): 195-209.

Cheng, Hsueh Fli. "Phenomenology in T'ien-T'ain and Hua-Yen Buddhism." In *Phenomenology of Life,* edited by Anna Teresa Tymieniecka, 215-227. Dordrecht: Reidel, 1984.

Chi, Richard See Yee. "Buddhist Logic and Western Thought." In *Buddhism and American Thinkers,* edited by Kenneth K. Inada 111-119. Albany, NY: State University of New York Press, 1984.

Clarke, J.J. *Oriental Enlightenment: The Encounter Between Asian and Western Thought.* New York: Routledge, 1997.

Cobb, John B. Jr. "'Mosa-Dharma' and Prehension: Nagarjuna and Whitehead Compared." *Process Studies* 4 (1974): 26-36.

———. "Process Thought and Buddhism." *Process Studies* 23 (1994): 69-71.

Cohen, Maurice. "Dying as Supreme Opportunity: A Comparison of Plato's *Phaedo* and the *Tibetan Book of the Dead*." *Philosophy East and West* 26 (1976): 317-327.

Conche, Marcel. *Nietzsche et le Bouddhisme*. La Versanne: Encre Marine, 1997.

De Mendonca, Albert. "Existential Elements in Buddhist Dialectics." *Philosophical Quarterly India* 25 (1952): 21-47.

Dilworth, David A. "Whitehead's Process Realism, the Abhidharma Dharma Theory, and the Mahayana Critique." *International Philosophical Quarterly* 18 (1978): 151-169.

Droit, Roger P. "Schopenhauer et la Boudhisme: Une 'Admirable Concordance.'" In *Schopenhauer*, edited by Eric von der Luft, 123-138. Lewiston, NY: Mellon Press, 1988.

———. *The Cult of Nothingness: The Philosophers and the Buddha.* Translated by David Streight and Pamela Vohnson. Chapel Hill: University of North Carolina Press, 2003.

Dumoulin, Heinrich S. H. "Buddhism and Nineteenth Century German Philosophy." Translated by Julia Ching. *Journal of the History of Ideas* 42 (1981): 457-470.

Elman, Benjamin A. "Nietzsche and Buddhism." *Journal of the History of Ideas* 44 (1983): 671-686.

Faure, Bernard. Trans. Janet Lloyd. *Double Exposure: Cutting Across Buddhist and Western Discourses*. Stanford, CA: Stanford University Press, 2004.

Ford, Lewis S. "Whitehead's Appropriation of the Teachings of the Buddha." *Religion in Life* 45 (1976): 184-190.

Foti, Veronique. "Heidegger and the Way of Art: The Empty Origin and Contemporary Abstraction." *Continental Philosophy Review*, 31 (1998): 337-351.

Fredricks, James L. "The Incomprehensibility of God: a Buddhist reading of Aquinas." *Theological Studies* 56 (1995).

Fu, Charles Wei Hsun. "Chinese Buddhism as an Existential Phenomenology." In *Phenomenology of Life,* edited by Anna Teresa Tymieniecka, 229-251. Dordrecht: Reidel, 1984..

Garfield, Jay L. "Epoche and Sunyata: Skepticism East and West." *Philosophy East and West* 40 (1990): 285-307.

Garner, Dick. "Skepticism, Ordinary Language and Zen Buddhism." *Philosophy East and West* 27, no. 2 (1977): 165-181.

Giles, James. "The No-Self Theory: Hume, Buddhism and Personal Identity." *Philosophy East and West* 43, no. 2 (1993): 175-200.

Glass, Newman Robert. *Working Emptiness: Toward a Third Reading of Emptiness in Buddhism and Postmodern Thought.* Atlanta: Scholars Press, 1995.

Goodchild, Philip. "Speech and Silence in the Mumonkan: An Examination of Use of Language in Light of the Philosophy of Gille Deleuze." *Philosophy East and West* 43, no. 1 (January 1993): 1-18.

Griffin, David R. "Buddhist Thought and Whitehead's Philosophy." *International Philosophy Quarterly* 14 (1974): 261-284.

Gudmunsen, Chris. *Wittgenstein and Buddhism.* New York: Harper and Row, 1977.

Hartshorne, Charles. "Whitehead's Differences from Buddhism," *Philosophy East and West* 25, no. 4 (1975): 407-413.

Heine, Steve. *Existential and Ontological Dimensions of Time in Heidegger and Dogen.* Albany: State University of New York Press, 1985.

Herman, A. L. "Skepticism and Madhyamika: How Not to Think about Things." *Philosophica* (India) 15 (1987): 139-161.

Heyman, Derek K. "Dual and Non-Dual Ontology in Sartre and Mahayana Buddhism." *Man and World* 30 (1997): 431-443.

Hirsch, Elisabeth Feist. "Martin Heidegger and the East." *Philosophy East and West* 20 (1970): 247-263.

Hsueh, Li Cheng. "Nagarujuna, Kant and Wittgenstein." *Religious Studies* 17 (1981): 67-85.

Inada, Kenneth K. "Whitehead's 'Actuality Entity' and the Buddha's Anatman." *Philosophy East and West* 21, no. 3 (1971): 303-316.

———. "The Metaphysics of Buddhist Experience and Whiteheadian Encounter." *Philosophy East and West* 25, no. 4 (1975): 465-488.

Innada, Kenneth K. and Nolan P. Jacobson, eds. *Buddhism and American Thinkers.* Albany: State University of New York Press, 1984.

Jacobson, Nolan Pliny. "The Predicament of Man in Zen Buddhism and Kierkegaard." *Philosophy East and West* 2, no. 3 (1952): 238-253.

———. "The Possibility of Oriental Influence in Hume's Philosophy." *Philosophy East and West* 19, no. 1 (1969): 17-37.

Kakol, Peter. "A General Theory of Worldviews Based on Mādhyamika and Process Philosophies." *Philosophy East and West* 52, no. 2 (2002): 207-223.

Kalansuriya, A. D. P. *A Philosophical Analysis of Buddhist Notions: The Buddha and Wittgenstein.* Delhi: Sri Satguru Publications, 1987.

Kamata, Yasuo. "Schopenhauer und der Buddhismus." *Schopenhauer Jahrbuch,* 65 (1984): 233-238.

Kapstein, Matthew. "The Trouble with Truth: Heidegger on Aletheia, Buddhist Thinkers on Satya." *Journal of the Indian Council of Philosophical Research* 9, no. 2 (1992): 69-85.

Katz, Nathan, ed. *Buddhist and Western Philosophy.* Atlantic Highlands, NJ: Humanities Press, 1981.

Kim, Hyŏnghyo. *Ha'idegŏ wa hwaŏm ŭi sayu* [*Heidegger and Huayan thought*]. Hwasŏng, South Korea: Ch'ŏnggye, 2002.

King, Winston L. "Hua-Yen Mutually Interpenetrative Identity and Whiteheadian Organic Relation." *Journal of Chinese Philosophy* 6 (1979): 387-410.

Kiowsky, Hellmuth. "Parallelen und Divergenzen in Schopenhauers Ethik zur Buddhistischen Erlosungslehre." *Schopenhauer Jahrbuch* 77 (1996): 255-260.

Ko, Hyŏnggon. *Sŏn ŭi segye: Sŏyang ch'ŏlhak kwa Sŏn* [*The World of Chan: Western philosophy and Chan*]. Seoul, Korea: Unjusa, 1995.

Kopf, Gereon. *Beyond Personal Identity: Dōgen, Nishida, and a Phenomenology of No-Self.* Richmond: Curzon Press, 2001.

Kotoh, Tetsuaki. "Language and Silence: Self-Inquiry in Heidegger and Zen." In *Heidegger and Asian Thought*, edited by Graham Parkes, 201-211. Honolulu: University of Hawaii Press, 1987.

Kreeft, Peter. "Zen in Heidegger's 'Gelassenheit'." *International Philosophy Quarterly* 11 (1971): 521-545.

Larrabee, M. J. "The One and the Many: Yogacara Buddhism and Husserl." *Philosophy East and West* 31, no. 1 (1981): 3-15.

Laycock, Steven. "Hui-Neng and the Transcendental Standpoint," *Journal of Chinese Philosophy,* 12 (1985): 176-196.

———. *Mind as Mirror and the Mirroring of Mind: Buddhist Reflections on Western Phenomenology*. Albany: SUNY Press, 1994.

———. *Nothingness and Emptiness: A Buddhist Engagement with the Ontology of Jean-Paul Sartre.* Albany, NY: State University of New York Press, 2001.

Lesser, A. H. "Eastern and Western Empiricism and the 'no-self' Theory." *Religious Studies* 15 (1979): 55-64.

Levin, David Michael. "Approaches to Psychotherapy: Freud, Jung and Tibetan Buddhism." In *The Metaphors of Consciousness,* edited by Rolf von Eckartsberg, 243-274. New York: Plenum Press, 1981.

———. "Liberating Experience From the Vice of Structuralism: The Methods of Merleau-Ponty and Nagarjuna." *Philosophy Today* 41 (Spring, 1997): 96-111.

Liebenthal, Walter. "Existentialism and Buddhism." *Visvabharati Quarterly* 22 (1956): 293-313.

Liu, Ming-wood. "The Harmonious Universe of Fa-tsang and Leibniz." *Philosophy East and West* 32, no. 1 (1982): 61-76.

Loy, David, R. *Lack and Transcendence: The Problem of Life and Death in Psychotherapy, Existentialism, and Buddhism*. Atlantic Highlands, NJ: Humanities Press, 1996.

———. *Non-duality: A Study in Comparative Philosophy*. New Haven: Yale University Press, 1988.

Mathur, D. C. "The Historical Buddha (Gotama), Hume, and James on the Self: Comparisons and Evaluations." *Philosophy East and West* 28, no. 3 (1978): 253-270.

May, Reinhard. *Heidegger's Hidden Sources: East Asian Influences on his Work,* trans. Graham Parkes. New York: Routledge, 1996.

McDaniel, Jay. "Mahayana Enlightenment in Process Perspective." In *Buddhism and American Thinkers,* edited by Kenneth K. Inada and Nolan P. Jacobson, 50-69. Albany, NY: State University of New York Press, 1984.

Mickunas, Algis. "Phenomenology of Zen." In *Japanese and Western Phenomenology,* edited by Philip Blosser, 263-274. Dordrecht: Kluwer, 1993.

Mistry, Freny. *Nietzsche and Buddhism: Prolegomenon to a Comparative Study.* Berlin, New York: de Gruyter, 1981.

———."Der Buddhist Liest Schopenhauer." *Schopenhauer Jahrbuch* 64 (1983): 80-91.

Mohanty, J. N. "Phenomenology and Existentialism: Encounter with Indian Philosophy." *International Philosophy Quarterly* 12 (1972): 485-511.

Mohanty, J. N. and D. P. Chattopadyaya, L. Embree, eds. *Phenomenology and Indian Philosophy.* New Delhi: Indian Council of Philosophical Research, 1992.

Morrison, Robert G. *Nietzsche and Buddhism: A Study in Nihilism and Ironic Affinities.* Oxford: Oxford University Press, 1997.

Nagasawa, Kunihiko. *Das Ich im Deutschen Idealismus und das Selbst in Zen: Fichte und Dogen.* Freiburg: Alber, 1991.

Nanajivako, Bhikku. "The Philosophy of Disgust: Buddha and Nietzsche." *Schopenhauer Jahrbuch* 58 (1977): 112-132.

———. "The Ethos of Knowledge in Kantian and in Buddhist Philosophy: Remarks on Some Theses from the Standpoint of European Philosophy." *Kantstudien* 77 (1986): 59-83.

Neville, Robert C. "Buddhism and Process Philosophy." In *Buddhism and American Thinkers* edited by Kenneth K. Inada and Nolan P. Jacobson, 120-142. Albany: State University of New York Press, 1984.

Odin, Steven. "Fantasy Variation and the Horizon of Openness: A Phenomenological Interpretation of Tantric Buddhist Enlightenment." *International Philosophy Quarterly* 21 (1981): 419-435.

———. *Process Metaphysics and Hua-yen Buddhism: A Critical Study of Cumulative Penetration vs. Interpenetration.* Albany: State University of New York Press, 1982.

———. "The Epochal Theory of Time in Whitehead and Japanese Buddhism: An East-West Study of Whitehead, Dogen, and Nishida." *Process Studies* 23 (1994): 119-133.

———. *The Social Self in Zen and American Pragmatism.* Albany: State University of New York Press, 1996.

Olsen, Carl. *Zen and the Art of Postmodern Philosophy: Two Paths of Liberation from the Representational Mode of Thinking.* Albany, NY: State University of New York Press, 2000.

Olson, Phillip. *The Discipline of Freedom: A Kantian View of the Role of Moral Precepts in Zen Practice.* Albany: State University of New York Press, 1993.

Olson, Robert F. "Whitehead, Madhyamika, and the Prajnaparamita." *Philosophy East and West* 25, no. 4 (1975): 449-464.

Parkes, Graham, ed. *Heidegger and Asian Thought.* Honolulu: University of Hawaii Press, 1987.

———. ed. *Nietzsche and Asian Thought.* Chicago: University of Chicago Press, 1991.

———. "Nietzsche and Nishitani on the Self-Overcoming of Nihilism." *International Studies in Philosophy* 25 (1993): 51-60.

———. "Nietzsche and East Asian Thought: Influences, Impacts and Resonances." In *The Cambridge Companion to Nietzsche,* edited by Kathleen Higgins and Bernd Magnus, 356-383. Cambridge: Cambridge University Press, 1995.

Pattison, George. "Eternal Loneliness: Art and Religion in Kierkegaard and Zen." *Religious Studies* 25 (1989): 379-392.

Puhakka, Kaisa. *Knowledge and Reality: A Comparative Study of Quine and Some Buddhist Logicians.* Delhi: Motilal Banarasidass, 1975.

Richards, Glyn. "Conceptions of the Self in Wittgenstein, Hume and Buddhism: An Analysis and Comparison." *Monist* 61 (1978): 42-55.

Saigusa, Mitsuyoshi. "Henri Bergson and Buddhist Thought." *Philosophy Studies* (Japan) 9 (1969): 79-102.

Schumann, Karl. "Husserl and Indian Thought." In *Phenomenology and Indian Philosophy,* edited by D. P. Chattopadyaya, L. Embree, J.N. Mohanty, 20-43. New Delhi: Indian Council of Philosophical Research, 1992.

Schurmann, Reiner. "Trois Penseurs du Delaissement: Maitre Eckart, Heidegger, Suzuki." *Journal of the History of Philosophy.* Part One, vol. 12 (1974): 455-477. Part Two, vol. 13 (1975): 43-60.

Smith, Joel R. "Human Insufficiency in Shinran and Kierkegaard." *Asian Philosophy* 6 (1996): 117-127.

Srivastav, C. P. "Plato and Nagarjuna on Samvrti and Paramartha: Some Converging Perspectives." *Indian Philosophical Quarterly* 25 (1998): 387-392.

Steffney, John. "Transmetaphysical Thinking in Heidegger and Zen Buddhism." *Philosophy East and West* 27, no. 3 (1977): 323-335.

———. "Man and Being in Heidegger and Zen Buddhism." *Philosophy Today* 25 (1981): 46-54.

Takeda, Ryusei. "Mahayana Buddhism and Whitehead's Philosophy." *Process Studies* 23 (1994): 72-86.

Teo, Wesley K. H. "Self-Responsibility in Existentialism and Buddhism." *International Journal for Philosophy of Religion* 4 (1973): 80-91.

Thompson, Evan. "Planetary Thinking/Planetary Building: An Essay on Martin Heidegger and Nishitani Keiji." *Philosophy East and West* 36, no. 3 (1986): 235-252.

Thurman, Robert. "Philosophical Nonegocentrism in Wittgenstein and Candrakirti in Their Treatment of the Private Language Problem." *Philosophy East and West* 30, no. 3 (1980): 321-337.

Umehara, Takeshi. "Heidegger and Buddhism." *Philosophy East and West* 20 (1970): 271-281.

Vohra, Ashok. "The Notion of Suffering in Buddhism and Marxism." *Dialectics and Humanism* 10 (1983): 97-102.

Waldo, Ives. "Nagarjuna and Analytic Philosophy." *Philosophy East and West* 25, no. 3 (1975): 281-290.

———. "Nagarjuna and Analytic Philosophy II." *Philosophy East and West* 28 (1978): 287-298.

Wang, Youru. *Linguistic Strategies in Daoist Zhuangzi and Chan Buddhism: The Other Way of Speaking.* RoutledgeCurzon, 2003.

Wienpahl, Paul. "Ch'an Buddhism, Western Thought, and the Concept of Substance." *Inquiry* 14 (1971): 84-101.

Wu, Kuang Ming. "The Cave and the Burglar: Plato Compared with Zen." In *Philosophy and Culture*, edited by Venant Cauchy, vol. IV. Montreal: Editions Montmorency, 1988: 223-228.

Yamaguchi, Minoru. *The Intuition of Zen and Bergson*. Tokyo: Herder, 1969.

Zimmerman, Michael E. "Heidegger, Buddhism, and Deep Ecology." In *The Cambridge Companion to Heidegger,* edited by Charles Guignon, 240-269. New York: Cambridge University Press, 1993.

Ziporyn, Brook. *Being and Ambiguity: Philosophical Experiments with Tiantai Buddhism.* Chicago, IL: Open Court Publishing Company, 2004.

Glossary of Chinese Characters

bei 背
ben 本
benwu zong 本無宗
benzhi zhiyong 本智之用
Biyan lu 碧巖錄
buke siyi 不可思議
bukeshuo 不可說
bupian buyi 不偏不倚
chao siju 超四句
Chanyuan zhuquan jiduxu 禪源諸詮集都序
Chanzong jicheng 禪宗集成
chaoyanyu 超言語
chengshi zong 成實宗
Chuanxin fayao 傳心法要
chu 觸
cun 存
Dacheng qixin lun 大乘起信論
Dacheng wusheng fangbian men 大乘無生方便門
Dacheng xuanlun: 大乘玄論
dan 膽
Dao An: 道安
dao xu tongliu 道須通流
dao 道
Daode jing 道德經
dao kedao feichangdao 道可道 非常道
Denshin hōyō (J.) 傳心法要
dingjie 定解
duanjian 斷見
Dōgen (J.) 道元
erdi yi 二諦義
erdi 二諦
Fa Chen: 法琛
Fa Lang: 法郎
Fa Wen: 法溫
Fa Zang 法藏
fa 法
Fahua 法花
Fang Litian 方立天
feiwu yi 非無義
feiwu 非無
feixiang feifeixiang 非想非非想
feiyou yi 非有義
feng 封
fengsu 風俗
fo 佛
fojiao zhexue 佛敎哲學
Foxing yu boruo 佛性與般若
fuyin baoyang 負陰抱陽
genjō kōan (J.) 現成公案

gong'an 公案
Guzunsu yulu 古尊宿語錄
Han Tingjie 韓廷傑
He Guoquan 何國銓
Hongzhou 洪州
Huangbo Xiyun 黃檗希運
huanyou 幻有
huatou 話頭
Huayan 華嚴
Huineng 慧能
ji fannao shi puti 卽煩惱是菩提
Ji Zang: 吉藏
jiaming 假名
jianwen juezhi 見聞覺知
jing 鏡
Jingde chuandeng lu 景德傳燈錄
jingtai 鏡臺
kaikou jiandan 開口見膽
Kamata Shigeo (J.) 鎌田茂雄
kongan (K.) 公案
kong yi bukong 空亦不空
kongji zhi zhi 空寂之知
kongjiazhong 空假中
kongkong 空空
konglun 空論
kongzong 空宗
kōan (J.) 公案
liangfei 兩非
lichao siju 離超四句
liduanchang 離斷常
linian 離念
Linji lu 臨濟錄
lizhijian 立知見
Mazu Daoyi 馬祖道一
mondō (J.)問答
Mou Zongsan 牟宗三
Nanyang heshang wenda zazhengyi 南陽和尙問答雜徵義
renxin 任心
renxing 人性
renyun zizai 任運自在
renyun 任運
Rinzai roku (J.) 臨濟錄
sanchong erdi 三重二諦
Sanlun xuanyi jiaoshi: 三論玄義校釋
Sanlun xuanyi 三論玄義
Sanlun 三論
Seng Zhao 僧肇
sheng 生
shengmie 生滅
Shenhui heshang chanhua lu 神會和尙禪話錄
Shenhui 神會
Shenxiu 神秀
shidi 世諦
shiren xingkong 世人性空
shisudi 世俗諦
shixiang 實相
Shoki no zenshi II: Rekidai hōbōki (J.) 初期の禪史 II: 歷代法寶記
Shōbō genzō (J.) 正法眼藏
sichong erdi 四重二諦
siju 四句
simenrudao 四門入道
sudao 速道
sudi 俗諦
suiyuan yingyong 隨緣應用
suozhi 所指
Taishō shinshū daizōkyō (J.) 大正新修大藏經
Takakusu Junjirō (J.) 高楠順次郎
Tang Junyi 唐君毅
tanyu 壇語
ti 體
Tiantai 天台
Ui Hakujū yakuchū zenseki shūsei maki (J.) 宇井伯壽譯注禪籍集成卷二
wangyan juelü 妄言絶慮
wangyou 忘有
Wanling lu 宛陵錄

Watanabe Kaigyoku (J.) 渡邊海旭
weiren benxing 爲人本性
Weishi 唯識
wu 無
wuliang zhu fodao 無量諸佛道
Wumen 無門
Wumenguan 無門關
wunian 無念
wusheng zi 無聲字
wusuoyi 無所依
wuxing 無性
xiang 相
xiangsheng 相生
xilun 戲論
xin 心
xing 性
xinji mingjingtai 心卽明鏡臺
xinjing yi feitai 心鏡亦非臺
xinti 心體
xinwu 心無
xu 虛
Xuzang jing 續藏經
Yanagida Seizan (J.) 柳田聖山
Yang Zengwen 楊曾文
yanyu 言語
yinian xianying 一念相應
Yin Shun 印順
yong 用
youdi 有諦
yuan 緣
yuanli liangbian 遠離兩邊
yuansheng wuxing 緣生無性
Zengen shosenshū tojo (J.) 禪源諸詮集都序
zheng 證
zhenxin 眞心
Zhi Daolin: 支道林
zhi 智
zhijian 知見
zhijie 知解
zhixin 直心
Zhi Yi 智顗
Zhong lun 中論
zhong 中
zhongdao foxing 中道佛性
Zhongguo chanxue sixiang yanjiu 中國禪學思想研究
Zhongguo chanzong shi 中國禪宗史
Zhongguo zhexue yuanlun: Yuanxing pian 中國哲學原論原性篇
Zhonghua Chuanxindi Chanmen shizi chengxitu 中華傳心地禪門師資承襲圖
zhu 著
Zhuangzi 莊子
zhufa xingkong 諸法性空
zixing benyong 自性本用
zixing 自性
Zongmi 宗密
Za ahan jing 雜阿含經

Credits

"Nāgārjuna and Deconstruction" is a revised version of "Nāgārjuna and Deconstruction" which appeared in *Philosophy East and West*, vol. 45, no. 2 (1995): 203-225

"Derridean and Mādyamika Buddhist Theories of Deconstruction" is a revised and expanded version of the essay "Derrida and Mādhyamika Buddhism: From Linguistic Deconstruction to Criticism of Onto-theologies" which appeared in *International Philosophical Quarterly*, vol. 33, no. 2 (June 1993): 183-195.

"Indra's Postmodern Net" is an abridged version of an essay, "Indra's Postmodern Net," which originally appeared in *Philosophy East and West*, vol. 43, no. 3 (July 1993): 481-510.

"Deconstructive and Foundationalist Tendencies in Indian and Tibetan Buddhism" is an abridged and updated version of an article, "Matching Concepts: Deconstructive and Foundationalist Tendencies in Buddhist Thought," which appeared in *The Journal of the American Academy of Religion*, vol. 57, no. 3 (1989): 561-589.

An expanded and modified version of "The Chan Deconstruction of Buddha Nature" appeared in the chapter four of *Linguistic Strategies in Daoist Zhuangzi and Chan Buddhism* (RoutledgeCurzon, 2003).

"emmanuel, robert," was first presented at the International Association for Philosophy and Literature (1999) and also at the Fourth International Convention of the Forum on Contemporary Theory at Konak (2001) and published in the *Journal of Contemporary Thought*, vol. 14 (Winter 2001): 83-91.

Contributors

Jane Augustine has studied and practiced in the Tibetan Buddhist tradition for thirty years and is a graduate of the Ngedön School of Higher Learning, founded by Chögyam Trungpa Rinpoche. She has a Ph.D. in literature, has held the H.D. Fellowship at Beinecke Library, Yale, and is editor of *The Gift by H.D.: The Complete Text* (University Press of Florida, 1998). Her two most recent books of poetry are *Arbor Vitae* (Marsh Hawk Press, 2002) and *Transitory* (Spuyten Duyvil, 2002).

Zong-qi Cai is Professor of Chinese and Comparative Literature at the University of Illinois, Urbana-Champaign. He is the author of *The Matrix of Lyric Transformation: Poetic Modes and Self-Presentation in Early Chinese Pentasyllabic Poetry* (Michigan, 1996) and *Configurations of Comparative Poetics: Three Perspectives on Western and Chinese Literary Criticism* (Hawaii, 2002), and the editor of *A Chinese Literary Mind: Culture, Creativity, and Rhetoric in Wenxin diaolong* (Stanford, 2001) and *Chinese Aesthetics: The Ordering of Literature, the Arts, and the Universe in the Six Dynasties* (Hawaii, 2004), and *How to Read Chinese Poetry: A Guided Anthology* (Columbia University Press, forthcoming). He has also published numerous articles on classical Chinese poetry, literary criticism, comparative literature and philosophy.

Simon Glynn is a Professor of Philosophy at Florida Atlantic University. His major area of focus is the application of contemporary European epistemology (Phenomenology, Existentialism, Hermeneutics, Structuralism and Post-Structuralism), to the Natural, Human and Social Sciences. In addition to a number of articles in collected volumes, and in journals such as *The Journal of the British Society for Phenomenology, Man and World, Analecta Husserliana* and *Continental Philosophy Review*, etc. his major publications include *Sartre: An Investigation of Some Major Themes, European Philosophy and the Human and Social Sciences*, and *Continental and Postmodern Perspectives in the Philosophy of Science*, edited with Babette Babich and Debra Bergoffen.

Gad Horowitz, born in Jerusalem in 1936, is Professor of Political Science at the University of Toronto. His publications include "Groundless Democracy," in Philippa Berry and Andrew Wernick, eds. *Shadow of the Spirit*, London: Routledge, 1993; "The Foucauldian Impasse," *Political Theory*, February, 1997 and *Basic and Surplus Repression in Psychoanalytic Theory: Freud, Reich, Marcuse*, Toronto: University of Toronto Press, 1977.

Roger R. Jackson is Stephen R. Lewis, Jr. Professor of Religions and the Liberal Arts of Carleton College in Northfield, Minnesota. He has written widely on Mahāyāna Buddhist thought and practice in India and Tibet, both in their traditional contexts and as they intersect with modern concerns. His most recent book is *Tantric Treasures: Three Collections of Mystical Verse from Buddhist India* (Oxford University Press, 2004).

E.H. Jarow has been an Assistant Professor in History of Religions at Vassar College since 1995. He was previously a Mellon Fellow in the Humanities at Columbia University and a Fulbright Scholar in India. He has published widely on Indian religious literature and Vaiṣṇavism and teaches an annual seminar on Buddhist Traditions in America. Publications include: "History of Sanskrit Poetry" (*Princeton Encyclopedia of Poetry and Poetics*, 1994), "Who is Vimalakīrti," and "Figuration in the Māhābharata" (*Journal of Vaiṣṇavism Studies*), and *Tales for the Dying: The Death Narrative of the Bhāgavata-Purāṇa* (SUNY Press, 2003)

Steven W. Laycock teaches philosophy at Leeward College of the University of Hawai`i System. He has devoted much effort to the elucidation of new, exciting and fruitful dimensions of inquiry on the horizon of traditional phenomenological and existential concerns and has contributed significantly to the elucidation of Buddhist philosophy in light of the concepts and techniques of the Western phenomenological tradition. His book, *Mind as Mirror and the Mirroring of Mind*, involves a sustained critical study of Husserl, Sartre, and Merleau-Ponty from a Buddhist perspective. *Nothingness and Emptiness* represents a focused critique of Sartre's early ontology from the standpoint of a developed conception of emptiness. And *Foundations for a Phenomenological Theology* represents a systematic meditation upon Husserl's theological musings.

David R. Loy is Besl Professor of religion and ethics at Xavier University in Cincinnati. He is the author of *Nonduality: A Study in Comparative Philosophy* (1988), *Lack and Transcendence: The Problem of Death and Life in Psychotherapy, Existentialism and Buddhism* (1996), *A Buddhist History of the West: Studies in Lack* (2002), *The Great Awakening: A Buddhist Social Theory*

(2003), *The Dharma of Dragons and Daemons: Buddhist Themes in Modern Fantasy* (2004, with Linda Goodhew), and various journal articles including "The Deconstruction of Buddhism" in *Derrida and Negative Theology* (1993). He is also the editor of *Healing Deconstruction* (Scholar's Press, 1996). He is a longtime student of Zen and qualified as a Zen *sensei* (teacher) in the Sanbo Kyodan lineage.

Ian W. Mabbett is a Reader in History at Monash University, Melbourne, Australia, with research interests in ancient India and South-East Asia and the history of Buddhism. In 2000-2002 he was Professor of Indian and Buddhist Studies (and from 2002 Emeritus Professor) at Aichi Bunkyo University, Nagoya, Japan. Among other publications, he is the author of *A Short History of India* (Cassell Australia; Praeger; Revised Edition, Methuen), *Truth, Myth and Politics in Ancient India* (Thomson Press, Delhi), and, with David Chandler, *The Khmers* (Blackwell); with J. G. de Casparis, he has contributed on ancient religion to *The Cambridge History of South-East Asia*, and with G. Baily he wrote a study of the *Sociology of Early Indian Buddhism* published by Cambridge University Press in 2003.

Robert Magliola is a specialist in both European hermeneutics/deconstruction and in Buddhist Studies; and has taught eighteen years in Asia. His "Afterword" commentary for this volume was prepared during his last year as Professor of Philosophy in the interfaith Graduate School of Philosophy and Religions, Abac Assumption University, Thailand, where he also underwent meditation training at Bangkok's Wat Mahadhatu. Prior to his years in Thailand, he was Distinguished Chair Professor at National Taiwan U., Taiwan, whence he made research-trips, sponsored by Taiwan's NSC, to England and France. A Carmelite lay tertiary, he is now ongoing interfaith retreatant/Dharma-disciple at Ling Jiou Mountain Buddhist Monastery (Kungliao, Taiwan and Manhattan, NYC), where he teaches mini-courses in Buddhism and organizes inter-religious symposia. He is also a Seminar Associate of the University Seminar in Buddhist Studies at Columbia U. His publications in philosophy include *Phenomenology and Literature* (Purdue University Press, 1977), *Derrida on the Mend* (Purdue University Press, 1984; 2000), and *On Deconstructing Life-Worlds: Buddhism, Christianity, Culture* (Scholars Press, 1997; Oxford University Press, 2000); and many book-chapters and journal articles.

Jin Y. Park is Assistant Professor of Philosophy and Religion at American University. She is the translator of *Getting Familiar with Death* and the author of journal articles including "Zen and Zen Philosophy of Language" and "Zen Language in Our Time: the Case of Pojo Chinul and Huatou Meditation." Her research areas include: Korean Zen Buddhism, Buddhist encounter with modernity in Korea, and problem of the moral agency in Zen Buddhism and postmodern thought.

Frank W. Stevenson has a Ph.D. in Philosophy from Boston College (1980) and teaches graduate courses on Nietzsche, poststructuralism and postmodern fiction at National Taiwan Normal University in Taipei. He has published essays on Chinese-Western comparative metaphysics in the *Journal of Chinese Philosophy*, *Canadian Review of Comparative Literature*, and *Tamkang Review*, as well as Nietzsche, Bataille, Deleuze, and theories of poetic language and the comic. In recent research on Sunzi and Zhuangzi and in a book concerned with self-reflexivity, irony, and comic absurdity in Poe's style, he moves between Derrida's problematics of meaning as iteration and citationality and Serres' reading of chaos theory (non-linear dynamics) in terms of sound and background noise.

Youru Wang, Assistant Professor, teaches Asian thought in the Philosophy and Religion Department at Rowan University, Glassboro, New Jersey. His area of specialty is Chinese Buddhist thought and early Daoist thought. He received his BA degree from the Department of Chinese Language and Literature, Fudan University, Shanghai, China and his Ph.D. degree from the Religion Department, Temple University, U.S.A. His articles have appeared in journals such as *International Philosophical Quarterly*, *Philosophy East and West*, *Asian Philosophy*, and *Journal of Chinese Philosophy*. His book, *Linguistic Strategies in Daoist Zhungzi and Chan Buddhism: The Other Way of Speaking*, was published in 2003 by RoutledgeCurzon.

Ellen Zhang is Assistant Professor of Religion at Temple University. Her major publications include: "Love and Death: The Dionysian Spirit of Juan Chi and Neo-Taoists," "The Neo-Confucian Concept of Body and its Ethical Sensibility," and "Icon without Logos, or Theology without Ontology."